THE INBETWEENERS SCRIPTBOOK

Damon Beesley and Iain Morris

CENTURY · LONDON

Published by Century 2012

2 4 6 8 10 9 7 5 3 1

First published in Great Britain in 2012 by
Century
Random House, 20 Vauxhall Bridge Road,
London SW1V 2SA

www.randomhouse.co.uk

Addresses for companies within The Random House Group Limited can be found at:
www.randomhouse.co.uk

The Random House Group Limited Reg. No. 954009

A CIP catalogue record for this book
is available from the British Library

ISBN 9781780891057

The Random House Group Limited supports The Forest Stewardship Council (FSC®), the leading
international forest certification organisation. Our books carrying the FSC label are printed on FSC®
certified paper. FSC is the only forest certification scheme endorsed by the leading environmental
organisations, including Greenpeace. Our paper procurement policy can be found at
www.randomhouse.co.uk/environment

Typeset in FS Albert by Palimpsest Book Production Limited,
Falkirk, Stirlingshire

Printed and bound in Great Britain by
CPI Group (UK) Ltd, Croydon CR0 4YY

THE INBETWEENERS
SCRIPTBOOK

Damon Beesley and Iain Morris are co-creators and writers of the multi-award-winning sitcom *The Inbetweeners*. Beesley and Morris met as producers on Channel 4's *The 11 O'Clock Show*. The two later launched their own company, Bwark Productions, in 2004 and landed the first series of *The Inbetweeners* in 2007.

To Caroline Leddy

Acknowledgements

I'll start by saying sorry. These acknowledgements will be brief. This is mainly down to me being a heady mix of lazy, busy and bad at life.

Firstly, because I rarely get to say it, thank you Iain. For the reasons listed above, I doubt I'd be writing this at all if it wasn't for you. Thanks for your enthusiasm, drive and talent. Thanks for consistently navigating life in the funniest way imaginable. Thanks for being my friend. Oooh, thanks.

Caroline Leddy for everything. I mean EVERYTHING.

Simon Bird, Joe Thomas, James Buckley and Blake Harrison for not making two fairly old men feel creepy for wanting to hang out with them. Oh, and for the stuff they do in the show too.

Chris Young for magnificent producer services.

Ben Palmer, possibly the nicest and most tolerant human I've ever met. Not too shabby at the old directing either.

Leo Martin, for too many reasons to list but especially for her tireless devotion to keeping everyone well fed.

Andrew Newman, Angela Jain, Danny Cohen for believing in us.

The residents of New Barn in the late 1980s who lost treasured flowerbeds or had to overhear what must have been a ludicrous overuse of curse words by teenage boys.

The New Barn Posse, for non-ironic use of a canary yellow Mini Metro* and a beige Austin Allegro* as primary modes of transport. (*Google 'em kids)

And finally, simply making it to the office every day would not be possible without the support of my incredible wife Nicole. Thank you for contractually agreeing to spend the rest of your life with me.

Damon

Foreword

Everyone in my line of work longs for a hit. A proper big hit. One that your auntie and your children's teachers have heard of (but must never see). They rarely come along, and unlike buses, they don't then come in threes. I knew for definite we were on to something big with *The Inbetweeners* when my doctor dropped the phrase 'bus wankers' into a consultation shortly after the second series went out.

Here are five observations I would like to make about the show and its makers, which simply don't warrant a paragraph of their own:

1. It speaks to both the 'young' and the 'once-young'. Who knew it?! We totally didn't plan it that way. Hooray!
2. The Eurostar trip to Paris in order to cast Patrice was pretty special. As was Patrice. This was definitely what's known as 'a perk'.
3. Bad news should only ever be sung. It sort of takes the edge off things. (Believe me, as a technique it's pretty fail-safe.)
4. If you don't know what Iain and Damon look like, read this carefully: if they had a child together it would look *exactly* like Matt Cardle.
5. If any friend or family member can spot my *Inbetweeners'* voice-over contributions as a pensioner, prostitute or chicken, I'll make them a banana cake.

The whole thing was bloody marvellous. Tons of people were essential and incredible, but my own special thanks go to my brilliant friend Chris Young, the show's producer, whose talent, energy and optimism know no limits: a man who simply doesn't understand the meaning of the phrase 'It can't be done.' (Of course he does. He's not a fucking idiot.) And to my Big Old Darlings, Iain and Damon, who, in their supremely gifted way, so generously offered up their life experiences on a plate for us all to adore.

Thank you so much for watching and supporting the show.

CAROLINE LEDDY
Executive Producer, *The Inbetweeners*
London, May 2012

Introduction

First off, I think I should say that writing an introduction to a book of scripts you've co-written is absolutely lovely and something I never even in my wildest dreams thought would happen. And what that means is I'm writing this introduction thinking primarily about the good times I've had with these scripts – the laughs, if you will – and not the many many times where I've sat with my head in my hands staring at the screen or the printed pages thinking, This is so terrible, how can we even show this to people, let alone film it? So, expect this introduction to be a little bit chirpier than you might expect from someone described in print by his long-term friend and writing partner Damon Beesley as 'pathologically pessimistic'.

I really didn't ever expect us to get the chance to write more than the one, pilot, episode. And even writing that, for me, was all about scratching an itch. Like I'm sure numerous friends around the country who make each other laugh do, Damon and I used to say (mostly after a couple of drinks) that we should write a sitcom. *We should write a sitcom.* We said it so often over a period of years but did so little about it that it got to the point where we thought that it wasn't ever going to happen. It was just a stupid idea. Now, it could have been my impending thirtieth birthday, or Damon moving out of the flat to live with his girlfriend (you won, Nicole, OK?), but one day we decided that there was really no reason not to do it. For my part I was propelled by mortality and knowing that I really didn't want to wake up in twenty years' time wishing I'd at least tried to write something, even if it was terrible shit. And I assumed it would be shit (there's that pessimism), because we'd never written anything long-form before. However, I decided that even if it turned out to be terrible, it was better to have tried and failed – then at least I wouldn't be left wondering. Corny as it sounds I was inspired by a couplet from one of the lesser-known Shakespeare plays, *Measure for Measure*: 'Our doubts are traitors and make us lose the good we oft might win by fearing to attempt.' (Although I saw recently that Gary Lineker's new wife has it tattooed on her tit, so it's obviously better known than I'd realised, certainly now.)

So we left our really nice, well-paid jobs to write this thing. We had both worked in comedy for many years – I started out making tea for Prince Edward then Skinner and Baddiel, Damon started out servicing Zig and Zag – and by the time we were thinking about writing, I was lucky enough to have a job as a commissioning editor for comedy at Channel 4.

Now, you might think that gave me an unfair advantage, and you'd be right, it did, but maybe not in the obvious ways. If what we'd written really was terrible shit, then E4 wouldn't have made it, no matter how well we knew the controllers. The ways that job actually gave me an advantage were threefold. Firstly, it involved working for comedy-producing legend Caroline Leddy – more on her later – and secondly, despite never having written anything narrative, my job at Channel 4 involved reading other people's scripts every day. Being exposed to that much material was a huge and fast lesson in narrative comedy. Obviously the quality varied, but I remember on my first day I was presented with the scripts to the original series of *Phoenix Nights*, written by Peter Kay, Neil Fitzmaurice and Dave Spikey. Reading them was an incredible eye-opener. Obviously I was a huge fan of sitcoms on TV, but seeing the words written down for one that hadn't been made yet was something different, and these scripts were something different again. Every line was a joke, every stage direction made me laugh. The way the dialogue was written was so economical, yet the whole script was visual as well as being verbal so I could 'see' the jokes happening. It was the most impressive thing I'd ever seen, and immediately set a benchmark for me. I started to think, OK, so this is the level we are talking about if you want to get a sitcom on Channel 4. *Phoenix Nights* was, and is, exceptional, and I wish I could say that every script I've ever delivered lived up to it.

Thirdly, my job at Channel 4 allowed me to meet Andrew O'Connor, Phil Clarke, Sam Bain and Jesse Armstrong – the team behind *Peep Show* (although Phil Clarke also introduced me to kickboxing at the Martial Arts Place, which changed my life for the better more fundamentally than I have time to express here). Sam and Jesse were relatively unknown at the time, compared to the genre-straddling colossi they are today, but were clearly great writers and from the first ten pages I read of what became *Peep Show*, I knew that I wanted to write like them. They were incredibly kind, letting me stick my nose into their work, offer up stories, even sit in on the casting sessions. On a prosaic level, Sam and Jesse taught me a process of writing with a partner that Damon and I have used for every script after our first one. Briefly put, it's coming up with the stories together, writing a longish scene-by-scene document, then quartering up the scenes to actually write the first draft. So I might write scenes 1–5, Damon will write 6–10, I'll write 11–15 and he'll do the rest. Then we'll rewrite and rewrite them together until the joins disappear. Phil and Andrew let me nose in on the way they produced *Peep Show*, and when I left Channel 4 without a job they kindly let me stay on the show as a script editor, something that has been as enjoyable as you'd imagine working out what disaster will next befall your favourite sitcom characters would be.

Returning to the second most important person in the writing of these scripts, Caroline Leddy, if you read her CV (*Brass Eye*, *Smack the Pony*, *Three Lions*, *Friday Night Dinner* and many more) it wouldn't be an exaggeration to use the cliché 'Queen of Comedy'. But that would imply a distance she doesn't have. Caroline to us is more a mixture of forensic scientist and sergeant major. To torture this analogy, she gets up to her elbows in the innards of our scripts from an early stage and helps us find out what's wrong as well as what's good. Then, when we feel we can't work out how to make things better, she pushes and cajoles us, and ultimately inspires us, to make the scripts and the show the best they can possibly be.

Something not a lot of people know is that almost all the voice-over is written after we've started editing the show, and is often added right up to the last second before delivery of the finished episode. This is due to Caroline pushing and pushing us to make each one funnier and funnier, sometimes almost to breaking point, but fundamentally we know that she's right and also that she's only doing it for the good of the show and therefore, us. If you're thinking of writing a script I cannot recommend highly enough finding someone who you trust, someone you think is hilarious, and someone who will give you a sometimes brutally honest assessment of what you've written. In Caroline we have all three and although we could have written these scripts without her input, they wouldn't have been very good, and the show wouldn't exist. So, in a very real sense, this book is for you, Caroline. Although, ironically, you've already read it twenty times.

The scripts don't exist in isolation, though, and you might notice that as the series progress the characters subtly change the way they talk. That's because of four young gentlemen who are four of the nicest and funniest people you'd ever care to meet. Writing the scripts didn't get easier as the series went on, but we definitely could 'hear' the characters more, and could hear them being funny, and that was due to the skill of Joe, Simon, James and Blake. Strictly speaking, they never wrote a line of these scripts, but without their input on the storylines before we wrote them, their ideas during rehearsal, their enthusiasm for the lines on-set and their occasional improvisation ('I wet your mum's bed – with my spunk' for example is all Buckley), these scripts wouldn't be of any interest to anyone. I can't thank them, and all the actors who brought these scripts to life, enough really, but I should try. So thank you from the bottom of my heart for making our silly lines funny and strangely more lovable than we would have thought possible.

So, nearly finally, to the most important person in the writing of what's in this book, Damon Beesley. Our process pretty much has always been perspiration over inspiration. We write ideas on Post-it notes, stick them up on the walls of a small room we rent away from the main production office, and then lock the door and stare at them until they start to form themselves into groups or scenes. We write those up, show that document to people we trust for comment (Robert Popper, Caroline, Shane Allen at Channel 4 and Chris, our producer), and if we get a broad thumbs up we lock ourselves back in the same room, quarter the script up as described above and start to type out a first draft.

Then we start the real work, which is rewriting and rewriting that draft until quite quickly we forget who wrote what in the first place. Going through this book I'd find it impossible to tell you exactly who wrote which joke – with the exception of about five brilliant ones from Damon that I remember very clearly from the first time I read them (including 'That's what you get for leading on paedos, you slut,' which has stuck for some reason). During the process of writing each series Damon and I would spend about four months shut together in that tiny office, the walls 90 per cent covered in those Post-it notes – which read things like 'Simon's bollock pop?' – facing each other across two small, impersonal desks under harsh white office lighting. Occasional visitors, and there weren't many, would be shocked not just by the size of the rooms but also by how bare they were apart from the Post-its. If people popped in, their faces would drop and immediately betray them, saying 'You work in here? It's horrible.' And they had a point. During the four months writing the film we didn't even open the security grilles on the windows. But it never bothered us, and in those rooms Damon and I worked as hard as I think you can when all you do is write knob jokes, and we made each other laugh, and occasionally we played Peggle, and we chatted about stuff, and we never fell out or had a fight. If we got sick of each other, or someone was having a bad day, the trip to Pret at lunchtime would remove any vague 'atmosphere' there might have been, so much so that looking back now I can't remember there ever having been such an atmosphere.

If you want my advice on writing with another person, then trust, as in most relationships, is at the heart of it. You are in it together, so when one of you says something you have to accept that he is not saying it to try and destroy the piece but because he believes it and so you have to question yourself and think, This person is intelligent and on my side, so why does he think that? I've been luckier than I could have ever imagined to have such a creative, funny, intelligent person to work with, and sitting now in America writing this, having not shut ourselves in a room for quite a while and not knowing when it will happen again, I miss our Pret a Manger lunches more than you know.

I'd also like to thank Jill and Malcolm Arconian not just for putting up with me when I was an Inbetweener, but also for lending us their home in Branscombe, Devon, to write 'Bunk Off' amongst other things, and Will Palin for his marginally less bucolic but no less useful house on Sheppey.

Really finally, I should thank the two women in my life, Pat Morris and Marchelle Bradanini, not just for their support but for the material. Mum's unswerving love, amongst other things, went to the point of suggesting to Damon he put a suppository up my arse if I ever got a migraine, and Marchelle was so keen to make me look vaguely fashionable that she once made me try on the same outfit as a mannequin in a clothes shop, including the tie and stupid glasses. Thank you both for everything. I know it's not been easy.

I hope you enjoy the scripts and that they make you laugh. Because really that's all it's been about.

IAIN MORRIS
Los Feliz, May 2012

SERIES 1

Episode 1

Ah, Episode One. Described during a dark time in the edit as 'like an unfunny *Grange Hill*'. Not written first ('Bunk Off' was the first), this episode came about when we knew that we had a series, and after much discussion decided that an episode where we explained why Will McKenzie was in this situation would be a good thing in terms of clarity, even if it meant that we'd have to put in a bit more exposition than we'd normally like – because inevitably it comes at the expense of 'jokes'. The *Grange Hill* comment came when we realised we had so much introduction to the 'sit' that it could be overbalancing the 'com' – and therefore whether anyone would actually watch it.

When we were writing it the idea was to try to introduce Will quickly, get some jokes in, definitely make it school-based, and try to hit some universal themes. The main theme for Ep One, which I think went relatively well, was the idea of getting served under age. We've all done it, or tried to do it, and I think the second half of the ep rattles along and deals with that rather nicely. The first half was trickier, and we spent an incredible amount of time in the cutting room (no one ever calls it that by the way, it's just called 'the edit') editing, re-editing and rewriting this episode.

The toilet scene was written and shot months after the end of the main body of filming, and the 'I'm Will and I'm having a shit' sign was made by our runner John Kennedy and shot on the wall of the edit suite. Excellent work by him, and we thanked him by naming the 'paedo' character in Series Two and Three after him.

——— OPENING MONTAGE ———

EXT. SCHOOL

WILL V/O   *Hi, I'm Will and here are some things I hoped wouldn't happen in my life. My father would leave my mother . . .*

SHOT OF WILL CRYING INTO HIS MUM'S ARMS.

WILL   I'm so sad.

WILL V/O   *. . . I'd be taken out of private education and forced to go to a normal school . . .*

SHOT OF WILL, WASTE PAPER BIN ON HIS HEAD.

WILL   Well this is nice.

WILL V/O   *. . . where the school nutter would take a bit of a dislike to me . . .*

SHOT OF MARK DONOVAN THREATENING WILL.

MARK DONOVAN   I'll rip your fucking throat out.

WILL V/O   *. . . but they do say whatever doesn't kill you makes you stronger. Except polio. And it's not been all bad . . .*

SHOT OF A GIRL KISSING WILL.

GIRL WITH RED-STREAKED HAIR   I'm gonna take you outside and I want you to fuck me.

WILL   Really?

WILL V/O   *. . . this is the story of how I made new friends. . .*

. . . like him . . .

SHOT OF JAY JUMPING ON HIS FRIEND'S CAR.

JAY   Friend, *fucking friend.*

WILL V/O   *. . . and him.*

SHOT OF NEIL.

WILL V/O   *And him . . .*

SHOT OF SIMON PUKING.

WILL V/O. *. . him not so much.*

SHOT OF MARK DONOVAN.

WILL V/O   *And definitely her.*

SHOT OF WILL AND CHARLOTTE.

WILL   Just to confirm, we are going to have sex?

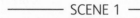

——— SCENE 1 ———

INT. HEADMASTER'S OFFICE

WILL V/O   *But back to the present. To put you in the picture, I've no friends, it's my first day and I'm in the Headmaster's office for a welcome chat with the rest of the new kids. Or, as they're otherwise known, the freaks . . .*

WILL IS WITH THE THREE OTHER NEW KIDS IN THE HEADMASTER'S OFFICE. ONE IS MASSIVE AND LOOKS LIKE HE MIGHT BE SPECIAL NEEDS, HE'S GRINNING SO MUCH. ANOTHER IS A KID WHO IS REALLY SHORT BUT HAS A MASSIVE HEAD THAT LOOKS LIKE THE HEAD OF A MAN TWENTY YEARS OLDER. AND THE THIRD IS A REALLY QUIET YOUNG GIRL WITH MASSIVE GLASSES.

MR GILBERT, THE HEAD OF SIXTH FORM, IS ALSO SITTING WITH THEM.

JOHN   You could be friends with us.

WILL V/O   *. . . yep, everyone's going to think I'm one of them. And in a well-meaning but disastrous move, as a new kid I've got to wear a massive green badge. At least I could discuss it with my Head of Sixth, Mr Gilbert. He seemed like an intelligent man . . .*

WILL   Mr Gilbert, you seem an intelligent man.

MR GILBERT   Ah, I seem intelligent. How lovely of you to say.

WILL   No, I just meant—

MR GILBERT   I mean I've long since been insecure about my capacity for learning, so it's nice to have it ratified by you, a child.

WILL   What I meant was, do you really think these badges that single us out as new kids are a good idea?

MR GILBERT   Yes. And if you have any more views on it I suggest you join the school debating society. Obviously you'll have to start one first.

THE BELL GOES.

WILL V/O   . . . *oh, my mistake, he's a wanker* . . .

WILL RELUCTANTLY PUTS HIS BADGE ON HIS BLAZER WHILE THE OTHER KIDS SEEM ENTHUSIASTIC ABOUT THEIRS, SORT OF SAYING HELLO TO EACH OTHER, ALMOST AS IF THEY ARE PRACTISING WHAT IT WILL BE LIKE WITH OTHER PEOPLE.

SUSIE   Hello John, I'm Susie.

WILL V/O   . . . *and so began my first day.*

——— SCENE 2 ———

INT. CLASSROOM

WILL OPENS THE DOOR TO FIND HIS NEW CLASSMATES, ABOUT TEN IN ALL, IN A NOT VERY BIG CLASSROOM.

WILL   Is this 6B?

CLASS MEMBER   Yeah.

WILL   Great. I'm Will. Cool. God, I just had to meet with the Head and his pet ape, Gilbert. What's his problem?

CLASS MEMBER   What?

WILL   That Gilbert. What a tosser.

EVERYONE IN THE ROOM HAS KIND OF STOPPED AND LOOKED ROUND AT WILL, WHICH HE HAS INTERPRETED AS POPULARITY AND SO NOW STARTS TO GRANDSTAND A BIT, THINKING THIS IS GOING BRILLIANTLY.

WHAT HAS ACTUALLY HAPPENED IS THAT MR GILBERT HAS COME INTO THE ROOM AND IS STANDING BEHIND HIM, AND EVERYONE HAS GONE QUIET.

WILL   I mean, 'Ooh, I'm Mr Gilbert, I'm such a big, huge, massive freak and I just love to suck the Headmaster's balls. And then . . .' Is he behind me?

HE TURNS. MR GILBERT GRINS A BIG GRIN.

WILL   Did you hear any of that?

MR GILBERT   Oh yes.

WILL   Can we start again?

MR GILBERT   As you can see from his rather natty badge, this is your new classmate, Will. As you share most of the same classes Cooper, you'll be looking after him.

SIMON   Sir, that's not fair.

MR GILBERT   Lesson number one of the Sixth Form: life is not fair.

SIMON   Sir, look at his blazer for starters. He's got an actual briefcase. His shoes are clumpy. His hair's a bit gay. And that badge. I mean the badge alone.

MR GILBERT   It's happening, get used to it.

THE BELL GOES. WILL GETS UP READY TO GO.

MR GILBERT   Oh, one more thing, the first-day-of-term drink down the Black Horse, this tradition is not only ridiculous, but illegal. Don't get excluded before you've even started.

WILL AND SIMON AND THE OTHER PUPILS ARE HEADING OUT OF THE CLASSROOM DOOR.

WILL   What's he talking about?

SIMON   Nothing.

WILL   Is everyone going for a drink tonight then?

SIMON   Erm, no. I have to go this way.

———— SCENE 3 ————

INT. SCHOOL CORRIDOR

WILL IS WALKING THROUGH THE SCHOOL CORRIDOR, PASSING GROUPS OF KIDS, MOST OF THEM YOUNGER THAN HIM, WHO ARE LAUGHING AT HIS BADGE.

WILL CONTINUES TO WALK THROUGH IT ALL, BUT ALL THE TIME HE TALKS UNDER HIS BREATH SARCASTICALLY.

KID A   Ooh, I'm Will.

WILL   Yep, thanks very much.

KID B   Ooh, hello Will.

WILL   Yes, that's very nice, thank you.

KID C   Nice badge, dickhead.

WILL   Lovely, fantastic. You must be what, Year 8?

KID D   Ooh, I'm Will, I've got the spacker badge.

WILL   Spacker, super, that's what they call it, a badge, so . . .

KID E   Briefcase wanker.

WILL   The baggage-themed insult. Thanks Mum, thanks a bunch.

———— SCENE 4 ————

INT. BOYS' TOILETS

WILL V/O   *Truth be told, the first-day nerves had got to me, so I went for what turned out to be one of the more eventful shits of my life.*

WE SEE WILL ENTERING THROUGH THE MAIN DOOR OF THE TOILETS. HE LOOKS LIKE A BOY WHO NEEDS A SHIT.

HE ENTERS A CUBICLE AND PULLS HIS TROUSERS DOWN. HE'S CLEARLY GOING TO HAVE A SHIT. AS HE DOES, THE DOOR BURSTS OPEN AND JAY, NEIL AND SIMON COME IN.

JAY   I'm just really good at shagging now, that's all I'm saying.

NEIL   Bollocks. How do you do it best then?

JAY   Just deep, try to get really deep, right up to the balls.

NEIL   And do you put the balls in?

JAY   What?

NEIL   I've heard you've gotta put the balls in really to make it work.

JAY   Yeah, can do, some girls like it, some don't.

A REACTION SHOT OF WILL IN THE CUBICLE LOOKING REALLY WORRIED AND SCARED BY THE CONVERSATION.

SIMON   What? Stop talking bullshit. Who are these girls you've fucked then?

JAY   Look, while you've spent the summer stalking Carli, I've been out porking loads of vag.

SIMON   One, I've not been stalking Carli, she's just a friend. And two, you've never fucked anyone. Nor have I, nor has Neil.

JAY   Shut up, you dickhead. I've fucked loads of g—

THE DOOR SMASHES OPEN AND DONOVAN AND A MATE COME IN.

JAY SHUTS UP AS DONOVAN WALKS PAST HIM. THERE'S A MOMENT AS DONOVAN CLOCKS THAT ITS GONE QUIET. DONOVAN GOES OVER TO THE URINAL AND STARTS TO PISS.

MARK DONOVAN   What the fuck are you doing? You trying to look at my cock?

SIMON   Ha, good one.

MARK DONOVAN   Fuck off.

THE THREE LADS LEAVE THE TOILETS.

WILL V/O   *I was beginning to wonder what sort of place I'd come to. And then I found out.*

DONOVAN'S MATE IS OVER BY THE CUBICLE AND CAN SEE WILL'S SHOES POKING THROUGH UNDERNEATH. DONOVAN SEES WHAT HE IS LOOKING AT, AND GETS HIS CAMERA OUT. HIS MATE LAUGHS AND DOES THE SAME. THEY JUMP ONTO THE TOILET IN THE CUBICLE NEXT TO WILL AND WE SEE THEM STICK THEIR

CAMERAS OVER THE TOP. WE SEE WILL'S REACTION AND THEN HIS POV OF THEM LAUGHING, TAKING PICTURES.

WILL   Come on, guys.

——— SCENE 5 ———

INT. SCHOOL CORRIDOR

WILL IS WALKING DOWN ANOTHER BUSY CORRIDOR, STILL GETTING ABUSE FROM RANDOM KIDS.

KID F   You're gonna die here Will.

WILL   OK.

KID G   That briefcase makes me wanna punch you.

WILL   Course it does.

KID H   What a spastic badge.

WILL   That's been pointed out already.

KID I   Your shoes are well shit.

WILL   Yep, the shoes.

WILL SPOTS SIMON UP AHEAD IN THE CORRIDOR, PUTTING HIS BOOKS INTO A LOCKER.

WILL   Simon.

SIMON   All right.

WILL   How's it going?

SIMON   What, since about five minutes ago? Yeah, fine.

WILL   Great. I'm trying to find the common room, can you show me where it is?

SIMON   Erm, not really.

WILL   Oh.

KID J   Posh twat.

SIMON   Look, it's this way but do me a favour, just hang back a bit, yeah?

WILL   Oh sure.

KID K   Wanker.

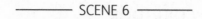

──────── SCENE 6 ────────

INT. SCHOOL COMMON ROOM

WILL V/O   *I still haven't managed to shake the freaks. It's not like I was aiming high, I just wanted to be friends with someone who didn't have a badge on.*

SIMON IS SITTING WITH JAY AND NEIL. HE LOOKS ACROSS TO THE OTHER SIDE OF THE COMMON ROOM WHERE WILL IS SITTING, LOOKING UNCOMFORTABLE WITH THE OTHER KIDS FROM THE HEAD'S OFFICE EARLIER.

SIMON   I might not go to this thing tonight, pretty knackered.

NEIL   We've just had ten weeks off.

JAY   Yeah but he's just spent the last ten weeks wanking three times a day. That's why he's knackered.

SIMON   Yeah, that's it. I've had 210 wanks and my cock's like a Peperami.

CARLI APPEARS. SHE'S A VISION OF LOVELINESS. WITH A COUPLE OF TOP BUTTONS UNDONE AND YOU CAN JUST SEE HER BRA. AND THIS HASN'T ESCAPED SIMON'S NOTICE.

CARLI   Whose cock's like what?

SIMON   Carli, oh, it's just, erm, nothing.

JAY   Are you coming to the pub tonight then? I'll be there.

CARLI   Great, that's great. Are you going Simon?

SIMON   Erm, not sure, sort of more into clubs than pubs.

JAY   Yeah, gay clubs. He's just shitting himself that he won't get served.

SIMON   No, it's not that.

CARLI   Come on, I'll buy you a drink. Can you do me a favour though?

SIMON   Sure, anything.

CARLI   OK, well you know what my mum's like, she'll freak if she hears I've been anywhere near a pub. So, don't mention it to your folks, yeah?

SIMON   Sure.

CARLI   Thanks hon. Oh, do you wear aftershave now?

SIMON   Oh, it's just Lynx.

AS SHE LEANS OVER TO GET A GOOD SNIFF, SIMON GETS A GOOD LOOK AT HER BRA DOWN HER TOP.

CARLI   That's nice.

THE BELL GOES.

SIMON AWKWARDLY STARTS TO CROSS HIS LEGS AND SLIGHTLY CROUCH FORWARD.

CARLI   Are you coming to sociology?

SIMON   Erm, no, I'm good here.

CARLI   Oh OK. Well I'll see you later then.

SHE LEAVES.

THERE'S A BEAT AS EVERYONE STRUGGLES TO PROCESS WHAT'S JUST HAPPENED.

JAY   Are you mental? She's so fit, why don't you just walk to class with her?

SIMON   Just don't feel like it.

JAY   Ah, what's wrong? Did you get a hard-on 'cos the pretty girl spoke to you?

SIMON   Can you fuck off?

JAY   Hang on, you haven't actually got a stalk-on, have you?

JAY PULLS SIMON'S HANDS FROM HIS CROTCH AREA AND WE GET A FLEETING
SIGHT OF AN ERECTION SPRINGING UP IN SIMON'S TROUSERS.

JAY   Oh my God, he's got a boner.

SIMON   Jay, please.

JAY   Oi, Simon's got a boner.

VARIOUS MEMBERS OF THE SIXTH FORM COME ROUND AND STARE AND LAUGH
AND POINT. WILL COMES OVER.

SOMEONE SHOUTS 'BONER'. THEN LOTS OF PEOPLE ARE SHOUTING 'BONER'.

JAY   Let's have a look, don't be shy, come on, let's have a look, show
us. Show us your boner.

WILL V/O   *. . . so I was left with a choice: stick with the freaks or try
to make friends with a boy they now called boner . . .*

WILL   Are you coming to sociology Simon? I'll save you a seat.

SIMON   Thanks.

WILL V/O   *. . . there you go, I suppose beggars can't be choosers . . .
and so my quest to make friends went, not worse, but certainly not
better. It was as if I had some kind of contagious disease and to be
seen with me was a form of social death. Which it is. But I was
amazed they worked it out so quickly. But it wouldn't stop me. Anyone
can be your friend, you just need to hang around them long enough.*

SHOT OF WILL HOLDING A CORRIDOR DOOR OPEN FOR A KID, THEN ENDLESS
KIDS PILING THROUGH SO HE CAN'T GET THROUGH HIMSELF AND IS JUST
HOLDING THE DOOR FOR LOADS OF THEM.

SHOT OF WILL SITTING DOWN AT A LUNCH BENCH AND KIDS IMMEDIATELY
GETTING UP AND MOVING AWAY.

———— SCENE 7 ————

EXT. SCHOOL

SIMON, NEIL, AND JAY ARE LEAVING SCHOOL AND WILL JUST ABOUT CATCHES UP
WITH THEM.

JAY   Oi, don't look left, Simon, there's a girl with a knee-length skirt on, you might just spunk in your pants.

WILL   Yeah, very good. Hi Simon.

SIMON   All right? This is Will.

WILL   Nice to meet you.

JAY   Ooh, briefcase.

NEIL   Yeah, briefcase.

WILL   Yes, it's a briefcase.

JAY/NEIL   Ooh, briefcase.

WILL   Right. These are your friends?

JAY   Where are we meeting tonight then?

NEIL   The Black Bull, it's just out on the London Road.

WILL   Oh, is this the drink thing? Great. What time?

JAY   You can get there whatever time you like, you're going on your own.

WILL   Oh, I just thought we could all—

JAY   No, you thought wrong.

SIMON   Shit, what happens if we don't get served? Carli will think I'm such a loser.

JAY   She'd be right.

WILL   She might not get served.

SIMON   Girls always get served. As soon as they get tits, they get served. And fit girls like her definitely always get served.

JAY   Well I'm gonna get served.

SIMON   And how do you know that?

JAY   I've got a fake ID, innit? A driving licence that says I'm eighteen years old.

NEIL   But you're not eighteen.

JAY Yeah that's right Neil, it's a fake ID.

WILL SEES HIS MUM (POLLY McKENZIE) PULLING UP AT THE GATES IN A
CONVERTIBLE SPORTS CAR.

WILL Oh no.

SIMON Is that your mum?

WILL I told her not to come and pick me up.

NEIL She's fit.

JAY Yeah, I'd fuck her.

WILL Thanks very much.

JAY No, but I would though, wouldn't you?

WILL Hmm, well, as she's my mum, no.

JAY But if she wasn't?

WILL She is though, so . . .

SIMON No, but what he's saying is, if she wasn't your mum, would
you fuck her?

WILL Oh are we still doing this?

NEIL So you would fuck her?

WILL No.

JAY Look, I just wanna know, if you get down between her legs,
spread them—

WILL Can we please stop talking about my mother's vagina?

IT'S GONE A BIT QUIET. HIS MUM LOOKS OVER. THE OTHER THREE ARE SMILING.

WILL Maybe see you tonight.

JAY You're not invited.

NEIL Unless you bring your mum.

——— SCENE 8 ———

INT. WILL'S MUM'S CAR

WILL   Did you have to pick me up?

POLLY McKENZIE   I just wanted to hear about your first day. I like your badge.

WILL   Why did you tell them I got bullied at Loreston?

POLLY McKENZIE   I thought you were.

WILL   No, I wasn't. I got wedgied a couple of times, but that was just a fad.

POLLY McKENZIE   Oh well, they wanted a reason and that's what sprang to mind.

WILL   Instead of 'I can't afford the school fees any more'?

POLLY McKENZIE   Yes.

WILL   I'm going to the pub tonight.

POLLY McKENZIE   With who?

WILL   Just some friends.

POLLY McKENZIE   Friends, already?

WILL   Yes, friends already.

POLLY McKENZIE   Well just make sure these so-called friends aren't just making fun of you.

WILL   Why would they be doing that?

POLLY McKENZIE   I just don't want you to get bullied again.

WILL   I was not bullied.

WILL   Can I borrow twenty quid?

—————— SCENE 9 ——————

INT JAY'S BEDROOM

WILL V/O   *For all the new Sixth Formers, this would be a massive night. It wasn't just the drink, this was an opportunity to reinvent yourself. A chance for a new start.*

JAY HAS THE BOX TO HIS OLD SCALEXTRIC SET ON HIS BED. HE'S CAREFULLY LIFTING OUT THE POLYSTYRENE PACKAGING TO REVEAL A COUPLE OF DODGY-LOOKING PORN MAGS. THEY LOOK WELL THUMBED. IN THE BOX IS WHAT'S OBVIOUSLY A FAKE DRIVING LICENCE. JAY KISSES IT.

————— SCENE 10 —————

INT. NEIL'S HOUSE

NEIL'S BY THE DOOR, POURING MONEY OUT OF A MONEY JAR. HE IS TALKING TO HIS DAD (KEVIN SUTHERLAND).

KEVIN SUTHERLAND   And I've told you money's tight.

NEIL   Do you want me to be called pikey by my mates? Do you?

BACK TO

INT JAY'S BEDROOM

JAY PICKS UP ONE OF THE MAGAZINES AND STARTS TO FLICK THROUGH IT, STOPS AT A PAGE, LOOKS AT HIS WATCH AND BEGINS TO UNDO HIS TROUSERS.

MRS CARTWRIGHT (OFF SCREEN)   Jay, I've got your dinner.

JAY (PANICKED)   Don't come in, don't come in.

WE HEAR THE SOUND OF FOOTSTEPS ON THE STAIRS. JAY IS SCRAMBLING TO PUT EVERYTHING BACK.

MRS CARTWRIGHT (OFF SCREEN)   All right, I won't come in.

JAY   Mum, can I borrow twenty quid?

BACK TO

INT. NEIL'S HOUSE

KEVIN SUTHERLAND   Here's £10, just promise me you won't spend it on the fruit machines.

NEIL   I can't do that, I'm afraid. Bye.

HE LEAVES.

——— SCENE 11 ———

INT. SIMON'S HOUSE

WILL V/O   *Of course it turned out we couldn't reinvent ourselves without our parents noticing . . .*

SIMON IS GETTING READY, PUTTING SOME OF THAT REALLY CHEAP GEL IN HIS HAIR. AS HE FINISHES, HIS MUM (PAMELA COOPER) POPS HER HEAD ROUND THE DOOR.

PAMELA COOPER   That's a lot of gel you've got in your hair.

SIMON   What?

PAMELA COOPER   Smells quite strongly too.

SIMON   Why are you telling this to me now?

PAMELA COOPER   I'm just mentioning it. I can see you've got a lot in, that's all.

SIMON   I don't, I mean I can't wash it now, can I? I've not got time. God, I don't know why you are like this sometimes.

HE GOES OUT AND SLAMS THE DOOR. THERE'S A BEAT. WE HEAR THE KEY IN THE LATCH AND THE DOOR OPENS AGAIN.

SIMON   Can I borrow twenty quid?

WILL V/O   *. . . and by borrow, we meant spend and never give back. Next stop, the pub.*

——————— SCENE 12 ———————

EXT. PUB CAR PARK

WILL V/O   *My plan to make friends was working. Little by little I was wearing them down . . .*

IT DOESN'T LOOK LIKE AN ESPECIALLY NICE PUB.

SIMON, JAY AND NEIL ARE IN THE CAR PARK. WILL ARRIVES FROM ROUND THE CORNER AND CALLS TO THEM.

WILL   Hey guys.

JAY   Not him?

SIMON   Oh, he's all right.

WILL   Sorry I'm late.

JAY   Fingering your mum.

WILL   Let me think, erm no. No I wasn't.

SIMON   Right, so what's the plan?

JAY   We don't need a plan. We go in there, buy some drinks and then wait for the gash to form an orderly queue.

WILL   Sorry, did he actually say 'gash'?

JAY   It'll be fine, relax.

SIMON   There is nothing relaxing about this. If we don't get served, I will be humiliated in front of the girl I've lusted after since she was eight.

NEIL   You fancy eight-year-olds?

SIMON   No, Neil, our families are friends and we were both eight.

NEIL   Yeah, but you still fancied an eight-year-old.

JAY   Come on, I've got ID, we'll be fine. You coming in, new boy?

WILL   I do have a name.

JAY   Sorry, are you coming then, briefcase mong?

WILL   Brilliant, after you.

———— SCENE 13 ————

INT. PUB

THEY WALK IN BUT STOP AT THE DOOR. THERE ARE LOTS OF TABLES FREE AND A PRETTY DEAD ATMOSPHERE, LOTS OF EMPTY TABLES. THERE ARE THREE PRETTY HARD-LOOKING BLOKES AT THE BAR, DRINKING INDIVIDUALLY, WHO ALL LOOK ROUND AS THEY WALK IN.

THE BOYS ARE KIND OF FROZEN IN THE DOORWAY.

WILL   Well this is nice.

SIMON   Maybe we should come back later.

JAY   Don't shit yourself, we're just the hard core. I'll get 'em in. What you having?

NEIL   Pint of lager.

SIMON   Pint.

WILL   Doesn't a pint seem like a lot when you think about it? I mean you wouldn't drink pint after pint of orange squash, would you?

JAY   What do you want?

WILL   Pint. Of Guinness.

SIMON   Guinness?

NEIL   Oh brilliant, a fruity.

NEIL THEN HEADS STRAIGHT OVER TO THE FRUIT MACHINE AND STARTS EXCITEDLY PUTTING MONEY INTO IT STRAIGHT AWAY.

DURING THE FOLLOWING WE CAN SEE THE BOYS NERVOUSLY LOOKING OVER TO CHECK THAT JAY IS GETTING SERVED.

JAY IS AT THE BAR, STANDING BETWEEN A COUPLE OF THE HARDER MEN.

JAY   Oi, bruv.

BARMAN   Yes, bruv.

JAY   Three pints of lager and a pint of Guinness.

BARMAN   Got any ID?

JAY   Yeah.

JAY GETS HIS FAKE ID OUT OF HIS POCKET AND HANDS IT OVER.

BARMAN   Brett Clement.

JAY   Yep.

BARMAN   And you know this is an Australian driving licence?

JAY   Yep.

BARMAN   So you're Australian?

JAY   That's right, mate.

BARMAN   So when's your birthday?

JAY   Fifteenth of bloody May 1989.

BACK OVER AT THE TABLE WITH WILL, SIMON AND NEIL.

WILL   Is he speaking in an Australian accent?

SIMON   Sounds like it.

BACK OVER AT THE BAR WITH JAY AND THE BARMAN.

BARMAN   Right. What do you want again?

JAY   Three jars of lager and a Guinness.

BARMAN   Are the other drinks for your mates?

JAY   You betcha, cobber.

BARMAN   Well I'm not serving them unless they've got ID as well.

BACK OVER AT THE TABLE WITH THE BOYS. JAY COMES BACK TO THE TABLE WITH A PINT.

SIMON   Where are our drinks?

JAY   Oh, did you want drinks too? Well you'd better go and fucking get them then.

SIMON   This is tragic, one pint between four of us.

WILL   As Jay has clearly failed, I will deal with this.

WILL GOES UP TO THE BAR.

WILL V/O . . . *I'd never been served in a pub before, but how hard could it be?*

WILL   Good evening. Could I have three pints, please?

BARMAN   Do you have any proof of age?

WILL   You have my word.

BARMAN   Any ID?

WILL   Look, my father's left my mother and I've been forced to go to a comprehensive school. I've attached myself to a fairly average group and all I'm trying to do is make a few new friends to make life bearable. You're human, you understand that. Now perhaps you can pour me three non-alcoholic lagers and we won't tell anyone about it.

BARMAN   Can't serve you at all if you're under age.

WILL   Right. You've driven me to this.

HE GOES IN HIS POCKET AND GETS OUT A SMALL BOOKLET CALLED 'TEENAGERS – KNOW YOUR RIGHTS'. IT'S WRITTEN IN THE SORT OF 'GRAFFITI' WRITING THAT ONLY A LOCAL COUNCIL COULD PRODUCE – I.E. VERY SHIT.

WILL   The law states sixteen-year-olds can legally drink cider, perry or mead in a pub if they're eating a meal. So I'll have three pints of cider and three carvery dinners, please.

BARMAN   It also states if it is bought by an adult and they are accompanied by an adult. No adult, no alcohol, I'm afraid.

WILL   This isn't over.

HE TURNS TO ONE OF THE OLDER HARD-LOOKING (POSSIBLY ALCOHOLIC) MEN AT THE BAR (STEVE).

WILL   Hello, sir. My name's William. I'll pay for your drinks all night if you'll just order me three pints of cider and three carvery dinners and then come and sit with my friends and me. You don't have to talk to us, you merely need to stay sitting with us.

MAN AT BAR   Yeah all right. Terry, I'll have three ciders, three carveries and four double rum and Cokes please, mate.

WILL   As many as four?

WILL RETURNS TO THE TABLE WITH STEVE.

WILL   Sorted.

SIMON   And who's that?

WILL   Oh this is . . . What's your name?

MAN AT BAR   Steve.

WILL   Steve. He'll be joining us.

SIMON   Why?

NEIL   All right, Steve.

SIMON   Where are our drinks?

WILL   It's a long story that involves Steve as well. Now before we get our cider—

NEIL   Cider?

WILL   Yes, cider, we've got to go to the carvery.

SIMON   Have you gone mental? What's Carli gonna think? Yeah, Simon's pretty cool, whenever he goes out he always has meat and gravy with his booze.

WILL   Well we're not going to get served unless we each get a carvery.

JAY   Nice work, briefcase.

SIMON   Oh for Christ's sake.

SIMON, WILL AND JAY GET UP TO GO TO THE CARVERY.

SIMON   You coming then Neil?

NEIL   Get mine for me.

SIMON, JAY AND WILL GO.

NEIL   All right?

STEVE   Yep.

NEIL   I just lost ten quid on the fruity.

STEVE   Oh really?

NEIL   Yeah.

STEVE LOOKS OVER AT THE FRUIT MACHINE, THEN GETS UP, GOES OVER AND STARTS PUTTING MONEY IN IT.

NEIL   Oi.

AS THE OTHERS APPROACH THE CARVERY, SIMON GETS A TEXT.

NEIL COMES OVER.

SIMON LOOKS AT HIS PHONE.

SIMON   Oh shit, it's from Carli.

JAY   Oh brilliant. Is she asking if your fit mate Jay is coming?

SIMON   No, she's saying it's so packed she can't see where we are.

HE LOOKS AROUND. THE PUB IS AS EMPTY AS IT WAS.

JAY   Is she a retard?

SIMON   She's in the Black Horse. Where are we?

NEIL   Black Bull.

SIMON   Right, so we're in the wrong pub. Let's go.

WILL   Well, let's not be hasty, we've got three carveries on the way.

SIMON   Neil, how could you confuse the Black Bull with the Black Horse?

NEIL   Oh come on, I was half right.

THEY RUN OUT TO THE NOISE OF STEVE WINNING BIG ON THE FRUITY.

———— SCENE 14 ————

INT. BLACK HORSE PUB

THE BOYS ENTER THROUGH THE DOOR QUITE FAST. EMBARRASSINGLY FAST.

LOTS OF TEENAGERS ARE THERE; THIS IS CLEARLY THE RIGHT PLACE.

SUDDENLY THERE IS A CHORUS OF 'BONER' FROM ALL OVER THE PUB AS THE BOYS STAND IN THE DOORWAY.

PEOPLE IN PUB   Boner. Boner. Boner.

WILL   Good start.

PEOPLE IN PUB   Boner. Boner.

SIMON   I'm going to find Carli.

NEIL   Whose round?

JAY   New boy's.

WILL   Again?

JAY   Yep.

WILL   Oh.

SIMON IS WALKING THROUGH THE PUB, LOOKING FOR CARLI, TO THE
OCCASIONAL COUGH OF 'BONER' AND 'STRAP IT DOWN' AS HE PASSES.

SHE SHOUTS OVER TO HIM. SHE'S SITTING DOWN ON A SOFA AT THE BACK OF
THE PUB. INCREDIBLY SHE HAS A SPACE NEXT TO HER.

CARLI   Simon, Simon.

SHE'S WAVING AND REALLY SMILING.

SIMON   Hi.

CARLI   Where have you been? Come and sit down. Hi.

HE SITS NEXT TO HER, THIS IS GOING BRILLIANTLY. SHE KISSES HIM ON THE
CHEEK AND HE CLOSES HIS EYES AS SHE DOES IT. WHEN SHE PULLS AWAY HE'S
KEPT THEM CLOSED FOR JUST A BIT TOO LONG, WHICH IS WEIRD FOR A CHEEK
KISS.

CARLI   Don't be shy, squeeze up.

SIMON   Oh really?

CARLI   Yeah, Tom's just coming back with the drinks.

A MASSIVE, HANDSOME RUGBY-PLAYING BLOKE WHO LOOKS A BIT OLDER COMES
OVER WITH A DRINK FOR CARLI.

WE SEE SIMON'S FACE FALL A BIT.

TOM SQUEEZES HIS MASSIVE AND IMPRESSIVE FRAME INTO THE SEAT NEXT TO
SIMON, SO SIMON IS CRUSHED BETWEEN HIM AND CARLI.

SIMON   Cool.

CARLI   Tom, this is Simon I was telling you about.

TOM   You all right, mate?

SIMON   Yeah, bit pissed, been to the Black Bull first just to sharpen up.

CARLI   Wow, this is a new Simon. I remember you used to cry when your dad poured whisky over the Christmas pudding.

SIMON   At least I didn't make myself sick in my plate when it had peas on it.

CARLI   Thanks for bringing that up.

NEIL AND JAY ARE BY THE QUIZ MACHINE, WATCHING ONE OF THE NEW KIDS PLAY.

NEIL   (ON SLOT MACHINE) Lee Sharpe, definitely Lee Sharpe.

JAY   Lee Sharpe.

IT'S THE WRONG ANSWER.

JAY   Oh, Roy Keane.

WILL IS AT THE BAR, SQUEEZING IN TO TRY AND GET SERVED.

WILL   Four pints please.

BARMAN   ID please.

WILL   You have got to be kidding me.

BARMAN   Can't serve you without ID.

WILL   Do you do food?

BARMAN   Kitchen's closed.

WILL   I'll just take the four pints then.

BARMAN   I'll just see your ID then.

WILL   Look, I've spent all night trying to buy one drink so I could take part in this poxy school tradition, so I'd like four pints of lager please.

PEOPLE ARE NOW LOOKING ROUND.

BARMAN   ID please.

WE ARE BACK WITH SIMON.

TOM   We should get going Carls.

CARLI   Oh yeah.

SIMON   You're going already?

CARLI   We've been here for two hours.

SIMON   Sure.

CARLI   Do you want a lift back Simon? Tom's got a car.

SIMON   Course he has. Nah.

TOM   Come on Carls. See ya, mate.

CARLI   See you later, Simon Pimon.

SIMON   Bye. See ya.

THEY LEAVE AND SIMON IS LEFT SADLY ON THE SOFA ON HIS OWN.

WE ARE BACK WITH NEIL AND JAY.

NEIL   Lee Sharpe. It's Lee Sharpe. Definitely Lee Sharpe.

JAY   Lee Sharpe. Lee Sharpe.

IT'S THE WRONG ANSWER.

JAY   Oh, Giggsy.

WILL IS STILL AT THE BAR.

IT'S NOT TOO BUSY AT THE ACTUAL BAR, BUT AROUND IT ARE A GROUP OF YOUNG TEENAGERS FROM THE SCHOOL.

WILL   Four pints of lager.

BARMAN   ID.

WILL   Look, just look around you. Everyone in this bloody pub is under-age.

WILL STARTS POINTING AROUND AT PEOPLE.

PEOPLE IN PUB   What? Shut up.

WILL   He's underage. She's underage. He looks a bit older cos he's uglier, but he's in the year below even me. (WILL STARTS TO WALK ROUND POINTING AT PEOPLE'S HEADS.) Look at that bum-fluff, 16. That bra's got padding in it. 16. His mum still buys his trousers. 16. 16. At a push, 17. 16, and this one, Mark Donovan, yeah he looks old and he's meant to be hard, but he's still only 16. All these people you've served, whatever bloody ID they used, are underage.

THE MUSIC IN THE PUB HAS STOPPED.

BARMAN   Right. We're closed. Everyone out.

WE HEAR GROANS.

EVERYONE LEAVES THE PUB QUICKLY.

MR GILBERT IS STANDING IN THE DOORWAY AS THE KIDS TRUDGE OUT.

MR GILBERT   Nice to see you again McKenzie. And congratulations on doing my job for me. I'll make sure you get another badge for this.

WILL   Sir.

MR GILBERT   Now get out, I want a pint.

WILL LEAVES.

MR GILBERT   Pint of lager please, Ian.

———— SCENE 15 ————

EXT. BLACK HORSE PUB

THE FOUR BOYS ARE WAITING FOR A LIFT HOME.

JAY   I don't care how fit your mum is, I wouldn't be seen dead in a car with you. Are you coming Si?

SIMON   Er nah, I said I'd look after supergrass here. I'd better not leave him on his own, just in case.

NEIL   Why are you staying with that bell-end?

WILL   I am here.

JAY   Yeah, I wish you weren't. See you later then.

NEIL AND JAY LEAVE.

WILL   What a first day. I'm such a twat.

SIMON   Yes you are. That was pretty specialist back there. 'His mum still buys his trousers' was a personal highlight.

WILL   Thanks. I made that up. Who was that guy with Carli?

SIMON   A friend, who didn't need ID. And had a car.

WILL   I'm sorry, mate.

SIMON   No it's OK.

MARK DONOVAN APPROACHES.

WILL   Please don't hit me.

WILL'S MUM (POLLY McKENZIE) ARRIVES IN HER CAR.

MARK DONOVAN   No, I'm not gonna hit you here, but I will get you. You won't know when it's coming, but it is coming. Some point in the next year, I will get you. Is that your mum? She is fit.

WILL   Thanks.

MARK DONOVAN   Lovely to meet you Mrs McKenzie. I will see you later Will, yeah?

POLLY McKENZIE   Nice to meet you. He seems nice.

MARK LEAVES.

WILL   He's the school psycho who just threatened to kill me.

POLLY McKENZIE   Well I'm glad you're making friends.

WILL   Do mums ever listen?

WILL AND SIMON GET INTO WILL'S MUM'S CAR.

WILL V/O   *I'd had an eventful first day. My quest for friends has lead to me alienating the entire school. And the psychotic Head of Sixth Form. And the really good news is, I'm now on the school nutter's 'to stab' list. If he doesn't shag my mum first. Maybe I should've just stuck with the freaks. At least things can only get better, or they could just stay the same. Or get worse.*

Episode 2

——— 'BUNK OFF' ———

This is the first piece of narrative comedy either Damon or I had ever written. And it's still a lot of people's favourite episode, meaning that we've been going downhill since the very start. This was also, uniquely, written by both of us. I typed, Damon stood behind and dictated. This is, I think, a very good way to write if you can get over the person behind you constantly pointing out your very obvious spelling mistakes.

This episode contains a lot of things that really happened, but also, unusually for the series, loses Jay and Neil for the majority of the second half. I think after this we thought of them more as a gang, and wanted them to each have some sort of storyline, so you can see a sort of evolution from this episode if you look hard enough.

I remember the exact moment that we decided that Simon should puke on Carli's brother. We had just finished writing the episode, and had each printed it off to read back. We came back into the kitchen in Branscombe and discussed what we thought, which was broadly that we liked it but the Simon/Carli stuff felt a bit underpowered for an ending with Carli's brother just crying. Crying children, even then, weren't enough for us. Then one of us, and I genuinely can't remember who, said, 'Simon could puke on the kid?' We thought that was pretty funny, not unrealistic, and probably a better ending, so we put it in knowing that if it was too much we could easily take it out. Then we walked down the hill to the Mason's Arms for lunch, arguably my favourite pub in the world, proud that we'd scratched the itch and written a script, but not confident that it would ever get made.

———— SCENE 1 ————

EXT. PARK

WILL V/O   *The local park, where people come to play football, hang out with their friends and most importantly, let their dogs shit . . .*

WE AREN'T TALKING RICHMOND PARK, OR EVEN HYDE PARK HERE. THIS IS A MUNICIPAL PARK, PROBABLY OPENED FOR THE SILVER JUBILEE.

WILL V/O   *. . . it's not a cool place, admittedly, but it is a good place to stare at girls, and if anything is worth braving this dog-shit minefield for, it's staring at girls . . .*

WILL, SIMON, JAY AND NEIL ARE PLAYING FRISBEE IN A WAY THAT ONLY TEENAGE BOYS CAN. THEY'VE ROLLED THE FRISBEE ONTO THE SAME PICNICKING COUPLE AT LEAST FOUR TIMES.

JAY   (LOOKING AT A GROUP OF HARD LADS PLAYING FOOTBALL) You lot are so gay. Why aren't we playing football?

WILL   Chasing men around a field with your top off, what could be more gay than that?

JAY   You.

WILL   Brilliant. Anyway, we're playing Frisbee 'cause girls can join in. Trust me, girls love this.

SIMON   Border collies love this. You're just scared to play football in case Donovan joins in and breaks your legs.

WILL   That's not true.

NEIL   Oh my God, check out the Jugasaurus Rex.

A GROUP OF GIRLS PASS BY INCLUDING CARLI D'AMATO. ONE OF THE GIRLS HAS QUITE A LARGE CHEST. THEY ARE DEFINITELY IN FRISBEE RANGE.

SIMON   Shit. And it's Carli.

WILL   Perfect. Watch this. Carli? Carli? Catch.

THE GIRLS LOOK OVER JUST AS THE FRISBEE LEAVES WILL'S HAND, GOES HIGH, AND THEN DOES THAT THING THAT THEY DO WHERE THEY ANGLE SLIGHTLY, CATCH THE WIND, AND SEEM TO BE ATTEMPTING A HUGE SWEEPING U-TURN WHILST ACCELERATING. IT'S NOW CLEAR TO EVERYONE THAT IT'S NOT GOING TO LAND ANYWHERE NEAR THE GIRLS BUT IS HEADING WAY OUT TO THE RIGHT.

EVERYONE SWINGS THEIR HEADS TO THE RIGHT TO SEE WHAT IT MIGHT HIT, AND THERE'S A WOMAN SITTING WITH HER DISABLED FRIEND, UNAWARE OF THE FLIGHT OF THE FRISBEE.

WE SEE WILL'S FACE AGHAST, SIMON STATIC AND JAY AND NEIL LEGGING IT IN THE TOTALLY OPPOSITE DIRECTION. THEY'RE GONE EVEN BEFORE THE IMPACT.

THE FRISBEE MAKES CONTACT WITH THE DISABLED GIRL'S FACE, HARD AND UNEXPECTEDLY FOR HER.

JAY   Oh fuck.

WILL, BEING WELL BROUGHT UP AND ALSO BEING THE OWNER OF THE FRISBEE, GOES RUNNING OVER.

SIMON STEALS A GLANCE AT CARLI AND THE GIRLS AND THEN DECIDES TO FOLLOW HIM.

THE GIRL'S FACE IS SCREWED UP IN PAIN.

GIRL IN WHEELCHAIR   Oh, oh.

WILL   Oh my God, I'm sorry. Sorry, sorry, sorry, sorry, sorry, sorry, I'm really, really sorry. I'm really, really, really sorry.

THE FRIEND, TAKING IT ALL IN, BEGINS TO YELL ABUSE AT HIM IN POLISH.

GIRL IN WHEELCHAIR'S FRIEND   (FOREIGN DIALOGUE) You idiot, oh my god.

WILL   So as I say, I'm sorry, I'm really, really sorry.

STILL THE SCREAMING CONTINUES. WILL LOOKS AT SIMON WITH A SORT OF SHRUG.

SIMON   It's fine, you've apologised about thirty times, come on.

WILL   I'm just going to get my Frisbee.

HE PICKS UP THE FRISBEE AND TURNS AWAY, AT WHICH POINT THE DISABLED GIRL STARTS SCREAMING AGAIN.

THEN THEY HEAR:

MARK DONOVAN   Oi, those wankers have nicked that girl's Frisbee. Hey.

WILL   It's my Frisbee. I've got a receipt. I've got a receipt.

HE STARTS PROPERLY RUNNING. SIMON NOW STARTS TO RUN TOO. THEY RUN AND RUN AND EVENTUALLY WILL CHUCKS THE FRISBEE OVER HIS SHOULDER WHILST RUNNING.

WILL V/O   . . . *and so, in what I can only describe as an attack of Frisbee rage, once again we found ourselves running from Donovan.*

———— SCENE 2 ————

EXT. ESTATE STREET CORNER

WALKING BACK FROM THE PARK, SIMON AND WILL ARE OUT OF BREATH. THEY APPROACH JAY AND NEIL, WHO ARE SITTING ON A WALL.

NEIL   All right.

SIMON   Not really.

NEIL   Oh, what's up?

WILL   Well think back Neil. Er, last time you saw us, before you legged it, a Frisbee was heading towards a disabled girl's face.

NEIL   Ah, did it hit her in the face then?

WILL   Bingo.

NEIL   Was the girl in the wheelchair all right?

WILL   No, I don't want to talk about it. I've lost a perfectly good Frisbee Aerobie Pro.

SIMON   Is the gayest sentence ever.

NEIL   Right, well that's it. We can't bunk off tomorrow now.

JAY   Ohh why?

NEIL   Well, 'cause it's bad karma innit. Threaten a spastic. Well, it could be a sign.

JAY   A sign that you've shit your pants.

WILL   I'll see you tomorrow, I'm heading home.

JAY   To wank over your mum's bras?

WILL   Er, well, as she's my mum, probably not.

JAY   Oh good, can I have 'em then?

WILL IS WALKING BACK AT A SAFE DISTANCE.

WILL   No, but you can have, um, that (GIVES HIM THE FINGER) and that (GIVES HIM THE OTHER FINGER). See you tomorrow.

SIMON   See ya.

NEIL   See ya.

——————— SCENE 3 ———————

INT./EXT. SIMON'S HOUSE

WILL V/O   *I'd only been in state education a month and yet the next morning, I found myself ready to break the law. OK, it was the truancy law, but it was still the worst thing I'd ever done . . .*

WILL, NOT IN SCHOOL UNIFORM, LOOKS AROUND SHIFTILY AND RINGS THE DOORBELL.

THE DOOR OPENS AND SIMON'S MUM (PAMELA COOPER) ANSWERS. WILL IS SURPRISED BY THIS AND EMITS A SURPRISINGLY SHORT AND HIGH-PITCHED YELP.

PAMELA COOPER   Hello William.

WILL   Hello Mrs Cooper. Is Simon in?

PAMELA COOPER   Yes, unless he ran away in the middle of the night. (SHOUTING) Simon.

SIMON HAS ARRIVED DIRECTLY BEHIND HER.

SIMON   Yes. Alright Will, come in.

SIMON'S MUM TAKES IN THE PAIR OF THEM, LOOKING THEM UP AND DOWN, REALISING THEY ARE NOT EVEN IN THE NOMINAL UNIFORM OF THE SIXTH FORM. SHE'S NO TIME FOR THIS.

PAMELA COOPER   Why aren't you in uniform?

WILL CRUMBLES IMMEDIATELY AND IS ABOUT TO COME CLEAN.

WILL   We're very sorry Mrs Cooper, it was Jay's idea.

SIMON   No, we're really sorry, we forgot to tell you, it was a non-uniform day.

SIMON'S YOUNGER BROTHER (ANDREW COOPER), WALKS PAST THEM IN VERY SMART UNIFORM, OUT OF THE DOOR AND TO THE CAR.

ANDREW COOPER   No it's not. Bye.

WILL LOOKS LIKE HE'S ABOUT TO CRY.

SIMON   (SHOUTS AFTER HIS BROTHER AS HE GETS INTO THE CAR) Yes it is, for Years 12 and 13. It is, you little shit.

PAMELA COOPER   Right, so it's a Year 12 non-uniform day?

For Christ's sake Simon, you're seventeen now and I don't want to play these stupid games.

SIMON   It's a bloody non-uniform day, all right?

PAMELA COOPER   I don't believe you. Will?

SIMON'S MUM STARES AT WILL. SIMON ALSO LOOKS AT WILL, WILLING HIM NOT TO CRUMBLE.

WILL   Yes, it's a non-uniform day.

SIMON   See.

PAMELA COOPER   Fine, fine, but if you've lied to me, I won't be angry, I will be really, really disappointed.

SIMON'S MUM LOOKS ENRAGED THEN SHE CLOSES THE DOOR BEHIND HER.

WILL   (DOES THE UNIVERSAL 'SPAZ' FACE AND NOISE) Urghhhh. How stupid is she, that she totally believed us.

SIMON   Er, that's my mum.

WILL   Sorry. Did you see the way I just lied to her? I totally did it. We're bunking off.

SIMON PICKS UP THE PHONE AND BEGINS TO DIAL.

WILL   Who you calling?

SIMON   School. I'll just say we're ill and won't be in today.

WILL   Huh. No really, who are you calling?

SIMON   Don't shit your pants; I'm only calling the school secretary, not fucking M15. (IN A HIGH VOICE AND UNDENIABLY RUSHING TO GET IT ALL OUT) Oh hello there, this is Mrs Cooper, Simon's mother, Year 12, Simon and his friend, William McKenzie have come down with food poisoning, must have been from the chicken.

WILL   You've put on your mum's voice.

──────── SCENE 4 ────────

INT. SCHOOL OFFICE

MEEK, ALL IN BROWN, THE MOUSY SCHOOL SECRETARY HAS ANSWERED SIMON'S CALL.

SCHOOL SECRETARY   Oh I'm sorry Mrs Cooper, now you say your son is ill?

SIMON   Yes.

SCHOOL SECRETARY   Oh well, Mr Gilbert the Head of Sixth is just here, I'll pass him over. Hold on one second.

SIMON   Oh no, there's really no need.

WILL   Look, if we hurry, we can still make it in time for English.

MR GILBERT TAKES THE PHONE. HE IS A MASSIVE MAN. HE LOOMS OVER HER.

MR GILBERT   Hello.

SIMON (VOICE GOING ALL THE TIME NOW) Hello, this is Mrs Cooper, Simon and his friend William are ill and won't be in today. Thank you. Goodbye.

MR GILBERT Mrs Cooper?

SIMON Yeah.

MR GILBERT What exactly is wrong with Simon?

SIMON (VOICE GONE NOW) Food poisoning.

MR GILBERT OK Simon, that's enough, I know you're bullshitting me. I think you better get into school.

SIMON Cheers, all the best, God bless.

MR GILBERT Simon, I'd get in before you make me—

SIMON HANGS UP VERY QUICKLY. HE KNOWS HE'S BUSTED BUT IS SORT OF KEEPING IT FROM HIMSELF, AND CERTAINLY FROM WILL.

WILL Well that was fucking dreadful.

SIMON I think he bought it though.

WILL In what way did he buy it?

SIMON I think he thought that was my mum.

WILL V/O . . . *so, with our terrible alibi in place, phase two of the plan was how to get some booze.*

──────── SCENE 5 ────────

INT. SIMON'S PARENTS' BEDROOM

THE BOYS ARE AT THE WARDROBE. WILL IS WEARING SIMON'S DAD'S LEATHER JACKET AND CHECKING HIMSELF OUT IN THE MIRROR. IT'S CLEARLY TOO BIG FOR HIM.

SIMON You look like you're on day release, they'll never serve you.

WILL Oh, what about this one?

WILL HAS PULLED OUT A SUIT HANGING ON THE RAIL.

SIMON No, not one of his suits, he'll go mental if he finds out.

WILL Shirts.

SIMON Not the suit.

WILL Yes.

SIMON Not the suit.

─────── SCENE 6 ───────

EXT. LOCAL HIGH STREET

WILL V/O *And so, in Simon's dad's suit and looking a bit like an Hasidic Jew, we headed for the off-licence.*

JAY AND NEIL ARE SITTING ON THE WALL IN FRONT OF THE OFF LICENCE. THE CAMERA SWINGS ROUND TO SEE SIMON AND WILL ARRIVE. WILL IS DRESSED IN A SUIT AND TIE, WITH A HAT.

JAY What, what are you wearing?

SIMON The suit's my dad's. He insisted. The hat's his though.

JAY What a bell-end.

WILL I'm just an adult man, stocking up on booze. This'll work, £10 each please.

THEY ALL HAND OVER THE MONEY UNSTINTINGLY, THIS IS CLEARLY PART OF THE PLAN. WILL TAKES THE CASH AND STRIDES CONFIDENTLY TOWARDS THE OFF LICENCE.

WILL (BEFORE HE ENTERS) . . . and as none of you offered to do it, you can fuck off.

JAY What?

WILL Nothing.

WILL V/O *Unlike those morons, I knew the key to getting served was confidence.*

———— SCENE 7 ————

INT. OFF LICENCE

THE BELL TINKLES, WE ARE IN A SORT OF THRESHER-TYPE WINE STORE. IN KEEPING WITH THE THEME, WILL IS DOING A BIT OF A VOICE:

WILL   Good day.

OFF-LICENCE OWNER   Sorry?

WILL   Good day.

OFF-LICENCE OWNER   Ah, hello.

———— SCENE 8 ————

EXT. STREET NEAR THE OFF LICENCE

SIMON, JAY AND NEIL ARE MUCKING ABOUT AND PUNCHING EACH OTHER. SIMON STOPS AS HE SPOTS SOMEONE IN THE DISTANCE.

NEIL   Shut up.

SIMON   Oh shit.

JAY   What?

SIMON   Nothing.

JAY   (LOOKING AND SEEING WHAT SIMON HAS SEEN: A PRETTY 40-SOMETHING WOMAN GETTING OUT OF HER CAR) That's Carli's mum, isn't it? Oi.

SIMON   Jay, please don't, she'll recognise me.

JAY (SHOUTING)   He wants to suck your Carli's tits.

CARLI'S MUM TURNS AND LOOKS OVER.

SIMON LOOKS AT HIS FEET WHILST JAY AND NEIL GIGGLE AND TURN AWAY.

SIMON   Unbelievable.

——— SCENE 9 ———

INT. OFF LICENCE

WILL V/O   *The key is to let the shop owner know who's in control. It's like a Jedi mind trick. I am an adult, you will serve me.*

WILL IS NOW A BIT SCARED AND IS IN THE MIDDLE OF THE SHOP. HE SPINS ROUND AND SPOTS THE KETTLE CHIPS AND PRINGLES, GRABS AN ARMFUL, THEN WALKS TOWARDS THE COUNTER.

OFF-LICENCE OWNER   Can I help at all?

WILL   Yes, I am a man who has recently bought a house in the local area and I'm having a house-warming party to which I'll be inviting a lot of the local adults to, hence the crisps.

OFF-LICENCE OWNER   Yes.

WILL   And I'll also probably need some alcohol as well, as well as the crisps etc.

OFF-LICENCE OWNER   Right, what sort of thing you looking for?

WILL   (SAYING THE FIRST THING HE SPOTS) Some Beefeater gin.

OFF-LICENCE OWNER   OK, so, how about two bottles?

WILL   Excellent.

OFF-LICENCE OWNER   Do you want some wine?

WILL   Christ no, we're not made of money. And I'll have some extra-strong mints, for those who are drink-driving.

OFF-LICENCE OWNER   Right. Comes to £29.50. Anything else?

WILL   What's on special?

OFF-LICENCE OWNER   I'll give you a bottle of Drambuie for £10 if you pay and are out of the shop in five seconds.

WILL   Done, my good man. I shall invite you to the party.

THE SHOP OWNER HANDS OVER THE BAGS AS HE TAKES THE MONEY.

WILL LEAVES.

——————— SCENE 10 ———————

EXT. STREET NEAR THE OFF LICENCE

WILL   Mission accomplished.

JAY   What's in all the bags then?

WILL   Just something to soak up the alcohol.

JAY GRABS A COUPLE OF THE BAGS AND RIFLES THROUGH THEM.

JAY   Crisps. Where's the beer?

SIMON   Have you spent all our money on fancy fucking crisps?

NEIL   You twat.

JAY   What the fuck's this?

WILL   Drambuie.

NEIL   And what's Drambuie?

WILL   It's a sort of whisky-based liqueur.

NEIL   And what's a liqueur?

JAY   It's what benders drink.

NEIL   Well why have we got that then?

SIMON   'Cos we're heading back to yours and it's your dad's favourite drink.

NEIL   Well my dad's not bent.

SIMON   He is a bit though.

NEIL   He's fucking not.

JAY   Right, let's look at the evidence. One, your mum left him because he loves cock.

NEIL   That's not true. Look, she was in a difficult place.

WILL   In bed with a bender.

SIMON   Your dad, who is a bender.

JAY   Two, he wears tight denim shorts to do the gardening.

SIMON   . . . and the only night he goes out all week is Wednesday and that's to play badminton.

THEY LAUGH.

NEIL   Right, my dad's not bent because he's got hundreds of porn mags at home and it's all straight.

SIMON   All straight.

NEIL   Well some lesbian.

SIMON   Well, I think we should go and have a look at it in that case.

NEIL   Well fine, come on then.

WILL   This should be good. I bet it's 90 per cent cock.

——— SCENE 11 ———

INT. NEIL'S HOUSE, LIVING ROOM

IT'S A 1980S SEMI-DETACHED HOUSE THAT IS VERY TIDY BUT REALLY QUITE DARK AND MISSING A WOMAN'S TOUCH.

WILL AND NEIL ARE MIXING THE DRINKS TOGETHER, POURING THEM IN SHOT GLASSES AND THEN HANDING THEM OUT. THEY ARE ALL NAILING THEM ON THE COUNT OF THREE AND THEN LOOKING LIKE THEY'VE SUCKED LEMONS.

NEIL   They must be round here somewhere. I don't know where they could have gone.

WILL   Maybe he swapped them for an Abba box set.

JAY   No, he probably shoved them up his arse. Drink.

ALL FOUR BOYS DOWN ANOTHER SHOT OF DRAMBUIE AND WINCE.

SIMON   So what we gonna do today then?

JAY   We can do anything we fucking well please.

WILL   Yeah, but specifically, what are we doing?

NEIL   We could get hold of some birds?

SIMON   Yeah, let's get some girls. Great. Where are all the girls?

WILL   At school.

JAY   Well, we'll wait for them to get out then.

SIMON   So we're not going to do anything till three thirty. We could have just gone to school then.

JAY   We can't fucking do this at school. Drink.

———— SCENE 12 ————

INT. SCHOOL OFFICE

MR GILBERT   (ON THE PHONE) Hello Mrs Cooper? Sorry to bother you at work. This is Mr Gilbert, Simon's Head of Sixth.

BACK TO

INT. NEIL'S HOUSE, LIVING ROOM

NEIL   You know, your mum is so fit, Will, I reckon she could be a prostitute.

WILL   Thanks.

SIMON   Have you wanked over Will's mum?

NEIL   No. Not yet.

WILL   Please don't have a wank over my mum.

NEIL   I can't promise that I'm afraid.

BACK TO

INT. SCHOOL OFFICE

MR GILBERT IS ON THE PHONE.

MR GILBERT   Yes hello, is that Mrs McKenzie, William's mother? Right, can I just check something with you, please?

BACK TO

INT. NEIL'S HOUSE, LIVING ROOM

JAY   When we go away with the Caravan Club, there's this bird and her sister, who I've shagged for about two years. Sometimes I get them to strum themselves while I watch.

SIMON AND NEIL ARE LISTENING INTENTLY AND ARE LAPPING IT UP.

WILL   Sorry, did you say you go on holiday in a caravan?

JAY   With the Caravan Club.

WILL   In a caravan, like a gypo. If my mum told me we were going caravanning, I'd call ChildLine.

JAY   Well shows how much you know, because it's a sense of freedom that you don't get with other holidays.

WILL   It's a sense of shitting in a bucket in a cupboard you don't get with other holidays. In England. With your parents.

JAY   Actually, it's a well-known fact that the Caravan Club is like a sex club, all over Europe, which is why I've lost my cherry and none of you sad acts have.

SIMON   Listen, I could have got laid loads of times.

JAY   No you couldn't.

SIMON   Yeah I could actually, but I wanna lose it with someone I love.

JAY   Oh what, like Carli?

SIMON   Maybe I do love Carli. She's gorgeous, she's smart, she's amazing.

WILL   Probably worth mentioning to her then, mate, if that's the way you feel.

JAY   Yeah, why not mention it? Worst that can happen, you get nothing, best that can happen, you get stinky fingers.

WILL   You really are one of the most disgusting humans I've ever met.

JAY   Oh look out, Prince Harry's had a few drinks and now he thinks he's hard.

WILL   I am hard.

JAY   So all this being scared of teachers and brown-nosing everyone's parents is just an act, is it?

WILL   I don't brown-nose anyone.

SIMON   You do a bit.

WILL   Good manners cost nothing.

JAY   A good shag costs nothing. A good shag with Carli, ay? (JAY JUMPS UP ON THE SOFA AND STARTS SINGING TO SIMON TO THE TUNE OF 'LONDON BRIDGE IS FALLING DOWN'). Carli's fanny on your face, on your face, Carli's fanny on your face...

 SCENE 13

EXT. NEIL'S HOUSE

WE SEE NEIL'S DAD (KEVIN SUTHERLAND) AND A THAI MAN WHO IS CLEARLY A WORKMAN (CARPENTER) WALKING UP THE DRIVE TO NEIL'S HOUSE. HE LOOKS ANGRY AS HE HEARS THE COMMOTION FROM INSIDE THE HOUSE, AND THEN ENTERS.

KEVIN SUTHERLAND   (TO CARPENTER) I keep catching myself on it. It's a bloody menace. Oh, hang on, I think someone's in.

BACK TO

INT. NEIL'S HOUSE, LIVING ROOM

JAY (STILL SINGING)   ... and your bellend. Carli's fanny on your face, on your face, on your face ...

THE DOOR OPENS AND NEIL'S DAD AND THE CARPENTER COME IN.

KEVIN SUTHERLAND   Neil, what the hell is going on? Oh, this place smells like a brewery and not a nice one. Jay, there is always trouble when you're around but Will, I'm especially surprised at you. (TURNING TO THE CARPENTER) I'm so sorry Steve.

WILL   (WITH THE DEVIL-MAY-CARE ATTITUDE OF THE FIRST-TIME TEENAGE DRUNK) Oh piss off.

KEVIN SUTHERLAND   What? Don't talk to me like that in my own house.

WILL   (BOLSTERED BY THE STIFLED LAUGHS OF THE OTHERS) Oh I'm so sorry, my manners. Piss off please.

KEVIN SUTHERLAND   I've had enough of your lip.

WILL   Oh you'd like my lip wouldn't you? Right round your bell-end. If Mr Chippy doesn't get there first. What's he going to knock up? A closet for you to hide in? You bumder.

———— SCENE 14 ————

EXT. NEIL'S HOUSE

WILL V/O   *In hindsight, I might have taken it a bit too far.*

NEIL IS INDOORS STILL. WE CAN HEAR NEIL'S DAD SHOUTING.

THE OTHER THREE BOYS RUN OUT.

SIMON   Amazing. Jesus Christ – bumder?

JAY   Yeah, fair play to you. That was pretty special. Bumder.

WILL   It's a mixture of bummer and bender. I think he'll be all right about it though, he can take a joke. That was taken as a joke.

JAY   My lips around your bellend? Yeah, it should be fine.

SIMON   I love Carli. I love Carli. Shit, I've gotta tell her, what if she feels the same.

WILL   Seems fairly unlikely.

SIMON   Life is about these moments. It's the things you don't do you regret.

WILL   . . . is the kind of cavalier philosophy that caused my father to leave my mother. You go for it.

JAY   Bumder.

──────── SCENE 15 ────────

EXT. CARLI'S HOUSE

WILL V/O   *And so we headed for Carli's house . . .*

WE FIND SIMON ON ALL FOURS WRITING ON THE PAVEMENT IN YELLOW SPRAY
PAINT: A BIG HEART AND 'I LOVE CARLI D'AMATO'.

SIMON   I feel a bit stupid doing this. This is fine, isn't it?

WILL   Yeah, yeah, yeah, definitely.

JAY   Yes, yeah, yeah.

THEY LAUGH BEHIND HIS BACK.

SIMON   You would tell me if I was being a dick?

WILL   Of course I would.

JAY   Yeah, yeah, yeah.

WILL   I think writing her surname is particularly important, I mean it
is her drive, but you wouldn't want there to be any Carli-based confusion.

JAY   Yeah, I reckon if you put a kiss, she'll definitely suck you off.

IN THE DISTANCE (AT THE END OF THE CUL-DE-SAC) JAY HAS SPOTTED CARLI
AND HER MATES COMING.

CARLI   What the fuck is that?

SIMON   What?

HE TURNS UP FROM ALL FOURS TO SEE CARLI. FOR HIM IT'S THAT MOMENT
WHEN IT DOESN'T MATTER HOW DRUNK YOU ARE, YOU SOBER UP INSTANTLY. HE
LOOKS AT HER AND THEN ACROSS THE PAVING STONES COVERED WITH A
MASSIVE HEART AND HER NAME.

CARLI   Simon, why are you vandalising my drive?

SIMON   Um.

CARLI   What's it say? What, you love me?

WILL AND JAY LAUGH.

SIMON   Look, I can easily wash it off and we can just pretend it never happened and I could not tell anyone and you could not tell anyone and my mates can not tell anyone and most importantly, your mates can not tell anyone.

CARLI'S FRIENDS GIGGLE.

CARLI   Simon, we've known each other for ages, why are you doing this now?

SIMON   Um, we were playing dares.

CARLI'S FRIEND   Did someone dare you to be the world's biggest saddo?

EVERYONE EXCEPT SIMON LAUGHS.

CARLI   So what, you are in love with me?

JAY   This couldn't have gone any better.

CARLI   Actually, I think this is pretty cool, Simon, sort of artistic, it's like Banksy or something.

SIMON   Ahh.

CARLI   (REALISING THAT SIMON IS SUFFERING) Why don't you come over to mine tonight, I'm babysitting for my brother and we can sort this out then, yeah?

SIMON   Really?

CARLI   Yeah, come round about eight. My folks will be out by then. Probably best to avoid them till this has washed away.

SIMON   Um, yeah, um, I'm not sure this washes away.

CARLI   Whatever. Well I'll see you later.

CARLI AND HER FRIENDS HEAD UP THE DRIVE GIGGLING.

SIMON STANDS UP AND DOES THE 'STEVE PETERSON', WHICH IS A MOVE NAMED AFTER A BLOKE WHO WAS ONCE ON *THE CRYSTAL MAZE* AND IS THE LEAST COOL CELEBRATION MOVE EVER. IT INVOLVES BITING YOUR BOTTOM LIP, CLAPPING, RAISING ONE KNEE AND THEN PULLING BOTH CLENCHED FISTS DOWN TOWARDS YOUR WAIST.

SIMON   Yes.

WILL   Incredibly, I think you might be in there.

JAY   Of course he's in there. She is wet for you, mate.

SIMON   I cannot believe this worked.

WILL   Maybe she was impressed by your artistic side.

JAY   No, bollocks, it's because you're drunk.

SIMON   Do you think so?

JAY   Yes, because you're wasted, like Pete Doherty, innit. Girls love it.

WILL   I think Pete Doherty is on heroin.

SIMON   I'm not sure I should do heroin, Jay.

———— SCENE 16 ————

INT. SIMON'S HOUSE, LIVING ROOM

SIMON AND JAY ARE RIFLING THROUGH THE DRINKS CABINET AND POURING BITS OF EACH SPIRIT INTO AN EMPTY LITRE BOTTLE OF TONIC.

JAY   Right, vodka, whisky and a load of crème de menthe. When she sees you after this, she'll be frothing at the gash.

SIMON   Are you sure my dad won't notice?

JAY   No, he'll never tell.

WILL   I think he might as his whisky now tastes of apple juice.

JAY   It'll be worth it.

BEHIND THEM SIMON'S BROTHER (ANDREW COOPER) ARRIVES.

ANDREW COOPER   What's that?

SIMON   Fuck off.

ANDREW COOPER   What you got there?

SIMON   And again, fuck off.

ANDREW COOPER You are in such shit.

SIMON That's a hat trick, fuck off.

ANDREW COOPER Mum knows you bunked off and also, everyone knows that you love Carli D'Amato.

SIMON I don't love her actually.

ANDREW COOPER Everyone knows, you spaz, you wrote it on the pavement outside her house. Even the Year 11s were laughing about how sad you are.

SIMON Yeah, well how sad is a date at her house tonight?

ANDREW COOPER You're such a sad.

SIMON No, you're the sad because, twat, you're such a little fuck, shit.

BUT IT'S TOO LATE BECAUSE ANDREW HAS GONE.

JAY He's made you look a right knob. So when are you gonna make the move then?

SIMON I dunno, I've got to get the kid brother out the way first.

WILL Well I could come and look after him for you.

JAY Bollocks.

JAY I'll take care of the kid while you take care of the . . . ooh, business. Mmmmm, business.

HE DOES A SEXY, BUT GRIM, HIP MOVEMENT. SIMON LOOKS AT HIM.

SIMON I think I better take Will.

JAY Fine, your funeral.

WILL V/O . . . *Jay was wrong, it wouldn't be a funeral, but it would be about as much fun as one.*

──────── SCENE 17 ────────

EXT. CARLI'S HOUSE

WILL V/O   *And so, that evening, we arrived at the house of the girl Simon had always loved and we were drunk, so very drunk.*

WILL AND SIMON ARRIVE AT CARLI'S. SIMON IS CLEARLY QUITE PISSED.

THEY WALK UP THE PATH AND RING THE BELL. CARLI ANSWERS.

CARLI   Hi.

SIMON   Hi.

WILL   Hello there.

CARLI   Oh, hello William. Are you coming in then Simon?

SIMON AND WILL GO TO ENTER, SIMON GOES IN. CARLI LOOKS AT WILL AS HE COMES IN.

CARLI   Are you his chaperone?

SIMON   No it's cool, babes, he's gonna watch the kid whilst we chat about, you know, our feelings.

CARLI   OK. Best not to call me babes though.

SIMON   Really?

CARLI   Really. Come on in then. Chris is in there watching TV Will. (TO SIMON) Come on you, let's get a drink.

──────── SCENE 18 ────────

INT. CARLI'S HOUSE, KITCHEN

CARLI   So Dad went totally ballistic about the driveway. I think you're still invited over for Christmas, but he's gonna make your parents pay for an industrial stone cleaner.

SIMON   Ha, it was worth it.

CARLI   Can you smell bleach?

SIMON PLACES HIS FINGER ON CARLI'S LIPS.

SIMON   Shhhh.

———— SCENE 19 ————

INT. CARLI'S HOUSE, LIVING ROOM

CARLI'S BROTHER (CHRIS D'AMATO), WHO IS ABOUT SEVEN, IS WATCHING TV. WILL ENTERS.

WILL   What are you watching?

CHRIS D'AMATO   Dunno, think there's been a big bomb.

WILL   Really? Oh, it's one of those recreations of a dirty bomb.

CHRIS D'AMATO   What's a dirty bomb?

WILL   Well, it's just a big nuclear bomb that terrorists would use to kill everyone in London.

BACK TO

INT. CARLI'S HOUSE, KITCHEN

CARLI   Have you been drinking spirits?

SIMON   Sorry, dunno what I was thinking. Would you like some?

HE PULLS OUT THE DODGY-LOOKING PLASTIC LITRE BOTTLE OF GIN FROM INSIDE HIS COAT.

CARLI   I'll stick to wine, thanks.

SIMON   Wine is for girls.

CARLI   I am a girl.

SIMON   This is a man's drink. If you don't want it, I'll have it and if you can't take me like this, well I'm sorry babes, but this is the package.

SIMON DOWNS FAR, FAR TOO MUCH OF THE GIN, DOES THE HEAD SHAKE A WET DOG WOULD BE PROUD OF, GRABS A BROWNIE AND THEN SWIGS SOME MORE. THIS IS CLEARLY NOT A GREAT PACKAGE.

BACK TO

INT. CARLI'S HOUSE, LIVING ROOM

WILL   Oops, there goes the tallest building in London. That'll be a few thousand dead.

CHRIS D'AMATO   My mum and dad are in London tonight. Would they be killed?

WILL   Oh yes, not only killed but obliterated. Merely a scorched shadow on the pavement. Dust.

CHRIS D'AMATO   So they are dead for ever?

WILL   Yeah, dead for ever.

CHRIS D'AMATO   (CRYING AND SCREAMING) My mummy, my daddy.

WILL   No. Shhhh.

CHRIS CONTINUES TO SCREAM.

CHRIS D'AMATO   Mummy, Mummy.

BACK TO

INT. CARLI'S HOUSE, KITCHEN

SIMON IS NOW HAMMERED BEYOND BELIEF.

SIMON   Come on Carli, you know why I'm here and I know why I'm here . . . and you know why I'm here. Kiss me.

HE LUNGES A BIT. SHE MOVES ROUND THE KITCHEN A BIT. THIS SUDDEN MOVEMENT FROM HIM HAS OBVIOUSLY SHAKEN HIM A BIT.

CARLI   Simon, you know I've got a boyfriend.

SIMON   Just finger yourself in front of me.

CARLI   Jesus, Simon.

SIMON   They do it in Caravan Club. Come on, I know you want to.

CARLI   Well, I don't want to, so . . .

SIMON   Yeah you do, you . . .

CARLI   Simon, are you all right?

HE PROJECTILE VOMITS IN AN ARC OVER THE KITCHEN WORKTOPS.

SIMON   Oh Christ.

HE THEN FINDS THE SINK AND VOMITS HARD INTO THAT. THEN HE'S HALFWAY UP AND WIPING HIS MOUTH, AND THEN AGAIN. AND THEN AGAIN.

THEN HE IS FULLY UPRIGHT AND LOOKS TOWARDS CARLI.

SIMON   I don't think I'm very well.

A BAWLING SCREAM IS HEARD FROM THE OTHER ROOM

CHRIS D'AMATO   (OFF SCREEN) Daddy, Daddy, Mummy.

CARLI   Chris?

SHE RUNS OUT.

──────── SCENE 20 ────────

INT. CARLI'S HOUSE, KITCHEN

CHRIS IS WELDED TO CARLI'S LEG, BUT LOOKS TO HAVE STOPPED CRYING.

SIMON IS LEANING OVER THE SINK, PICKING OUT SICK WITH HIS HANDS.

WILL IS WIPING DOWN THE KITCHEN WORKTOPS AND RETCHING A BIT AS HE DOES SO.

WILL   Look, I'm really sorry, I was just telling him about terrorists and stuff.

CARLI   You were telling a seven-year-old about terrorists? He won't sleep for a week now, you idiot. Have you unblocked the sink yet, all the lumps?

SIMON   I'm really sorry, I think maybe I ate something. Could we maybe sit down and talk about us and have you got any Nurofen, it's just I—

SIMON TURNS A BIT AND IS SUDDENLY SICK ON TOP OF CHRIS'S HEAD. HE STARTS BAWLING AGAIN AND CARLI TURNS TO THEM.

SIMON   Oh dear.

WILL   I think we'll be off now.

SCENE 21

EXT. STREET

WILL   Right, I think we better get you back to mine and cleaned up.

SIMON   Oh God, my head. I've ruined it.

I love her and I've ruined it with her. Oh God. Oh, she's so amazing.

WILL   I'm going to say this to you as a friend – shut up. Today's been a fuck-up from start to finish, we need to write it off. OK, today's gone, it isn't going to get any worse.

THEY TURN THE CORNER AND SEE A COUPLE OF PARKED CARS.

WILL   Oh shit. Isn't that your mum's car?

SIMON   Yeah and that's Neil's dad's car. Oh shit.

WILL   Oh shit.

SCENE 22

INT. WILL'S LIVING ROOM

NEIL'S DAD IS SITTING CHATTING TO SIMON'S MUM AND DAD.

KEVIN SUTHERLAND   Well it's every Wednesday and we play a sort of . . . I suppose it's a best of three games and . . .

ALAN COOPER   Right.

KEVIN SUTHERLAND   . . . and changing facilities are not too bad . . .

ALAN COOPER   Yeah, yeah.

KEVIN SUTHERLAND   . . . so, you know, all in all it's a good thing.

THE BOYS ENTER FOLLOWED BY WILL'S MUM, AND THE ATMOSPHERE IMMEDIATELY CHANGES AS THE ADULTS GO INTO 'PARENT' MODE.

PAMELA COOPER   Right, sit down, you two.

WILL V/O   *Sometimes in life, you have to sit down and take your punishment like a man. Unfortunately, this was not one of those times . . .*

ALAN COOPER   Well, you've had quite a day off. You've lied to your mothers, bought alcohol illegally, abused Neil's dad, stole my suit, defaced the pavement outside Carli's. Am I missing anything?

WILL   We also hit a spastic with a Frisbee.

POLLY McKENZIE   I feel totally let down William.

WILL   It wasn't our fault Mum.

POLLY McKENZIE   And what you said to Kevin here. I thought I'd brought you up better than that.

WILL   It isn't our fault.

ALAN COOPER   Why's it not your fault then?

SIMON   (INDICATING NEIL'S DAD) It all happened 'cause he touched us.

ALAN COOPER   What?

KEVIN SUTHERLAND   Me?

SIMON, WHO IS NOW BASICALLY A MESS, AND CAN'T SEE HOW ANOTHER LIE COULD MAKE THINGS WORSE, PICKS UP A SORT OF ORNAMENTAL RAG-DOLL THAT WILL'S MUM HAS ON THE SOFA BY THE CUSHIONS.

SIMON   He touched us here (INDICATING FRONT OF THE DOLL) and here (INDICATING THE DOLL'S CHEST) and (TURNING THE DOLL) here, (WHISPERING) the bum hole.

KEVIN SUTHERLAND   You evil little shits.

ALAN COOPER   I'll deal with this Kevin. Now listen to me, you two, that is an extraordinary allegation and you should think very carefully before you repeat it. Just because Kevin's gay, it doesn't mean he goes—

KEVIN SUTHERLAND   Wait, no, I'm not gay.

ALAN COOPER   It's all right, Kevin, we're all friends, it doesn't matter.

KEVIN SUTHERLAND   No, but I'm not gay, I was married for nearly—

WILL   Oscar Wilde was married.

POLLY McKENZIE   That is enough, William. Although he is right Kevin, and obviously that's fine.

KEVIN SUTHERLAND   Well no, no, I'm not gay.

SIMON   All right, don't have a hissy fit.

PAMELA COOPER   Just because Kevin is gay, it doesn't make him automatically a paedophile.

KEVIN SUTHERLAND   I'm not a paedophile.

ALAN COOPER   So if you want to repeat those allegations, then we'll take them seriously, but if you want to tell us the truth, that it never happened, we'll move on to the other things you're in trouble for.

THERE'S A TENSION EVIDENT IN THE ROOM; BREATH IS AUDIBLY BEING HELD.

WILL   OK. The truth is, we're alcoholics. You have to help us. All we can think about is where the next drink is going to come from. We're literally out of control. Today we even talked about heroin. There's a long road ahead of us, but with your support and your love, we think we can make it, so please, as our parents, help us.

THE ADULTS LOOK ON THIS PATHETIC SIGHT IN AMAZEMENT, BEFORE BREAKING INTO SPONTANEOUS LAUGHTER.

WILL AND SIMON LOOK ASHAMED AND ARE STILL CRYING A BIT.

WILL V/O   . . . *and so we were so pathetic, even my mum, who has no sense of humour, was laughing at us.*

 SCENE 23

INT. SCHOOL COMMON ROOM

WILL BUMPS INTO SIMON OUTSIDE THE COMMON ROOM. SIMON LOOKS LIKE SHIT.

WILL   Hello, you look well.

SIMON   Thanks. How's your mum?

WILL   Not happy, but fit, like a prostitute.

ONCE INSIDE, THEY SPOT NEIL AND JAY AND HEAD OVER TO THEM.

WILL   How's your dad?

SIMON   Really not happy, but at least he's not bent like Neil's.

WILL AND SIMON SHARE A LAUGH AS THEY JOIN NEIL AND JAY. NEIL LOOKS
BEMUSED, BEFORE TAKING IN HOW ROUGH SIMON LOOKS.

NEIL   What? Shit Si, you don't look well, mate. What happened?

JAY   He was up all night, fucking Carli's brains out.

SIMON   Huh, not quite.

WILL   Obviously by not quite he means he puked on her brother's
head and then went home and accused Neil's dad of being a paedophile.

JAY   You dickhead.

NEIL   What a knob. Oi, my dad's not a paedo.

MR GILBERT ENTERS THE COMMON ROOM AND INSTANTLY SPIES THEM.

MR GILBERT   Ah boys, good of you to join us today.

SIMON   Oh shit.

MR GILBERT APPROACHES AND LOOMS OVER THEM.

MR GILBERT   Shit indeed. Now boys, you are in the Sixth Form, so actually, you're under no legal obligation to attend school. Sutherland,
Cartwright, if you want to piss away your chance of gaining some qualifi-
cations and improving your lives, then be my guest. I still get paid at the
end of the week.

NEIL   Really? Oh great.

JAY   Brilliant. Thanks sir.

SIMON   I knew no day could go as badly as yesterday did.

MR GILBERT   However, Cooper, McKenzie, phoning the school and pretending to be your parents? Oh, that my little friends is fraud. I think we better go and see the Head.

SIMON AND WILL TRUDGE OFF BEHIND MR GILBERT WHILE JAY AND NEIL LAUGH.

WILL V/O   *They say it's the things you don't do in life that you regret. Well that's clearly not true, I regret hitting that girl with the Frisbee and I regret hurling insults at Neil's dad . . .*

SHOT OF THE GIRL IN THE WHEELCHAIR BEING HIT BY WILL'S FRISBEE AND SHOT OF WILL INSULTING NEIL'S DAD.

WILL   Bumder.

WILL V/O   *. . . and I'm pretty certain that Simon regrets almost everything he did that day . . .*

SHOT OF SIMON SPRAYING 'I LOVE CARLI D'AMATO' ON CARLI'S DRIVE AND SHOT OF SIMON PUKING OVER CARLI'S BROTHER.

SIMON   Oh dear.

WILL V/O   *. . . but they also say, all's well that ends well. Hang on, this didn't even end well.*

SHOT OF THE PARENTS LAUGHING AT SIMON AND WILL, AND FINALLY A SHOT OF THE TWO BOYS SITTING OUTSIDE THE HEAD'S OFFICE.

Episode 3

Initially, due to time constraints, E4 only commissioned five episodes. I know, right, who does that? Well, after we'd started writing and it was going OK, Caroline Leddy and Angela Jain (then head of E4) came back and said did we think we could knock off another one to make the usual six? And the answer was obviously yes, because when you've worked in TV a while you understand that the best way to deal with channels is to say yes when they offer you anything and work out the details afterwards.

It turned out not to be as hard as we thought because 'Caravan Club' was far too long, and we were going to cut some stuff that we liked such as Simon getting a crappy car (which seemed like a universal thing for all but the luckiest of suburban teenagers) and it would be a shame to waste it. So it turned up here. For the record Damon's was a Metro, mine was my mum's Polo, and Simon Cooper's was a Fiat Cinquecento 'Hawaii', which of course doesn't actually exist. We thought that 'Hawaii' was the kind of sticker car dealers put on smaller cars to try to make you feel like it's a sports car, but they fool no one, least of all the owner. We wanted the car to be the same colour as Damon's Mini Metro, but the Cinquecento didn't actually come in that colour. Showing commitment above and beyond the call of duty, Richard Drew and his art department team resprayed the original car 'nan's piss yellow' (and the now iconic red door was also Richard's idea).

So we had the first half, but what to stick it on? Well that came relatively easily, for two reasons. One, I grew up very near Thorpe Park, and both Damon and I love roller coasters. We had the thought (and by the way this isn't the most artistic way to write sitcoms) that if we wrote something set at Thorpe Park they might let us on the roller coasters repeatedly and for free. And they did. Two, I'm not proud of it, but I once had a very similar (but, honestly, worse) tantrum to Will's at some Down's syndrome people on the front of the Superman ride at Six Flags in California.

Obviously I didn't know who I was shouting at (I'm not that bad), but it was (and remains) the worst moment of my life – and for the two friends I was on holiday with, one of their fondest memories. But as I was catapulted at 90 mph along the track, milliseconds after realising what I had done, I did just manage to say 'I'm the worst human being in the world.'

——— OPENING MONTAGE ———

WILL V/O   *So, I'm halfway through my first term at a new school . . .*

SHOT OF WILL WALKING INTO THE SCHOOL. SHOT OF PUPILS INSULTING WILL.

PUPIL   Nice badge dickhead.

WILL V/O   *. . . and, well, it could have been worse . . .*

SHOT OF MARK DONOVAN THREATENING WILL.

MARK DONOVAN   I will get you.

WILL V/O   *. . . I still have all my limbs . . . just . . .*

SHOT OF MARK AND HIS MATES RUNNING AFTER WILL.

WILL V/O   *. . . I've met loads of new people . . .*

SHOT OF WILL'S 'BADGE' FRIENDS FROM EPISODE 1, AND SHOT OF SIMON PUKING OVER CARLI'S BROTHER.

WILL V/O. . . *and best of all no one's tried to fuck my mum yet . . .*

SHOT OF WILL'S MUM WAVING AT HIM AND NEIL WATCHING HER.

NEIL   She's fit.

SHOT OF MARK DONOVAN WATCHING WILL'S MUM.

MARK DONOVAN   She is fit.

SHOT OF WILL.

WILL   Don't have a wank over my mum.

WILL V/O   *. . . and unlike my old school, there were girls here. And if there's one thing I now know about girls, and let's face it there is only one thing I now know about girls, it's that boys who drive are a whole lot more attractive than those who don't . . .*

——— SCENE 1 ———

INT./EXT. DRIVING INSTRUCTOR'S CAR

WILL V/O   *As he was the oldest, our chances of getting a car to impress the ladies rested on Simon's shoulders . . . oh and his stupid uncoordinated size-ten feet . . .*

SIMON IS HAVING A DRIVING LESSON AND TRYING TO PARALLEL PARK.

THE DRIVING INSTRUCTOR IS GENTLY ENCOURAGING HIM.

DRIVING INSTRUCTOR   Careful. Gently does it. Careful. Little bit more.

SIMON IS STICKING HIS TONGUE OUT OF THE SIDE OF HIS MOUTH AND IS CONCENTRATING HARD.

SIMON   I'm just not great at parallel parking.

SIMON STALLS IT.

SIMON   Bollocks.

WE HEAR LOADS OF LAUGHTER AND WE CUT WIDER TO SEE THAT JAY, NEIL AND WILL ARE STANDING ON THE SIDE OF THE ROAD WATCHING AND LAUGHING.

SIMON   Shut up.

JAY   (PASSING SIMON HIS MOBILE) Si, it's me nan. She wants to know if you want some help parking.

THEY ALL LAUGH EXCEPT SIMON.

DRIVING INSTRUCTOR   Steady on, boys. It's not easy for Simon. OK, let's try again.

SIMON STARTS THE CAR AND SORT OF JUMPS IT BACKWARDS AS HE'S LEFT IT IN GEAR. THERE'S A CRASHING NOISE. HE'S HIT THE PARKED CAR BEHIND.

SIMON   Oh shit.

DRIVING INSTRUCTOR   Right. OK, off we go Simon, into first.

WILL   Shouldn't you leave a note?

DRIVING INSTRUCTOR   No, we're driving off. Quickly now. Drive, drive.

THEY DRIVE OFF WITH A SQUEAL OF WHEELS.

WILL V/O   *. . . so it looked like it might be quite some time before we were picking up girls in a car.*

———— SCENE 2 ————

INT. SCHOOL COMMON ROOM

THE USUAL STUFF IS HAPPENING. GROUPS OF KIDS SITTING AROUND: THE GOTHS, THE EMOS, ALL IN THEIR LITTLE GROUPS.

NEIL ENTERS AND JOINS JAY, SIMON AND WILL.

NEIL   Oi Jay, I have just had the best lesson ever. Jack Stephens dropped his ruler next to Miss Timms and when she bent over to pick it up, I saw loads of leg on her way down and a little bit of tit on the way up.

JAY   You lucky git.

NEIL   Oh yeah, and it's all locked away up here in the visual wank bank.

SIMON IS READING THE HIGHWAY CODE.

WILL   I thought you'd passed your written test.

SIMON   Yeah, I did, but I've got the practical tomorrow. I thought this might give me a few tips.

JAY   I don't think there is a section on how not to be a whining little bitch.

SIMON   Brilliant.

WILL   If you pass we could go on a road trip.

SIMON   Could do. Maybe we could see what Carli's doing and go somewhere with her.

JAY   Look, a car is like a mobile pulling machine. Forget about Carli, forget about all the girls at this school. There is a whole world of pussy out there.

WILL   He's right. Although he expressed it like a terrible misogynist.

JAY   Thank you.

NEIL   Why don't you come to Thorpe Park? There's always loads of birds there.

WILL   Oh my God yes, Thorpe Park.

NEIL   I can get you free tickets.

WILL   How?

NEIL   I work there.

JAY   Mopping up sick?

NEIL   Some sick.

SIMON   How come you never mentioned you work at Thorpe Park before?

NEIL   I used to work at Asda and you never asked about that.

JAY   I s'pose your old man needs the money.

NEIL   He doesn't actually.

SIMON   But paying for rent boys can't be cheap Neil.

NEIL   Oi, my dad's not bent.

JAY   Why's he paying for rent boys then?

NEIL   He's not.

SIMON   What, they give him freebies?

WILL   Look, I think we should lay off Neil a bit. Is it right Neil, that Thorpe Park has one of only two pulley-launch coasters outside North America?

NEIL   I don't know.

WILL   It is right.

SIMON   I don't know if my dad will let me go anyway.

JAY   What's it got to do with your dad?

SIMON   He's paying for my car. He might not let me do long journeys yet.

JAY   Surely he'll want you to get sucked off by a little lovely on the teacup ride.

SIMON   Are there really loads of girls there Neil?

NEIL   Oh yeah. Sometimes on the rides their boobs pop out. You only get a split second of tit 'cause they're going at about seventy miles an hour, but it's still good though.

WILL   This is perfect. Simon passes his test, drives us to Thorpe Park. Neil gets us freebies and I get to ride—

JAY   A man's cock in the bushes.

WILL   —the Nemesis Inferno. This is going to be awesome.

SIMON   If I pass my test.

THE BELL GOES.

JAY   Roller coasters and tits. This is going to be brilliant.

SIMON   If I pass my test.

─────── SCENE 3 ───────

EXT. DRIVING TEST CENTRE

WILL V/O   *Despite our excitement, we knew it would take a miracle for Simon to pass his test. But miracles often come in unlikely packages . . .*

SIMON IS OUTSIDE HIS INSTRUCTOR'S CAR, MEETING THE TESTER (TRACEY). SHE IS A MIDDLE-AGED, SLIGHTLY FRUMPY-LOOKING WOMAN.

TRACEY   Hello Simon. I'm Tracey, your examiner for today's test.

SIMON   Hello.

TRACEY   Don't look so nervous. I'm not going to eat you.

SIMON   Ha.

TRACEY   So how are you feeling? Ready to be, um, examined.

SIMON   I'm a bit nervous.

TRACEY   It's perfectly natural sweetheart.

TRACEY MOVES BEHIND SIMON AND PUTS HER HANDS ONTO HIS SHOULDERS.

TRACEY   We just need to loosen you up, ease into it. (MASSAGES SIMON'S SHOULDERS) Now the first part of the test is a doddle. All you've got to do is sing out the registration plate of that blue car.

TRACEY STARTS TO MASSAGE SIMON'S SHOULDERS.

SIMON   OK, it's . . . it's EOS, no, 51 CUZ. Shit, it's a V not a U, isn't it?

TRACEY   Well technically yes, but you get a pass on that one for having such pretty eyes. Right, to the Batmobile Robin.

SIMON   Sorry?

TRACEY   Off you pop to your car.

SIMON WALKS FORWARD AHEAD OF TRACEY, WHO STANDS THERE ADMIRING HIS ARSE AS HE WALKS.

TRACEY   Nice.

CUT TO INSIDE THE CAR.

SIMON IS STRUGGLING TO GET THE SEAT BELT ON AND TRACEY LEANS ACROSS HIM TO PULL THE BELT DOWN.

TRACEY   Oh, why don't you just let me help you with that?

SIMON IS PINNED TO HIS SEAT, HOLDING HIS HANDS UP AROUND HIS SHOULDERS SO AS NOT TO TOUCH TRACEY. EVENTUALLY SHE BUCKLES HIM IN AND THEN SITS BACK INTO HER SEAT.

TRACEY   So Simon, have you got a girlfriend?

SIMON   Is this part of the test?

TRACEY   No, but I will fail you if you say yes. Right, just slip it into first and pull out of the centre slowly.

SIMON GOES TO PULL AWAY AND STALLS THE CAR.

SIMON   Shit. Stalled it.

TRACEY   False start, just relax. Try again.

TRACEY LEANS IN AND PUTS HER HAND ON SIMON'S KNEE.

TRACEY   Oh, oh, you're shaking.

SIMON   I've failed, haven't I?

TRACEY   Ssh, ssh, silly. No one's going to fail here. (TOUCHES SIMON'S LEG)

TRACEY SLIDES HER HAND FURTHER UP SIMON'S LEG. HE LOOKS TERRIFIED.

SIMON   Right, I'm not sure that's helping with the nerves actually.

TRACEY   Simon, if you don't want my help, you've only to say. But trust me, I know how difficult this test can be.

THERE'S A BEAT AS SIMON THINKS ABOUT IT. HE LOOKS RESIGNED TO HIS FATE. HE STARTS THE CAR AGAIN.

TRACEY   Good boy, you steer and I'll do the pedals, that's the tricky bit.

SIMON LOOKS CONCERNED AND WE PULL WIDE TO SEE THE CAR JERKILY PULL OUT OF THE TEST CENTRE.

WILL V/O   . . . Simon never did tell us what happened on his driving test.

——— SCENE 4 ———

EXT. SIMON'S HOUSE

SIMON'S MUM (PAMELA COOPER) IS STANDING OUTSIDE THE FRONT OF HER HOUSE. IT'S A NICE SUBURBAN DAY. SIMON'S BROTHER (ANDREW COOPER) IS PLAYING WITH A NINTENDO DS LITE, JUST HANGING AROUND THE FRONT PORCH/DRIVE.

A CAR WITH 'JOHN WHITE' WRITTEN ON THE TOP AND FLANKED BY L-PLATES PULLS INTO THE CLOSE AND DROPS SIMON OFF AT THE DOOR. SIMON GETS OUT.

SIMON LOOKS DOWNBEAT TO HIS MUM FOR A SECOND (HE'S PRETENDING TO BE SAD AS A LITTLE JOKE) THEN SMILES AND JUMPS UP AND DOWN.

SIMON   I passed.

PAMELA COOPER   Yaay.

SIMON   I passed first time, so you owe me that, you little shit.

HE GRABS THE DS LITE FROM ANDREW.

ANDREW COOPER   Hey, I didn't shake on it.

SIMON   A bet's a bet. Unlucky.

PAMELA COOPER   Oh well done Simon. We knew you'd pass. Your dad's just bringing round your new car.

SIMON   Oh God Mum, this is brilliant.

ANDREW COOPER   That is not fair.

SIMON   You're not allowed to touch it.

PAMELA COOPER   Well we're very proud of you. It's a Fiat or something, but he says it is second-hand.

SIMON   God Mum, that doesn't matter. This is so cool.

THERE'S A 'TOOT, TOOT' FROM AN AMAZINGLY RUBBISH HORN AND SIMON'S DAD (ALAN COOPER) DRIVES ROUND THE CORNER IN A FIAT CINQUECENTO 'HAWAII'.

ANDREW BEGINS TO LAUGH REALLY AGGRESSIVELY.

ANDREW COOPER   That is the gayest car I've ever seen.

SIMON   Oh no. Dad really? Really?

ALAN COOPER   It might not look much. It's a great little runner and you won't be able to get up enough speed in it to kill yourself.

SIMON   I don't want it.

ALAN COOPER   Come on. It's a special edition, a Hawaii. I bet your mates at school will think it's cool.

SIMON   I can't go to school in it.

PAMELA COOPER   Well if I was a girl I'd think whoever drove this was pretty trendy.

SIMON   Are you trying to wind me up? Why are you saying these things?

PAMELA COOPER   Well I think you should just be a bit more grateful, to be honest.

SIMON   (LOOKS INSIDE THE CAR) Oh Christ it's got a tape deck.

PAMELA COOPER   See, that's good.

SIMON   No, it's not. You can't even buy tapes any more.

PAMELA COOPER   Oh you're being melodramatic again. Now why don't you go and show Will. I bet he'll be jealous.

ANDREW COOPER   Yeah, he'll be really jealous of how yellow it is.

ALAN COOPER   Now be careful. That's the most valuable present you'll ever get.

SIMON   I fucking hope not.

ALAN COOPER   I heard that.

 SCENE 5

EXT. WILL'S HOUSE

WILL V/O   *The good news was that Simon had passed. The not so good news was bright yellow and parked in my driveway . . .*

WILL   Well I don't think it's too bad.

SIMON   It's not great though, is it?

WILL   No, but don't look at the external realities. Think of the immense possibilities.

SIMON   What?

WILL   Yes it's a Cinquecento Hawaii, but it's also freedom. It's a possibility of driving our own destiny. We can be what we want now.

Push our lives literally in the direction we want them to— Oh Christ, is that a tape deck?

MARK DONOVAN AND HIS MATES ARE WALKING BY. MARK IS DRINKING A LUCO-ZADE SPORT.

MARK DONOVAN Check out the bendermobile.

THEY ALL LAUGH.

GIRL Looks like a paedo's car.

WILL He's just jealous because his family haven't discovered fire yet.

MARK DONOVAN You fucking what McKenzie?

DONOVAN COMES STORMING OVER. HE MEANS BUSINESS.

WILL Nothing, nothing.

WILL'S MUM (POLLY McKENZIE), COMES OUT OF THE HOUSE.

MARK'S FACE DROPS THE SNARL AND HE TURNS TO GREET HER. WILL IS RELIEVED AT FIRST, BUT OBVIOUSLY A BIT WARY OF MARK STILL.

MARK DONOVAN Oh hello Mrs McKenzie.

POLLY McKENZIE Oh hello Mark. Is this your car?

POLLY IS NOW STANDING IN FRONT OF THE HAWAII.

MARK DONOVAN Oh no, it's Cooper's.

POLLY McKENZIE Oh, shame about the colour Simon.

SIMON Right.

WILL Mum, we're just off to Thorpe Park and we're running a bit late, so we should probably go now.

POLLY McKENZIE Thorpe Park? To ride roller coasters? Is it safe?

WILL Yes, it's incredibly safe.

POLLY McKENZIE Well, won't you be frightened? You cried when you went on the ghost train.

DONOVAN AND HIS FRIENDS LAUGH.

WILL I was five years old. Mum, please.

POLLY McKENZIE   Oh I just worry about you petal. Oh actually I should get you a jumper.

POLLY HAS TURNED ROUND TO GO BACK TO THE HOUSE.

WILL   Go. Just drive before she gets back.

SIMON TRIES TO ACCELERATE HARD OUT OF THE DRIVE BUT IS GETTING NOWHERE AS HE HASN'T REMOVED THE HANDBRAKE.

DONOVAN SPITS OUT A MOUTHFUL OF HIS DRINK ONTO THE WINDSCREEN. SIMON TAKES OFF THE HANDBRAKE, DRIVES OFF AND HAS TO PUT THE WIND-SCREEN WIPERS ON.

WILL V/O   . . . *Simon's dad needn't have worried. There was no danger of him getting up enough speed to kill himself. Despite the fact Thorpe Park will be shutting in a few hours.*

——— SCENE 6 ———

EXT. JAY'S HOUSE

ON THE DRIVE WE SEE A CARAVAN.

JAY, WILL AND SIMON ARE COMING DOWN THE DRIVE. THE HAWAII IS OBSCURED FROM VIEW BY THE CARAVAN.

JAY   Where's your new car then Si?

SIMON   Round here.

JAY   Fuck me. Do you get a free Barbie when you buy one of these? Shotgun.

THEY GO TO GET INTO THE CAR. SIMON HEADS FOR THE DRIVER'S SIDE AND WILL HOLDS THE PASSENGER DOOR OPEN FOR JAY.

WILL   After you.

JAY   I called shotgun.

WILL   What?

JAY   Shotgun. It means I get the front seat.

WILL   In what way could it possibly mean that?

JAY Just does.

WILL Look, we drove over here with me in the front seat. We've come to pick you up. We've picked you up. Now in you get and I return to my previous position.

JAY It's not happening, freak. I called shotgun.

SIMON He's right, he did call it.

WILL What? You're backing him?

SIMON Get in the back Will.

JAY PUSHES WILL'S HEAD TOWARDS THE OPEN CAR DOOR.

WILL Ow, ow. I'm getting in. Get off. I've had morphallaxis. My bones will pop out.

──────── SCENE 7 ────────

INT./EXT. SIMON'S CAR

WILL V/O *So we had a car. It was a shit car, but it was still a car. All we needed now were some girls . . .*

THEY ARE WAITING TO PULL OUT ONTO A BUSY ROAD. SUDDENLY THEY NOTICE THAT THE CAR IN FRONT OF THEM HAS FOUR ATTRACTIVE GIRLS IN IT.

JAY Aye aye, up ahead. A car full of muff. Pull alongside them Si.

SIMON I can't, I'm not turning left. It's against the Highway Code.

JAY Well just beep them.

SIMON No.

JAY Don't be such a pussy.

HE LEANS OVER TO PUSH THE HORN. SIMON FIGHTS HIM OFF.

SIMON Oi, no, get off.

JAY All right, all right.

HE SITS BACK AS IF HE'S GIVEN UP ON PUSHING THE HORN. THEN HE SUDDENLY LEAPS FORWARD AND LEANS ON IT. THE HORN SOUNDS FOR AGES, HE LAUGHS AND SIMON TRIES TO COVER HIS FACE AS THE GIRLS TURN ROUND.

SIMON   Oi.

JAY   Hello lovelies.

THE GIRLS DRIVE OFF.

JAY   Follow them.

SIMON   All right, I suppose.

SIMON STALLS IT.

SIMON   Shit, stalled it.

JAY   Oh you dickhead, they're getting away.

WILL   Jesus, you make it sound like we're about to attack them.

JAY   I can't believe you lost the muff wagon.

SIMON   Well what were we going to do anyway? Follow them till they're forced to drive to a police station.

JAY   They love it, you tool. It's called flirting.

WILL   Yeah, a terrifying and unsolicited form of flirting.

JAY   And if you didn't drive like such an old woman we might actually catch up with them.

SIMON   I'm not going to risk our necks for some random girls.

JAY   Yeah, well I'd give a left bollock for them, so get a fucking move on.

WILL   Actually I think that's them up ahead.

JAY   Yes, we've caught up with them. Do a left.

SIMON SLOWS AND STOPS AT THE JUNCTION.

JAY   What you doing? Pull out.

SIMON   No.

WILL   There's a space, you can go now.

SIMON   No, it's not safe.

JAY   Are you winding me up? Look, go now.

WILL   Thorpe Park's going to be closing soon Si.

SIMON   Look, fuck off, all right. I've just passed my test and I'm not going to crash 'cause you twats can't wait two minutes.

JAY   Just fucking go.

WILL   Well, there's a gap – quickly.

SIMON   All right, for fuck's sake.

HE FLOORS IT AND WITH A SCREECH OF TYRES THEY TURN RIGHT INTO THE TRAFFIC.

THERE IS A BEAT THEN WE PULL WIDE AND SEE THAT HE'S DRIVEN INTO A FUNERAL CORTEGE, RIGHT BEHIND THE HEARSE, AND IN FRONT OF THE CHIEF MOURNERS' CAR. THERE ARE FLOWERS SPELLING THE WORD 'DAD' INSIDE THE HEARSE.

WILL LOOKS BEHIND TO SEE A CAR WITH A WOMAN CRYING IN THE BACK AND A HARD-LOOKING MAN RED WITH RAGE STARING OUT FROM THE FRONT PASSENGER SEAT.

WILL   Oh shit.

SIMON   Now look what you've made me do. Oh God.

JAY   Why are they going so fucking slowly?

WILL   Yeah, I mean it's almost as if they don't want to see their dearly departed fly out the back on to the A320.

SIMON   Oh God.

WILL V/O   . . . it wasn't a great start to our first road trip, and knowing our luck they'll be burying them at Thorpe Park.

———— SCENE 8 ————

INT./EXT. SIMON'S CAR (AT THORPE PARK)

WILL V/O *It's fair to say overtaking dead bodies wasn't Simon's strong point. By the time we finally got to Thorpe Park we only had two hours of valuable roller-coaster time left.*

THEY ARE PULLING INTO THE HUGE CAR PARK AT THORPE PARK.

JAY I can't believe you lost the muff, you bell-end. They were giving us the come-on.

SIMON Yeah, by driving away as fast as possible.

JAY They wanted us to chase them. But it's hard to have a chase when you don't go over thirty.

SIMON It's thirty for a reason.

WILL Look, I think we should remember today is about roller coasters. And Simon's got us here safely.

SIMON I thought it was about me passing my test.

WILL Yes, as well, but mainly it's about Nemesis Inferno.

JAY No, today is about tits and we're in luck. Get them.

WE SEE THE GIRLS FROM EARLIER PARKING UP AND GETTING OUT OF THEIR CAR.

SIMON Right.

SIMON DRIVES PAST THE PARKING SPOT AND THEN TRIES TO REVERSE PARK. HE DOES THIS VERY BADLY. HE THEN DRIVES FORWARD A BIT AND TRIES AGAIN. AND AGAIN.

THE GIRLS ARE LAUGHING AND THEN START TO MOVE OFF.

JAY Park it. Quickly, you dickhead.

SIMON Fuck off.

SIMON GOES TO REVERSE ONE MORE TIME.

JAY I'm not waiting any longer.

JAY OPENS THE DOOR JUST AS SIMON REVERSES VERY FAST. THE OPEN DOOR HITS A POST AND IS TORN OFF.

THEY ALL GET OUT OF THE CAR TO SURVEY THE DAMAGE.

SIMON   Oh no. Oh shit.

WILL   Oh dear. Your dad's not going to be pleased, is he?

SIMON   God, look what you've done. Christ, I've only had it a day.

SIMON GOES TO GET BACK INTO THE CAR.

JAY   You're in the shit. Where are you going?

SIMON   My dad's going to go mental. I've got to get this fixed.

WILL   But the roller coasters?

SIMON   I don't care. I have to get this fixed.

WILL   But Simon, we've come so far.

JAY   Neil's sister's boyfriend is a mechanic, he'll fix it.

SIMON   Is he?

WILL   Well there you go then. We'll go and find Neil. His sister's boyfriend will fix the car and your dad will be none the wiser. And as we've travelled all this way, we might as well enjoy the rides.

SIMON   But my car.

WILL   Simon, look at me. Look at me. I guarantee the Nemesis Inferno will cheer you up.

JAY   Or think about them little lovelies. They're in there with their tits and that.

WILL   Come on, let's go and find Neil for you.

SIMON   Can't we just phone him?

WILL   He's at work Si. He can't take personal calls. We're going to have to go in there if we want to talk to him.

SIMON   Well what about my car door? What if someone nicks it?

WILL   We'll take it with us. They'll definitely have a place to store it.

SIMON   Fine. For fuck's sake.

HE PICKS UP THE DOOR AND THEY MOVE OFF.

——————— SCENE 9 ———————

EXT. THORPE PARK–TICKET BOOTH

TICKET SELLER   We have baby changing and disabled access for limited rides.

WILL   Right. Not really what I asked though.

TICKET SELLER   We don't have anywhere to store car doors.

WILL TURNS ROUND TO THE OTHERS. SIMON IS STANDING THERE HOLDING A DOOR.

WILL   Turns out they don't have anywhere to store car doors.

SIMON   Knew it. Fine. We'll take turns carrying it then.

JAY   I'm not carrying it.

SIMON   Fuck not carrying it. You're paying for it as well, mate.

JAY   Me, why?

SIMON   Because you ripped it off.

JAY   You reversed.

SIMON   Yeah, but you're the one who ripped it off.

WILL   Hey, let's not argue. Let's just get in there, have some fun.

JAY   Face it, if you could park properly this wouldn't have happened.

SIMON   Yeah, well I'm the only one who can drive, so you can fuck off.

JAY   I can drive. I took an army driving course when I was ten.

SIMON   Bollocks, you still wet the bed when you were ten.

JAY   Yeah, I wet your mum's bed with my spunk.

SIMON   Yeah, brilliant.

THE THREE OF THEM WALK INTO THORPE PARK.

——— SCENE 10 ———

EXT. THORPE PARK

WILL V/O   *When we got into the park, I realised it had been worth ruining the dignified man's funeral for. It was amazing. We may have lost the . . . hmm . . . tits, but the roller coaster was still in our sights. First up we had to find Neil, if only to stop Simon bitching about his car.*

WILL, SIMON AND JAY ARE APPROACHING MR MONKEY'S BANANA RIDE. SIMON IS LOOKING A BIT KNACKERED FROM CARRYING THE DOOR.

JAY   I'm not paying for it.

SIMON   Yes you are.

JAY   Good luck with that.

WILL   Let's just find Neil.

WE SEE ONE OF THE THEME PARK MASCOTS, MR MONKEY, A MAN IN AN 8FT MONKEY COSTUME, BEHAVING VERY STRANGELY. HE'S LEAPING AROUND AND BEATING HIMSELF. A COUPLE OF YOUNG CHILDREN ARE IN FRONT OF HIM AND START TO CRY AS HE LOOKS TOTALLY DERANGED.

MR MONKEY   Help, ah.

SIMON   What's that?

MR MONKEY   Help, ah . . .

WOMAN   Are you all right, Mr Monkey?

MR MONKEY   Ah. Ah.

WILL   Does he need help?

MR MONKEY   Oh help, help. No, not my balls, not my balls, ah . . .

JAY   He's gone mental. Poor fucker.

MR MONKEY IS WAVING FRANTICALLY AND THRASHING AROUND ON THE GROUND.

MR MONKEY　Ah, ah. (TAKING THE MONKEY HEAD OFF) Wasp, wasp.

IT'S NEIL.

JAY　Neil.

NEIL　Wasp, in me costume.

SIMON, JAY AND WILL SIMPLY CANNOT BELIEVE IT. THEY ARE IN STITCHES.

——— SCENE 11 ———

INT. CHANGING ROOM

NEIL IS GETTING CHANGED OUT OF HIS MR MONKEY OUTFIT.

WE CAN SEE A FEW RED WELTS ON HIS BODY. JAY, WILL AND SIMON LOOK ON.

NEIL　Oh God that hurts. Stupid bloody wasps.

SIMON　Neil, I need to speak to you about your sister's boyfriend.

THEY WATCH NEIL UNDRESSING AND IT BECOMES CLEAR AS HE REMOVES THE BOTTOM PART OF THE COSTUME THAT HE IS NAKED UNDERNEATH. HE CLEARLY HAS NO SHAME ABOUT IT AND IS STANDING FACING THEM QUITE OPENLY.

JAY　Oh Jesus, Neil.

SIMON　Christ, you're naked under there.

WILL　I really don't think it's a good idea to be naked if you're working with kids.

NEIL　But Mr Monkey isn't naked; he's got a waistcoat and a hat.

WILL　No, not Mr Monkey Neil. You.

NEIL　But I'm in the suit.

WILL　Yes, naked.

NEIL　Look I'm in agony here. (POINTING TO THE FIRST AID BOX) Put some of that cream on my stings.

WILL　God, all right then.

NEIL The worst ones are on my back . . . and arse.

JAY Fuck that. Look, you lot can stay here and finger Neil's arse if you want to, but I'm off to find the clunge.

HE LEAVES IN A RUSH.

SIMON Neil seriously, can you put it away so we can talk. Put some clothes on.

NEIL All right, all right.

HE GOES TO HIS LOCKER AND OPENS IT. IT IS EMPTY.

NEIL (LAUGHING) Oh not again.

WILL What?

NEIL They're always doing this round here. They're bonkers. They've nicked my clothes.

SIMON Where will they have put them?

NEIL (SHAKING HIS HEAD, LAUGHING) I don't know last time this happened they burnt them.

SIMON Burnt them?

WILL Please hurry up. We can't go on the roller coaster if you're naked.

NEIL Oh don't worry, I'll get something out the lost-property bin. There's always stuff in there.

NEIL CROSSES IN FRONT OF WILL AND BENDS OVER TO GET SOMETHING OUT OF THE BIN. HIS ARSE CRACK IS TERRIFYINGLY CLOSE TO WILL'S FACE.

——————— SCENE 12 ———————

EXT. THORPE PARK

WILL V/O *With the stench from Neil's arse still hot in my nostrils, we headed for Nemesis. Though technically dressed, the clothes Neil had picked from lost property made him look surprisingly like a Brazilian male prostitute . . .*

NEIL IS DRESSED IN A SINGLET, A PAIR OF SPEEDO BRIEFS AND A PAIR OF TRAINERS WITH SOCKS.

JAY HAS BEEN WALKING AHEAD, LOOKING AROUND ANIMATEDLY.

JAY   I've just seen the clunge head towards Nemesis.

WILL   Oh, sounds like they're thrill-seekers too.

JAY   I hope they're cock-seekers too.

WILL   Brilliant.

JAY RUNS OFF TO FOLLOW THEM.

JAY   See ya.

SIMON   Neil, I seriously need to speak to you about my car.

NEIL   What?

SIMON   Your sister's boyfriend works in a garage, doesn't he?

NEIL   Yeah, he works in a garage.

SIMON   Will he be working tonight?

NEIL   Probably. He works most evenings.

WILL   Brilliant, perfect, that's sorted. The park's about to close, so we'll go on Nemesis now and then we can deal with your car later. But we'll go on the Nemesis now.

SIMON   I suppose so.

WILL'S PHONE RINGS.

WILL ANSWERS THE PHONE. THE BOYS LOOK AT WILL.

WILL   Hello. Yes I got your text. Yes I'm safe. No I'm not crying.

WILL V/O   . . . *so far the only terrifying experience I'd had all day was seeing Neil's cock and balls. But now the Nemesis Inferno was tantalisingly close.*

──────── SCENE 13 ────────

EXT. THORPE PARK

THE BOYS ARE AT THE ENTRANCE TO THE NEMESIS INFERNO RIDE.

TANNOY ANNOUNCEMENT   This is your last chance to queue for Nemesis Inferno. The ride is now closing.

JAY   Shit, still an hour queue.

WILL   That's nothing. I was waiting three hours for the Indiana Jones ride at Disneyland Paris.

JAY   You are mental.

NEIL   Mental.

WILL   Why's enjoying things mental?

JAY   This place is full of muff, but you're only interested in roller coasters.

WILL   Girls are everywhere Jay. The best rides in the country are only here.

NEIL   You sound like you're forty.

WILL   Well I'm queuing and I'm getting in a separate queue for the front four seats. The front's the best.

TANNOY ANNOUNCEMENT   This ride is now closing.

WILL   Si, you coming?

SIMON   Are you sure your sister's boyfriend will be working tonight, Neil?

NEIL   Yeah, I told you he works evenings.

WILL   Well that's sorted then. Now can we please get on the ride.

JAY   Shotgun the outside seats?

WILL   No, you can't shotgun a roller coaster.

JAY   Well I just did.

——— SCENE 14 ———

EXT. NEMESIS INFERNO RIDE

THEY FINALLY GET TO THE FRONT OF THE QUEUE.

WILL   Oh yes, you know this is one of the only two versions of this roller coaster outside of the US and I promise, although it's taken a little bit longer—

JAY   Half a fucking hour longer.

WILL   —to queue for the front, it will be worth it. Unencumbered thrills and we can come back all year thanks to Neil.

NEIL   Come on, we're up.

WILL WALKS FORWARD TO THE FRONT OF THE RIDE.

THE RIDE ATTENDANT INTERCEPTS HIM AS HE WALKS TO THE FRONT, HOLDS HIM WHERE HE IS AND THREE PEOPLE CLEARLY COME FROM THE OTHER SIDE AND SIT IN THE FRONT ROW OF THE RIDE.

ASSISTANT   Room for one more at the front.

WILL   Sorry?

ASSISTANT   One more at the front.

WILL   How can there possibly be room for only one more at the front?

ASSISTANT   Well, there's three people on the front, so there's a spare seat there.

WILL   Yeah, yeah, let's just rewind a bit shall we? Why are there now three people at the front?

ASSISTANT   Sir, if you could just get on.

WILL   They've pushed in. We've spent over an hour queuing specifically for the front and they've pushed in.

ASSISTANT   Sir.

WILL   Get them off. Get them off and make them move. Fucking pushing in.

SIMON (AWARE OF THE SCENE NOW BEING CREATED) Will it doesn't matter. We'll sit at the back.

ASSISTANT Sir, if you could just—

WILL Are they so dumb they think it's OK to push in? Make them move.

JAY Shut up you plum and get on the ride.

ASSISTANT Sir, it's the last ride of the day, please get on.

SIMON Will, honestly it doesn't matter, just get on.

WILL Fine, fucking fine. I'll just . . . I'll just get on. I'll just get on and sit at the front next to these inconsiderate arseholes.

HE WALKS TO THE FRONT, STRAPS HIMSELF IN, THEN LOOKS ACROSS TO GIVE THE PEOPLE WHO SAT AT THE FRONT A DIRTY LOOK ('OR MAYBE YOU THREE SHOULD...')

HE SEES THAT THE THREE IN THE FRONT ARE TWO KIDS WITH DOWN'S SYNDROME AND A VERY NICE, GOOD-LOOKING HELPER BLOKE.

WILL I'm the worst human being in the world.

JUST AS HIS FACE FALLS, THE RIDE SHOOTS OFF.

A MONTAGE OF THE PEOPLE ON THE FRONT AS THE RIDE GOES ROUND, WITH WILL LOOKING DREADFULLY GUILTY AND NOT ENJOYING IT.

 SCENE 15

EXT. NEMESIS INFERNO RIDE

WILL V/O *When I look back on my life, I'm pretty sure that ride will be a low point. But with a bit of luck the others wouldn't find out who I'd insulted . . .*

THE RIDE ENDS.

THE THREE PEOPLE AT THE FRONT GET OFF.

WILL SLOWLY EMERGES BEHIND THEM.

SIMON They were on the front? Oh no Will, no.

JAY   Oh my God.

SIMON   Oh Will.

JAY   Oh my God.

WILL   Don't.

PEOPLE ARE LOOKING AT WILL WITH DISGUST.

SIMON   Arseholes.

JAY IS KILLING HIMSELF LAUGHING.

JAY   This is the best. You're going to hell.

WILL   Please don't.

──────── SCENE 16 ────────

EXT. THORPE PARK

WILL V/O   . . . *so I'd finally got to ride the Nemesis, which wasn't as much fun as I'd hoped. It will be a long journey home. Made longer by Simon carrying the door and my heavy sense of shame.*

THE FOUR BOYS ARE TRUDGING BACK ACROSS THE ACRES OF NOW EMPTY CAR PARK, SIMON CARRYING THE CAR DOOR AND NEIL STILL WEARING HIS LOST PROPERTY OUTFIT.

JAY   Well it can't be too hard to find. It's the colour of my nan's piss.

NEIL   Why are you watching your nan piss?

SIMON   Oh Christ, what am I going to say to my parents? Will the door go back on?

JAY   Stop shitting yourself. Like Neil said, his sister's boyfriend will be able to fix it.

NEIL   He won't be able to fix that.

SIMON   What? You said he'd be able to fix it, no problem. You said he worked in a garage.

NEIL   He does, BP garage. He mucks about with cars, but he won't be able to fix that in a million years. The door's come off.

SIMON   Oh this is a disaster. My dad's going to go mad.

JAY   It will be fine. We'll find someone else to fix it. I know a bloke who builds Formula One cars. He owes me a favour.

SIMON   I don't think your make-believe friend will fix this.

WILL   Look, we'll find a proper mechanic on the way back. It can't be too hard.

SIMON   As long as it's fixed good as new and my parents don't know, that's all I care about.

WILL   (COMING UP TO SIMON'S CAR) Oh look here it is car park D.

WILL   Ah, oh dear.

SIMON PUTS DOWN THE CAR DOOR.

SIMON   What the fuck has happened?

HE LOOKS AT THE CAR. THE INSIDE HAS BEEN STRIPPED, THE STEERING WHEEL IS GONE, ONE OF THE SEATS HAS GONE, THE REAR-VIEW MIRROR HAS GONE, THE HUBCAPS AND TWO OF THE WHEELS ARE GONE.

SIMON   Holy shit, what's happened?

WILL   At least they left the tape deck.

SIMON   I don't believe this. There's no explaining this to my dad.

WILL   I mean, who and why?

JUST THEN A 'HAPPY FOUNDATION' BUS DRIVES PAST THEM.

LEANING OUT OF THE WINDOW ARE THE TWO DOWN'S KIDS FROM EARLIER AND THEIR HANDSOME HELPER. THEY WAVE SIMON'S STEERING WHEEL AND HUBCAPS AT SIMON AND WILL AS THEY DRIVE PAST, THEN GIVE THEM THE FINGER.

WILL   Yes. That makes sense.

JAY   Fuckers. Let's get 'em.

SIMON   Jay, I'm not going to chase after them and fight the Happy Foundation bus.

NEIL   How we getting home then?

WILL V/O   *It's true, girls do like cars. They just don't like shitty little yellow cars that ruin funerals and don't have all the doors they were made with. Girls are also less keen on boys who wear speedos, border-line sex pests and people who insult the disabled . . .*

SHOT OF WILL INSULTING THE DISABLED KIDS ON THE NEMESIS RIDE.

WILL   Inconsiderate arseholes.

WILL V/O   *. . . but it's not all bad. What we learnt today is there isn't a car on the planet that can make us cool whatever state it was in.*

SIMON   (ON THE PHONE) Dad, what you need to know is it wasn't my fault. Well I'm sorry, but it wasn't my fault.

Episode 4

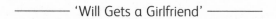

This episode (one of my favourites) was inspired by a mishmash of my early romantic life (which is definitely giving me getting dumped by a couple of girls too grand a name), and Damon's 'friend' story (which actually did happen to him). Damon and his teenage mates wound up a member of their group so much about a new 'friend' he'd just said hello to on their estate that he jumped up and down on said 'friend's' car. It's a bit mental, and we weren't 100 per cent sure if it would work in a sitcom, but what we did know is that teenage mates will take the piss out of each other constantly, over anything, and if you show some weakness or that you're annoyed by it that's only going to make it worse. We also liked the idea that a word with such positive connotations as 'friend' (surely only a good thing?) could be used to bully and irritate.

Names are a weird thing when you're writing, because before you film anything, what's called a 'negative check' is done by a legal team on all the names you've given the characters. What the negative check does is make sure that you aren't unintentionally (or intentionally) libelling someone. So if either of us had known someone called Charlotte Hinchcliffe with big jugs who everyone said slept with a rugby team, then we wouldn't have been allowed to use the name. As it happens we thought Charlotte felt like a nice name, and one of my closest friends is a guy called Christian Hinchcliffe, who had just become a new father. I told him we were using his surname, and he said he was happy with that, but it was a shame that we hadn't called the character Saskia Hinchcliffe after his daughter. Then he saw the episode, and what was said about the character of Charlotte Hinchcliffe, and was absolutely delighted it wasn't his lovely daughter's name.

——— SCENE 1 ———

INT. PARTY HOUSE, LIVING ROOM

WILL V/O   *It was a typical Saturday night in suburbia and Wendy's party was the kind of shit party that happened most weekends. Her parents were upstairs waiting for the house to be trashed and they'd be down at 11.30 anyway to turf us all out. We were downstairs bored senseless and wondering how we'd ever get laid and anyone who is in any way cool was somewhere else.*

WILL IS STANDING, SIMON IS SITTING ON AN ARMCHAIR, WITH NEIL ON THE ARMREST. THEY ARE NOT REALLY TALKING TO EACH OTHER, JUST LOOKING OUT INTO THE (QUITE SMALL, VERY UNCOOL) PARTY. THERE ARE MAYBE SEVEN OTHER KIDS THERE.

THE GIRL WHOSE PARTY IT IS (WENDY) GOES OVER TO NEIL.

GIRL   Can you get off the armrest please?

NEIL   Sorry.

WILL   Although it was nice of you to invite me, this doesn't seem like a very cool party.

SIMON   Oh I'm sorry, did you cancel a night out with Paris Hilton to be here? Wendy, do you have any more beer?

WENDY   I think there's a box of my dad's small beers left but don't drink it all 'cos Charlotte Hinchcliffe and her mates will be here soon.

NEIL   Yeah, right, like she's going to come.

WILL   Why wouldn't she come?

SIMON   She's fit and popular, therefore she won't be coming.

JAY COMES OVER.

JAY   Who won't be coming?

WILL   Charlotte Hinchcliffe.

JAY   Ahh, I'd make her come, all over my face. You know she has to get special bras made because not only are her tits so big, but they are perfectly round.

NEIL   Like porn star tits.

JAY   And she's a slag. She once munched off the whole rugby team.

WILL   Can that be true?

JAY   No word of a lie.

NEIL   I heard that.

WILL   Our school doesn't even have a rugby team.

JAY   Well it was another school then.

WILL   Which one?

JAY   Look, it happened, all right?

WILL   Well then you should be able to tell me where it happened.

NEIL   Well you can ask her yourself when she gets here.

SIMON   Except she won't be here.

A BOY POPS HIS HEAD IN THE DOOR AND WAVES AT JAY.

JAY'S FRIEND   Jay, I'm off mate. See you soon.

JAY   All right then mate.

JAY GIVES A THUMB UP.

SIMON   Who was that?

JAY   Just a friend.

NEIL   You've made a new friend.

SIMON   Ooh a friend? Since when have you had other friends? Ooh friend.

JAY   I knew him from when we were doing trials at West Ham. He's moved into the area. He's just some guy.

SIMON   Some guy?

WILL   Oh he's just some guy.

SIMON   He's just some guy.

WILL   That's all it is.

SIMON   Just a friend from when Jay had trials at West Ham that never happened.

WILL   Don't forget the thumbs up.

NEIL, WILL AND SIMON, ALL DOING THE THUMBS UP AT JAY:

SIMON   Ooh friend. Ooh, new friend.

NEIL   Weeee.

WILL   Ooh friend.

SIMON   Please be my friend, ooh friend.

WILL   Ooh friend.

JAY   Fuck you lot, where's the beer?

SIMON   We're out.

WILL   I'm going to the loo.

JAY   What, for a wank? You wanker.

WILL   (SMILING BACK AT HIM AND GIVING THE THUMBS UP) Friend.

SIMON   See if you can find some more beer on the way back.

NEIL   Check the washing machine, that's where I'd hide it. No one ever puts any in the fridge.

WILL LOOKS QUIZZICALLY AT NEIL THEN SHAKES HIS HEAD AS HE LEAVES.

AFTER WILL HAS LEFT THREE REALLY QUITE PRETTY GIRLS COME IN, ONE OF WHOM IS CLEARLY THE 'LEADER' (CHARLOTTE HINCHCLIFFE). SHE IS CONFIDENT AND SEEMS LIKE A GOOD, FUN, INTELLIGENT GIRL.

SIMON   Fucking hell, she has turned up. This is now officially the coolest party we've ever been to.

JAY   Try and look cool, then.

THEY ALL STRIKE POSES, NONE OF WHICH ARE VERY COOL.

─────── SCENE 2 ───────

INT. PARTY HOUSE, KITCHEN

WILL IS IN THE KITCHEN. THERE ARE TWO EMPTY BOTTLES OF WINE, A FEW EMPTY CANS AND ABOUT TWELVE EMPTY BOTTLES OF THOSE SMALL FRENCH BEERS YOU GET.

WILL SHAKES THE CANS – NOTHING – THEN STARTS RIFLING THROUGH THE CUPBOARDS. NOTHING.

HE HATES HIMSELF FOR DOING IT, BUT HE EVEN HAS A FEEL AROUND INSIDE THE WASHING MACHINE. TO HIS SURPRISE HE PULLS OUT A SINGLE, TINY CAN OF LAGER.

WILL V/O   *As expected, the kitchen was a booze-free zone apart from one small beer in the washing machine which was presumably Neil's. I assumed there wouldn't be anything in the fridge but what the hell, and to my surprise I hit the jackpot.*

FINALLY, HE TAKES A LOOK AT THE FRIDGE, FIGURING HE MIGHT AS WELL CHECK. THERE'S A BOTTLE OF CHAMPAGNE IN THERE. HE GETS IT OUT AND IS JUST OPENING IT AS BEHIND HIM HE HEARS:

CHARLOTTE   I think you've got my champagne.

WILL TURNS ROUND AND SEES THIS VISION. HE LOOKS A BIT PANICKED AND THEN THE CORK POPS OUT. SHE CLOCKS THIS.

WILL   Oh, God, um, sorry.

CHARLOTTE   Well you've opened it now, you might as well grab a glass.

WILL   Right, er yes, thanks, sorry. Did you know the original champagne glass is said to be modelled on Marie Antoinette's breast?

CHARLOTTE   Do you always start off a conversation by talking about breasts?

WILL   No. How's it gone?

CHARLOTTE   Quite badly.

WILL   Right.

BACK TO

INT. PARTY ROOM, LIVING ROOM

SIMON IS STARING AT ONE OF CHARLOTTE'S FRIENDS, WHO LOOKS A BIT BORED, AND WHEN SHE CATCHES SIMON'S EYE SHE LOOKS AWAY.

SIMON   She's amazing.

NEIL   Who?

SIMON   That girl. Her eyes are beautiful.

NEIL   You get weird around girls. Like a stalker.

SIMON   No I don't.

JAY   Yeah you do. Where's that muppet with our drinks?

JAY LEAVES TO GO TO THE KITCHEN.

BACK TO

INT. PARTY HOUSE, KITCHEN

JAY WALKS INTO THE KITCHEN AND KIND OF STOPS DEAD IN THE DOOR FRAME.

WILL IS CHATTING TO CHARLOTTE AND THEY BOTH SEEM TO BE VERY RELAXED AND ENJOYING THEMSELVES, LAUGHING ETC.

WILL   I haven't told my old friends I've joined a state comprehensive yet. They think I'm here doing voluntary work for UNICEF.

CHARLOTTE   You pretentious twat.

JAY   Oi, did you get us any beers?

WILL   Hi Jay.

JAY   Listen, if you really want a laugh, you should come and chat with me. I'm about fifty times funnier than him.

CHARLOTTE   Is he for real?

WILL   Regrettably yes.

JAY   I'm totally for real. Everybody knows I'm funnier. Even you'd say so, wouldn't you Will?

WILL   Er well, no, not really.

CHARLOTTE   All right then, funny boy. Make me laugh without undressing.

JAY STANDS THERE. IT LOOKS LIKE HE'S LOST CONFIDENCE, BUT THEN HE JUST STARTS DOING A FAIRLY ACCURATE IMPRESSION OF THE CRAZY FROG:

JAY   Ehmmm, num, num, nehmmmm, nehmmmmm... etc

WILL AND CHARLOTTE LOOK ON IN CONFUSION AS JAY CARRIES THIS ON FOR A GOOD FIFTEEN SECONDS. EVEN JAY CAN SEE THAT THIS ISN'T GETTING QUITE THE REACTION HE'D HOPED FOR. HE EVENTUALLY STOPS.

JAY   Crazy Frog.

CHARLOTTE   OK, er, if Will ever stops being funny, I'll let you know. Come on you.

WILL AND CHARLOTTE LEAVE THE KITCHEN.

——————— SCENE 3 ———————

INT. PARTY HOUSE, LIVING ROOM

SIMON AND NEIL ARE WATCHING SEMI-AGAPE AS CHARLOTTE AND WILL SIT AND TALK ALMOST OPPOSITE.

HE'S SITTING ON THE FLOOR, EFFECTIVELY AT HER FEET, BUT SHE SEEMS TO BE REALLY ENJOYING THE CONVERSATION. HE CERTAINLY IS.

SIMON   What the hell is going on?

JAY   Fuck knows. Her and her mates must be having a snog-a-twat competition.

SIMON   Well that can't be happening or someone would have claimed you. This is brilliant news.

JAY   How is Will getting off with Charlotte 'big jugs' brilliant news?

SIMON   'Cos it means things really have changed. Girls might be about to notice us for who we actually are.

JAY   Well you're fucked then because you're a twat.

SIMON   Nice.

JAY   (SEEING CHARLOTTE LEADING WILL OFF) Oh my God.

NEIL   I thought she was seeing someone in our year.

JAY   Yeah, I heard she was seeing Donovan.

NEIL   No. Who is it?

SIMON   Is it Donovan Neil? Because he's a nutter and we should warn Will.

NEIL   It's someone.

JAY   Is it Donovan?

NEIL   I can't think.

SIMON   Donovan?

NEIL   Let me think.

JAY   Donovan?

NEIL   That guy.

SIMON   Donovan.

NEIL   What's his name?

──────── SCENE 4 ────────

INT. PARTY HOUSE, UPSTAIRS LANDING

WILL AND CHARLOTTE COME UP THE STAIRS. THEY ARE HOLDING HANDS.

WILL   (STRAIGHTENING UP AND ADDRESSING CHARLOTTE SERIOUSLY) Look, this isn't a practical joke, is it?

SHE LOOKS BEMUSED. WILL LOOKS OVER HIS SHOULDERS TO SEE IF ANY OF HER FRIENDS ARE STANDING BEHIND HIM ON THE STAIRS.

WILL   Because if it is then I'm fine with that, it would just be nice to know so we can all have a laugh about it, admittedly at my expense, and then get on with our lives.

CHARLOTTE   No, it's not a practical joke.

WILL   Oh great, sure, no, didn't think it was.

CHARLOTTE LEANS OVER AND KISSES HIM.

WILL   I like that kiss.

CHARLOTTE   So did I and if you're lucky you might get more.

WILL   Oh my God – sex?

CHARLOTTE   I'm not going to have sex with you Will.

WILL   No, no, of course not.

CHARLOTTE   How about we, er . . . don't have sex in here?

SHE OPENS THE DOOR AND DRAGS WILL INTO A BEDROOM.

WILL   All right.

BACK TO

INT. PARTY HOUSE, LIVING ROOM

SIMON   Was it Donovan Neil?

NEIL   I'm trying to think who it was.

DONOVAN WALKS INTO THE ROOM.

NEIL   Oh yeah, it was Donovan.

SIMON   You fucking idiot.

JAY   Will's dead.

SIMON   Oh shit, we should do something.

DONOVAN CASTS A MEAN GLARE AROUND THE ROOM.

NEIL   Well, after he gets beaten up, we could take him to hospital.

DONOVAN HAS BEEN CHATTING TO CHARLOTTE'S MATES AND LOOKING OVER AT
THE BOYS. HE COMES OVER TO TALK TO SIMON.

SIMON   Oh fuck, fuck, fuck. Right, don't say anything.

NEIL   OK.

MARK DONOVAN   All right?

SIMON   Yeah, yeah, I'm all right.

MARK DONOVAN   I heard your mate is with Charlotte.

SIMON   Um, don't know, I don't think so.

JAY   Yeah, they're upstairs.

MARK DONOVAN   Cheers.

DONOVAN LEAVES. SIMON AND NEIL LOOK AT JAY.

JAY   What?

──────── SCENE 5 ────────

INT. PARTY HOUSE-UPSTAIRS

MARK DONOVAN   So sorry, Mr and Mrs Dean.

MRS DEAN   That's OK Mark. Hope you're having a nice time. The, er, loo's on the left.

MARK DONOVAN   Thank you very much.

DONOVAN LEAVES POLITELY THEN STRIDES ALONG THE LANDING. HE OPENS ANOTHER DOOR, THEN CLOSES IT AND WALKS DOWN THE CORRIDOR. WE CAN HEAR VAGUE SNOGGING SOUNDS. DONOVAN OPENS THE DOOR AND SEES WILL AND CHARLOTTE ON THE EDGE OF THE BED.

THERE IS A FAIR DISTANCE BETWEEN THEIR BODIES, BUT THEY ARE KISSING AND WILL HAS HIS HAND ON CHARLOTTE'S BREAST, OUTSIDE OF HER CLOTHING. IT'S JUST THERE. STATIC. MARK LOOKS AT HIM. WILL STILL HAS HIS HAND ON CHARLOTTE'S BREAST. WILL SLOWLY PULLS IT AWAY.

CHARLOTTE   What are you doing here?

MARK DONOVAN   I, I came to see you. (TO WILL) Leave.

CHARLOTTE   (TO WILL) No stay. (TO DONOVAN) Mark, it's finished. Now please go.

MARK DONOVAN   No, I'm not leaving till you tell me it's over and you mean it.

CHARLOTTE   It's over and I mean it.

WILL   I think you should leave.

MARK DONOVAN   What, you are telling me to leave, yeah?

WILL   Yes.

MARK DONOVAN   Or what?

CHARLOTTE   Mark, please don't hit him, just go.

MARK DONOVAN   Or what?

CHARLOTTE   Mark, please, for me. Just go.

MARK DONOVAN   Yeah, yeah. Right, all right, I'm leaving, I'm leaving.

WILL   Good, because I was going to call Wendy's parents and don't think that I won't.

MARK DONOVAN   OK, mate, two things, yeah, One, be nice to her 'cos she is kind and fragile and gentle, not like people think. And two, if you tell anyone I said that, I will kill you. I will kill you.

DONOVAN IS GETTING A BIT CHOKED. HE LEAVES.

WILL   What a dickhead.

CHARLOTTE DOESN'T LOOK SO SURE.

 SCENE 6

INT. PARTY HOUSE, LIVING ROOM

DONOVAN WALKS PAST QUICKLY AND LEAVES.

JAY   Fucking hell, he's leaving.

SIMON   No screams and he's not covered in blood. Will must have got away with it.

NEIL   Or Donovan killed them both silently.

THE GIRL THAT SIMON WAS STARING AT EARLIER CASTS A CONCERNED GLANCE AT THE BOYS.

SIMON   She is so beautiful and she keeps looking at me.

JAY　She's only looking to see if you've stopped staring at her.

SIMON　She's still looking.

JAY　Because you're freaking her out.

SIMON　I think we've got a connection. Her eyes. Why don't we go over?

NEIL　No, I don't need to pull, I've got a sure thing lined up.

JAY　A midweek wank.

NEIL　No. I've entered that charity *Blind Date* thing at school.

JAY　That's tragic.

NEIL　Well that's where you're wrong, because I get the choice of three girls to take out on a date, so I don't need to spend my Saturday evening scaring girls like Simon does.

SIMON　What if she's feeling the same and neither of us does anything about it?

JAY　She's fit and she's the year above. She'll never go for you.

SIMON　Look, Will, Will yeah, has pulled Charlotte Hinchcliffe. Anything could happen tonight. I'm going over.

HE GETS UP AND GOES TO WALK OVER TO THE GIRL. SHE'S NOT LOOKING HIS WAY, BUT AS HE GETS CLOSE TO HER AND OPENS HIS MOUTH TO SPEAK SHE TURNS ROUND.

CHARLOTTE'S FRIEND　Go away.

─────── SCENE 7 ───────

EXT. PARTY HOUSE

WILL V/O　*With Simon's humiliation, the party was over, and some of us had done better than others.*

JAY　I don't get it. Charlotte Tits could have had me and she went for that. Come on then, what did you get?

WILL　Well, a gentleman never tells.

JAY   A bender never tells.

WILL   Brilliant.

NEIL   Look, come on, did you get a chew on her boobies or not?

WILL   I can neither confirm nor deny.

JAY   Bender.

SIMON   Look, don't listen to them, this is brilliant. Are you seeing her again?

WILL   I've got to call her tomorrow. She said we should hook up soon.

THEY APPROACH SIMON'S DAD (ALAN COOPER)'S CAR – ONE OF THOSE FOUR-DOOR SPORTS CARS.

SIMON   Oh amazing. Oh and don't tell my dad anything yet. It'll only set him off.

WILL   Of course.

———— SCENE 8 ————

INT. ALAN COOPER'S CAR

SIMON IS IN THE PASSENGER SEAT. JAY, WILL AND NEIL ARE VERY SQUASHED IN THE BACK.

ALAN COOPER   Good night?

SIMON   No, boring.

JAY   Will pulled.

SIMON LOOKS IN AMAZEMENT AT JAY.

ALAN COOPER   Did you Will? Good work.

WILL   Um, thanks.

ALAN COOPER   Yeah when I was your age I used to love house parties. Getting off with some bird, one of the upstairs' rooms, underneath the coats.

SIMON   Dad, can we not . . .

ALAN COOPER Oh in fact I think I met your mum at a house party Simon.

SIMON Jesus Christ.

ALAN COOPER Ohh, she was wild, but after that she didn't just like keeping it upstairs. No, we did it in the kitchen, in the garage. I think we notched one up in the greenhouse once.

SIMON Right, stop the car, I'm going to walk home.

ALAN COOPER Oh come on Simon, me and your mum like doing it too you know.

JAY, WILL AND NEIL LAUGH.

SIMON Dad. You're so embarrassing.

JAY Your mum loves it.

——— SCENE 9 ———

EXT. SCHOOL

WILL V/O *Two days have now passed since I kissed Charlotte, which meant it probably wasn't a wet dream . . .*

THE BOYS ARE HANGING AROUND THE SCHOOL GATES AS CHARLOTTE WALKS TOWARDS THEM.

CHARLOTTE Hello stranger. Hello boys.

JAY, NEIL, SIMON, WILL Hello.

WILL SORT OF SPLITS OFF FROM THE REST OF THE BOYS WITH CHARLOTTE.

WILL V/O *. . . pulling me at a party of geeks was one thing, but how would she treat me at school?*

WILL Hi, hi, how are you? What have you been up to?

CHARLOTTE Well, on Sunday me and Sarah went up to London, bought some vibrating love eggs and put them in on the train back.

WILL And where did you eat in London?

CHARLOTTE   Did you hear what I said?

WILL   Yeah, yeah, it just sounded like a private matter so I thought best not to intrude.

CHARLOTTE   Does it intimidate you when I talk about sex?

WILL   No, not at all. I'm just interested in London restaurants and stuff.

CHARLOTTE   You have had sex before, haven't you?

WILL   Yes, yes, loads. I've done it with two different girls.

CHARLOTTE   I've had eleven lovers already.

WILL   Five girls actually. Sorry, it was five, not two.

CHARLOTTE   All right, stud. Who are they then?

WILL   Well there was a girl I met in Australia.

CHARLOTTE   Australia?

WILL   Yeah, I went there on holiday.

CHARLOTTE   When was that?

WILL   2005.

CHARLOTTE   So you were thirteen.

WILL   I was very mature for my age.

CHARLOTTE   Oh, older woman then, was she?

WILL   No, she was a couple of years younger actually.

CHARLOTTE   So she was eleven.

WILL   Christ no, I mean, yes, I suppose she must have been. Jesus, eleven.

CHARLOTTE   And what about the other four? Had they reached puberty when you slept with them?

WILL   God yes, they were very recent. One was a couple of weeks ago, another one was a few days ago.

CHARLOTTE   I see. Well I reckon you should come round on Friday night and you know.

WILL   God. You mean, you know, on, on Friday?

CHARLOTTE   Yeah, why not? It's no big deal.

WILL   Not a big deal.

CHARLOTTE   I'm not a virgin and you're not a virgin.

WILL   I am so not a virgin.

CHARLOTTE   I believe you.

SHE KISSES HIM ON THE LIPS AND LEAVES.

IN THE BACKGROUND WE CAN SEE A SCOWLING MARK DONOVAN, WHO IT LOOKS LIKE CHARLOTTE GLANCED OVER AT BEFORE KISSING WILL.

——— SCENE 10 ———

INT. SCHOOL DINING HALL

SIMON   What you doing?

NEIL IS READING AND HAS QUITE A LARGE STACK OF HARDBACKS WITH HIM, CLEARLY FROM THE SCHOOL LIBRARY.

NEIL   I'm reading.

SIMON   That's what I meant.

NEIL   I don't know why anyone bothers with this shit. It's like a slow version of TV.

SIMON   Then why bother?

NEIL   For *Blind Date*. It'll make me sound clever if I say I read and girls like clever blokes.

WILL   But once a girl speaks to you Neil, she'll realise you're not a clever bloke.

NEIL   Exactly, that's why I'm saying that I read books.

WILL   No, not exactly, because you'll still seem stupid even though you've lied about reading books.

NEIL   Exactly.

WILL   Oh OK then Neil, that clears it up. Good plan.

JAY   Are you coming round mine tonight? Play Pro Evo?

SIMON   Depends. Will your friend the footballer be there?

NEIL   Ah friend, football friend.

WILL   Ooh best friends for ever and ever.

SIMON   Ooh friend.

JAY   Fuck off, all right, he's not my friend.

SIMON   All right, you're touchy about your friends.

NEIL   Come round mine tonight, my dad's out.

WILL   Oh at last.

NEIL   No, I mean going out.

SIMON   Cottaging?

NEIL   No, he's playing badminton actually.

WILL   Sounds like a euphemism.

JAY   Look, we're not going round yours. Your house stinks.

NEIL   It does not.

SIMON   No offence, mate, but it does smell odd.

NEIL   Like what?

JAY   Just smells like being poor.

NEIL   Fuck off.

WILL'S PHONE BEEPS.

WILL   Shit.

SIMON   Charlotte again?

WILL Yeah, I don't know why she doesn't just come over and say hello.

JAY Because she doesn't want to be seen dead with you.

WILL Well on Friday she'll be doing more than being seen dead with me.

SIMON You're having sex?

NEIL Nice.

SIMON Does she know you're still a virgin?

WILL Nope. I told her I got laid last week.

SIMON Last week. Shit.

JAY Here's a tip for you. The more fingers up, the better. They fucking love it. Try to get at least three. What I'm telling you, all the birds I've shagged love that.

SIMON So no birds love that then.

JAY Well your mum loved it.

SIMON Brilliant.

WILL Knowing my luck, she'll dump me by Friday anyway.

SIMON Yeah, especially if she's using you to get back at Donovan.

WILL What?

SIMON Well it's obvious, mate, everyone can see it. I mean it's still great for you 'cos you get a go on those fantastic tits.

WILL That's not true.

SIMON Yeah it is, no offence, mate, but you don't look much like her type. She goes for big rugby players.

JAY Fifteen at a time sometimes.

WILL Fuck off. Fuck off the lot of you. You don't know her.

SIMON Listen, mate, I'm only trying to look after you.

WILL   No you're not, you're just jealous because a fit girl fancies me and not you.

SIMON   Oh come on, don't be a dick.

WILL   It's not all about looks, you know, and beautiful women like Charlotte understand that. Maybe if you weren't so obsessed by that arsehole Carli who's just stringing you along, you'd see that.

SIMON   Fine. Fine, get your stupid fucking heart broken, I don't care. I've had mates before you and I'll have mates after you've fucked off.

HE TURNS TO LEAVE. JAY AND NEIL ARE PRETENDING TO SHAG THE BOOKS. THE IDEA IS THAT THIS ISN'T A GREAT SET OF MATES.

NEIL   Books get me girls. Books get me girls.

WILL V/O   *It was true. Simon did still have his old friends . . . and he was welcome to them.*

SCENE 11

INT. WILL'S LIVING ROOM

WILL V/O   *Friday rolled around and I was all dressed up for my, you know, date with Charlotte.*

WILL HAS HIS BEST GET-UP ON.

WILL   Bye Mum.

POLLY McKENZIE   Oh you smell nice. Where are you off to?

WILL   Just to meet a friend.

POLLY McKENZIE   Is it a girl?

WILL   No.

POLLY McKENZIE   Is it a boy?

WILL   No. It's a girl. Alright, her name's Charlotte.

POLLY McKENZIE   Charlotte. Oh, is she pretty?

WILL   Yes. She's beautiful actually. She's one of the most popular girls at school.

POLLY McKENZIE   Oh Will. Don't go for the good-looking girls, 'cos everyone's after them. Someone like you will have much more of a chance if you go for the plainer girls.

WILL   Someone like me?

POLLY McKENZIE   Trust me, good-looking girls just break your heart. Let the good-looking boys go out with the good-looking girls.

WILL   Are you saying you think I'm not good-looking?

POLLY McKENZIE   Darling, I think you're beautiful.

SHE KISSES HIM.

WILL   Right, thanks Mum. See you later.

HE LEAVES.

 SCENE 12

EXT. ESTATE CORNER

SIMON, JAY AND NEIL ARE SITTING ON A LOW FENCE LOOKING BORED. NEIL FLICKS SIMON'S EARLOBE.

SIMON   Can you not?

JAY'S FRIEND PULLS UP IN HIS CAR

JAY'S FRIEND   All right Jay.

JAY   (FORGETTING HIMSELF FOR A MINUTE) All right. Nice car.

JAY'S FRIEND   Do you like it? Just got new rims for it.

JAY   Yeah, it's well nice.

SIMON   (TO NEIL, UNDER HIS BREATH BUT LOUD ENOUGH THAT JAY CAN HEAR) Ooh friend.

NEIL   Ooh car friend.

SIMON   Ooh car friend, shall we play football?

JAY'S FRIEND   I've just got to pop home now, but you can have a drive later if you like.

JAY   Yeah, maybe.

SIMON   Ooh thanks, friend.

JAY   Cheers.

NEIL   Car friend, football.

SIMON   Cheers, friend.

JAY'S FRIEND   See you later then.

JAY   Yeah.

JAY'S FRIEND DRIVES OFF AND JAY TURNS TO THE OTHERS.

JAY   (SHOUTING) He's not my fucking friend.

JAY STORMS OFF

SIMON   All right.

NEIL   Ooh friend.

SIMON   Friend. Friend, weird friend.

NEIL   Ooh friend, friend.

NEIL AND SIMON PISS THEMSELVES LAUGHING AS THEY FOLLOW JAY.

——————— SCENE 13 ———————

INT. CHARLOTTE HINCHCLIFFE'S BEDROOM

WILL   Just to confirm, we are going to have sex.

CHARLOTTE   Yes, I can confirm that.

WILL   (UNDER HIS BREATH) Told you Mum.

CHARLOTTE   Did you just call me 'Mum'?

WILL   No, no, God no.

CHARLOTTE   Are you all right?

WILL   Yeah I'm fine. Are you going to hurt me?

CHARLOTTE   If you want me to.

WILL   No, no, sorry, no, I meant . . .

CHARLOTTE   I know what you meant Will. Come on.

WILL   I really, really like you. You know, I adore you a lot.

CHARLOTTE   I like you too. Come on.

MOVEMENT UNDER THE TINIEST OF COVERS SHOWS THAT HE IS GETTING ON TOP OF HER.

WE SEE CHARLOTTE'S FACE FACING UP AND THE BACK OF WILL'S HEAD MOVING UP AND DOWN QUITE A LARGE DISTANCE. THIS IS HAPPENING IN SILENCE.

WE PULL WIDE AND SEE THAT WILL STILL HAS HIS SOCKS ON AND HIS ARMS RIGID BY HIS SIDES. HE IS PUSHING OFF HIS FEET AND EFFECTIVELY POGO-ING ON TOP OF HER.

AFTER ABOUT TEN SECONDS:

CHARLOTTE   Will, stop. Look, don't move your whole body, just kind of move your hips, you know.

WILL   Right. Sorry.

CHARLOTTE   Yeah, you know.

WILL   Just my hips?

CHARLOTTE   Yeah.

WILL   How would that work?

HE TRIES TO MOVE THEM, DOESN'T QUITE SEE HOW THAT COULD WORK.

CHARLOTTE   Well you sort of just . . . look forget it. You haven't done this before, have you?

WILL   No. Sorry, I lied. Shall we have another go?

CHARLOTTE   I think the moment's gone to be honest.

WILL   Sorry to ask, have I just lost my virginity?

CHARLOTTE   I'm not going to count that one.

WILL   Can I count it though?

CHARLOTTE   Probably not, no.

WILL   Oh, OK. Shall we cuddle?

CHARLOTTE   Look, I'm going to get dressed. You should go before my mum gets back.

CHARLOTTE GETS UP, AND GOES TO GET DRESSED.

WILL LIES THERE A MOMENT AND LOOKS A BIT SAD.

CHARLOTTE   And Will, don't tell your mates, yeah?

WILL   My mates, not sure I have any.

CHARLOTTE   Will you put your pants on please?

——— SCENE 14 ———

EXT. ESTATE STREET

JAY IS MARCHING AHEAD OF NEIL AND SIMON.

NEIL   Friend.

SIMON   Friend.

NEIL   Friend.

SIMON   Made-up football friend.

JAY   Just give it a fucking rest, will you.

THEY COME ACROSS JAY'S FRIEND'S CAR PARKED ON THE STREET OUTSIDE WHAT IS PRESUMABLY HIS HOUSE.

SIMON   Hello, isn't that 'Friend's' car?

NEIL   Ooh new-rims car friend.

JAY   I'll show you how much of a friend he is. Fucking friend.

JAY GETS ONTO THE BONNET OF HIS FRIEND'S CAR AND JUMPS UP AND DOWN.

JAY   Oh friend. Friend. Fucking football friend.

THE CAR ALARM GOES OFF AND JAY'S FRIEND COMES OUT, AGAPE.

SIMON   I never thought he'd get that wound up.

NEIL   Yeah.

JAY'S FRIEND IS STANDING BESIDE HIS CAR WHILE JAY JUMPS ON THE BONNET. HE LOOKS A BIT CONFUSED AND SCARED.

JAY'S FRIEND   Jay, what are you doing?

JAY   Ooh friend, friend, I'm not your fucking friend, all right? All right? Ooh friend, friend . . .

NEIL   (TO SIMON) So, are they friends or not?

JAY IS STILL JUMPING ON THE CAR.

JAY   . . . new car friend, let's go for a drive sometime, friend. See you, friend. See you later, friend. Ooh, ooh, friend, friend, friend, fucking friend.

SIMON AND NEIL RUN OFF.

——————— SCENE 15 ———————

INT. SCHOOL HALL

WE SEE A POSTER FOR THE BLIND DATE EVENT.

ABOUT A HUNDRED KIDS ARE IN THE AUDIENCE.

WILL V/O   *Later that week it was the school's Blind Date show and I was there to see how Neil's brilliant book-reading plan went, even though I wasn't talking to him . . .*

ON STAGE NEIL IS CHOOSING, AND IS ASKING HIS FINAL QUESTION BEFORE HE PICKS. MR GILBERT LOOMS OVER HIM.

THERE ARE THREE GIRLS: TWO QUITE HOT, ONE REALLY SPECCY AND A BIT YOUNG-LOOKING (SUSIE).

NEIL   And finally the same question to number three.

SUSIE   People say Anna Karenina because of my aristocratic elbow, but I secretly like to think I'm more Jane Eyre.

SUSIE SMILES. NEIL MAKES A 'WHAT THE FUCK WAS THAT?' FACE TO THE AUDIENCE.

MR GILBERT   Right, have you made your decision?

NEIL   Um . . . I don't know.

MR GILBERT   Oh come on, I know it's for charity but we've still got another one to go. Get on with it.

NEIL   Um . . . number three.

MR GILBERT   She's doing her A levels four years early. And she loves Russian literature. It's Susie.

WE CUT TO WILL IN THE AUDIENCE. HE'S SITTING AMONGST THE BULLIED STUDENTS FROM EPISODE 1, INCLUDING JOHN.

WILL   (SITTING WITH HIS PHONE, WHISPERING A MESSAGE) Hi Charlotte, it's me, Will. I don't want to be a stalker but I was wondering if you could get back to me and just so you know, I'm on the mobile now and not the home number. OK, bye then.

MR GILBERT   (ON STAGE) Time for us to meet the boys, so boys, out you come. Yes, hurry up, no swearing . . .

SIMON AND JAY WALK IN. THEY WALK BY WILL, BUT SIT NEAR HIM. THE ATMOSPHERE IS FROSTY.

SIMON   Alright?

MR GILBERT   Hurry up, no swearing . . .

WILL   Alright.

JAY   Where's your girlfriend then?

WILL   She's meeting me here actually. She'll be here in a minute.

SIMON   We won't hang around then.

SIMON AND JAY GO AND SIT A FEW SEATS AWAY.

JOHN AND ANOTHER KID LEAN FORWARD EXCITEDLY.

MR GILBERT   (ON STAGE) Number one, what's your name, where do you come from?

NICK   Hi I'm Nick, I'm from Twickenham and I like, I like . . .

BACK ON WILL.

JOHN   (TO WILL) Have you got a girlfriend?

WILL   Yeah, oh yeah.

JOHN   What's her name?

WILL   Charlotte. Charlotte Hinchcliffe actually. She's a Year 13.

JOHN   Is she pretty?

WILL   Yes, she's very pretty John.

JOHN   And do you love her?

WILL   Yeah, yeah, I think I do.

BACK ON STAGE, MR GILBERT HAS THE MICROPHONE.

MR GILBERT   So those are the boys. Let's meet the lucky lady that gets to choose one of them. It's Charlotte from Year 13.

JOHN   Just like your girlfriend.

WILL HAS A MOMENT OF TUNNEL VISION, THAT MOMENT WHEN YOU THINK 'NO, NO, NO' JUST BEFORE SOMETHING BAD HAPPENS. SIMON LOOKS ACROSS AT HIM.

ONTO THE STAGE WALKS CHARLOTTE HINCHCLIFFE.

MR GILBERT   What's your name and why are you here?

CHARLOTTE   My name's Charlotte Hinchcliffe and I'm here for a bit of fun.

JOHN   That's your girlfriend. Why's she on a dating thing?

WILL   I don't know John.

MR GILBERT   Now Charlotte, tell us a bit about yourself, and keep it clean.

CHARLOTTE   Well I'm single, I've been messing around with a few boys and now I'm looking for a real man who's going to show me a good time.

LOTS OF THE AUDIENCE LAUGH.

MR GILBERT   I said keep it clean.

CHARLOTTE   I'm looking for a big strong man who really knows what he's doing.

MR GILBERT   I won't tell you again. Right. OK, let's have your first question.

THIS IS ALL TOO MUCH FOR WILL, WHO GETS UP AND RUNS OUT, LAUGHTER RINGING IN HIS EARS.

WILL V/O   *. . . and that was the end of my first love affair. To date my only love affair. There was only one thing to do – run to my mum and cry.*

——————— SCENE 16 ———————

INT. WILL'S LIVING ROOM

WILL IS CRYING INTO HIS MUM'S ARMS.

WILL   I'm so sad. I feel sad. You were right Mum.

POLLY McKENZIE   I know it hurts petal, but it will get better, I promise.

WILL   I just started to make friends and I dumped them all for this girl.

POLLY McKENZIE   Why don't we move you to another school?

WILL   Stop trying to make me move schools.

POLLY McKENZIE   I don't want you bullied again.

WILL   I was not bullied.

THE DOORBELL RINGS.

WILL'S MUM GOES TO ANSWER IT.

——————— SCENE 17 ———————

INT/EXT. WILL'S HOUSE

IT'S SIMON AT THE DOOR, AND JAY IS HANGING AROUND OUTSIDE.

SIMON   Oh hello Mrs McKenzie. Is William in?

WILL APPEARS AT THE DOOR.

POLLY McKENZIE   I'll leave you to it.

WILL   What?

SIMON   Just wanted to know if you wanted to come out.

WILL   Um . . .

SIMON   Neil's date is that weird girl who's taking her A Levels four years early. It turns out she's about twelve. He's at Milwaukee Fried Chicken.

JAY   She's so young, her mum's had to go with her. The three of them are all probably sitting there now round a bargain bucket.

SIMON   You should come.

WILL   (BREAKING INTO A SMILE) Actually that does sound quite funny. Mum, I'm off out.

SIMON   Brilliant.

WILL SHUTS THE DOOR BEHIND HIM AND THEY WALK OFF DOWN THE ROAD.

WILL   How's your football friend?

JAY   Ah, I don't think we're friends any more. I had to borrow three hundred quid to get his car fixed so he won't call the police.

SIMON   It was amazing, you should have seen it.

JAY   He's a really nice bloke. I don't know why I did it.

WILL   You've got mental problems.

WILL V/O   *I learnt many things from my first heartbreak. I learnt a little about love . . .*

SHOT OF WILL AND CHARLOTTE KISSING, AND A SHOT OF SIMON WALKING OVER TO CHARLOTTE'S FRIEND.

CHARLOTTE'S FRIEND   Go away.

WILL V/O   *. . . a bit about anatomy. A lot about friendship . . .*

SHOT OF JAY JUMPING OVER HIS FRIEND'S CAR.

JAY   Ooh friend, fucking football friend.

WILL V/O . . . *and absolutely nothing at all about sex . . .*

SHOT OF WILL TRYING TO HAVE SEX WITH CHARLOTTE.

CHARLOTTE   Will, stop.

WILL V/O . . . *apart from rubbing up against the perineum doesn't count as losing your virginity.*

Episode 5

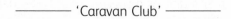

After writing the pilot we were commissioned by Channel 4, and specific-ally Caroline Leddy, to write a couple more episodes. We were still a long way from having a series commissioned, but sometimes channels do things like that because it speeds the whole process up if they do decide that they want a series.

We flirted with the idea of 'table writing' them with a team, and even went so far as to have an ideas day with some other writers (and the excellent writer Emma Millions actually wrote an episode from that process which we never used – sorry, Emma), but in the end decided that we should just write them together as it felt like we knew these characters better than anyone, and it would probably be easier.

Why Caravan Club? Well, it seemed both very suburban middle-class (lower middle maybe) and also a nice opportunity to be the place where Jay could say his fictional sexual adventures took place, because it sounded both very low-rent and like somewhere the others could never turn up to check the veracity of his statements. Kids can be really cruel, and when everyone else is going to the Mediterranean on holiday, going to a caravan park in England would, we thought, mark you out for bullying. But Jay being Jay, he tried to turn something that could be perceived as a weakness into a strength by adding, for example, two sisters who strum themselves off, something the others were unlikely to get in Cyprus. We'd started to play with that idea in 'Bunk Off', but we thought it would be interesting to see what happened when Jay was confronted with his bullshit (although, actually, Caravan Club does turn out OK for Neil).

In terms of truth, this ep is chock-full of things that really happened to the two of us. I'm not sure I can disclose exactly what happened to whom, but I will say that I did once skid up and down a parquet floor at a party when I'd just been offered sex by a girl.

——— OPENING MONTAGE ———

INT. SCHOOL

SHOT OF WILL WALKING INTO THE SCHOOL.

WILL V/O *Hi, I'm Will and as a special treat I now get to finish my A levels at a state comprehensive . . .*

SHOT OF A GIRL INSULTING WILL.

GIRL Posh twat.

WILL V/O *. . . everyone's made me feel very welcome . . .*

SHOT OF A BOY INSULTING WILL.

BOY Briefcase wanker.

WILL V/O *. . . I have made some friends . . .*

SHOT OF JAY JUMPING OVER HIS FRIEND'S CAR.

JAY Ooh, friend.

WILL V/O *. . . unfortunately it turns out they're bigger losers than me . . .*

SHOT OF NEIL'S ARSE AS HE BENDS IN FRONT OF WILL'S FACE, AND SHOT OF SIMON PUKING.

——— SCENE 1 ———

INT. SCHOOL COMMON ROOM

WILL V/O *. . . which means while other people get to play pool and hang out, I get to spend my free periods tied to a chair with a rubbish bin on my head . . .*

THE USUAL STUFF IS HAPPENING. GROUPS OF KIDS ARE SITTING AROUND: THE CHAVS, THE GOTHS, THE EMOS, ALL IN THEIR LITTLE GROUPS.

IN THE CENTRE OF THE ROOM, TIED TO A CHAIR, IS WILL. HE HAS A WASTE PAPER BIN ON HIS HEAD. EVERYONE IS CARRYING ON AROUND HIM, IGNORING HIM.

NEIL, JAY AND SIMON WALK IN.

SIMON   What happened to you?

WILL   I tripped.

NEIL   Really?

WILL   No, not really Neil. Donovan's tied me to a chair. He says no one's allowed to touch me. The prick.

SIMON   Just so you know, he's stood about ten foot away from us.

WILL   Shit, he didn't hear that, did he?

SIMON   Yeah, he's heard that one.

NEIL, JAY AND SIMON LOOK OVER AND SEE MARK DONOVAN GLOWERING FROM THE OTHER SIDE OF THE ROOM. JAY GIVES HIM A THUMBS UP.

NEIL   Come on, we'll get you out.

NEIL MAKES A MOVE TOWARDS THE CHAIR AND SIMON SPOTS MARK DONOVAN SHAKING HIS HEAD.

SIMON   Er better not Neil. Sorry, we're not allowed to untie you.

THE THREE BOYS WHO AREN'T TIED TO A CHAIR SIT DOWN.

WILL   Fair enough. So what we up to this weekend?

SIMON   We could go to Bluewater.

WILL   A shopping centre? Great, you know how much I love chavs.

JAY   Bluewater's not chavvy. It's quality, I go there all the time.

WILL   I rest my case.

SIMON   To be fair they've now got a Nando's.

WILL   The hallmark of quality!

SIMON   I actually like Nando's.

JAY   Yeah well whatever you sad acts get up to this weekend, I won't be there.

WILL   Oh no, but who'll supply the witticisms?

JAY   I'll be up to my nuts in some guts, shagging those two sisters from Caravan Club. It's the Camber Sands meeting this weekend which is always like a massive orgy.

WILL   Except it's not though, is it? It's holidays for old people.

JAY   I'm sorry? Did someone say something? Was bin boy giving it the big 'un?

WILL   It's just funny how you never get any girls around here, and yet away on Caravan Club you're like some sort of gypsy Russell Brand.

JAY   Yeah, well, I wouldn't shag any of the skanky girls round here, mate. Except for your mum . . . obviously.

NEIL   Get in the queue.

WILL   Brilliant.

JAY   If you don't believe me then you lot should come down to Camber Sands. Even bin boy might get some sex.

SIMON   All right, I'm definitely up for that.

NEIL   Yeah, love to.

JAY   Oh well you don't have to.

WILL   No, if I have to sleep in a caravan to prove you're lying, then I'm willing to make that sacrifice.

JAY   Fine, good. Come down, then we'll see who's lying.

WILL   Yes, you, you're lying.

THE BELL RINGS.

SIMON   Mark, can we untie him now?

MARK GIVES A SAGE SHAKE OF THE HEAD.

MARK DONOVAN   Nah.

SIMON   Sorry mate, see you at lunch.

WILL   See you then.

A LOOMING PRESENCE HAS APPEARED IN THE DOORWAY. IT'S THE 6'8" MR GILBERT.

SIMON   Oh shit, it's Gilbert.

WILL   Good, now Donovan's in trouble.

SIMON   Oh don't grass.

MR GILBERT HAS COME OVER.

MR GILBERT   Cooper, Sutherland, Cartwright . . . and who have we under here?

WILL   McKenzie sir.

MR GILBERT   Oh let me guess, no one saw how this happened? I suppose you tripped?

WILL   No sir, what happened is—

MR GILBERT   Sorry McKenzie? You're about to grass, are you?

WILL   Sir?

MR GILBERT   There's one thing no one likes, it's a grass, so I will ask you how this happened and you will reply 'I tripped'.

WILL   But sir, if no one reported crimes the justice system would collapse and—

MR GILBERT LIFTS THE BIN OFF.

MR GILBERT   I'll ask you again. How did this happen?

WILL   I tripped.

MR GILBERT   Tut-tut, clumsy.

WILL V/O   . . . *thanks to Gilbert's disdain for informers, I was left tied to the chair for the rest of the day.*

EVERYONE LEAVES.

WILL   Guys?

─────── SCENE 2 ───────

INT./EXT. SIMON'S CAR

WILL V/O *The one good thing is we called Jay's bluff. This was the classic win-win situation. If by some miracle Caravan Club was full of girls then we might get laid, but if it was full of weird old people and chavs, which it would be, then Jay would never live it down.*

So with high hopes we hit the open road in Simon's shitty little yellow car . . .

WE SEE SIMON'S YELLOW FIAT HURTLING DOWN THE A2 IN KENT. THE PASSENGER DOOR IS SPRAYED IN PRIMER AND THE HUBCAPS ARE MISSING. THEY PASS A SIGN TO FOLKESTONE, DOVER ETC.

SIMON IS DRIVING, WILL IS IN THE BACK SEAT AND NEIL IS SITTING SHOTGUN. WILL IS SQUEEZING HIMSELF BETWEEN THE FRONT TWO SEATS SO THAT HE CAN JOIN IN THE CONVERSATION.

NEIL How fast can this thing go then, do you reckon?

SIMON Well it's a special edition, so I reckon it could probably top a ton.

NEIL Bollocks!

SIMON It easily could, it's a pretty good car.

WILL I thought your dad had forbidden you from going over fifty?

SIMON Yeah well he's not here, is he?

NEIL And it couldn't do it anyway.

SIMON Right, we'll see.

HE FLOORS IT ON THE MOTORWAY AND WE SEE THE THREE OF THEM GETTING EXCITED AND THEN SLIGHTLY SCARED AS THE SPEEDOMETER CREEPS TOWARDS 100 MPH.

AT THIS POINT THE CAR IS SHAKING LIKE A PLANE ON TAKE-OFF.

WILL Eighty's pretty good. We can . . . we can leave it there.

NEIL Go on Si!

WILL   Oh my God, we're going to die!

Simon, if you survive and I don't, give this message to my mum – Simon killed me.

SIMON   My arm's are hurting a bit now!

NEIL   Ninety-eight . . . ninety-nine . . .

NEIL/SIMON   One hundred miles an hour!

SIMON EXHALES IN EXTRAORDINARY RELIEF, EASES OFF THE ACCELERATOR AND THE CAR SLOWS SHARPLY.

WILL   Oh thank Christ.

SIMON   Told you.

NEIL   Yeah, not too bad.

WE HEAR A MUSICAL RINGTONE. IT'S A LEONA LEWIS TRACK.

SIMON   Can you get that?

WILL   It's from Jay. No idea what it says but I'm pretty sure it's not English. There's an I, then an H, then a V . . .

NEIL   Oh give it 'ere.

He says he wants us to pick him up at the garage just outside Camber Sands and he'll show us how to get to the caravan park.

WILL   Thank you Dr Doolittle.

NEIL   What?

WILL   He talks to the animals.

NEIL   I'm not following you.

THE RINGTONE SOUNDS AGAIN.

Oh . . . and he's also buying a jumbo pack of ribbed johnnies – does anyone else need some?

——————— SCENE 3 ———————

EXT. PETROL STATION

WILL V/O *. . . despite Simon's best efforts we made it to Camber Sands alive. We'd arranged to meet Jay at the service station and though Simon could just about drive a car, getting petrol into it still remained a mystery . . .*

SIMON HAS CLEARLY PARKED ON THE WRONG SIDE FOR HIS CAR'S PETROL CAP AND IS DESPERATELY TRYING TO STRETCH THE HOSE ACROSS THE CAR.

THE BOYS HAVE PILED OUT OF THE CAR AND ARE WATCHING HIM.

JAY STROLLS UP OUT OF THE SHOP.

JAY Christ, forgot about this shit heap. I don't think even I can help you get laid in that.

SIMON IS STILL STRUGGLING WITH THE PETROL HOSE.

WILL Have you ever used one of these before?

SIMON It's fucking broken. This should reach!

JAY You sure you actually passed your test?

SIMON Yes.

JAY How many times did you have to suck off the instructor?

NEIL You want to park it a bit closer Si.

SIMON Yeah, thanks Neil.

A VOICE COMES OVER THE TANNOY:

WOMAN ATTENDANT Pump number six, please park closer.

NEIL Told you.

JAY This is embarrassing. I'm going to go check out the clunge mags.

NEIL Oi, wait for me.

WOMAN ATTENDANT Pump number six, do you need assistance?

JAY WALKS INTO THE SHOP. NEIL FOLLOWS.

WILL I think I might go and stretch my legs a bit too.

——————— SCENE 4 ———————

INT. PETROL STATION SHOP

INSIDE THE SHOP NEIL AND JAY ARE LAUGHING ABOUT SOMETHING IN ONE OF THE TOP-SHELF MAGS.

WILL   What's so funny then?

JAY   It's your mum in this mag.

WILL   Yes, very droll, well done.

NEIL   No, look, it really looks like your mum's face.

THEY LOOK AT SOME HORRIBLE PICTURES, BUT IN A CERTAIN LIGHT THEY COULD BE OF WILL'S MUM.

WILL   (UNNERVED) Ha, ha, yes. Hmmm er, no.

JAY   Oh that is definitely your mum's snatch.

SIMON ENTERS.

SIMON   (SLIGHTLY INCREDULOUSLY) I just got a text from this girl at the Caravan Club.

JAY   Oh yeah, is it Becky?

SIMON   Yeah.

JAY   Yeah I texted your photo. What's she say?

SIMON   'Hi Simon my name is Becky, liked your photo, Jay says you've got a cool car as well, see you later,' smiley face.

WILL   Well she's seen a picture of you, let's get back one of her.

NEIL   With her tits out.

WILL   Might be a bit early in the relationship for that Neil.

JAY   She is filthy.

WILL   Still a bit early I reckon.

SIMON   What shall I write?

JAY   'Spread 'em, I'll be there in half an hour.'

WILL   Or . . . 'So lovely to hear from you, will be a pleasure to meet up.'

JAY   'PS I'm a poofda.'

WILL   Don't put the PS.

SIMON   All right I've put: 'Can't wait to meet up, how do I know what you look like?' Smiley face at the end?

NEIL   Smiley with a wink, it's cheeky.

WILL   No, the winky face is the mark of a moron.

SIMON   I've sent it.

THEY ALL STAND AROUND SELF-CONSCIOUSLY WAITING. THEN THE RINGTONE GOES AS A TEXT COMES BACK.

WILL   Is that Leona Lewis?

SIMON   Oh it's a picture of her with her sister Suzanne.

NEIL   Are they kissing?

THEY ALL SUDDENLY SCRAMBLE TO GET BEHIND SIMON TO SEE THE PICTURE.

JAY   Where? Let me see.

NEIL   Oh please be lesbo.

SIMON   Oh fit enough.

JAY   I told you there was fit birds, and there's plenty more where they came from.

SIMON   I think I am actually gonna get laid.

NEIL   Oh my God, sisters! That's so horny.

JAY   First rule of the Caravan Club is that everyone gets some.

WILL   Second rule of Caravan Club is don't tell anyone about the first rule 'cos it's a massive lie.

JAY   Yeah well, we'll see about that, won't we?

WILL   Yes we will.

SIMON IS GOING TO PAY. THERE IS A BIT OF A QUEUE BEHIND HIM.

SIMON   Pump number six please and these.

JAY   And them.

HE CHUCKS IN A COPY OF *BARELY LEGAL* AND LEGS IT OUT OF THE SHOP.

SIMON LOOKS MORTIFIED.

THE ASSISTANT, A MIDDLE-AGED LADY, LOOKS AT THE MAGAZINE, SEARCHING FOR THE COVER PRICE.

WOMAN ATTENDANT   Want a bag for these?

————— SCENE 5 —————

EXT. CARAVAN SITE

WILL V/O   *OK, admittedly Jay knew some girls, but driving into the caravan park it didn't look like the kind of place you'd have an orgy, it looked like a field with some old tents in it . . .*

THE BOYS TURN DOWN THE DRIVE AND INTO THE CAMPSITE. THEY EXIT SIMON'S CAR.

JAY   Welcome to my world.

WILL   Where are all these women then?

JAY   There's loads, just look around you.

WILL   Where?

JAY   Everywhere. What about her?

SIMON   She's about twelve Jay.

JAY   Nah she's older than that, believe me.

WILL   Christ, what sort of camp have we come to?

WALKING NEARBY ARE TWO GIRLS (BECKY AND SUZANNE) WHO ARE PRETTY AND ABOUT THEIR AGE. THEY SEEM LIKE 'NICE' GIRLS.

JAY   Oh here they come. Becky, Suzanne . . .

BECKY AND SUZANNE   Hi Jay.

JAY   This is Simon I was telling you about.

SIMON   Hello.

BECKY   Hello, thanks for your texts, nice car.

SIMON   Thanks, it's not actually from Hawaii, it just says it on the back.

BECKY   I like it. Are you guys coming to the party later?

SIMON   Yeah, definitely.

BECKY   Great, I'll see you later then.

THE GIRLS LEAVE.

JAY   That one has fucked everyone. I've slung one up her a few times myself.

WILL   And who exactly is everyone Jay?

THEY LOOK AROUND THE CAMPSITE TO SEE PREDOMINANTLY OLD PEOPLE, INCLUDING A REALLY SWEET OLD MAN.

WILL   That old man over there? Has he had a go on her?

JAY   Look, I promise you that when you go back from this place you'll be begging your parents to buy a caravan.

SIMON   I'm not sure Neil's dad could afford a caravan.

WILL   If he thought of it as a mobile closet I'm sure he'd find the money.

NEIL   My dad's not bent.

WILL   Well we only have your word for that, Neil.

NEIL   My dad's not bent.

SIMON   Yeah, you would say that though.

AT THIS MOMENT WE SEE JAY'S MUM (MRS CARTWRIGHT) POP HER HEAD OUT OF THE FAMILY'S CARAVAN AND CALL OVER TO JAY.

MRS CARTWRIGHT   Jay, dinner's ready.

JAY   All right then, dickheads, Mum's made you tea, so park up and I'll meet you in the caravan.

WILL   Tea in a caravan. I've finally hit rock-bottom.

——————— SCENE 6 ———————

INT. JAY'S CARAVAN

IT'S YOUR STANDARD DOUBLE BERTH CARAVAN.

THEY ARE ALL SQUEEZED UP AT ONE END OF THE SORT OF U-SHAPED BANQUETTE THING, AND THE FOOD IS BEING SERVED ON PLASTIC PLATES FROM A PICNIC SET.

MRS CARTWRIGHT   There you go boys. Some lovely salad to go with your sausages.

WILL   Thanks Mrs Cartwright.

MRS CARTWRIGHT   It's my pleasure.

UNDER THIS CONVERSATION WE HEAR THE SOUNDS OF STRAINING THEN A COUPLE OF FARTS, THEN A COUPLE OF REALLY LOUD SPLOSHES. THEN THE NOISE OF SOME MOVEMENT, THAT SORT OF NOISE YOU GET WHEN PLASTIC WALLS ARE BEING PUSHED HARD AGAINST.

WILL   This is really delicious Mrs Cartwright.

NEIL   Cool, crisps! Have you got any ketchup?

JAY'S DAD (TERRY CARTWRIGHT) COMES OUT OF THE TOILET, WHICH IS RIGHT NEXT TO WHERE THEY ARE EATING. HE'S A BIG MAN AND WE GET A SENSE THAT SOME SORT OF PRIMAEVAL STRUGGLE HAS JUST TAKEN PLACE. HE'S MAYBE SWEATING A BIT. AS HE OPENS THE DOOR, THE SMELL HITS THEM ALL. IT'S EYE-WATERING, BUT THEY ARE TRYING TO BE POLITE.

SIMON   (UNDER HIS BREATH) Jesus Christ.

WILL   (UNDER HIS BREATH) My eyes are burning.

TERRY CARTWRIGHT   All right boys? You coming to the dance tonight then?

WILL   Yes Mr Cartwright.

JAY   I've lined Simon up with a girl, Dad.

TERRY CARTWRIGHT   Finally someone's gonna take advantage of all the birds down here. Jay's about as much use as a nun's tits.

HE LAUGHS.

MRS CARTWRIGHT   Oh leave him alone Terry, you're embarrassing him.

WILL   Delicious crisps, Mrs Cartwright.

MRS CARTWRIGHT   Thanks Will.

TERRY CARTWRIGHT   Yeah, she opened the packet herself! (HE LAUGHS AGAIN) Don't you boys just love it out here? Sense of freedom you don't get with other holidays.

JAY   Right, well, we'd best be getting ready Dad. Maybe see you later?

TERRY CARTWRIGHT   Yeah, I'll be there, fighting the girls off with a shitty stick.

WILL   (TO SIMON AS THEY LEAVE) I don't think he'll need that stick.

WILL V/O   . . . *looking back, I should have realised that Mr Cartwright's explosive bowels were a sign of things to come.*

——— SCENE 7 ———

INT. HALL

WILL V/O   *So the big night was finally here. The Caravan Club disco and all its delights of the flesh lay just inside a giant garden shed . . .*

A HALL IS BEING USED AS A DISCO; IT LOOKS PRETTY SHITTY.THERE IS A DJ AT ONE END AND SOME EIGHT–YEAR-OLD KIDS DANCING/CHASING EACH OTHER AROUND IN THE MIDDLE.

AT THE FAR END NEAR A DRINKS TABLE ARE SOME ADULTS WHO ARE PROBABLY THE PARENTS OF THE KIDS. THEY ARE DRINKING AND CHATTING.

THERE ARE A FEW BITS OF BUNTING AROUND THE PLACE, AND A HUGE PLATE OF SNACKS, AND OTHER BITS INCLUDING HUMMUS, ON THE TABLE NEAR THE ADULTS.

THE BOYS HAVE A CAN OF BEER EACH.

WILL   As predicted, this is shit.

SIMON   I drove all the way here for this?

JAY   It's just getting started, give it a minute.

THE MUSIC CHANGES – ITS JUSTIN TIMBERLAKE, SEXY BACK.

NEIL   Oh tune!

NEIL IS OFF AND DOING HIS NEIL DANCE, WHICH INVOLVES MOVING SIDE TO
SIDE LIKE A SPACE INVADER, WAVING HIS HANDS AROUND IN FRONT OF HIM IN
VERTICAL PATTERNS SO IT LOOKS AS IF THEY CROSS AND UNCROSS.

WILL   He's actually quite good. I'm going to get some hummus.

WILL GOES OFF TO WHERE THE ADULTS AND FOOD ARE.

BECKY AND SUZANNE TURN UP AT THE DOOR AND GO OVER TO THE OTHER SIDE.
JAY AND SIMON SPOT THEM AND WAVE BUT DON'T GO OVER. SUZANNE IS
PRETTY BUT A BIT LARGER THAN THE MORE DOLLED-UP BECKY.

JAY   Your ride for the evening is here.

SIMON   Do you really think she'll shag me?

JAY   Course. Why else do you think they come caravanning?

SIMON   Fresh air?

JAY   That text was her way of telling you it is on.

SIMON   Shit. Amazing. I feel a bit weird though, 'cos I always
thought I'd lose it with Carli.

JAY   Listen to me (HE POINTS TO BECKY DANCING. SHE LOOKS SWEET) that
bird Becky's an animal, she'll fuck you til you're blind, and teach you all
sorts, when Carli finds out she's going to be two things – jealous and
wet because now she'll know you're a stud.

SIMON   Do you really think so?

JAY   Course. Also, Carli doesn't really fancy you so if you're waiting to
lose it with her, you're gonna be waiting till you're dead.

SIMON   I think she likes me a bit though.

JAY   No she doesn't, she thinks you're a twat. Becky likes you and she likes sex, it's the perfect combination. Just don't go for anal straight away.

SIMON   OK. Thanks man.

JAY   No problem. Look here they come. Don't worry, I'll distract fatty boom-boom with the buffet.

THE GIRLS COME OVER AND THEY START TO CHAT.

WILL V/O   . . . *so, amazingly, it looked like Simon might actually pull if he could bring himself to speak to her . . . as for the rest of us . . . I wasn't holding my breath.*

———— SCENE 8 ————

INT. HALL

WILL IS WITH THE GROUP OF ADULTS.

WILL   Well I'd imagine it's the sense of freedom that you don't get with other holidays.

WOMAN   Can I get you some more hummus, William?

WILL   Delicious, thank you very much.

AT HIS ELBOW APPEARS A REALLY QUITE ATTRACTIVE GIRL, BUT A LITTLE BIT 'ALTERNATIVE' LOOKING. MAYBE VEERING TOWARDS GOTH WITH A LOT OF PIERCINGS AND STREAKED RED HAIR. SHE'S ABOUT THE SAME AGE.

GIRL WITH RED-STREAKED HAIR   Why are you talking to the pensioners?

WILL   Oh just . . . just taking the piss.

GIRL WITH RED-STREAKED HAIR   What, by eating hummus?

WILL   Yeah.

GIRL WITH RED-STREAKED HAIR   Would you rather eat hummus or take me somewhere quiet?

WILL   I think I'd rather take you somewhere quiet.

GIRL WITH RED-STREAKED HAIR   Come over here then.

HE FOLLOWS HER TO A BIT OF A CORNER.

WILL   Sorry I, I didn't catch your name. I'm Will and I like hummus. There I've said it!

GIRL WITH RED-STREAKED HAIR   Well, two things. For the next few hours I don't need you to be charming or sophisticated or even interesting, I just need you to be willing, can you handle that?

WILL   I think so.

GIRL WITH RED-STREAKED HAIR   Good. And second – kiss me.

WILL   Right. OK.

SHE GRABS HIS HEAD AND PULLS HIM TOWARDS HER. THEY AGGRESSIVELY SNOG AND WILL STARTS NERVOUSLY BUT GETS MORE INTO IT. THEN HE PULLS AWAY.

GIRL WITH RED-STREAKED HAIR   What you doing?

WILL   I just need a moment.

GIRL WITH RED-STREAKED HAIR   I'm gonna take you outside and I want you to fuck me.

WILL   Really?

GIRL WITH RED-STREAKED HAIR   Yes, really.

WILL   Hang on, I mean we, we barely know each other, we should get to know each other a bit first, shouldn't we?

THE GIRL SHRUGS.

WILL   I mean, come on, we're, we're young. Let's have some fun and then fall exhausted into each other's arms. I've got an idea – did you ever used to skid as a child? I used to love it.

HE TAKES OFF HIS SHOES.

WILL   Come on! Let's skid! (HE SKIDS) Woooh, wooh! Get your shoes off, it's liberating.

HE RUNS AND SKIDS ACROSS THE HALL. NO ONE'S REALLY PAYING ATTENTION, BUT THE GIRL LOOKS BORED. HE SKIDS BACK TOWARDS HER. THEN BACK AGAIN, AND THIS TIME AS HE TURNS SHE GETS UP AND WALKS OFF.

WILL   Where you going? Don't you want to skid?

GIRL WITH RED-STREAKED HAIR   No.

WILL   What about our love-making?

GIRL WITH RED-STREAKED HAIR   Love-making? Gone off it. Sorry.

SHE LEAVES THE HALL.

WILL   Oh.

WILL IS CRESTFALLEN. THEN HE TURNS ROUND AND SEES THAT SOME OF THE SMALLER KIDS HAVE TAKEN HIS SHOES AND ARE RUNNING AROUND WITH THEM.

WILL   Oi, my shoes! Give me back my shoes!

WILL IS DESPERATELY PLAYING PIGGY-IN-THE-MIDDLE TO TRY AND GET HIS SHOES BACK.

WILL V/O   *Somehow in three minutes I'd gone from guaranteed sex to being bullied by eight-year-olds, and I'm still not entirely sure how that happened.*

——— SCENE 9 ———

INT. CAMPSITE SHOWER BLOCK

WE SEE JAY ENTERING THE SHOWER ROOM/TOILET BLOCK. AS HE GETS INSIDE HE RUNS ACROSS A HALF-NAKED TERRY CARTWRIGHT, WHO IS TOWELLING OFF AFTER A SHOWER.

JAY   Oh all right Dad? Thought you were coming to the party?

JAY GOES OVER TO THE URINAL TO HAVE A PISS.

TERRY CARTWRIGHT   Yeah I was. I popped my head in the door and saw you chatting up some fat bird so I didn't want to cramp your style.

JAY   I wasn't chatting her up, I was keeping her busy while Simon was talking to her mate.

TERRY CARTWRIGHT   Don't be embarrassed, son, if I was as bad with the ladies as you I'd have moved on to the fatties months ago.

JAY LOOKS A BIT HURT.

WILL ENTERS.

WILL   Oh hello Mr Cartwright. Jay.

TERRY CARTWRIGHT   You all right Will? You got any action then?

WILL   Um, yeah, I pulled a girl actually.

JAY   Fuck off! No way!

TERRY CARTWRIGHT   So where is she now then, cleaning up her beaver for you?

WILL   Er, no, she went off.

TERRY CARTWRIGHT   Oh well, plenty more fish in the sea. Jay's harpooned himself a whale.

JAY   Give it a rest Dad. I already told you it's not like that.

TERRY CARTWRIGHT   Yeah and I told you not to be so fussy and to get stuck in. You're more likely to get somewhere with a fatso 'cos they're grateful for the attention, even from a loser like you.

JAY   Dad!

TERRY CARTWRIGHT   They say any port in a storm, and she was the size of a fucking port! I know what you're up to, you think 'cos she's so massive she'll count as two shags, well she doesn't!

JAY   I get plenty of girls.

TERRY CARTWRIGHT   No you bloody don't, and even if you did what could you do with that thing? It's like a McDonald's chip!

JAY   Dad!

TERRY CARTWRIGHT   You definitely take after your mum in the cock-size department, she ain't got one either.

JAY   Dad, can you just leave me alone for once?

TERRY CARTWRIGHT   Oooh! All right, all right. Bloody hell, he's just like his mum, make one little joke and he has a shit fit.

JAY   Fuck this!

JAY STORMS OUT. TERRY CARTWRIGHT LOOKS A BIT SHOCKED, BUT
UNPERTURBED NONETHELESS.

WILL   Are these the only toilets then?

WILL, WITHOUT HIS SHOES ON, PICKS HIS WAY THROUGH THE URINALS. WE SEE
HIS SOCKS GET WET IN THE WATER/PISS THAT IS SPREAD ACROSS THE FLOOR.

WILL   Oh God!

TERRY CARTWRIGHT   I'd give trap number two a couple of minutes.
I had eggs for lunch.

——————— SCENE 10 ———————

INT. HALL

SIMON IS SLOW-DANCING WITH BECKY. THEY ARE MOVING VERY SLOWLY ROUND.

AS THEY TURN, WE CAN SEE BECKY'S HAND SLIDE DOWN AND GIVE SIMON'S
BUM A SQUEEZE. THEY LOOK AT EACH OTHER AND START TO AGGRESSIVELY SNOG
IN THE WAY THAT ONLY TEENAGERS CAN.

WE THEN PULL WIDE AND SEE THAT THE ONLY OTHER PEOPLE DANCING TO THIS
SONG IN THIS REALLY VERY-WELL-LIT HALL ARE A VERY OLD COUPLE, AND TWO
PARENTS/GRANDPARENTS WITH THEIR KIDS AT ARMS' LENGTH.

AS SIMON AND BECKY SNOG AND TURN, WE SEE SIMON OPEN HIS EYES AND GET
AN IDEA OF JUST HOW EXPOSED AND EMBARRASSING THIS IS. HE STARTS TO
PULL AWAY AND BECKY FOLLOWS HIM BECAUSE SHE'S STILL SO INTO IT. HE
PULLS OFF WITH A LOUD SLURP.

SIMON   Shall we go outside then?

BECKY   Yeah, all right.

SHE TURNS TO GO OUT. SIMON GIVES JAY A THUMBS UP BEHIND HER BACK. JAY
IS SORT OF WAITING BY THE DOOR. BECKY GOES OUT FIRST, THEN AS SIMON IS
LEAVING HE TURNS TO JAY:

SIMON   Fucking hell! Is this really happening? I'm going to have
sex, aren't I? At last. Thanks for sorting this Jay.

JAY, SMILING BROADLY AND TAKING IN THE COMPLIMENT, PALMS SIMON SOMETHING. IT'S A CONDOM.

JAY   Fill this up for me.

SIMON   Thanks so much mate, nice one.

——— SCENE 11 ———

INT. CAMPSITE SHOWER BLOCK

BACK IN THE SHOWER ROOM/TOILET BLOCK. WILL'S AT THE URINAL, JAY'S DAD JOINS HIM AND SLAPS HIM ON THE BACK.

TERRY CARTWRIGHT   Gotcha!

JAY'S DAD STARTS TO HAVE A PISS.

WILL   Mr . . . Mr Cartwright, you . . . you seem to be splashing me a bit.

TERRY CARTWRIGHT   Who stole your shoes?

WILL   Oh . . . just some kids.

TERRY CARTWRIGHT   Kids? You let them get away with that? Laughing at you while you're standing in your piss?

WILL   I think it's mostly your piss.

TERRY CARTWRIGHT   Go and get 'em, show 'em who's boss.

WILL   Yeah, OK, I will.

JAY'S DAD LETS OUT A HUGE FART.

TERRY CARTWRIGHT   Better out than in.

WILL   I'm going to go now then.

──────── SCENE 12 ────────

INT. HALL

WE SEE NEIL STILL DOING HIS OWN DANCE ROUND THE HALL, OBLIVIOUS, AND THE GIRL WHO WAS TALKING TO WILL EARLIER.

GIRL WITH RED-STREAKED HAIR   I'm curious, are you subversively mocking this place or are you actually enjoying yourself?

NEIL   I'm sorry I have no idea what you're talking about.

──────── SCENE 13 ────────

EXT. HALL/SPORTS FIELD

SIMON IS OUTSIDE GETTING OFF WITH BECKY IN QUITE A DARK AREA. THEY ARE STANDING. SIMON IS QUITE EXCITED AS WE CAN TELL FROM HIS GRUNTS, BUT SHE SEEMS QUITE INTO IT TOO. THEN THERE IS A TEARING NOISE.

BECKY   You've ripped my top!

SIMON   Oh God, sorry, you just turn me on so much.

BECKY   My parents will see this!

SHE'S KIND OF HALF TURNED AWAY TO TRY TO GET SOME LIGHT ON IT TO SEE HOW BAD IT IS. WHILE HER BACK IS TURNED, SIMON IS CLEARLY FIDDLING WITH HIS CROTCH AREA.

SHE TURNS BACK AND HE TURNS BACK. SHE SCREAMS.

BECKY   What the hell are you doing?

WE SEE SIMON WITH HIS TROUSERS ROUND HIS ANKLES AND ERECTION PUSHING OUT AGAINST HIS SHIRT.

SIMON   It's a condom, I thought we should be safe.

BECKY   Why have you got a condom on? I'm not going to have sex with you.

SIMON   You're not? But Jay said . . .

BECKY   Jay said what?

SIMON   Well he said . . .

BECKY   What? What did Jay say?

——————— SCENE 14 ———————

INT. HALL

BECKY COMES RUSHING IN, LOOKING BEDRAGGLED. SIMON COMES IN BEHIND HER. BECKY GOES OVER TO HER SISTER, AND THEY POINT AT JAY AND WALK TOWARDS THEIR PARENTS.

SIMON IS APOPLECTIC.

JAY   Hey, how's it feel to be a man then?

SIMON   You fucking liar. Shagged her and her sister have you? Loads of times, yeah?

JAY   Untold.

SIMON   Really? 'Cos she didn't seem that keen and her sister's thirteen years old.

JAY   Well I haven't actually shagged her and her sister exactly, but other similar girls.

SIMON   Well thanks for the condom. I'll be lucky if I'm not on some sort of paedophile register by the end of the night.

Oh fuck, she's talking to her parents! We'd better go.

JAY   Where's Neil?

SIMON   Don't know and don't care. Let's get out of here. Will, we're off.

WILL IS STILL VAINLY TRYING TO GET HIS SHOES BACK.

SIMON   Will, come on!

WILL LOOKS AT THEM, AND WRESTLES A FAT-ISH KID TO THE GROUND IN ORDER TO GET HIS SHOES BACK.

THE KID SCREAMS AND STARTS TO CRY AND THE ADULTS LOOK ROUND AT HIM, THEN AT WILL. THEY AREN'T TOO HAPPY.

WILL   Prick!

———— SCENE 15 ————

EXT. JAY'S CARAVAN

WILL V/O   *And just when I thought things couldn't get any worse I then had to spend a night in a caravan with Jay's dad and his irritable bowel.*

JAY, SIMON AND WILL ARE GETTING OUT. IT'S CLEARLY QUITE EARLY.

WILL   Thanks very much for your hospitality Mrs Cartwright. See you soon Mr Cartwright.

JAY'S DAD LEANS OUT OF THE CARAVAN.

TERRY CARTWRIGHT   Cheers lads. Oh and Simon . . . don't worry about that Becky business, her dad's calmed down now. We were all your age once, least you had a pop, unlike soppy bollocks here.

SIMON   Um, thanks.

TERRY CARTWRIGHT   Yeah, don't mention it. Now just try not to rape anyone on the way out.

THE BOYS ARE WALKING OFF TO THE CAR.

SIMON   I don't see why I should ever talk to you again, let alone give you a lift home.

JAY   Look, you're just angry because you didn't get laid.

SIMON   Yeah that's it.

WILL   Well let's just get out of this dump, and please God don't let me ever have to come back to a caravan park.

THEY GET TO THE CAR. NEIL IS APPROACHING THEM FROM THE SHOWER BLOCK.

NEIL   All right?

SIMON   Where have you been?

NEIL   Oh I slept in the car. Shall we go then? Shotgun.

JAY AND WILL RELUCTANTLY GET IN THE BACK.

———— SCENE 16 ————

INT. SIMON'S CAR

THE CAR IS DRIVING ALONG.

SIMON   My seat's a bit wet.

WILL   Mine is too.

JAY   Yeah, it's wet here as well.

SIMON   Neil, did you wet yourself in my new car?

NEIL   It's not really new.

SIMON   Did you wet yourself?

NEIL   No, but I did have a bird back in here.

SIMON   You fucked a girl in my car?

NEIL   No it's too small. Did a lot of fingering though. She wanked me off a few times.

SIMON   Oh my God!

WE CUT WIDE TO THE CAR SKIDDING TO A HALT ON THE HARD SHOULDER AND THE BOYS ALL JUMPING OUT.

JAY   Fucking hell.

SIMON/JAY/WILL   Oh no! Bloody hell.

SIMON IS WIPING HIS HANDS ON THE GRASS VERGE.

SIMON   Thanks Neil.

JAY   Who was she then?

NEIL   Well some sort of punky redhead, she was nice.

WILL   She was mine! Oh God.

SIMON   Oh shit, we can't stay here!

JAY   Well I'm not getting back into Spunkmobile!

SIMON   Clean it up Neil.

NEIL   Why?

SIMON   Because you have spunked on my seats! Oh God, this weekend has been a disaster.

WILL   Well one good thing is we found out the Caravan Club is shit, and that Jay is a liar.

JAY   Oh I'm such a liar? That Neil got some.

WILL   No, no . . .

JAY   I said Neil got some.

WILL   . . . you, you lied.

SIMON IS TRYING TO GET BACK INTO THE CAR, BUT RECOILING FROM THE DAMP SEAT.

SIMON   Clean it up Neil!

NEIL   It's your car.

SIMON   It's your spunk!

NEIL   Some of it could be her juice.

JAY   Did Neil get any?

WILL   That's not the point.

JAY   Yes or no, did Neil get some?

WILL   You lied.

SIMON   And I want petrol money.

NEIL   What for?

SIMON   For petrol! Money for petrol.

WE PULL OUT FROM THE HARD SHOULDER AND LEAVE THESE TWO ARGUMENTS RAGING OVER THE CINQUECENTO AS TRAFFIC ROARS PAST.

WILL V/O   *I'm not sure what we learnt from this whole sorry episode, apart from never take advice from Jay . . .*

SHOT OF WILL AND BECKY OUTSIDE THE HALL.

SIMON   But Jay said . . .

BECKY   Jay said what?

WILL V/O   . . . *when you are offered sex don't skid . . . and never, never follow Mr Cartwright into the toilet . . .*

SHOT OF WILL SKIDDING, AND SHOT OF WILL IN JAY'S CARAVAN.

WILL   My eyes are burning.

WILL V/O   . . . *but as we stood arguing on the side of the A2 one thing was for sure: Neil can produce an unholy amount of spunk.*

WE ARE BACK WITH THE FOUR BOYS ARGUING BY SIMON'S CAR.

SIMON   And I want this cleaned now.

NEIL   No, it's in your car, so it's yours.

SIMON   Oh so if I spunk on you that's yours, is it?

NEIL   No.

SIMON   You are just fucking disgusting.

Episode 6

——————— 'The Prom' ———————

When we started writing the series we wanted it to be about a time of life, Sixth Form, and so we knew that it had a limited lifespan. But, like Rutger Hauer in *Blade Runner*, we weren't going down without a fight. So the first series was the first term of the Lower Sixth, and if the miracle happened and we got another series the plan was to do the second half of the year. If things went well from there who knew where we'd be, but at least we'd have the option for two more series. Though I should reiterate that at the time of writing this episode we assumed we'd get one series and maybe two if we were very very lucky, but we never spoke of the show doing any better than that.

At my school the main 'prom' was at Christmas, and I was on the organising committee for it. It was stressful beforehand and absolutely mental on the night, and we thought that throwing himself into something like this was exactly the kind of thing Will would do both for his CV and to try and gain some semblance of respect from his peers.

I don't remember this as being a particularly tortuous ep to write because it had a number of storylines/ideas from the previous eps to tie up (Simon/Carli, Jay's sex life, Will and Charlotte), meaning there was a lot to play with.

But I do remember a great note from our script editor, Robert Popper (of robertpopper.com fame), which was to push the 'Thanks, Phil' scene for all it was worth, and get Gilbert to make Will apologise. We did this, and it went on much longer than we'd originally imagined it and was much much funnier for it. So thanks, Robert, Thobert.

I think, rewatching it recently, it's a bit soppier than we'd normally allow ourselves to be. Will, as he says, 'wins' in it, the Carli/Simon moment features rather lovely performances from Emily and Joe, and the ending is a nice set piece showing friendship, which is what the show was about in the first place. Also, it ends with a sentence starting

'I haven't washed my cock yet . . .', which again I'm quite proud of as it shows you can use the most horrific language you like and still make something rather sweet.

——— OPENING MONTAGE ———

SHOT OF WILL WALKING TO SCHOOL.

WILL V/O   *It was the end of my first term and my personal report card read: Making new friends, C minus, must try harder. Being one of the cool gang . . .*

SHOT OF JAY DOING THE CRAZY FROG, AND A SHOT OF SIMON PUKING.

JAY   Num, num, hehhhme.

WILL V/O   *. . . D . . .*

SHOT OF A YOUNG BOY INSULTING WILL.

YOUNG BOY   Nice badge, dickhead.

WILL V/O   *. . . not losing my virginity . . .*

SHOT OF CHARLOTTE HINCHCLIFFE.

CHARLOTTE   Will you put your pants on please?

WILL V/O   *. . . A star. But things were looking up. I'd been elected chairman of the school's Christmas prom committee.*

——— SCENE 1 ———

EXT. MENSWEAR SHOP

WILL V/O   *All right, I was the only candidate, but still, I really wanted to look the part, which meant hiring my first ever suit, and Simon's dad said he knew just the place.*

THEY ARE STANDING OUTSIDE ONE OF THOSE RUBBISH, TOTALLY ANACHRONISTIC, MENSWEAR STORES THAT YOU GET IN SUBURBAN TOWNS.

SIMON'S DAD (ALAN COOPER)'S CAR IS PARKED OUTSIDE. AND THE BOYS ARE STANDING NEXT TO IT.

SIMON   Are you sure this is the best place to hire suits?

ALAN COOPER   Listen, I've been coming here for years. Old Mr Sethi knows me very well, he'll do you a good deal if you mention my name.

NEIL   It looks a bit old-fashioned.

ALAN COOPER   Neil, the stuff in here never goes out of fashion, it's timeless.

JAY   Yeah well I don't care 'cos I've already bought a suit.

ALAN COOPER   Once, Sethi went mental 'cos I brought a suit back covered in grass stains, if you know what I mean. Blimey, imagine that, if you got to hire the exact same suit I was wearing the first time me and your mum . . .

SIMON   All right, all right, we're going in.

—————— SCENE 2 ——————

INT. MENSWEAR SHOP

THE BOYS ARE BEING SERVED BY A SPRIGHTLY BUT ELDERLY INDIAN GENTLEMAN (MR SETHI). HE STILL HAS QUITE A STRONG ACCENT.

WILL EXITS THE SMALL CURTAINED DRESSING ROOM, WEARING A QUITE OLD-LOOKING BLACK SUIT WITH SHINY BRASS BUTTONS. JAY AND NEIL LAUGH A BIT AS HE COMES OUT.

WILL   What do you think?

MR SETHI   Oh yes very nice. It is a lovely fit.

WILL   I'm not too sure about the lapels.

MR SETHI   Too jazzy?

WILL   They are a little too jazzy, yes. Is this the sort of suit a chairman would wear?

MR SETHI   But of course, definitely for a chairman.

NEIL   Here we go.

WILL   Because you see I'm the chairman of this committee that's organising our school's Christmas prom this year.

JAY   And that's it, you've now officially told everyone you've ever laid eyes on.

WILL   I just think it's important that people know, that's all.

JAY   Yeah I'm the DJ, that's far more important.

WILL   I said you might get to DJ.

SIMON EXITS THE NEXT-DOOR DRESSING ROOM. HE ALSO LOOKS TERRIBLE, AND HIS OLD-FASHIONED SUIT DOESN'T FIT AT ALL.

MR SETHI   Oh yes, very, very nice.

SIMON   I think it's kind of hideous. Is it velvet?

MR SETHI   Oh, too jazzy?

SIMON   Yeah, yeah, too jazzy.

MR SETHI   And for you, my young friend, shall I find you something also?

NEIL   I suppose so, but I need something special, yeah? Something that's gonna make me stand out.

MR SETHI   Oh I will get you something extra-special. Something just for you.

MR SETHI DISAPPEARS INTO THE BACK OF THE SHOP.

JAY   You said I could fucking DJ, now don't go back on your word.

SIMON   Oh let him DJ, he's part of my plan to seduce Carli.

WILL   What's he going to do, hold her down?

SIMON   You know I get breathless every time I think of her and when I see her my heart does little flips.

JAY   Are you bent?

SIMON   Shut up.

JAY   It's just that right then you sounded really really bent.

WILL   Won't her boyfriend be there?

SIMON   Who?

WILL   Well her boyfriend. The massive rugby player.

SIMON   Oh him. Yeah, no, I don't think they're going out. Or if they are, then they aren't really. Oh I don't know, but she never really says that they definitely are. So maybe they aren't.

WILL   Yes. I mean that's the most positive possible way of looking at it.

MR SETHI, RETURNS.

HE HOLDS UP A HIDEOUS OLD-FASHIONED SUIT.

MR SETHI   Here we are, just for you, perfect . . . Too jazzy?

─────── SCENE 3 ───────

EXT. SCHOOL

WILL V/O   *With the prom a few days away I was stressed. But I wasn't the only one with things on my mind.*

THE BOYS ARE WALKING IN TO SCHOOL.

NEIL   You know, I think I'm ready for a relationship.

JAY   You mean you think you're wanking too much?

NEIL   Yes.

SIMON   Talking of which.

WE SEE A MODERATELY ATTRACTIVE WOMAN (MISS TIMMS) GETTING OUT OF A CAR.

JAY   Oh Miss Timms.

NEIL   Oh she is so fit. It should be illegal for her to teach biology. I almost knocked one out there and then when we did the reproduction system.

WILL   As something of an outsider I'd say that actually she isn't very fit at all, she's just the only adult female in the school under thirty.

NEIL   She is so fit.

WILL   No she isn't. I mean she's fine but she's no . . .

JAY   Oh she'd definitely get it.

WILL   If we could all just concentrate above the waist for a second. I need you all at a planning meeting this lunch. I've got you some brilliant jobs lined up.

SIMON   Like what?

WILL   Well, giving out the vouchers that can be exchanged for alcohol.

JAY   Shit, if we control the beer vouchers, we get a pick of the birds. The drunk birds.

WILL   That sounded just a little bit rapey.

JAY   Well say what you like Professor Words, thanks to you we're gonna be drowning in babes.

WILL   I just want the night to be a success. I've no interest in babes.

JAY   Well that's handy, 'cos they've got no interest in you.

WILL   Oh, sorry, who here has pulled Charlotte Hinchcliffe? Who? Huh? Me, that's who.

JAY   Yeah, she only did it for a bet.

WILL   That's not true.

SIMON   Oh God, let's not get into all that again.

JAY   It is true.

WILL   It's not fucking true. People don't get fingered for a bet Jay. With the possible exception of your sister.

JAY   Take that back.

WILL   Actually, I do take it back. Your mum, on the other hand, she'd probably get fingered for a packet of biscuits.

SIMON/NEIL   Ooh. (LAUGHING)

——————— SCENE 4 ———————

INT. SCHOOL CLASSROOM

WILL V/O   *Obviously no one cool wanted to help organise the prom, so when it came to recruiting a crack team, I wasn't exactly spoiled for choice.*

THE CLASSROOM IS EMPTY EXCEPT FOR EIGHT PUPILS SITTING ROUND THE PLANNING TABLE.

WILL, NEIL, JAY (LOOKING BORED) AND SIMON ARE AMONG THEM.

JOHN IS SITTING ON ONE SIDE OF THE BANK OF DESKS. HE SEEMS TO BE COMPARING TWO MÜLLER FRUIT CORNERS. HE LOOKS A LITTLE PERTURBED AND CONCERNED, UNABLE SEEMINGLY TO DECIDE WHICH TO EAT. HE THEN POURS THE CORNERS INTO BOTH AT THE SAME TIME, GETS TWO SPOONS OUT AND EATS THEM SIMULTANEOUSLY, WITH TWO SPOONS IN HIS MOUTH. HE THINKS FOR A MOMENT THEN SEEMS SATISFIED WITH THE RESULT AND CONTINUES.

WILL V/O   *But while there may be no I in team, luckily there was a me. And if I was to stop these morons from screwing up my big night, every fine detail had to be planned.*

WILL   Right, welcome. As you all know this is the first ever Christmas prom. Two things are going to make this event successful: teamwork and exceptional leadership. The first thing we need to discuss is the agenda and how that— yes, John?

JOHN HAS HIS HAND UP.

JOHN   Are we gonna have food?

WILL   Yup, yup, we will. If you look at the agenda that's item four, so we'll get to that.

JOHN   Because I think we should have food and I was wondering what type everyone thought we should have.

WILL   Yep, yep, as I say that is on the agenda so we'll get to that.

JOHN   Lasagne's nice and so are burgers. You don't need a plate for burgers, which gives them an edge on lasagne.

WILL   Yes John, please, we'll get to that.

JOHN   But you can eat burgers off a plate too.

JAY   Listen lard arse, there will be food, so shut the fuck up so we can get this over with.

JOHN   I just wanted you all to—

JAY   Shut up!

WILL   Right. OK. Item one, venue. We're having it in the school hall obviously. Item two, band.

JAY   We don't need a band, I'm DJing.

WILL   After ten thirty.

JAY   I shall be DJing the whole thing.

WILL   Well, they're booked now.

JAY   Oh you're shit at this. I'd be much better, I've organised hundreds of parties.

WILL   This is the first ever Christmas prom, not a chimp's tea party. What we want is a good, structured evening.

JAY   What we want is a big mucky disco and a piss-up.

SIMON   Hang on, when have you organised parties?

JAY   All the time.

SIMON   I've known you for ten years and I have never seen you organise a party.

JAY   Bollocks. What about my birthday party last year?

SIMON   Your mum organised that.

JAY   Yeah under my supervision and that was a wicked party.

NEIL   I fingered a bird.

JAY   See? And also I organised the Caravan Club parties.

WILL   Remember we have been to a Caravan Club party.

SIMON   And it was shit.

NEIL   I fingered a bird.

JAY   Well there you go.

WILL   Look Jay, now's not the time. Item three.

SIMON   Seriously Will, why are we here? You've clearly decided it all already.

WILL   No I haven't. There's still loads I need your help with.

SIMON   Like what?

WILL   Like who cleans up the next day.

SIMON   What item's that?

WILL   Twenty-eight.

SIMON   Oh for Christ's sake, just get on with it.

WILL   OK. Item four, food.

JOHN   Oh good.

──────── SCENE 5 ────────

INT. CANTEEN

THE BOYS ARE GETTING THEIR TRAYS AND MOVING ALONG THE LUNCH LINE.

WILL HAS A SALAD AND JAY IS EATING HIS CHIPS AS HE'S GOING ALONG.

IT LOOKS LIKE THE ARGUMENT HAS BEEN GOING ALL DAY. NEIL AND SIMON LOOK TIRED BY IT.

JAY   She did it as a bet.

WILL   One more time, that's not true.

JAY   Say what you like, I know it was a bet, ask her.

WILL   I will.

JAY   Well there she is over there, go ask her now.

WE SEE LOVELY VIVACIOUS CHARLOTTE IN THE LUNCH LINE.

WILL   I'm not going to ask her now, I'll ask her later. Or tomorrow at the prom.

JAY   Right, course.

CARLI WALKS IN WITH A FRIEND (SAMANTHA).

SIMON   Right, here goes, phase one.

HE GOES OVER.

SIMON   Carli.

SHE TURNS ROUND.

CARLI   Oh hi Simon.

SAMANTHA   All right, sick boy boner?

SIMON   Huh, yeah. Listen, this dance, you are going, aren't you?

CARLI   Yeah.

SIMON   Great, great. Maybe we could go together?

CARLI   I could do with a lift actually, yeah, thanks.

SIMON   Right a lift, yeah.

CARLI   Tom's car's broken so that'd be perfect.

SIMON   Great, gotta get here early to help Will set up, so I'll pick you up about four.

CARLI   Four? You want me to get to a prom that starts at eight, at four o'clock?

SIMON   Well that's what time I'll be getting there. There'll be loads to do.

CARLI   So what? I could turn up in my evening dress four hours early and help you blow up balloons?

SIMON   Yeah you could help scrub the floors. It might be fun, you know, all together.

SAMANTHA   Are you mentally ill?

SIMON   Ha ha, good one.

CARLI   Tell you what, I'll see you there, in the evening.

SIMON   Great, great, I'll see you there then.

SHE LAUGHS AND WALKS OFF WITH SAMANTHA, SHAKING HER HEAD.

JAY, WILL AND NEIL HAVE GOT TO THE CANTEEN TILL. JAY PUTS HIS LAST CHIP
INTO HIS MOUTH AND SLIDES THE EMPTY PLATE UNDER HIS BURGER PLATE.

JAY   You know, since he's met you, he's become much more of a dick.

WILL   Really?

NEIL   Yeah he does seem to think more and, like, express himself.

WILL   Isn't that a good thing?

JAY   Does it look like a good thing?

WE SEE SIMON CLASPING HIS HANDS OVER HIS FACE AND THEN DOUBLING
OVER.

JAY IS PAYING FOR HIS DINNER.

DINNER LADY   I'm charging you for the chips.

JAY   (CHEWING A CHIP BUT NONETHLESS OUTRAGED) I never had chips.

———— SCENE 6 ————

INT. SCHOOL COMMON ROOM

MR GILBERT IS AT THE HEAD OF THE CLASS.

MR GILBERT   Right then, so tomorrow is your Christmas party. Or
prom if you will insist on speaking like our transatlantic cousins. Myself
and Miss Timms will be attending.

NEIL   (UNDER HIS BREATH) Yes.

MR GILBERT   To make sure you enjoy yourselves sensibly. Now obviously we want you to have fun, but in order to make it enjoyable for
everyone we have a few rules. One, everyone will get two alcoholic drink
tokens and no more. Frankly, the last thing I want is to be cleaning up
your dreadful sick or even worse, you putting your arms around me and
telling me that I'm all right for a teacher and that you love me. Two,
this is a school dance and not the last days of Rome.

WILL LAUGHS, MR GILBERT LOOKS AT HIM, EVERYONE ELSE LOOKS BEMUSED.

MR GILBERT   What I mean by this is no heavy petting, and I will be the judge of what constitutes heavy.

JAY   (COUGHING AT THE BACK) Pervert.

MR GILBERT   I heard that. But if I see anything that I consider too much you will be sent home. Is that clear?

STUDENTS   Yes sir.

MR GILBERT   Is that clear?

STUDENTS   (LOUDER) Yes sir.

MR GILBERT   Good. Have a nice evening. I'll leave you in the hands of the chairman of the organising committee, and God help you, William McKenzie.

WILL   Thanks Phil. Now—

MR GILBERT   Sorry?

WILL   Thanks for that Phil.

MR GILBERT   Phil?

WILL   Oh, it's just because the dance is outside of school time, so I assumed—

MR GILBERT   Well you assumed wrong 'Will'. Very wrong.

WILL   Sorry . . . (TURNING TO THE ASSEMBLED SIXTH FORM) Right then . . .

MR GILBERT   Say my name properly.

WILL   Mr Gilbert.

MR GILBERT   Say thank you.

WILL   Thank you.

MR GILBERT   Say thank you Mr Gilbert.

WILL   Thank you Mr Gilbert.

MR GILBERT   Better.

MR GILBERT LEAVES.

WILL   OK. Just a few things to make sure it runs smoothly. I've got the schedules here.

AS WILL IS TALKING, EVERYONE ELSE STARTS TALKING AND LEAVING. HE'S LEFT STRANDED AT THE PODIUM.

THEN IT'S CLEAR THAT MARK DONOVAN HASN'T LEFT. DONOVAN APPROACHES WILL.

MARK DONOVAN   I've not forgotten about you. I'll be watching you tomorrow and if I see you anywhere near Charlotte Hinchcliffe I'll rip your fucking throat out. Have a nice time.

HE LEAVES. WILL LOOKS SCARED.

WILL   Well that's good.

WILL V/O   *Brilliant, mate, it wasn't just my reputation on the line at the prom, now it was my life.*

——— SCENE 7 ———

INT. SCHOOL HALL

WILL V/O   *It was the moment of truth, prom night had arrived and as I watched my crack team setting things up it's fair to say I was shitting myself . . .*

THE SCHOOL HALL IS EMPTY OF PEOPLE APART FROM THOSE FEW WHO ARE SETTING UP – JOHN OVER BY THE FOOD COUNTER, A FEW PEOPLE PUTTING UP BALLOONS, JAY SORTING THROUGH HIS RECORDS.

WILL IS OVERSEEING THE RAISING OF A BIG 'RUDGE PARK INAUGURAL CHRISTMAS PROM' BANNER.

WILL   David, David, don't lean on that, it'll come down. Who's written the toilet signs? Where are the toilet signs?

SIMON   We're in the school, everyone knows where the toilets are, they piss in them every day.

WILL   Not everyone will know, we're meant to have signs. (SHOUTING) Pen, pen! (FINDING ONE) It's fucking run out, how can this be happening? Tonight is a fucking disaster.

SIMON   It's fine, it's all fine, it looks good.

WILL   Look, people are going to judge tonight and therefore me as either a huge success or a massive failure.

SIMON   You've got balloons, you're already one up on any event the school's ever had before. Just relax.

WILL   Also it's very hard to relax knowing that Donovan might very well kick the shit out of me at some point.

SIMON   Oh right, that makes much more sense.

WILL   Anyway, how come you're so calm? I thought you'd be shitting yourself about your plan to get Carli.

SIMON   No, no, I'm fine. Jay's got his end sorted and I know exactly what to say.

WILL   Right, are you sure you should trust Jay with what could be the tenderest moment of your life?

SIMON   Yeah yeah, yeah yeah, he'll be fine. It's a good plan. And can it be worse than puking on her brother's head?

WILL   Maybe, you haven't told me what it is yet.

THE DOORS FLY OPEN AND WE SEE A FIGURE SILHOUETTED AGAINST THE BACKGROUND. HE IS WEARING A TIGHT ALL-IN-ONE ICE-SKATING BODY SUIT, CUT TO THE NAVEL, WITH A BOW TIE. IT'S NEIL.

EVERYONE STOPS AND LOOKS.

JAY   What the fuck are you wearing?

SIMON   Oh my God and I thought our suits were shit.

JAY   Oh, your cock, it looks so tiny, it's like an acorn.

SIMON   Have you gone mental?

NEIL   No, this is cool, I saw it in *Nuts*. Girls will fancy me because I stand out.

JAY   You'll stand out because your cock is minuscule.

NEIL   Will you stop looking at my cock?

SIMON   Mate, I think that's brave, really brave.

JAY   It's so shit.

NEIL   Actually maybe I'd better go stick a couple of socks down there. Any jobs for me?

WILL   Wash your hands afterwards.

NEIL   Got ya . . . Will, where's the toilets?

HE LEAVES. THERE'S A CRASH AS THE 'CHRISTMAS PROM' SIGN FALLS DOWN.

WILL   Oh for fuck's sake.

———— SCENE 8 ————

INT. HALL

THE PARTY APPEARS TO BE IN FULL SWING. THE BAND ARE PLAYING. IT LOOKS LIKE A LOT OF FUN.

NEIL IS DOING HIS DANCE FROM CARAVAN CLUB.

WILL IS RUSHING AROUND.

WILL V/O   *Despite being organised by my team of geeks, it actually looked like people were enjoying the party . . . mind you, I couldn't afford to relax . . .*

WILL   John, John! Stop eating the burgers.

WE SEE JOHN WITH A FEW BURGERS IN HIS MOUTH.

WILL EXITS THE HALL.

NEIL   He's stressed.

SIMON   Yeah and to be honest I think it's a pretty good party.

NEIL   Oh and it just got even better. Here's Miss Timms.

SIMON   She actually looks quite fit.

NEIL   Very fit. (HE TAKES A HUGE GULP OF HIS BEER)

BEAT.

NEIL   Oh very fit indeed. (HE TAKES ANOTHER HUGE GULP)

JAY COMES OVER.

JAY   I'm on soon, are you ready Si? Have you found Carli yet?

SIMON   Not yet, but she'll be here soon.

JAY   Another drink?

SIMON   Better not, I don't want a repeat of what happened last time. You OK with the plan?

JAY   Yeah, yeah, I'm on it.

SIMON   You've got the timings and everything?

JAY   Yeah, to the second.

SIMON   Please don't fuck it up.

JAY   I won't fuck it up. Go on, go and find her.

SIMON   Right, here goes.

WILL V/O   . . . *as Neil was about to discover, the problem with drinking for Dutch courage is the next level of drunk up from that is Dutch dickhead . . .*

WE SEE NEIL APPROACHING THE SEXY TEACHER MISS TIMMS, AND OBVIOUSLY ASKING HER TO DANCE. SHE ACCEPTS AND THEY DANCE, DISCO NOT SEXY.

WILL V/O. . . *so far, so good. The band rocked, people largely found the toilets without a sign and best of all, my throat remained unripped out . . . Now all I had to worry about was Jay's DJing.*

WE SEE JAY DJING AND ENJOYING IT.

WILL   This isn't on the approved play list, no one likes this one, Jay. Well that's it, it's a disaster.

WILL TURNS AND FINDS HIMSELF FACING CHARLOTTE

CHARLOTTE   Hello stranger.

WILL   Oh um . . . hello. Is . . . is Mark not around?

CHARLOTTE   Why, were you gonna ask him to dance?

WILL   Ha ha, no, no I wasn't.

CHARLOTTE   Are you all right?

WILL   Yeah, I just don't know whether this is any good. I mean, what makes a cool party?

CHARLOTTE   You and your bloody party Will. It's great, just enjoy yourself.

WILL   You're just being nice.

CHARLOTTE   Why would I want to be nice to you? Trust me, I've been to loads of shit parties and this really isn't one.

WILL   Really?

CHARLOTTE   Yeah. You've done well. For a geek. Come on, we're going for a dance.

CHARLOTTE TRIES TO LEAD WILL OFF BY THE HAND BUT HE DOESN'T BUDGE.

WILL   Oh I, I don't really dance to be honest. And I've got stuff to sort out.

CHARLOTTE   Fine, but you owe me a dance later, agreed?

WILL   Agreed . . .

SHE GOES TO MOVE OFF, AND WILL CALLS AFTER HER:

WILL   Oh Charlotte?

CHARLOTTE   Yeah?

WILL   You know 'us'.

CHARLOTTE   Yeah.

WILL   I wasn't a bet, was I?

CHARLOTTE LOOKS AT HIM AND THEN COMES OVER, GIVES HIM A LITTLE KISS ON THE LIPS, NOT LIKE A SNOG BUT LIKE THOSE GIRLS WHO YOU THINK JUST KISS PEOPLE ON THE LIPS DO.

CHARLOTTE   Look, just enjoy your party and we'll have a dance later, OK?

SHE DANCES OFF INTO THE MIDDLE OF A LOAD OF KIDS.

———— SCENE 9 ————

INT. HALL BY THE FOOD COUNTER

JAY IS OBVIOUSLY TAKING A BREAK FROM DJING AND IS AT THE FOOD COUNTER NEAR JOHN.

JAY   Oi, give us a burger.

JOHN   You could say please.

JAY   Just give me one. I've gotta be back up there in three minutes.

JOHN   Not until you say please. Manners cost nothing.

JAY   Oh for fuck's sake. Can I have a burger, please?

JOHN SMILES.

JOHN   Course you can. Would you like ketchup on that?

JAY   Yeah go on then. Please.

THEY SMILE AT EACH OTHER AGAIN.

JOHN   Your DJing seems to be going well.

JAY   Yeah it's all right. Made a few cock-ups.

JOHN   Well no one's noticed.

JAY   It's weird but I feel better when I'm doing it. And I'm not so tense.

JOHN   My counsellor used to say that frustration often comes from wanting to be noticed.

JAY   Yeah, yeah, that's it. It's probably why I exaggerate a bit.

JOHN   To feel special?

JAY   Yeah, it's like sometimes I feel like the kids here don't pay attention to me, like I'm so dumb I don't matter. I guess making a few things up at least makes them notice.

JOHN   Do you fancy a beer? I've still got my two tokens, I don't mind sharing.

JAY   Yeah, yeah, cheers.

JOHN   I understand how you feel, you know. Back in a mo.

JOHN GOES OVER TO THE BAR. AS HE LEAVES, A GIRL COMES OVER TO TALK TO JAY. IT'S CARLI'S MATE SAMANTHA FROM EARLIER.

SAMANTHA   You're DJing, aren't you?

JAY   Yeah.

SAMANTHA   I used to DJ at a top nightclub in Ibiza.

JAY   Oh yeah?

SAMANTHA   I could probably get you a regular spot, you look like you're really into it.

JAY   Yeah. Yeah, it's all about being sensitive. I find it hard to trust, but when it's just me and the music, I'm sorted.

SAMANTHA   Are you bent?

JAY   What?

SAMANTHA   Just right then you sounded really really bent.

JAY   Yeah I heard. Do you wanna come up to the decks with me?

SAMANTHA   Yeah, all right.

JOHN COMES BACK WITH THE BEERS.

JOHN   Got them!

HE PASSES JAY A BEER, WHICH JAY PASSES TO SAMANTHA, AND THEN HE TAKES JOHN'S BEER. JOHN LOOKS A LITTLE SURPRISED.

JOHN   You didn't say please. What about opening up and trusting?

JAY   Oh fuck off, you fat wanker.

HE LEADS SAMANTHA TOWARDS THE DJ BOOTH. JOHN IS LEFT LOOKING A BIT FLAT.

———— SCENE 10 ————

INT. HALL

SIMON IS LOOKING FOR CARLI, WHO IS MOVING THROUGH THE CROWD BUT
NOT WITH TOM OR ANY OTHER NOTICEABLE MEN.

SIMON Carli . . . Carli.

SHE STOPS, AND TURNS AS HE TOUCHES HER ARM.

CARLI Simon.

SIMON You got here all right then?

CARLI Looks like it.

SIMON Where's Tom?

CARLI Oh that dick. He is out with his rugby mates. I left them just
as they were going to start drinking beer out of each other's bum
cracks.

SIMON Right, that's a bit weird isn't it?

CARLI I don't care, I'm not interested.

SIMON Right. Great.

SHE'S CLEARLY NOT HAVING A GREAT EVENING.

CARLI So did you want anything in particular?

SIMON Yeah, yeah, I did want something.

SIMON TURNS TO GET JAY'S ATTENTION. AS SIMON TURNS BACK TO CARLI, THE
MUSIC STOPS.

CARLI Why has the music stopped?

SIMON I stopped it because I need to say that, I just wanted to say
to you that . . .

CARLI Are you going to ask me to finger myself again?

SIMON No, God no. No. I just need to say that . . . um . . .

CARLI Simon, I've had enough of dickheads today. What is it? Why
are you being so weird?

SIMON HAS A BIT OF A LOOK AT THE KIDS ALL AROUND HIM WHO ARE LAUGHING A BIT.

SIMON   Oh, no, no, it's nothing.

CARLI   Nothing.

SIMON   I was going to say something but it's gone now.

CARLI   No, what were you going to say?

SIMON   I was, I was going to say—what the fuck is Neil doing?

SIMON IS LOOKING OVER CARLI'S SHOULDER WHERE WE CAN SEE NEIL OPPOSITE MISS TIMMS. THEY HAVE BEEN DANCING BUT NOW IT LOOKS LIKE HE'S GOING TO LUNGE.

CARLI TURNS ROUND JUST IN TIME TO CATCH NEIL LUNGING FOR THE TEACHER.

NEIL   Come here.

MISS TIMMS   Neil!

NEIL   Oh go on.

MISS TIMMS   Neil, what are you doing?

NEIL   I love you. Please.

HE LUNGES AGAIN AND SHE PUSHES HIM OFF.

LOADS OF PEOPLE ARE NOW POINTING AND LAUGHING.

KID   Boner.

ANOTHER KID   Boner.

SHE LOOKS DOWN AND NEIL'S ERECT PENIS IS PRETTY CLEAR IN HIS TIGHT OUTFIT, AS IS THE SOCK THAT HAS SLIPPED DOWN HIS LEG.

SIMON   Oh God.

HE GOES OVER TO NEIL TO SAVE HIM, BUT MR GILBERT GETS THERE FIRST.

ANOTHER KID   What a boner.

MR GILBERT   Every year, every year someone has a pop, don't they? Come on Sutherland, let's get you a glass of water.

NEIL AND MR GILBERT LEAVE. EVERYONE IS STILL LAUGHING.

SIMON TURNS TO SEE CARLI OVER WITH TOM. SHE'S GIVING HIM A MASSIVE BOLLOCKING.

CARLI   What's the problem? I wanted you to come here with me tonight, yeah. You decide to go out with your friends instead.

TOM   What's wrong with that?

CARLI   What do you mean what's wrong with that? I had to come here on my own.

TOM   I . . .

SIMON SMILES AND LEAVES.

———— SCENE 11 ————

INT. HALL

WILL LOOKS BROADLY HAPPY. DONOVAN APPROACHES. HE GRABS WILL AND PUTS HIM UP AGAINST THE WALL BY HIS NECK.

MARK DONOVAN   I fucking warned you about talking to Charlotte. You are taking the piss.

WILL   I did— I didn't, I wasn't. She came over to me. (DESPERATELY) Mr Gilbert. Mr Gilbert.

JOHN   Hey, put him down.

DONOVAN LOOKS ROUND TO SEE WHO IT IS.

MARK DONOVAN   Or what?

KID A   Yeah, leave him alone.

CHORUS OF VOICES NOW RISING.

KID B   What's wrong with you? He ain't even done nothing.

KID C   Don't be a dickhead Donovan.

KID D   Oi wanker Donovan.

KID E   Yeah, fuck off Donovan.

DONOVAN TURNS ROUND AND NOW FACES QUITE A NUMBER OF KIDS. HE PUTS WILL DOWN.

KID F   Leave the specky short arse alone. He's organised a good party.

KID G   Yeah, briefcase is all right Donovan.

KID H   Wanker.

KID I   Don't be a tit.

DONOVAN THEN SEES CHARLOTTE, WHO SHAKES HER HEAD AND LEAVES. HE GOES AFTER HER.

MARK DONOVAN   Charlotte?

WILL   (TO THE PARTY GOERS) Thanks, that was really kind. And really great. And I, I sort of knew that I'd have to say a few words of thanks at some point tonight. So I prepared a little speech that . . .

HE IS LOOKING IN HIS JACKET FOR A SPEECH, AND FINDS IT, THEN LOOKS UP, AND SEES THAT EVERYONE HAS GONE.

WILL   Oh . . . again. Of course.

HE SMILES.

——— SCENE 12 ———

EXT. SCHOOL

PEOPLE ARE LEAVING.

A KID IS BEING CARRIED OUT OF THE HALL BY CONCERNED PARENTS.

STUDENT   Sorry, Mummy.

MAN   Don't worry, son.

MR GILBERT SURVEYS THE SCENE.

MR GILBERT   Well done, children, a fairly innocuous jamboree of adolescent nonsense. Fear not, the relationships that some of you have entered into tonight, well they may seem like everything now. But they'll be over in a matter of weeks. And if we can just make it home without tagging people's property, yeah, I may go to bed relatively hate-free . . .

MR GILBERT SPOTS TWO PUPILS SNOGGING EACH OTHER'S FACES OFF

Oi, you two! Do you want me to fetch up my dinner? Go home!

——— SCENE 13 ———

INT. SCHOOL GYM

SIMON AND WILL ARE LYING ON THE TRAMPOLINE, LOOKING UP AT THE CEILING.

WILL   I'm allowed to enjoy this, aren't I?

SIMON   Oh yeah, well done, mate, top night.

WILL   Tonight I win. Party was good; Charlotte probably not a bet; and best of all Donovan didn't beat me up.

SIMON   That last one you can only enjoy over the holiday. He'll kill you next term.

WILL   Oh. Did you really enjoy it though?

SIMON   Yeah, I had a laugh. Why do you think I hadn't?

WILL   Oh you know, it didn't exactly go to plan with Carli.

SIMON   Well, I was standing there ready to say all this stuff to her. And it just wouldn't come out. And then I thought, Am I really that bothered?

NEIL ARRIVES AND GETS ON THE TRAMPOLINE.

SIMON   And then Neil sort of fucked the teacher.

NEIL   Oi, leave me alone.

SIMON   Honestly she looked like she was going to slap you. But I think your erection scared her off.

WILL   What were you thinking?

NEIL   I dunno, I think it was the suit.

SIMON   It was definitely too jazzy.

WILL   Hah.

NEIL   I thought Miss Timms would like it.

WILL   Even though she's thirty, is going out with Gilbert, would go to prison for snogging you?

NEIL   Gilbert was all right about it actually.

WILL   Are you looking forward to biology next term?

NEIL   Not really.

SIMON   Should be interesting.

JAY ENTERS.

JAY   Oi oi, guess who just got a blowie behind the decks?

SIMON   Well not you, obviously.

JAY   Guess again.

SIMON   Jay, you're my mate, but please, for once just don't lie. What happened?

JAY   Blowie.

SIMON   I said please don't lie.

JAY   Alright, alright, she gave me a hand job, not a blowie.

NEIL/WILL   Aaaaahhhh!

SIMON SHAKES HIS HEAD.

SIMON   Knew it was bollocks.

JAY   What? I just got a hand job on the school stage, that's better than any of you.

WILL   Bollocks, it's already come down from a blow job. You'll be telling us it was outside the trousers next.

JAY   It was.

NEIL   That doesn't count.

SIMON   Oh well that's not even a hand job then. What has just happened there my friend is you've spunked yourself.

JAY   That counts.

WILL   Doesn't count.

JAY   Oh, well I haven't cleaned my cock yet so . . . does this count?

HE JUMPS ON THE TRAMPOLINE, RUNS OVER TO WILL AND TRIES TO PUSH HIS GROIN IN WILL'S FACE. WILL SQUEALS AND LEAPS UP; SIMON AND NEIL LEAP UP AS WELL. JAY CHASES THEM ROUND.

THEY ARE ALL LAUGHING.

SERIES 2

Episode 1

——— 'Field Trip' ———

We were told that we had a second series the August after the first series went out. It was obviously great news, but the slightly less good news was that E4 wanted the new series to be broadcast earlier than the last one or they didn't want it at all. So that meant we had to be shooting in December, which as we didn't have a single storyline idea meant that the writing time would be much tighter than it had been before. We got organised, probably more so than ever before or since, and after chatting through some ideas with each other for a week called in Robert Popper, Greg Davies and the four leads to talk through what we were thinking but also for them to give us some of their anecdotes and to discuss what universal moments exist in the lives of teenage boys. They were all really helpful, and useful, and some of the stories from the boys were genuinely shocking. James Buckley, I'm looking at you.

Anyway, for this episode we had an idea it would be about a field trip and it seemed that Swanage had pretty much cornered the market in field trips. Everyone had been at least once, and Greg, being a teacher originally, had been, by his guess, about fourteen times. So Swanage it was, but of course due to budgetary constraints (if you're based in London the further you go from London the more expensive it gets) we ended up shooting in Littlehampton, where I had had many happy childhood trips. But not at the end of January, in minus temperatures. I've said it before and I'll say it again, Joe Thomas is a legend for putting up with us.

However, if the idea of a field trip was universal, Damon's experiences on one weren't. In brief, on a trip to a small fishing town, he and some friends took out a boat, accidentally caught a fish, which shit itself, and then they killed it. Weird, certainly, but also true and such a funny anecdote about teenage hopelessness that we felt sure it was worth trying to work into an episode. That said, logistically it seemed ambitious to the point of being impossible to film a boat with fish, and people falling overboard, and we expected to have the customary conversation with production that you have when you write something a bit bigger than customary. The conversation normally starts with you writing, for example, 'The plane explodes on the runway'. You deliver that, and then eventually you're told that due to budgets and health and safety etc what you can actually film will have to be 'The bike scrapes a wall'. However, our new director, Ben Palmer, came in one day, and with Damon and me braced for the bad news, he told us that he'd worked out how we could film boats and falling in and fish. And from that moment on we loved him.

In terms of how the episode came out, I think it's one of my favourites. We had thought of it as coming later in the series, but Channel 4 said it should go first because they found it the funniest and thought that it would be a great way to announce the new series, and I think they were right. I'm rarely really happy with anything we've done, but in my most optimistic moments I think that the escalation of the situation in the boat, driven by four excellent performances, is as funny as we've got and maybe, maybe, is the sort of thing people might want to watch and talk about in years to come.

——— SCENE 1 ———

EXT. SCHOOL CAR PARK / INT. COACH

WILL V/O   *Hi, I'm Will. And yes, it's a briefcase. I'm still at a normal, terrifying comprehensive, 'cause my mum hasn't scraped enough money together to send me back to my old private, and let's face it, better school . . .*

. . . however, I have made friends here, and in some ways this term will be better than the last. And in many other ways, a lot, lot worse . . .

. . . but before all that, my first hurdle of the new term involved a freezing cold day in January, a coach, and Jay calling me a bender.

NEIL, SIMON AND WILL ARE STANDING AROUND READY TO BOARD A COACH.

JAY ARRIVES.

JAY   Morning, benders.

SIMON   All right?

JAY   This is it. The Swanage field trip is legendary for carnage. It's the only reason I chose geography.

WILL   Seems a flimsy reason, unspecified 'carnage'.

JAY   Yeah well, I'll tell you one thing that won't be flimsy. My cock. There's this sexy housewife down there and every year she fucks one bloke from our school.

WILL   How could you possibly know that?

JAY   My mate went last year and he banged her. He said she was the best he'd ever had, a right fit mature bird who does it because she loves young meat.

SIMON   Oh bollocks. For one, you don't even have a mate in Year 13.

JAY   Yeah I do, Chris Groves.

SIMON   Never heard of him.

JAY   Well he's not going to hang out with a twat like you, is he?

WILL   So let me get this straight – your imaginary friend fucked an imaginary older woman in Swanage, so you decided to do geography A level. Good plan.

SIMON   We should try and have a laugh down there, though, do something different.

WILL   We could go on a boat trip? I've checked online. You can hire boats from the harbour.

JAY   The internet really is wasted on you.

SIMON   No, I dunno, we should just, like, try to get off with the local girls, or get some booze or something.

WILL   Everything we're shit at here, but by the seaside? Yeah, can't wait.

NEIL   We could let a load of fireworks off in our room.

SIMON   Could do. Might be a bit pointless.

THE COACH DOOR OPENS AND THEY START TO BOARD. NEIL FOLLOWS AND WILL TURNS ROUND TO FACE HIM.

WILL   Neil, where are you going?

NEIL   Getting on the coach.

WILL   But you don't do geography or sociology.

NEIL   I know that.

WILL   So what are you doing on the coach to the geography and sociology field trip?

NEIL   Oh, well Jay was going on about how mental it all was and I really really wanted to go, so I asked Mr Kennedy if I could come and help him out.

SIMON   Paedo Kennedy? He said yes presumably?

NEIL   He did actually.

WILL   Who's Paedo Kennedy?

SIMON   Geography teacher. And paedo.

WILL   I don't believe that the school would actually employ a paedo-phile.

JAY   They have done.

WILL   The thing is, they haven't, have they?

SIMON   He was caught in the music cupboard wanking over the school orchestra.

WILL   When?

SIMON   Before we started.

WILL   Convenient. What's he asked you to do, Neil?

NEIL   He's got to collect a load of samples down there.

JAY   What, of your spunk?

SIMON   Collected in his mouth.

JAY   And hair.

NEIL   Behave.

———— SCENE 2 ————

INT. COACH

WILL V/O   *So even though Neil was now a suspected paedo's play-thing, we boarded the coach with high hopes. It might have been a new term and a new year, but some things never change . . .*

THE BOYS BOARD THE COACH AND SIT DOWN ON THE BACK ROW.

WE SEE CARLI BOARD AND TAKE HER SEAT. SIMON WAVES AT CARLI BUT CARLI DOESN'T SEE IT, SO HE HAS TO PULL OUT OF THE WAVE AND PRETEND IT WAS JUST AN ARM MOVEMENT.

WILL   It's still going well with Carli then is it?

SIMON   Shut up.

MR KENNEDY BOARDS THE COACH BEHIND MR GILBERT.

JAY   Here he is.

SIMON   Oh watch out, Neil.

MR KENNEDY SPIES NEIL AND DOES A THUMBS UP. NEIL LOOKS A BIT
EMBARASSED. KENNEDY SITS DOWN AT THE FRONT.

NEIL   Oh don't do that.

SIMON   Ooh thumbs-up friend.

WILL   Ooh weird old inappropriate friend.

SIMON   Ooh spunk-samples friend.

NEIL   Oh why did he have to do a thumbs up?

JAY   Because that's what'll be going up your arse first.

NEIL   It's going up your arse first.

NEIL AND JAY START TO PLAY FIGHT, BUT ARE BROUGHT TO A HALT BY THE
APPEARANCE OF MARK DONOVAN ON THE COACH, BOARDING WITH MATES AND
A SWAGGER.

THEY START MAKING THEIR WAY TO THE BACK SEAT.

WILL V/O   . . . *but in all the excitement, we had forgotten the first
rule of coach travel. Hard kids at the back* . . .

SIMON   Oh shit.

NEIL   I'm off.

WILL   No, stay. There is no reason for us to move and we're not
moving.

AS WILL IS SAYING THIS, THE OTHER THREE HAVE ALREADY STARTED TO MOVE.

MARK DONOVAN HAS REACHED THEM.

MARK DONOVAN   Move.

WILL   Why should we move?

MARK DONOVAN   Do you want me to give you a reason?

WILL   Well I'm not leaving without one.

MARK DONOVAN   I don't think you understand.

WILL   I don't think that you understand that we got up early to secure these seats. There's no reason—

MARK DONOVAN GRABS WILL BY THE TIE AND DRAGS HIM FORWARD, CHOKING HIM SLIGHTLY.

WILL   (THROUGH STRANGLED VOCAL CHORDS) Yep, good point, fine.

MARK DONOVAN SORT OF THROWS WILL PAST AND SITS DOWN.

JAY   Oh fuck, where are we going to sit now?

MR GILBERT   What is going on? Will you lot sit down.

NEIL   Our seats have been taken sir. There's nowhere left.

HE'S ALMOST RIGHT, BUT THERE ARE THREE OR FOUR EMPTY SEATS YET TO BE TAKEN. ONE IS NEXT TO JOHN, AND ONE NEXT TO MR GILBERT. ALL OF THESE ARE PRETTY NEAR THE FRONT, MR GILBERT'S BEING AT THE VERY FRONT.

MR GILBERT   Yes there is, there's loads at the front. Sit next to John.

JAY   I'm not sitting next to John. His fat arse takes up two seats.

JOHN   I've got feelings too, you know.

MR GILBERT   Fine, you're sitting next to me.

JAY   Oh what?

MR GILBERT   Well it's me or Mr Kennedy. Now come on, hurry up. And McKenzie, sit down.

JAY SITS DOWN AT THE FRONT, AS SIMON AND NEIL FIND SEATS. WILL PLONKS HIMSELF DOWN WITHOUT LOOKING AND SEES THAT HE IS SITTING NEXT TO A RATHER PRETTY GIRL.

WILL   Hello.

LAUREN   Hi.

WILL   Um, who are you?

LAUREN   I'm Lauren Harris. I'm new.

WILL   Hi, I'm Will McKenzie. Scary being new, isn't it?

LAUREN   It is a bit.

WILL   The way the kids threaten to beat you up and call you names like briefcase wanker?

LAUREN   Oh, it's not been like that.

WILL   No, it wasn't for me either.

THE COACH EVENTUALLY ROLLS OUT OF THE SCHOOL GATES.

—————— SCENE 3 ——————

INT. COACH / EXT. ROAD

WILL V/O   *. . . I was more used to field trips to places like the Alps or Barcelona than shitty English seaside towns. But as we headed to Swanage there was definitely a sense of excitement. A feeling that anything could happen. For the first couple of hours. Then it became just another incredibly tedious coach journey.*

WE SEE THE COACH TRAVELLING DOWN THE MOTORWAY, THEN CUT BACK INSIDE TO SEE SIMON OCCASIONALLY LOOKING BACK OVER HIS SHOULDER AT CARLI, WHO IS LAUGHING WITH HER FRIENDS AND TOTALLY OBLIVIOUS TO SIMON.

NEIL LOOKS LIKE HE'S ACTUALLY ENJOYING HIMSELF.

JAY OPENS HIS MOUTH AS IF HE'S ABOUT TO SAY SOMETHING TO MR GILBERT.

MR GILBERT   (WITHOUT EVEN LOOKING AT JAY) Don't even think about trying to talk to me.

HE WALKS DOWN THE COACH TOWARDS THE TOILET. JAY JUMPS UP AND STARTS TO WALK DOWN THE COACH BEHIND MR GILBERT'S BACK TOWARDS NEIL AND SIMON.

JAY   Hey, who wants to swap seats?

SIMON   Nah, you're all right.

JAY   God, it's so boring up there. Wait a minute, who's Spongebob shithispants talking to?

THE OTHER BOYS LOOK ROUND. THEY SEE LAUREN AND WILL TALKING.

NEIL   Oh she's fit.

SIMON   Yeah she is.

NEIL   Here, this'll get her attention.

SIMON   Oh Neil, don't be embarrassing.

NEIL   Oi, everyone, watch this.

MOST OF THE COACH PASSENGERS, INCLUDING WILL AND LAUREN, LOOK AT NEIL.

NEIL LOOKS OUT OF THE WINDOW AT THE PASSING LORRY. HE MAKES A GESTURE TO THE LORRY DRIVER WHERE HE PULLS AN IMAGINARY HORN. THE LORRY DRIVER RESPONDS WITH A REAL HONK OF HIS REAL HORN. NEIL LOOKS DELIGHTED AND SO DO MOST OF THE COACH PASSENGERS.

LAUREN   What's going on?

WILL   Oh Neil's just being silly.

LAUREN   Is he doing the horn thing? That's really funny.

WILL   Yeah it's really funny silly, isn't it? Silly in a funny way?

LAUREN   Do it again Neil.

WILL   Yeah do it again Neil.

NEIL DOES IT AGAIN WITH THE SAME RESPONSE. EVERYONE LAUGHS. IT'S REALLY GOOD.

JAY LOOKS ROUND AND SEES THAT HE HAS A CAPTIVE AUDIENCE, NOT JUST FROM THE COACH IN GENERAL, BUT FROM A COUPLE OF GIRLS INCLUDING LAUREN.

JAY   Here, if you like that, I got a good one. Watch this.

PASSING THE SCHOOL COACH IS A MINIBUS LOAD OF PENSIONERS. IT'S NOT EXACTLY RACING PAST. JAY SMILES AND WAVES AT THEM. AS THEY SMILE AND WAVE BACK, JAY GIVES THEM THE FINGER AND THEN THE WANKER SIGN. THEY LOOK HORRIFIED AS HE LAUGHS AND PLAYS TO THE GALLERY.

THE GIRLS LOOK DISGUSTED AND TURN AWAY.

JAY   What? They loved it.

MR GILBERT IS RETURNING FROM THE LOO AND WALKING DOWN THE AISLE NOW.

MR GILBERT   Cartwright. Sit down.

——— SCENE 4 ———

EXT. HOSTEL CAR PARK

WILL V/O   *So far the only unspecified carnage we had witnessed was what John had left in the coach toilet. But Jay wasn't giving up on finding his mythical seaside milf.*

WILL, SIMON, NEIL AND JAY ARE MILLING AROUND OUTSIDE THE COACH.

NEIL   So where do you think this nympho hangs out then?

JAY   Not sure. High street maybe? Or down by the ice-cream stall on the front. Apparently, right, she comes up to you and asks for a lick of your Cornetto. It means she's offering a cock in mouth situation. It's like a code.

WILL   Brilliant.

LAUREN GETS OFF THE COACH AND WALKS TOWARDS THE BOYS.

LAUREN   Oh Will. Bit embarrassing, but do you mind if I sit with you at lunch? You know, 'cos I've got no mates and all that.

WILL   God no, no problem at all.

JAY   You can sit on my lap if you like?

LAUREN   No thank you. I thought you should know that thing you did on the bus was really sad and pathetic and not funny. I'll see you later.

LAUREN WALKS OFF.

JAY LOOKS STUNNED.

JAY   Frigid.

——— SCENE 5 ———

INT. HOSTEL CANTEEN

WILL, JAY, NEIL AND SIMON ARE SITTING ON THEIR OWN, A SMALL DISTANCE AWAY FROM MOST OF THE OTHER KIDS.

SIMON   Looks like you won't be getting off with Lauren.

JAY   Who cares, she's just a little girl. Didn't come down here for girls, mate, I get enough of them back home. Nah, I've come down here for a woman.

SIMON   She is fit though.

WILL   What?

SIMON   Lauren's fit, isn't she?

WILL   I saw her first.

SIMON   What? I only said she was fit.

FROM OUT OF NOWHERE LAUREN APPEARS WITH A TRAY.

LAUREN   Hi guys.

WILL   Hi.

SIMON   Here, sit down here.

WILL GIVES SIMON A LOOK THAT SAYS 'I'M WARNING YOU'.

JAY   Oh, er, I'm just off actually.

LAUREN   Oh, no, don't leave on my account.

JAY   Oh nah, it's not that. I've just got to see a man about a dog and then a woman about a pussy.

LAUREN   I do know what that means.

JAY   Right. You coming Neil?

NEIL   Yeah.

JAY AND NEIL LEAVE. LAUREN SITS DOWN.

SIMON   I'm Simon by the way.

LAUREN   Hi Simon.

SIMON   Sorry about those two.

LAUREN   It's all right, I've got a younger brother so I'm used to it. Well, he's eight, so he's a bit more mature like, but you know.

WILL   (DOING YODA FROM *STAR WARS* AND TRYING TO GET LAUREN'S ATTENTION) Feisty one you are.

LAUREN   What?

WILL   (DOING YODA FROM *STAR WARS* AGAIN) Feisty one you are.

LAUREN   Why are you talking like that?

WILL   It was Yoda.

LAUREN STARES BLANKLY AT WILL.

WILL   From *Star Wars: A New Hope*? It's the same impression I was doing on the coach for about an hour.

LAUREN   Oh, was that what that was? Oh good. I thought you might, y'know, have a problem.

WILL   Ha ha, no.

LAUREN   Or Asperger's maybe?

WILL   Wrong again!

LAUREN   Have you ever been tested for anything?

WILL   Good one.

LAUREN   Oh I was gonna ask, would one of you two do the survey with me? You know, as I've got no mates and all that.

SIMON   I will.

LAUREN   Oh really.

SIMON   Yep.

WILL   I don't think you can actually.

LAUREN   Why not?

SIMON   Yeah, why not?

WILL   Um maybe because of what I mentioned earlier?

SIMON   Jay fucking an old woman?

WILL   Ooh ladies present. No, um, the other thing.

SIMON I have no idea what you're talking about. Look, Lauren doesn't know anyone, don't be a dick.

WILL I'm not being a dick Simon, I'm just saying who am I going to do my survey with?

JOHN HOVES INTO VIEW. WILL SPOTS HIM.

WILL Oh no.

JOHN Mr Gilbert says I'm to pair up with you because I'm not very good with directions and I might get lost.

WILL Great.

JOHN AND WILL LEAVE.

THEY WALK PAST CARLI, WHO HAS NOTICED SIMON AND LAUREN CHATTING AND LAUGHING OVER THEIR LUNCH.

JOHN Can I borrow your forms? I spilt ketchup on mine.

——— SCENE 6 ———

EXT. SWANAGE HIGH STREET

WILL V/O *So Simon got to hang out with lovely Lauren, while I had to stop a fat kid wandering into the sea . . .*

. . . meanwhile, Jay was searching for that rarest of beasts, a sexy middle-aged woman.

NEIL AND JAY HAVE THE SURVEY IN THEIR HANDS.

NEIL Hurry up, Jay, I've got to get back to old Kennedy in fifteen minutes.

JAY All right, I'll try this one.

JAY SEES AN ATTRACTIVE WOMAN, ABOUT FORTY, PUSHING A PUSHCHAIR. HE APPROACHES HER.

JAY Excuse me.

WOMAN Yes?

JAY   Um, we're doing a survey for school. Can you answer a few questions?

WOMAN   Will it take long?

NEIL   It can take as long as you like.

WOMAN   Sorry?

JAY   First question, what form of transport did you take into town today?

WOMAN   I drove.

JAY   And how often do you use public transport?

WOMAN   Um, rarely.

JAY   And do you wear stockings and that?

WOMAN   Is this about transport?

JAY   It's just the questions written down. Er, one last one . . .

WE CUT OVER TO WILL, WHO IS LOOKING BACK AT JAY AND NEIL WITH THE WOMAN. HE SEES THE WOMAN SLAP JAY AND STORM OFF. WILL WINCES AND THEN SMILES.

SIMON SPOTS WILL AND COMES OVER TO JOIN HIM.

SIMON   Alright.

WILL   Oh hello, where's Lauren?

SIMON   Oh she went to get a drink. She's nice, isn't she?

WILL   I thought you were only interested in Carli?

SIMON   Oh well sort of, but Lauren's all right, you know? Easy to talk to.

WILL   Did you mention me at all?

SIMON   No.

WILL   Right.

SIMON   She said that she thought I was really good-looking.

WILL   Oh.

SIMON   I was not expecting that.

WILL   This is a bit weird because I really like her but I think she might like you.

SIMON   Right, well, if you think she fancies me then I should probably go for it.

WILL   Perhaps, except I'm saying that I like her.

SIMON   I should go for it though.

WILL   Any thoughts on the 'me liking her' part?

SIMON   Um, no, sure, good point. But she is fit, so you can see my problem.

WILL   Not really.

SIMON   Yeah, but you know how it is.

WILL   How? How is it?

SIMON   You know. Look, why don't we just see what happens later back at the dorm. She might not be interested in either of us.

WILL   I suppose that's true, let's just wait and see. And no hard feelings if she goes for me?

SIMON   Oh I'm not worried about that.

─────── SCENE 7 ───────

INT. HOSTEL DORM

THE DORM IS MORE OR LESS EMPTY APART FROM WILL, SIMON AND JAY. NEIL WALKS IN.

NEIL   All right? Found that nympho yet?

JAY   Not yet.

WILL   Surprisingly.

SIMON   Where have you been Neil?

NEIL   Me and Kennedy went to the beach and then went swimming.

WILL   Sorry?

SIMON   Swimming?

NEIL   Yeah.

WILL   Just the two of you?

NEIL   Yes.

JAY   Paedo Kennedy took you skinny-dipping?

NEIL   No. He gave me a spare pair of trunks.

WILL   What, speedos?

NEIL   They were actually.

ALL THE BOYS ARE NOW LAUGHING.

WILL   I'm beginning to see what he gets out of this arrangement Neil, but what's in it for you?

NEIL   This.

NEIL GETS OUT A BOTTLE OF VODKA FROM HIS RUCKSACK.

NEIL   He got me it from the offy.

JAY   Nice.

SIMON   Cool.

WILL   Shit.

JAY   Now here comes some carnage.

NEIL   He said don't tell Gilbert though.

WILL   Don't tell him about the inappropriate swimming or about the planned sexual assault when you're drunk?

NEIL   Both.

JAY   This is brilliant. We can get well pissed.

WILL   Although technically it does mean that we are now pimping Neil out.

SIMON   I'm cool with that.

NEIL   Me too.

WE HEAR A KNOCK ON THE DOOR.

WILL   Shit, hide it.

WE HEAR LAUREN'S VOICE FROM OUTSIDE THE DOOR.

LAUREN   (OFF SCREEN) Simon? Will? It's Lauren. Are you guys in there?

SIMON OPENS THE DOOR TO LET LAUREN IN.

SIMON   Alright.

LAUREN   Hey. There's a load of noise down the hall, sounds like a party. Do you fancy it?

WILL   (DOING YODA FROM *STAR WARS*) Party hmmmmm? Cool that sounds.

JAY   You know you are never, ever going to get laid.

WILL V/O   *Jay was wrong. Statistically there was a good chance I would get laid. Eventually.*

——— SCENE 8 ———

INT. HOSTEL CORRIDOR

WILL V/O   *So we had the booze and the girls, well, a girl. Now all we needed to get this party started was a party.*

THE BOYS AND LAUREN ARE IN THE CORRIDOR OUTSIDE THE PARTY DORM DOOR. FROM BEHIND THE DOOR WE CAN HEAR LAUGHTER AND MUSIC.

WILL WALKS CONFIDENTLY UP TO THE DOOR AND KNOCKS. THE DOOR OPENS AN INCH.

DAVID GLOVER   What?

WILL   Um, we're here for the party.

DAVID GLOVER   (TO SOMEONE INSIDE) It's that posh little prick.

MARK DONOVAN   (OFF SCREEN) Ask him if he's got any pictures of his mum.

DAVID GLOVER   He's got a bottle of vodka.

WILL SMILES UNCOMFORTABLY TO LAUREN. THE DOOR OPENS AND IT'S MARK DONOVAN.

MARK DONOVAN   Here they are, team twat. What's that you've brought for me?

WILL   Well it's Neil's vodka. We thought we could maybe come in and join the party . . .

DONOVAN GRABS THE BOTTLE OF VODKA FROM WILL.

MARK DONOVAN   Thank you, wankers.

DONOVAN SLAMS THE DOOR SHUT.

SIMON   Well that went well.

LAUREN   So I reckon the party's probably over for us then?

WILL   We could do something else. Pool? Table tennis? I think I saw the board game Risk downstairs.

JAY   Fuck that for a laugh. I'm going to find that yummy mummy who wants me to spunk on her tummy.

WILL   A rapey rhyme. How lovely.

NEIL   Yeah, come on, let's bunk it.

JAY AND NEIL HEAD OFF DOWN THE CORRIDOR.

LAUREN   Um, I think I'll call it a night guys. Maybe see you at break-fast? Do you want to walk me back to my dorm maybe?

WILL   My pleasure.

LAUREN   Oh, I meant Simon.

SIMON   Er yeah, OK.

WILL   Great, we'll both walk you back then.

WILL, SIMON AND LAUREN LEAVE.

—————— SCENE 9 ——————

INT. HOSTEL CORRIDOR

WILL, SIMON AND LAUREN ARE IN THE CORRIDOR, IMMEDIATELY OUTSIDE
LAUREN'S DORM DOOR.

LAUREN I'll see you tomorrow then, Will.

WILL Definitely. See you tomorrow.

LAUREN Simon, can I speak to you before you head back?

SIMON Yeah, course.

THERE'S AN AWKWARD MOMENT.

LAUREN Good night then Will.

WILL Oh no, it's OK, I'll wait for Si. You can say anything you want to
in front of me. We're mates.

LAUREN OK. Simon, do you fancy hanging out tomorrow maybe, in
the free time. Just the two of us?

WILL (TO HIMSELF BUT MAKING SURE LAUREN AND SIMON HEAR) Bit rude.

SIMON Erm yeah, that would be good. I'd love to do that.

LAUREN Cool. Meet you by the harbour after lunch?

SIMON By the sea?

WILL That's where they tend to position them Si, makes it easier for
the boats.

LAUREN Well goodnight then Will.

WILL Yeah whatever.

LAUREN Goodnight Simon.

SIMON Yeah, goodnight.

LAUREN LEANS IN TO KISS SIMON GOODNIGHT. SHE THEN PUTS HER ARMS
AROUND HIM AND GIVES HIM A BIG HUG.

WILL LOOKS ON ANXIOUSLY.

WILL   Come on then Si, let's get going.

LAUREN   It's been so nice meeting you Simon.

SIMON   I know. I mean, I feel the same.

SIMON AND LAUREN CONTINUE TO HUG.

WILL   Getting late now Si, off we go . . . Si?

AND STILL THEY HUG. WILL CARRIES ON REGARDLESS.

WILL   Si? Come on now mate! (AS HE WALKS OFF) Right, see you back at the dorm then. I'll leave a knife right by my bed, just pop it in my back later mate. Right between the shoulder blades. Night then Lauren.

WILL V/O   *So Simon got a hug. A hug . . .*

. . . not sex. But from the way he went on about it you'd think she'd sucked his foreskin or something.

──────── SCENE 10 ────────

<u>INT. HOTEL DORM</u>

IT'S 2 A.M. IN THE BOYS' DORM. THE LIGHTS ARE OUT AND EVERYONE IS ASLEEP EXCEPT SIMON, WHO IS HALF WHISPERING TO WILL.

SIMON   Can you believe it? I think she really likes me.

WILL   Yeah, I think it's time to get some sleep now Simon.

SIMON   Funny that she—

THERE'S A FAINT KNOCK ON THE DOOR. THE DOOR OPENS AND A SHAFT OF LIGHT SPILLS IN FROM THE HALLWAY. MR KENNEDY ENTERS. HE SOUNDS A BIT DRUNK.

MR KENNEDY   Hello. It's only me boys.

HE CROSSES THE DORM TO NEIL'S BED AND PERCHES ON THE END. NEIL STIRS, AS MR KENNEDY SEEMS TO HAVE HIS HAND RESTED, ABOVE THE COVERS, ON NEIL'S LEG.

MR KENNEDY   Just, er, on my way to bed. Thought I'd check how you are.

JAY HAS NOW WOKEN UP AND SEEN MR KENNEDY.

MR KENNEDY   Ooh. Swimming's tiring. Are your legs tired?

NEIL   I think they're OK.

MR KENNEDY   Yes. Quick massage before bedtime? Tired legs. Ooh.

HE STARTS TO RUB NEIL'S LEGS A BIT, OVER THE COVERS. THE BOYS ARE
FREAKED OUT AND JUST STARE AT HIM.

MR GILBERT COMES IN. HE PICKS KENNEDY UP.

MR GILBERT   Come on John.

MR KENNEDY   Rub-down, shift the lactic acid.

MR GILBERT   Not now John.

HE PUTS HIS ARM AROUND KENNEDY'S SHOULDER AND LEADS HIM FROM THE
ROOM. MR GILBERT LOOKS BACK INTO THE ROOM OVER HIS SHOULDER WITH A
LOOK THAT SAYS 'IF ANY OF YOU SAY ANYTHING, I'LL KILL YOU'.

WILL   Was that a dream or did that just happen?

JAY   That was your wet dream.

WILL   No it wasn't.

NEIL   He rubbed my legs.

JAY   Well that's what you get for leading on paedos, you slut.

WILL   Shouldn't we report him?

NEIL   And he did give us that vodka.

WILL   That's called 'grooming' Neil.

NEIL   Is it?

WILL   Yes.

NEIL   Oh. Goodnight.

———— SCENE 11 ————

EXT. HOSTEL

WILL V/O   *Neil didn't seem too emotionally scarred by the night's events. Unlike me.*

SIMON AND WILL ARE HANGING AROUND OUTSIDE THE HOSTEL.

WILL IS EATING SOME TOAST, WHICH SOME SEAGULLS SEEM QUITE KEEN ON, AND TALKING TO SIMON.

SIMON   You are all right with me seeing Lauren later, aren't you?

WILL   Yes. Course.

SIMON   She's pretty cool actually.

WILL   Is she?

SOME SEAGULLS DESCEND AND EYE WILL'S TOAST. WILL VIOLENTLY TRIES TO KICK ONE AWAY.

WILL   Fuck off, you beady-eyed little shit.

SIMON   Um, are you sure you're all right with it?

CARLI COMES OVER TO TALK TO SIMON.

CARLI   Hi Simon.

SIMON   Hello.

CARLI   Haven't seen you at all this trip. Where've you been?

SIMON   Um, just here.

CARLI   What are you doing this afternoon?

SIMON   Nothing.

WILL   Is that correct?

SIMON   Yes.

WILL   I'm sure you've got something on this afternoon.

SIMON   No, I don't think so.

CARLI It's the free time later, and as we haven't hung out for ages I thought, like, why don't I see what Simon's doing?

SIMON Did you?

CARLI Yeah.

WILL That's a real shame, Carli, because Simon's hanging out with, is it Lauren, this afternoon.

CARLI Oh, right, is that the new girl? I saw you talking to her.

SIMON Did you?

CARLI Yeah.

WILL So Simon can't come as he's got a date.

CARLI Are you going on a date with her Simon?

SIMON No, not a date. Just hanging.

CARLI Sorry Simon, I didn't realise it was a date thing.

SIMON No, listen to me, it's not a date. It can't be a date because anyone's welcome – me, you, Lauren, who may or may not be coming.

WILL She is definitely coming.

SIMON She might not and I don't care either way if she does. Carli, it would be great to hang out with you this afternoon. See you down the front at three?

CARLI See you later then.

CARLI LEAVES.

SIMON Well thanks for nearly fucking that up for me, mate.

WILL I just don't want things to get confusing. You can't meet up with both of them, can you?

SIMON Shit. I don't know. I can't cancel Lauren, can I?

WILL Look, Carli means something to you. You should go out with her. I'll sort Lauren out.

SIMON Yeah. That's the right thing to do, isn't it?

Will you talk to Lauren then?

WILL   Course. I'll let her down gently for you, mate.

———— SCENE 12 ————

EXT. HOSTEL

WILL IS SPEAKING TO LAUREN.

WILL   He's going out with somebody else and he couldn't tell you to your face. He's a twat. So I said I'd do it because I think you deserve an explanation.

LAUREN   Oh . . . OK. Well that's a shame. Thanks Will.

WILL   Look, I've hired a boat this afternoon, why don't you come out on it with me?

LAUREN   I'm not sure.

WILL   Go on, please?

LAUREN   Oh all right then.

WILL   Great. They hire the boats out down by the quay. Oh and if you see Simon, best not to mention I said he was a twat.

LAUREN   See you later then.

———— SCENE 13 ————

EXT. ICE CREAM KIOSK BY SEAFRONT

WILL V/O   *Meanwhile, Jay was still on the hunt for his sex-starved ice-cream lady. . .*

JAY AND NEIL ARE STANDING NEAR AN ICE-CREAM KIOSK. MANNING THE KIOSK IS A WOMAN WHO APPEARS TO BE ABOUT SIXTY YEARS OLD (OLD WOMAN).

NEIL   I don't know. She looks too old.

JAY   We've been here two days and she's the first bird we've seen hanging out here.

NEIL   She looks like she's only got one leg.

JAY   She's probably just got an old face. Must be 'cos of all the jizz she's had on it. I bet her body is still pretty fit.

SIMON APPROACHES. HE'S LOOKING PRETTY PLEASED WITH HIMSELF.

SIMON   Thought I'd find you here. How's the sex search going?

NEIL   Jay thinks it's her.

SIMON   Ha. You must be joking. She's ancient.

JAY   Nah, if she put on a bit of fake tan and slipped into some sexy undies I'd definitely give it a go. It must be her, I've given everyone else the eye.

SIMON   She looks like she could give you her actual eye.

JAY   This is it. It's now or never.

JAY HEADS OVER TO THE KIOSK.

NEIL   Get us a ninety-nine Jay.

CUT TO JAY AT THE KIOSK.

OLD WOMAN   What can I get you?

JAY   A cornetto please?

OLD WOMAN   One cornetto. Is that all?

JAY   Do you wanna lick it?

OLD WOMAN   Sorry?

JAY   My cornetto – do you wanna lick it?

OLD WOMAN   Oh, that's kind. I've had enough ice cream today though sweetheart.

JAY   Oh right, bit late am I?

HE HANDS OVER THE MONEY. THERE'S A BEAT AS JAY IS ABOUT TO GIVE UP.

HE GIVES IT ONE LAST GO.

OLD WOMAN   (CONFUSED) Do you want something else?

JAY   Are you the woman who sucks schoolboys off?

OLD WOMAN   Sorry?

JAY   Can you suck me off?

THE OLD WOMAN LOOKS GENUINELY CONFUSED. JAY GIVES IT A SECOND BEFORE HE REALISES THAT HE'S MADE A MISTAKE. THEN HE STARTS TO WALK OFF QUITE QUICKLY.

WILL V/O   *So it looks like Jay's search for a nympho had hit a brick wall . . .*

SIMON   . . . so it's not her then?

JAY   No.

WILL V/O   *. . . a very old and confused brick wall.*

———— SCENE 14 ————

EXT. SWANAGE HARBOUR/BOAT

WILL IS WEARING A LIFE JACKET AND STANDING IN A SMALL WOODEN BOAT WITH AN OUTBOARD MOTOR. IN THE BOAT ARE A COUPLE OF OARS, A REEL OF FISHING LINE AND SOME MORE LIFE JACKETS. IT DOESN'T LOOK VERY GLAMOROUS. NEIL, SIMON AND JAY ARE WALKING ALONG THE QUAY.

SIMON   Yes, a date with Carli. You have no idea how long I've waited for this.

NEIL   We have. You never shut up about her.

THEY SEE WILL IN THE BOAT, PREPARING IT.

NEIL   Oh my God. What does he look like?

JAY   Aye aye. Permission to come aboard, Captain Cockwash.

WILL   Permission denied, I'm leaving in a minute.

SIMON   You're going to go on a boat trip on your own?

NEIL   That's tragic.

WILL   I'm not going on my own actually.

JAY   Who you going with then?

WILL   Lauren.

SIMON   What? After you told me to not see her?

WILL   I didn't say that.

SIMON   Yes you did. You said I should choose Carli instead.

WILL   Only because she's the one you want to be with.

SIMON   Yeah, and you want to be with Lauren, so you scared me off.

WILL   No, not at all.

SIMON   I dunno, I think that's a bit dodgy mate.

NEIL   Let's have a go then.

WILL   Nope.

JAY   Yeah come on, don't be a dick.

WILL   No.

NEIL   Oh go on, I love boats. I used to go fishing with my dad.

JAY   Fisting?

NEIL   Fishing.

SIMON   Oh come on Will, just take us up to the sea. As you stitched me up.

WILL   No, she's going to be here in fifteen minutes.

JAY   Oh I get it, he's scared.

WILL   I'm not actually. And that incredibly childish attempt at reverse psychology will not work.

———— SCENE 15 ————

EXT. BOAT/HARBOUR/OPEN SEA

WILL V/O   *All right, so it did work.*

THE FOUR BOYS ARE SLOWLY CHUGGING ALONG IN THE BOAT. THEY ARE GENUINELY ENJOYING THE RIDE, ALTHOUGH SIMON IS STILL A BIT MOODY WITH WILL. WILL TAKES IN A DEEP BREATH, ENJOYING THE SEA AIR. STANDING ON THE HARBOUR WALL ARE A FEW LOCAL FISHERMEN. WILL WAVES AT THEM.

WILL V/O *It was quite good fun actually. Even the locals seemed pleased to see us.*

WILL Ahoy ahoy. . . !

FISHERMEN Afternoon.

THEN JAY WAVES, THEY WAVE BACK. THEN HE GIVES THEM THE WANKER SIGN. THEY LOOK ANGRY.

WILL V/O *. . . for about ten seconds anyway. Brilliant.*

WILL Brilliant. Well, that was great. Let's head back then.

SIMON What? You said we could go out to sea.

WILL Well we can't. And put your life jacket on. The sea can be a cruel mistress.

JAY PICKS UP THE REEL OF FISHING LINE.

JAY What's this? Is this the sail?

NEIL It's a fishing line. Give it here.

WILL Neil! Do not throw—

NEIL THROWS THE LINE OVERBOARD AND IT REELS ITSELF OUT.

JAY What happens now?

NEIL Nothing. You have to have bait on it.

WILL Please don't muck around. There's a £150 deposit on the boat.

THEY HAVE ROUNDED A MEANDER AND NOW CAN CLEARLY SEE THE SEA. SIMON HEADS TO THE PROW OF THE BOAT EXCITED.

SIMON Oh cool, the sea. Let's get out there.

SIMON'S A LITTLE UNSTEADY. HE LEANS OVER THE FRONT AND JAY AND NEIL START TO ROCK IT. SIMON TURNS ROUND, BUT'S HE'S REALLY UNSTEADY ON HIS FEET.

SIMON Oi, fuck, no, don't.

WILL Stop rocking the boat. I knew this would happen, I'm turning this round.

NEIL AND JAY KEEP LAUGHING AND SIMON KEEPS YELLING AT THEM TO STOP.

AS WILL TURNS THE ENGINE TO STEER BACK, JAY WRESTLES WITH HIM A BIT, AND WILL HITS THE ACCELERATOR A BIT TOO HARD AND THE BOAT IS THROWN FORWARD. SIMON CATCHES HIS FOOT AND FALLS INTO THE SEA. THE ENGINE STALLS DUE TO THE OVER-REVVING.

NEIL Ooh fuck.

JAY Ha ha.

WILL Oh God. Oh no. Sorry Simon.

SIMON BOBS UP.

SIMON Holy fucking shit that's cold.

WILL Get him out Neil.

SIMON Why did you do that? Was it because of Lauren?

WILL No! God no. It was an accident.

THE THREE BOYS PULL SIMON OVER AND INTO THE BOAT. HE LOOKS FREEZING COLD AND REALLY YOUNG AND CONFUSED.

JAY You total bell-end.

SIMON I thought we were friends?

WILL I'm sorry. Shit, we'd better head straight back in.

JAY Enjoy your swim?

SIMON What? I'm really cold. Like to my bones.

WILL He's going to get hypothermia unless we get him out of those wet clothes. Neil, undress him.

WILL AND NEIL START TO UNDRESS SIMON.

JAY I knew it.

WILL What?

JAY   You've been waiting for this. Knew you were bent for him.

WILL   It's basic first aid. I was in the scouts and we did this.

JAY   I bet that's not all you did in the scouts.

WILL   No, you're right, we did knots too.

SIMON   I'm cold. Could someone get me some hair gel?

JAY   Oh don't take his pants off Neil, you're not your dad.

WILL   He has to, it's the safest way. Put that coat round him Neil. I'll get the engine started.

NEIL POPS A COAT ROUND SIMON AS WILL TRIES TO PULL THE STARTER MOTOR FOR THE ENGINE.

NEIL   Don't worry, I'll cover him up.

WILL   Oh fuck, why won't this start? Jay, get that line in.

JAY   All right. Don't shit yourself.

JAY GRABS THE FISHING LINE.

WILL   How's this happened.

JAY   I think it's caught on something.

WILL   It must be caught round the engine.

SIMON   Can I huddle up to someone please? I'm really cold. Is anyone else really cold? Like really cold?

JAY TAKES THE REEL AND GIVES IT A HUGE TUG. HE AND NEIL REEL THE REST OF THE LINE INTO THE BOAT AND ON THE END OF IT IS A MASSIVE FISH. EVERYONE PANICS. THE HUGE FISH IS FLAPPING IN THE MIDDLE SECTION OF THE BOAT. NEIL IS THE ONLY ONE WHO REMAINS CALM.

JAY   Wooah

WILL   Jesus Christ.

SIMON   Oh my.

WILL   How the hell has that happened?

NEIL   Dunno. It didn't have any bait on it.

JAY   Get it out.

NEIL   It's all right. It's just a fish.

WILL   It's a fucking terrifying massive fish Neil. Get rid of it.

JAY   It's shit itself.

NEIL   It's all right.

JAY   Fuck that. We're in serious trouble here.

NEIL   Oh what?

JAY GRABS THE FLARE GUN FROM UNDER THE SEATS.

WILL   That's only for emergencies. For emergencies!

JAY FIRES ONE OFF HIGH INTO THE SKY. THEY ALL STAND BACK AND LOOK AT IT.

WILL   Oh brilliant.

NEIL   Oh my gosh.

SIMON   That looks warm.

WILL   Why the fuck did you do that?

JAY   To get the sea police out?

WILL   And say what? Help, we've caught a fish? And we're already in the harbour. What are they going to do with us, tow us four feet closer to shore?

(THEY SEE THE LIFEBOAT STATION METRES AWAY)

JAY   (POINTING AT THE FISH) What if it's a shark?

WILL   It's not a shark Jay.

JAY   Oh get it out Neil.

NEIL   I'd better kill it. It's the kindest thing to do. It won't survive back in the sea now.

NEIL LEANS DOWN TO THE FLAPPING FISH. HE LOOKS A PICTURE OF COMPASSION, UNTIL HE VIOLENTLY PUNCHES THE FISH IN THE HEAD. SEVERAL TIMES. IT STILL FLAPS ABOUT A BIT SO HE HAS TO GO FOR ROUND TWO. THE

OTHERS ARE MAKING GROANING NOISES AT NEIL'S BARBARIC MERCY-KILLING. EVENTUALLY THE FISH IS DEAD.

WILL Well that was a much more dignified end for him.

SIMON You just punched a fish to death.

NEIL Now we can take it back and eat it.

JAY I'm not eating that; it's come out the fucking sea.

WILL INSPECTS THE ENGINE, TRIES TO START IT AGAIN BUT CAN'T.

SIMON I'm cold. Mummy, can you get the potty.

WILL Stay with it Simon, we'll get you help. Oh fuck. Fuck it.

LAUREN IS ON THE QUAYSIDE.

LAUREN Are you OK Will?

WILL Fine thanks. Be back for you in a minute.

LAUREN You know you've sent a flare up?

WILL Yep, thanks Lauren. Won't be a minute.

LAUREN Is that a fish?

WILL (LOSING IT NOW) Yes Lauren, it's a fucking fish. Give me a minute.

SIMON Are we going to have to swim back? It's very cold in there.

JAY We'll just row back. On holiday in Spain one year, me and a mate took a pedalo out and we went to Africa.

WILL Do you think you could spare us the bullshit for one minute while I try to figure out how not to die at sea.

SIMON Oh Carli's there, look. Hi Carli.

AS HE WAVES, THE COAT WRAPPED ROUND HIM FALLS OFF AND HE'S NAKED AGAIN, APART FROM A SOCK THAT COVERS HIS COCK.

JAY Oh Neil, you put a sock on it!

SIMON Is it a bit draughty?

WILL   He's in trouble. We've got to huddle round him till the lifeboat gets here, and then we have to explain that we called them away from their proper jobs because we caught a fish.

NEIL   Come here mate.

THEY GO TO HUG SIMON.

JAY   Uh, I can see his knob head.

SIMON   If anything I'm colder than before.

WILL   Well huddle in closer then.

JAY   No one better find out about this.

WILL   What, apart from everyone over there?

THEY ARE INDEED NOT VERY FAR AWAY. WE CAN FAINTLY HEAR SOME JEERING AND LAUGHING FROM THE HARBOUR WALL. WE CUT TO A WIDE SHOT OF THE BOAT. WE CAN SEE THE FOUR BOYS HUDDLING TOGETHER.

NEIL   Now we just wait for the sea police.

——————— SCENE 16 ———————

EXT. HARBOUR

WE SEE THE LIFEBOAT MEN HELPING THE BOYS UP THE STEPS BY THE HARBOUR WALL. SIMON HAS ONE OF THOSE FOIL BLANKETS ROUND HIM. ALL OF THE PUPILS, MOST NOTABLY CARLI AND LAUREN, ARE STANDING ASHORE WATCHING. MR GILBERT AND MR KENNEDY ARE THERE, AND A SMALL CROWD OF LOCALS HAS GATHERED TO LAUGH TOO.

AS HUMILIATIONS GO, THIS IS PRETTY SPECIALIST.

SIMON   I'm worried this might look a bit weird.

WILL   No it's totally fine. We just all went out for a boat ride about twenty minutes ago and now we've been dragged back to shore, the boat's covered in fish brains and you're totally naked.

SIMON   And Carli and Lauren are going to think this is pretty cool, right?

WILL   Oh yeah. Pretty cool.

WILL V/O   *The definition of a field trip is an educational journey allowing students to observe events outside their usual experience, and so in that sense, Swanage was a complete success . . .*

. . . we observed my brilliant Star Wars *impression . . .*

SHOT OF WILL DOING HIS YODA IMPRESSION.

WILL   Feisty one you are.

WILL V/O   *. . . Jay getting slapped, Neil punching a fish and Simon's penis in a sock. And after all that observation, we had learnt one thing – turns out Mr Kennedy is a paedophile . . .*

BACK AT THE HARBOUR, MR KENNEDY STEPS FORWARD WITH A TOWEL WHICH HE DRAPES OVER NEIL'S SHOULDERS, THEN STARTS TO DRY HIM BEFORE MR GILBERT LEADS HIM AWAY.

NEIL   It's all right sir, I didn't even get wet.

MR GILBERT   John.

WILL V/O   *. . . but at least some good came of it. Lauren had to move away shortly afterwards and Simon never saw her again.*

Episode 2

————— 'Work Experience' —————

Another episode that came out of our trying to think 'What are universal experiences at that age?' Greg Davies and Robert Popper, again, were particularly useful for this story. I think Greg mentioned that when he worked as a teacher work-ex placements often got mixed up, but in general they did nothing to rectify them. And Robert told us a story of a friend of his who had been mercilessly bullied during his work experience, culminating in him being thrown in a duck pond. Which is not, I think, by anyone's standards a necessary part of learning about the world of work.

Another universal theme that we liked, and certainly remembered from our youth, was the idea of there being a group of local 'hard lads' and the potential nightmare of thinking that one of them was going to beat you up. I got in a few scrapes, mainly of my own making and crushingly embarrassing to look back on, but Damon once had a full-blown after-school fight. I know it's nothing to be proud of, but I can't imagine the terror of knowing that at the end of the day you had to have a fight with a 'hard lad'. Damon claims he won, but there's no way of checking. And anyway, violence is never the answer.

 SCENE 1 ————

INT. SCHOOL COMMON ROOM

WILL V/O *Wouldn't it be good to know exactly how unpopular you are with the opposite sex compared to your classmates? Well luckily for me someone invented Valentine's Day. My favourite annual humiliation.*

THE BOYS ARE IN THE SIXTH FORM COMMON ROOM. IT'S FAIRLY BUSY, BUT THERE'S NO TEACHER, SO THEY ARE IN VERY RELAXED POSITIONS. JAY IS SITTING WITH A PILE OF VALENTINE'S CARDS.

JAY (READING ALOUD) 'Roses are red, violets are blue, your dong is massive, I want to blow you. Love from your secret slut'.

NEIL I didn't get none, I can't believe you got so many.

WILL Yes, it is hard to believe.

JAY Dear Jay, I've just baked you a finger pie, why don't you cum' – spelt c-u-m – 'and taste it'.

NEIL Oh mate, that's so horny. Who do you think that's from?

SIMON Your dad?

NEIL Yeah, funny.

WILL Let me look at these.

WILL GRABS THE PILE OF CARDS AND READS ONE OUT.

WILL 'Jay you massive stud, please please spaff on my tits. From your Valentine's bitch. PS and on my face'.

NEIL That one's my favourite, I like the way she remembered the face.

WILL It's just funny how all these cards seem to be in the same scrawly handwriting. Your secret admirers are all very young or have severe learning difficulties. Which I admit is a possibility.

JAY   Nah, the handwriting's bad because they were strumming one out as they wrote them.

SIMON   It's not you writing them with your left hand then?

JAY   You lot are just jealous because I got loads and you got none.

WILL   Oh I got a card.

SIMON   If it's from your nan it doesn't count.

WILL   I didn't get any then.

SIMON   Well I actually did get a card. A proper one.

JAY   Total bollocks.

SIMON   Yeah? What do you call this then?

SIMON PRODUCES A CARD FROM HIS RUCKSACK.

WILL   Interesting.

NEIL   Wow. Who's that from?

SIMON   Hannah Fields in the year below.

NEIL   Sniff it to see if she rubbed her fanny on it.

WILL   Neil!

BEAT. SIMON LOOKS AT NEIL. THEN SNIFFS THE CARD.

SIMON   Nah, just a bit of perfume.

WILL   So what are you going to do about it?

SIMON   Nothing. Apart from making sure Carli doesn't find out.

JAY   I think she'll be too busy sucking on her boyfriend's knob to notice.

SIMON   Shut up.

JAY   What? All I'm saying is he'll have his cock right deep in her gob and then in her vadge. Out the vadge and straight back into the gob.

SIMON   Thanks.

NEIL   Oh yeah, that reminds me.

NEIL HANDS WILL A VALENTINE'S CARD.

NEIL   Give this to your mum for us.

WILL   Are you serious? Oh you are.

NEIL   Don't tell her who it's from though.

WILL   No, course not. Anything else Neil? Would you like me to ask her out for you?

NEIL   Would you?

WILL   Um, let me think about that. Would I? No. No I fucking wouldn't.

MR GILBERT ENTERS. THE KIDS STRAIGHTEN THEMSELVES UP.

MR GILBERT   Morning. And shut up.

HE WALKS AROUND THE ROOM HANDING OUT A PHOTOCOPIED SHEET THAT SHOWS EVERYONE WHERE THEY WILL BE ASSIGNED FOR THEIR WORK EXPERIENCE.

MR GILBERT   Right everyone, your work experience placements have now been finalised. And as 99 per cent of you left it to the careers officer, I don't want to hear any whingeing about where you are heading.

WILL FLIPS THROUGH THE SHEET UNTIL HE FINDS WHAT HE WAS LOOKING FOR. ONLY IT'S CLEARLY NOT WHAT HE EXPECTED AND WE SEE HIS FACE DROP AND HAND RAISE.

WILL   Sir, there seems to be some mistake.

MR GILBERT   Oh? Is the mistake that you have chosen to ignore me saying 'no whingeing'?

WILL   Ha. No sir, it says here I'm going to work in a garage?

MR GILBERT   Yes.

WILL   Come on, me a garage? Me? Does that seem likely?

MR GILBERT   What's your point McKenzie?

WILL   I wrote to the local paper, sir. To shadow a journalist there. Maybe even write a few pieces myself.

MR GILBERT   All right, let me have a look. I don't get paid extra for this you know. OK, it says here that Sutherland is expected at the news-paper, case closed.

WILL   Well then there's clearly been some sort of mix-up. I don't mean to be rude, but look at him. No offence.

NEIL   None taken.

MR GILBERT   What did you put down as your first choice, Sutherland?

NEIL   Airplane driver.

MR GILBERT   And that is?

NEIL   Someone who drives planes.

MR GILBERT   You mean a pilot.

NEIL   Do I?

MR GILBERT   What was your second choice?

NEIL   Working with cars.

MR GILBERT   Right. Have you ever wanted to work at a newspaper?

NEIL   No sir.

MR GILBERT   Have you ever read a newspaper?

NEIL   Not really.

MR GILBERT   Ok, does seem there's been some sort of mistake here somewhere.

WILL   Well that's OK, mistakes happen. So shall I go to the paper tomorrow?

MR GILBERT   No, you go to the garage. It's all booked.

WILL   Is this a joke?

MR GILBERT   Do I make a lot of jokes?

WILL   But sir . . .

MR GILBERT   I can't change the placements.

WILL   Can't or won't?

MR GILBERT   You pick, it's the same result.

NEIL HAS HIS HAND UP.

MR GILBERT   Sutherland?

NEIL   Does this mean I won't be driving any planes?

———— SCENE 2 ————

INT. SCHOOL CORRIDOR

WILL   Well this is a fuck-up. What kind of experience am I going to get at a garage? Apart from a depressing working-class one.

NEIL   At least you get to look at all them horny calendars.

JAY   Why do you want to work on a paper for anyway? I thought you wanted to go into the family business?

WILL   Which is?

JAY   Prostitution.

WILL   Yep, nice one.

SIMON   Look, it'll be shit anyway. The clue's in the name, 'work' experience.

JAY   Oh well it won't be shit at my dad's firm Si. We'll have a right laugh. When I worked there last summer I spent every day jumping JCBs over cement mixers.

WILL   Well that's a lie.

JAY   And got paid a grand at the end of the week.

WILL   Another lie.

JAY   Well, I had a wank this morning thinking about your mum's tits. Is that a lie?

WILL   I hope so.

JAY   It's not.

WILL   Oh good.

WE SEE TWO YEAR-SEVEN KIDS WALKING TOWARDS OUR BOYS.

SIMON, WHO HAS NOT REALLY NOTICED THEM AND IS STILL ENJOYING JAY'S JOKE, BUTTS SHOULDERS WITH ONE OF THE KIDS (DANNY). DESPITE HAVING QUITE HARD-LOOKING FACES, THEY ARE STILL KIDS AND ONLY ABOUT 5FT TALL.

SIMON   Sorry mate.

DANNY   I'm not your fucking mate.

SIMON   He's touchy.

JAY   Yeah, it's probably 'cos he's such a short arse.

THEY BOTH SORT OF LAUGH. WE SEE DANNY AND HIS MATE STANDING IN THE CORRIDOR SHOUTING BACK AT SIMON.

DANNY   What d'you say?

SIMON   What?

DANNY'S MATE   He's taking the piss Danny.

DANNY   Fucking do you.

SIMON   (WALKING AWAY AND TALKING TO THE OTHERS) Yeah whatever.

IN THE BACKGROUND WE SEE DANNY AND HIS MATE TURN AND CARRY ON THEIR WAY.

DANNY   Wanker.

SIMON   What was his problem?

JAY   Don't cry Simon.

SIMON   Yeah, good one.

WILL SPOTS CHARLOTTE DISAPPEARING ROUND A CORRIDOR.

WILL   Um, catch you up in a bit.

HE RUNS OFF.

JAY   Oh that's right, run after her, that's not creepy.

——— SCENE 3 ———

INT. SCHOOL CORRIDOR

WILL V/O *I may not have received any Valentine's cards . . . but that didn't mean I hadn't sent any.*

WILL Charlotte.

WILL (LOUDER) Charlotte.

WILL CATCHES UP WITH CHARLOTTE.

CHARLOTTE Oh hello.

WILL Happy Valentine's Day. Did you get any cards?

CHARLOTTE Yeah, maybe ten?

WILL Ten?

Yeah, yeah, me too.

But did you get any flowers?

CHARLOTTE I think you know I did. It was really sweet, and I was going to say that if you're not doing anything maybe we could hang out this Friday night?

WILL I think I'm free. Yep, yes I am.

CHARLOTTE OK, well, I'm working behind the bar at this local Valentine's disco thing. It's under-eighteens, so it might be a bit lame, but if you fancied popping along to keep me company?

WILL A date?

CHARLOTTE No Will, not a date. Just two friends hanging out.

WILL Great. See you on Friday then. It's a date.

CHARLOTTE No, it's not a date.

WILL Cool.

──────── SCENE 4 ────────

EXT./INT. GARAGE

WILL V/O *She said it wasn't a date, but we both knew it was a date. Before that, though, I had to make the most of my new pointless, shitty manual job.*

WILL LOOKS AT THE EXTERIOR OF THE GARAGE AND SHUDDERS. HE WALKS IN CARRYING HIS BRIEFCASE. TWO MEN ARE BUSY WORKING, WEARING BLUE OVERALLS. THEY LOOK UP AT WILL AS HE WALKS IN. HE SMILES AT THEM. THEY IMMEDIATELY TURN BACK TO WHAT THEY WERE DOING.

WILL Hello! Will McKenzie, I'm here for work experience.

SUDDENLY FROM THE OFFICE ANOTHER SLIGHTLY OLDER MAN (JIM) COMES BOUNDING OVER WITH A HUGE SMILE.

JIM Hello, you must be Will, great to meet you. I'm Jim, this here's Wolfie and Steve.

WILL Hi Jim, hi Steve, hello Wolf.

WOLFIE Wolfie.

WILL Wolfie? Right, gotcha.

JIM You'll have a right old laugh here, long as you don't mind a bit of the blue talk. You're not a poof are you?

WILL No.

JIM Not a problem if you are, just be a bit harder to join in some of the banter. So is there any part of car mechanics you're especially interested in as it goes?

WILL To be honest none of it, as it goes.

JIM More interested in bikes is it?

WILL No, the media. Or law. Look, no offence, but I'm never going to work in a place like this.

JIM Place like this?

WILL   You know, a place like this. Manual, dirty. Not stupid exactly, but not academic by a long chalk. It's not that I am better than this, it's just that I am much cleverer than you need to be to work here.

JIM   Steve here has got a BTEC.

WILL   Exactly. Look, I suspect the mix-up will be sorted today, and I'll be gone by tomorrow.

JIM   I see, well you don't mind helping out today then?

WILL   No, course not. Just the once, eh?

JIM   Right then Chomdley-Warner, first job is that we need some stuff picking up from the suppliers.

WILL   Fine. I'll just get a pen and paper then. Great.

JIM   OK, we need two tins of tartan paint.

WILL   Tartan paint times two.

JIM   Spirit-level bubbles.

WILL   Bubbles for spirit-level.

JIM   Do you need anything Wolfie?

WOLFIE   Yeah. Ask him for a reach around.

WILL   A reach around.

JIM   Don't forget you really need that.

WILL   Fine. So it's two tins of tartan paint, some bubbles for spirit-levels and a reach around.

JIM AND STEVE ARE STIFLING THEIR LAUGHTER. WOLFIE IS LAUGHING.

JIM   You might as well ask for a long weight while you're there.

WILL   Great.

HE TAKES A COUPLE OF STEPS TOWARDS THE DOOR, THEN STOPS AND TURNS AROUND.

WILL   Ah, this is a joke, isn't it?

JIM   What?

WILL   These items are jokes, aren't they? They're not real things, are they? They don't exist.

JIM   Dunno what you mean.

WILL   Now I know that these initiation ceremonies exist in certain types of workplace, and don't get me wrong, I enjoy the camaraderie, but you'll have to get up pretty early to fool me.

JIM   Nope, fair enough, you've caught us out.

WOLFIE   Yep, fair cop.

JIM   Too sharp for us. I tell you what, why don't we initiate you with a pint at lunch instead?

WILL   Great.

JIM   We'll go to the Crown. The barmaid in there has got a smashing pair of tits.

WILL   O-K.

─────── SCENE 5 ───────

INT. LOCAL NEWSPAPER OFFICE

WILL V/O   *So while I was getting a City & Guilds in tits, Neil was at the newspaper happily wasting the opportunity of my lifetime.*

A MAN IN HIS FORTIES (TOBY), IS SITTING AT HIS DESK TYPING ON A PC. SOMEONE POPS THEIR HEAD ROUND THE CORNER.

WOMAN   Toby, your work experience is here.

TOBY   Oh. Fine, alright.

TOBY WALKS IN TO THE RECEPTION AREA OF THE OFFICE (JUST ROUND THE CORNER REALLY) AND NEIL IS SITTING THERE.

TOBY   Hi, you must be Neil, I'm Toby.

NEIL   Alright.

TOBY   So, tell me, what are you looking to get out of this assignment Neil?

NEIL Oh don't worry, I won't steal nothing.

TOBY Ha.

TOBY SEES THAT NEIL ISN'T LAUGHING.

TOBY No, what I meant was, is there anything specifically you'd like to do while you're with us, or an area of journalism you are particularly interested in?

NEIL Nah, not really.

TOBY Right. And do you have any questions you'd like to ask me about anything?

NEIL How long's my lunch hour?

TOBY An hour.

——— SCENE 6 ———

EXT. CARTWRIGHT'S PLANT HIRE YARD

WILL V/O *Meanwhile, Jay really had arranged some great work experience for Simon. Freezing his arse off at a disgusting plant-hire yard.*

SIMON AND JAY ARE LUGGING BAGS OF RUBBLE INTO A SKIP.

SIMON This is shit. I don't want to do this for a living.

JAY Ah that's all right, we'll be able to drive the diggers soon I reckon.

JAY'S DAD (TERRY CARTWRIGHT) SWINGS HIS HEAD OUT OF THE PORTAKABIN AND ADDRESSES THEM.

TERRY CARTWRIGHT Oi Jay, what you stopped for? This is meant to be work experience, not standing-around-being-a-useless-twat experience. You don't need any experience at that, you're the expert.

JAY Sorry Dad, we've only stopped for a minute, this is well knackering.

TERRY CARTWRIGHT Well you'd better get used to it, because with your brains you'll be fucking lucky to get a job throwing shit into a skip.

SIMON   This isn't exactly how you described it Jay.

TERRY CARTWRIGHT   Get many Valentine's cards this year then Simon?

SIMON   Just the one.

TERRY CARTWRIGHT   That's one more than Jay's ever got.

JAY   I got plenty.

TERRY CARTWRIGHT   Don't worry son, there's a girl out there for you somewhere. You just need to find a desperate bird that likes the smell of BO and blokes with tiny cocks. Now get back to work, I ain't paying you to sit on your scrawny arse all day.

SIMON   Nice.

JAY'S DAD GOES BACK INSIDE. JUST AT THAT MOMENT WE SEE NEIL WALK INTO THE YARD.

NEIL   Alright.

SIMON   What are you doing here? I thought you were on work experience over at the newspaper.

NEIL   I have been. They let me go home at lunch.

JAY   You jammy bastard.

NEIL   Oi Si, what's all this I hear about you having a fight with Danny Moore?

SIMON   What? Who's Danny Moore?

NEIL   He's been mouthing off about how he's gonna do you in.

SIMON   Who is he? I don't even know who he is.

NEIL   That kid you bumped into and then called a short arse.

SIMON   That was Jay.

JAY   Oh well you'll have to go and knock him out now Si, teach him a lesson.

SIMON   Neil, if you see him just tell him he's made a mistake.

NEIL   I'm not getting involved. I heard he's from a well-hard family in Northwood. His brother did time.

JAY   Ooh Northwood, been nice knowing you Si.

SIMON   What's this? My dad's bigger than your dad? What are we? Twelve?

NEIL   I think he is twelve actually.

JAY   You're not scared are you Si?

SIMON   No, it's just I'm not going to look cool beating up a kid.

JAY   And you couldn't.

SIMON   Yes I fucking could. Now can we just leave it? I'm not fighting anyone.

JAY AND NEIL MAKE A CHICKEN NOISE.

SIMON   Oh yeah, nice one, mature.

——— SCENE 7 ———

EXT. THE CROWN PUB

WILL V/O   *Compared to Simon, my first day was turning out OK. After a morning of pretending cars were broken and overcharging middle-class women, we had bonded over a pint.*

WILL IS WALKING OUT OF THE PUB WITH THE MECHANICS BEHIND HIM.

WILL   Well, thanks for that. That was a much more civilised way to welcome me. It's a shame we won't get to do it again, but as I said— what? Wait—

HE IS INTERRUPTED AS THEY HAVE GRABBED HIM. ONE OF THEM IS PULLING HIS JUMPER AND T-SHIRT UP OVER HIS HEAD SO HIS ARMS ARE TRAPPED AND WE CAN'T SEE HIS FACE, THEN TIES THE ARMS SO HE CAN'T MOVE BUT IS FLAILING. THE OTHER ONE TAKES HIS TROUSERS OFF.

WILL   What? Oh no, a kidnap. What are you, the cockney Al-Qaeda?

LAUGHING, THEY PICK WILL UP (NOW JUST IN HIS PANTS) AND POP HIM IN THE BOOT OF THE CAR THEY HAVE DRIVEN OVER IN.

JIM   Don't shit yourself, we're just going for a little drive.

JIM SHUTS THE BOOT.

SCENE 8

EXT. POND

WILL IS TAKEN OUT OF THE BOOT NEAR A POND AND IS THROWN INTO THE
POND IN HIS PANTS.

STEVE/WOLFIE   Hello mate.

WILL   Come on guys, is this really necessary? What about my allergies. Let's talk about this. Please – my allergies.

JIM   Wasn't expecting that, was you mastermind? See you tomorrow.

WILL MANAGES TO DRAG HIMSELF OUT OF THE POND.

SCENE 9

INT. MR GILBERT'S OFFICE

WILL V/O   *Institutionalised bullying wasn't quite the work experience
I had in mind. But I knew how to deal with bullies. I got my mum to
tell the teacher . . .*

MR GILBERT IS WITH NEIL'S DAD (KEVIN SUTHERLAND) AND WILL'S MUM (POLLY
McKENZIE), WHO ARE SEATED ON THE OPPOSITE SIDE OF THE DESK. GILBERT
LAUGHS OUT LOUD. POLLY McKENZIE LOOKS AT HIM.

POLLY McKENZIE   I was hoping you would be able to do something
about it Mr Gilbert.

MR GILBERT   I'm sorry.

KEVIN SUTHERLAND   I just wonder what he said to them?

POLLY McKENZIE   I don't think he said anything Kevin.

MR GILBERT   Oh come on, we both know Will, he must have said
something.

POLLY McKENZIE   He had to walk back through the town centre sopping wet and barely clothed Mr Gilbert.

MR GILBERT   Ha.

POLLY McKENZIE   I'd hoped you'd take this more seriously. He wrote to the paper especially to get work experience and instead I'm picking frogspawn out of his underpants.

MR GILBERT   Would you excuse me. Just, just for a second.

MR GILBERT LEAVES AND AS HE SHUTS THE DOOR BEHIND HIM WE CAN HEAR HIM LAUGHING OUT LOUD. THERE'S A BEAT WHERE POLLY AND KEVIN LOOK AT EACH OTHER AS THEY ARE BOTH SITTING IN THE SMALL OFFICE. MR GILBERT RETURNS.

MR GILBERT   Look, I don't want it to seem as if I'm passing the buck, but it is really up to their employers. I'll ask if they'll consider swapping the students, but I can't promise anything. Now if you'll excuse me, I do have a meeting to attend to.

MR GILBERT LEAVES AND AS HE WALKS OUT OF THE DOOR HE MAKES THE UNIVERSAL HAND SIGNAL FOR 'WELL, I HAVE WASHED MY HANDS OF THAT ONE'.

KEVIN SUTHERLAND   Oh what a pickle. I'm not sure I should send Neil to the garage. Those men sound like brutes.

POLLY McKENZIE   Oh I think it was just high jinks.

KEVIN SUTHERLAND   What, three dirty men throwing a young naked boy into water? The mind boggles.

POLLY McKENZIE   I never said Will was naked.

KEVIN SUTHERLAND   Oh, I thought you did.

WILL V/O   . . . *um, not quite the outcome I'd hoped for . . .*

. . . Neil's dad imagining me naked.

──────── SCENE 10 ────────

INT. NEIL'S LIVING ROOM

WILL V/O   *When it comes to love, they say a gentleman never tells, but unfortunately I wasn't a gentleman. I was a twat.*

THE FOUR BOYS ARE PLAYING PRO EVO SOCCER ON THE PLAYSTATION 3 IN NEIL'S FRONT ROOM. NEIL SCORES A LATE WINNER.

WILL   Guess who got themselves a date with Charlotte Hinchcliffe.

JAY   Mark Donovan?

WILL   Nope.

NEIL   I bet it is Donovan, he's probably balls deep in her right now.

WILL   No, the answer is me.

SIMON   No way.

WILL   Yes way. Of sorts. Of sorts way.

SIMON   How?

WILL   I have no idea. Honestly I don't, and I'm not going to stop and ask her. For some reason she likes me at the moment so I'm going to do everything I can to try to keep it that way.

SIMON   Sounds like a good plan.

JAY   So when is it then?

WILL   What?

NEIL   The date.

WILL   Friday night.

NEIL   What we up to Friday night?

SIMON   Same as every Friday night, nothing.

NEIL   Maybe we could go.

WILL   In what world would I want you to come along?

JAY   It's not for you, it's for us. It'll be funny to watch you fuck it up again.

NEIL   Yeah, you might cry.

WILL   Well thanks for the vote of confidence, but you won't want to come along as I'm meeting her at this under-eighteens night she's working at. It will be very uncool, even for us.

NEIL   Sounds all right to me.

SIMON   At least we'll definitely get in.

WILL   No, no, no. You honestly won't like it.

JAY   We might even get some.

SIMON   Won't they be a bit young?

JAY   Nah. If there's grass on the pitch, play ball.

SIMON   Right, and what if there isn't?

JAY   By the time you find out it'll be too late anyway.

WILL   Surely you've got something better to do this weekend than watch me try to get off with Charlotte?

BEAT AS NO ONE ANSWERS.

WILL   Great. No? Fine. See you there then.

 SCENE 11

INT. GARAGE

WILL V/O   *So before my date with Charlotte, and it was a date, I had to endure one last day with the savages. Although I was pleasantly surprised to find Jim and Wolfie in serious debate.*

WILL WALKS IN TO THE GARAGE. JIM AND WOLFIE ARE MAKING TEA, AND THERE ARE A COUPLE OF PAGE THREE TYPE CALENDARS ON THE WALL. THEY SEEM TO BE FAIRLY ANIMATED.

JIM   Alright Will, you'll like this, we're just having 'a discussion'.

WILL   Oh really?

JIM Yeah. Which titties would you spunk over? The pert little ones, or the big and bouncy. Right old handful, plenty to play with.

WILL They both look nice.

JIM Better than anything you'll ever get, mate.

WILL All right then, I'd spunk over the big ones, and they aren't better than I'd get actually.

JIM Bollocks. Here Steve, speccy here—

WILL I've told you about that . . .

JIM —reckons he's had better than that.

WILL I have.

JIM Fuck off, you're a virgin.

WOLFIE Classic virgin.

WILL Well that's where you're wrong. I did it last year. With a girl I'm seeing tonight actually.

JIM Yeah, sure.

WILL Yep. She's fit, she's older than me and she goes like a porn star.

JIM Oh right.

WILL Yep, and she's got massive titties and I, well, I fucked her hard and all night long.

JIM What are you and this dirty little horn bucket up to this weekend then? I might come and check her out.

WILL Going to an under-eighteens disco where she works, so unfortunately you won't be able to.

WOLFIE I could go.

WILL What?

WOLFIE I could go. I'm seventeen.

WILL You're *seventeen*? You're seventeen?

WOLFIE Yeah, I just look older.

WILL   There's looking older and then there's that. You look about thirty.

JIM   Lovely. Wolfie'll pop by and check out this tart you've been boning then.

WILL   Good.

JIM   Maybe Wolfie will pull her.

WILL   Except he won't do that because she loves me.

JIM   She loves you? Ooooooh, think I'm going to cry.

WILL   I mean she loves to, erm, fuck me.

JIM   Yeah, course she does.

——————— SCENE 12 ———————

INT. CIVIC HALL

WILL V/O   *That evening at the civic hall, I hoped Neil would enlighten me about what I'd be up to next week. Admittedly he'd never enlightened me about anything ever before, but you never know.*

WILL, SIMON, JAY AND NEIL GO IN. IT'S BUSY, BUT THEY ARE COMFORTABLY THE TALLEST THERE. THE MAJORITY OF THE PEOPLE ARE THIRTEEN OR MAYBE FOURTEEN.

WILL   So, how's the newspaper Neil? Have they asked you to write anything?

NEIL   Nah, nothing boring like that. I'm on the internet most of the day. This afternoon I smashed some old desks up in a skip and then they let me go home at four.

SIMON   Are we the oldest here?

WILL   Possibly.

SIMON   It's even more shit than I knew it would be.

WILL   I honestly don't know why you came.

JAY   To see you get blown out by Charlotte Titties again.

WILL   Please try not to fuck this up for me. Charlotte actually asked me here, so there's a chance, admittedly a very slim chance, that she wants to pull me.

SIMON   Or maybe she needs a mechanic to service her car.

WILL   Good one.

JAY   I'd service her all right. I'd slide my dipstick in right deep—

WILL   Well, thanks for coming guys, really appreciate it. I'm going to go and find Charlotte.

JAY   Up to you. At least it looks like there is some tidy minge here.

WILL   Yes, it's tidy because there's no hair on it.

———— SCENE 13 ————

INT. CIVIC HALL

JAY, SIMON AND NEIL ARE WANDERING ABOUT A BIT. IT IS VERY CLEAR THAT THEY ARE OLDER THAN THE MAJORITY OF THE KIDS HERE.

NEIL   Oi Si, Hannah Fields is over there.

NEIL POINTS OVER AT SOME GIRLS, A COUPLE OF WHOM SEEM TO BE ABOUT THE SAME AGE AS THEM.

JAY   Is that who your Valentine's was from?

SIMON   Oh yeah, shit. Oh, she looks quite fit actually.

JAY   Right, I'll go over and tell her that you fancy her then.

SIMON   No, hang on.

JAY   Why?

SIMON   Well, you going over and telling her that I fancy her seems a bit, y'know, childish.

JAY   When in Rome mate. That's how you've got to play it with younger girls. You go over— Shit, she's coming over here.

THE BLONDE GIRL (HANNAH) IS INDEED HEADING THEIR WAY.

HANNAH   So did you get my Valentine's card then?

SIMON   Oh yeah, great. Thank you.

HANNAH   Do you want a drink?

SIMON   I've got one thanks.

HANNAH   No, I mean a proper drink.

SHE GOES INTO HER BAG AND PULLS OUT A HALF-LITRE BOTTLE OF VODKA. IT'S HALF DRUNK.

SIMON   Oh, right. Yeah, thanks.

SHE POURS HIM A LARGE SPLASH, TAKES HIS DRINK AND DOWNS IT.

HANNAH   You're fit.

SIMON   Sorry?

HANNAH   Forget it.

SHE GRABS SIMON BY THE FACE AND SNOGS HIM. HE LOOKS SHOCKED BUT EXCITED. SO DO NEIL AND JAY.

HANNAH   Come on.

SHE TAKES HIM OVER TO THE SIDE OF THE HALL AND STARTS AGGRESSIVELY SNOGGING HIM.

HANNAH   I think you are well sexy. I used to stare at you in assembly.

SIMON   (A LITTLE TENTATIVE BECAUSE HE'S BEING MAULED A BIT BY THIS GIRL) Right.

HANNAH   Oooh, you're so horny. Tongue me.

SIMON   Um, how old are you?

HANNAH GRABS HIS HEAD AND JUST STARTS SNOGGING HIM.

CUT TO WILL WALKING OVER FROM THE BAR TO JOIN JAY AND NEIL. THEY ARE LOOKING OVER AT THE SNOG.

WILL   Blimey, that didn't take long.

JAY   Well compared to you and Charlotte anything's quick.

WILL   Softly softly, catchey monkey.

NEIL   I didn't know you spoke Spanish.

JAY   See, I told you this was a great place to get your fingers stinky.

NEIL   Oh my God, she's going for his cock.

CUT TO SIMON AND HANNAH. HANNAH HAS NOW UNTUCKED SIMON'S SHIRT, AND SEEMS TO BE FUMBLING WITH HIS FLIES.

SIMON   Oooh, what you doing? Should we go somewhere more private?

HANNAH   Oooh, I want you.

SIMON   Right. Yeah. No. Careful, no one's touched that before, it might go off.

HANNAH   OOOH good.

SIMON   Oh yes. Crikey, careful.

CUT TO JAY, WILL AND NEIL, WHO ARE WATCHING.

WILL   Are they allowed to do that in here?

JAY   Fuck me, she's going to wank him off. The jammy git's pulled an experienced cock handler.

WILL   Or someone so hugely inexperienced she thinks this is the best way to pull an older boy.

JAY   Either way, it's a win-win situation.

WILL   It's not really though, is it.

WE SEE JAY, WILL AND NEIL'S PERSPECTIVE OF SIMON AND HANNAH. SHE IS KIND OF LEANING ON HIM AND MOVING HER HAND AROUND UNDER HIS SHIRT, GRABBING AT HIS CROTCH AREA. SIMON IS LOOKING OVER HER SHOULDER AT THE BOYS, MAKING ALL SORTS OF FACES - SOME THAT SAY 'WHAT'S HAPPENING?', SOME THAT SAY 'OOOH THAT'S NICE', AND SOME THAT SAY 'FUCK, THAT HURT'.

JAY   Thanks to me we are watching Simon get wanked off.

WILL   Yes, well, we really do have a lot to thank you for.

BEAT.

JAY   Getting a bit weird now.

NEIL   I don't like it when he makes eye contact.

WILL   None of us do Neil.

ALL OF A SUDDEN AND OUT OF NOWHERE, DANNY MOORE GOES PILING INTO SIMON, KNOCKING HIM TO THE FLOOR. AS SIMON'S TROUSERS ARE PRACTICALLY ROUND HIS KNEES, HE FALLS OVER ONTO HIS ARSE. SIMON DESPERATELY COVERS HIS COCK WITH ONE HAND AND TRIES TO PULL UP HIS TROUSERS WITH THE OTHER. DANNY PUTS THE BOOT IN WHILE SIMON IS ON THE FLOOR. SIMON YELPS.

DANNY   Call me short arse now! Come on then, you fucking coward.

DANNY PUTS THE BOOT IN TO SIMON ONE MORE TIME, BEFORE A BOUNCER COMES OVER AND DRAGS HIM OFF. THIS DOESN'T TAKE LONG AS HE IS A CHILD.

HANNAH   Oh please, not his face.

DANNY   (SHOUTING OVER BOUNCER'S SHOULDER) I'm going to fucking do you mate. Northwood are in the house, you're fucking dead.

HANNAH   How embarrassing.

HANNAH LEAVES.

SIMON GETS TO HIS FEET. WILL, NEIL AND JAY HAVE COME OVER. NEIL IS LAUGHING.

NEIL   That was brilliant.

SIMON   Was it?

JAY   Fucking hilarious, he totally did you.

SIMON   Have they chucked him out?

JAY   Doubt it, not gonna chuck him out for that. That was just a scuffle.

SIMON   He kicked me in the cock.

JAY   Good shot to get you in the cock.

SIMON   What happened to Hannah?

JAY Um, I think you blew it when you got knocked out by a twelve-year-old.

SIMON I fucking slipped.

NEIL Uh-oh, he's talking to a load of Northwood lads.

WE SEE DANNY TALKING TO A HARD-LOOKING SET OF LADS.

SIMON What?

NEIL And they don't look twelve to be fair. Fucking hell Si, you muppet.

NEIL We're so dead.

WILL What do you mean we're dead? That should be the end of it. Simon has taken a beating, a child's honour has been restored . . .

SIMON I didn't take a beating.

JAY Yeah you did.

NEIL This is Northwood we're talking about. It's not the end of it, it's the start.

SIMON Fuck. What are we going to do?

WILL Shall I get Charlotte?

SIMON Why, is she hard?

WILL No Simon, she'll be able to get them thrown out. I'll go and find her, you lot go and hide somewhere.

SIMON Hide?

WILL Yes, hide.

NEIL Toilets?

WILL HEADS OFF TO FIND CHARLOTTE.

——————— SCENE 14 ———————

INT. CIVIC HALL, BAR

WILL FINDS CHARLOTTE AT THE BAR.

WILL   Charlotte.

CHARLOTTE   All right, someone's desperate for a diet coke.

WILL   No, look, Simon got attacked by a kid . . .

CHARLOTTE   What, in here? What did he do, headbutt him in the knee?

WILL   Ha, no. He kicked him in the cock actually . . . But listen . . .

CHARLOTTE   Will, please say that you aren't going to ask me to protect you from some children?

WILL   A bit.

WE SEE WOLFIE ARRIVE BEHIND WILL.

WOLFIE   All right Chomdley-Warner?

WILL   Oh no.

WOLFIE   Is this your bird then?

WILL   No, no, no, no, no.

WOLFIE   Nice to meet you. You're exactly like Will said you was.

CHARLOTTE   Right, I hope that's a compliment.

WOLFIE   (GETTING HIS MOBILE PHONE OUT) Oh yeah it is. Listen you wouldn't mind having a quick word with our boss Jim on the old blower would you?

WILL   Ha, ha, ha, ha. Please don't.

IT'S TOO LATE AS WOLFIE IS ALREADY ON THE PHONE.

CHARLOTTE   New friend?

WILL   From my work experience. It's not really a friend.

WOLFIE   (HANDING THE PHONE TO CHARLOTTE) Jim for you.

WILL LOOKS AGHAST.

WILL   Ignore everything he has to say, it's all total bollocks I promise.

CHARLOTTE   Hello. Right. No, I'm not his girlfriend, no. No, we didn't have sex. He did, did he? No that didn't happen. No, I'm not a porn star.

SHE HANGS UP AND HANDS THE PHONE BACK TO WOLFIE.

WILL   Charlotte, listen, I was working in a garage, you don't understand what it's like . . .

CHARLOTTE   How many chances do you think you get to be a dick-head Will?

WILL   One more?

CHARLOTTE   Wrong. You are a nasty little virgin. See you later.

SHE THROWS A GLASS OF DIET COKE OVER HIM AND WALKS OFF.

WILL   Right, fair enough. OK, best of a bad lot. Deal with what we have. Wolfie, you've got to help me and my mates out, we're in trouble.

WOLFIE   Nah, I'm off, mate. I only popped in to check out your missus.

WILL   Right, well thanks for popping by and ruining my love life.

WOLFIE   No problem.

WILL   I hope you and your ignorant boss get a good laugh out of it. 'Cos I'll tell you who'll be laughing last – me. Because I'm not the one working in a shitty garage doing manual labour for the rest of my life.

WOLFIE   See you Monday.

WOLFIE LEAVES.

WILL   No, no you won't. Because I'll be at a local paper. That's right, a local newspaper.

WILL V/O   *So my date, yes date, was a disaster. But at least my friends weren't hiding in the toilet . . .*

WILL GETS A TEXT FROM SIMON. IT READS: 'IN THE TOILET. HAS CHARLOTTE SORTED IT?'

WILL V/O . . . *oh, they were . . . um, there was only one person who could help us now.*

WILL MAKES A CALL ON HIS MOBILE.

—————— SCENE 15 ——————

<u>INT. CIVIC HALL TOILET CUBICLE IN GENTS</u>

NEIL, SIMON AND JAY ARE IN THE CUBICLE.

SIMON   Thanks for stepping in, by the way, mate.

JAY   I was going to dive in the second you put your cock away.

NEIL   Budge up a bit Jay, I really need a piss.

JAY   You're not pissing in here Neil.

NEIL   Why not? It's a toilet.

SIMON   Go outside if you have to.

NEIL   But what if they come in? I don't see why I can't just piss in here.

SIMON   Because I do not want to see piss coming out the end of your cock.

NEIL   I could sit down and do it.

SIMON   What?

NEIL   I do that sometimes. You know, for a treat.

SIMON   Oh fuck, just get on with it then.

EVERYONE SHUFFLES AROUND WHILE NEIL UNDOES HIS TROUSERS AND SITS ON THE TOILET. THERE'S A SILENCE. NOTHING HAPPENS. NO TINKLING SOUND.

JAY   Are you going yet?

NEIL   I can't go. You lot are putting me off.

THERE'S A KNOCK ON THE CUBICLE DOOR.

SIMON   (WHISPERING) Shit, who's that . . . ?

NEIL   Could be Northwood.

SIMON   (IN A HIGH PITCHED VOICE) Who is it?

WILL   It's obviously me.

THEY OPEN THE DOOR FOR WILL AND WE SEE NEIL HAVING A SIT-DOWN PISS WITH HIS TROUSERS ROUND HIS KNEES, AND JAY AND SIMON STANDING EITHER SIDE OF HIM.

WILL   What is happening in here?

SIMON   Has Charlotte sorted it?

WILL   No. I've sorted it though.

SIMON   What have you done?

WILL   I've called my mum. She's going to come and pick us up.

SIMON   What?

JAY   Oh this is tragic.

SIMON   You've called your mum? Your mum is coming to rescue us from the toilet of an under-eighteen disco because we're being bullied by twelve-year-olds. No one must ever know about this.

JAY   Look Si, you should just go outside and take your beating from a child like a man, and then we can all leave.

SIMON   I would've taken him down there and then if it wasn't for Northwood backing him up.

JAY   How were you going to take him down Si? Spunk in his eyes?

SIMON   Oh shit. What if Carli finds out about me and that girl?

JAY   Oh no, maybe she still won't go out with you.

SIMON   Oh God, this is a fucking disaster. Oh no actually, it's OK, it's fine. I've worked it out, I just need to move away and change schools.

WILL   My night hasn't exactly been brilliant Simon. At least next week will be better, get my teeth into some journalism.

NEIL   Oh yeah, I was meant to tell you about that. The paper want to keep me on, so there's no room for you.

WILL   Tell me you're joking.

NEIL   Nah, they said I was the best work experience they'd ever had or something.

TANNOY ANNOUNCEMENT   This is an urgent message for William McKenzie. Could William McKenzie please make his way to the front entrance, as his mother is here to pick him and his friends up. That's William McKenzie, a Year 12 at Rudge Park, please come to the front where your mother is waiting to collect you.

AS THIS MESSAGE IS PLAYED OUT WE HEAR A ROAR OF LAUGHTER FROM THE HALL OUTSIDE.

WILL   Oh for fuck's sake.

WILL V/O   *It had been a strange week. I hadn't experienced much actual work, but I had learnt some valuable lessons. Never work with children or animals . . .*

SHOT OF WILL BEING THROWN IN THE POND.

SHOT OF DANNY KICKING SIMON.

SHOT OF WILL AT THE GARAGE.

WILL   Hello, Wolf.

WOLFIE   Wolfie.

WILL V/O   *. . . don't call your valentine a porn star . . .*

SHOT OF CHARLOTTE THROWING A DRINK AT WILL.

CHARLOTTE   You are a nasty little virgin.

WILL V/O   *. . . and despite what I previously thought, a girl touching a penis is not always a good thing.*

SHOT OF SIMON GETTING A HANDJOB FROM HANNAH.

Episode 3

———— 'Will's Birthday' ————

As I've said, the way we write is that after a few initial chats about ideas we lock ourselves away in a small office, sitting directly opposite each other, then hammer it out. In the early stages of this process we cover the walls with Post-it notes often containing nothing more than a word or a phrase. Over the first few weeks these somehow come together in groups that seem to complement each other, and we then turn them into episode outlines. The full outlines eventually take their places on another wall, looking much more formal, whilst the 'ideas wall' is left patterned with a few orphaned Post-its.

Before we embarked on writing the second series we had a strong idea about five stories, but no real idea of a sixth. We thought, adorably, that it would come to us, but it didn't. And then at one point in the autumn Chris Young, our producer, told us that time was running out and we really needed a sixth ep and because of the planning etc we had about a week to write it. Which, even by our standards, wasn't very long at all. In fact, it was about three weeks less than we would have liked.

So, we looked at the orphan wall and incredibly among the few Post-its left were three containing the words 'Will's birthday', 'French exchange' and 'pretending your mate has done a shit'. And from these humble beginnings we nailed the whole script in about a week, the first and last time that's ever happened. Maybe it was how lightly we treated it, but somehow it's ended up as one of my favourites ever. A romp, if you will.

———— SCENE 1 ————

INT. COMMON ROOM

WILL V/O *To the untrained eye, it may look like just another day at school. But actually it was a very special week . . .*

. . . or in Neil's case, a very 'special needs' week.

THE COMMON ROOM IS BUSY. WE SEE NEIL SITTING DOWN ON THE SOFT SEATING, STARING INTENTLY AT HIS NINTENDO DS LITE. WILL AND SIMON ARE SITTING NEXT TO HIM.

NEIL Oh bollocks, no way is that right.

JAY COMES THROUGH THE DOOR AND JOINS THEM ALL. NEIL DOESN'T LOOK UP, HE IS STILL ENGROSSED IN HIS DS LITE, BUT ALSO CLEARLY FRUSTRATED BY IT.

SIMON You all right Neil? What you playing?

NEIL (FRUSTRATED WITH THE GAME) Oh behave. That's well too hard.

SIMON Brain Training?

NEIL Stupid thing. Ah no. Why's that wrong?

WILL What does it say your brain age is Neil?

NEIL I got it up to twelve a minute ago.

WILL Twelve? Twelve years old?

JAY Have you caught Down's syndrome or something?

SIMON Has it asked you if Santa is real yet?

WILL Don't listen to them Neil. He does exist.

JAY Yeah – he's just sorted out our Saturday night out with the gift of gash.

JAY POPS DOWN A FLYER HE WAS HOLDING. IT SAYS 'SEXY LOU-LOU'S SATURDAY SOIREE'. IT HAS THE TIME AND THE ADDRESS (AS WELL AS A PHOTO OF SOME GIRLS TRYING TO LOOK SEXY) AND THEN IN BOLD LETTERS AT THE BOTTOM, JUST BELOW LARGE TYPE SAYING 'DRESS SEXY' IT SAYS 'STRICTLY INVITE ONLY'.

NEIL Sexy soirée? That sounds sexy.

SIMON (LOOKING AT FLYER) Fucking hell, is that Louise Graham? She doesn't normally look like that.

JAY Oh she'd definitely get it. Right in the bumhole.

WILL Lucky girl.

SIMON This is amazing, we've actually been invited to a cool party.

JAY Yeah, kind of. I nicked this out of Sadie Cunningham's bag in registration. I thought we should try and go.

SIMON Oh right, so it's another cool party we're specifically not invited to? Good job Jay.

WILL HAS BEEN SITTING THIS ONE OUT AND FINALLY INTERRUPTS:

WILL Erm, isn't there something else on Saturday night anyway?

SIMON Don't think so.

WILL It's my birthday. I'm having a dinner party. I sent you all the invites a month ago.

NEIL Is that really happening? I thought it was a joke.

JAY It's a joke that we've got to go to a dinner party rather than a sex party.

WILL Two things. One, it's not going to be a 'sex party' is it, it's Louise Graham we are talking about. And two – even if it is, you were invited to my dinner party first.

NEIL Just cancel yours Will, you can have your birthday any weekend.

WILL Thanks Neil. Simon, you don't want to go to Louise Graham's do you?

SIMON Me? No, God no. No. Not unless you're going to cancel yours?

WILL I'm not.

SIMON Sure, sure. Oh, except my French-exchange bloke arrives today and I'm meant to look after him all week.

WILL   Bring him along, it will be nice to have some sophistication at the party.

SIMON   I'm not sure if he's that sophisticated, some friend of my mum's asked if we'd look after him. He might be a massive twat.

JAY   So what, he's the French version of you?

WILL   Oh and don't forget you've all got to bring a girl. I'd like it to be a proper dinner party.

NEIL   Can I ask your mum?

WILL   No.

———— SCENE 2 ————

INT. SIMON'S KITCHEN

WILL V/O   *So after school we went to say bonjour to Patrice.*

THE BOYS ARE SITTING WITH A BLOKE IN A LEATHER JACKET. HE LOOKS QUITE COOL. THIS IS PATRICE, SIMON'S FRENCH EXCHANGE KID.

NEIL   What's France like then, Patrice?

PATRICE SHRUGS INSOUCIANTLY.

NEIL   Cool. And are French birds dirty?

PATRICE   *Quoi?*

JAY   He doesn't get any. Look at him, he's all greasy. Birds don't go for that, French or not.

WILL   *Bonjour, Patrice, je m'appelle Will. Est-ce qu'il y a quelque chose que tu veux faire pendant ton sejour?*

PATRICE   *Je n'aime pas les arabes.*

WILL   *Pardon?*

PATRICE   *Les arabes, je n'aime pas les arabes.*

WILL   Yeah, that's what I thought you said. I think you'll be OK round here.

SIMON What did he say?

WILL Do you not speak any French?

SIMON No. I think that's why my mum was so keen for him to come over, try to teach me a bit. I've picked up *clope* so far.

WILL What does that mean?

SIMON Cigarette. He smokes like a chimney.

PATRICE Simon. You have porn?

SIMON Oh for fuck's sake, I keep saying no I don't.

PATRICE Internet?

SIMON No.

JAY You can't get any porn on the internet?

WILL That's not the internet you're thinking of Si. Are you maybe trying to get porn on the washing machine?

SIMON My mum and dad have got a filter on it, can't see any.

JAY Ah that is fucking tragic. What are you, eleven?

PATRICE *Je vais fumer une clope.*

SIMON Yeah, all right, mate.

NEIL See you later, Patrice.

PATRICE TAPS OUT A FAG AS HE LEAVES.

SIMON He seems a bit weird. He asked if I'd tried the 'sleeping beauty'.

NEIL Oh it's good that.

SIMON What, you know it?

NEIL Yeah. You sit on your arm till your hand goes dead. Ten, fifteen minutes is normally enough. And then when you wank it feels like someone else is doing it.

WILL How do you know these things?

JAY Oh everyone knows the sleeping beauty, that's old.

WILL   Is it?

JAY   Yeah, my mate's brother invented it. He and his mates used to be called the Dead Hand Gang.

WILL   They had a gang based on masturbation? There's nothing gay about that.

JAY   Yeah, well he's in the air force now, so how gay is that?

WILL   Still quite gay.

——————— SCENE 3 ———————

INT./EXT. SIMON'S CAR

WILL V/O   *So my dinner-party guest list was shaping up nicely. Four idiots and a racist Frenchman.*

THE FOUR BOYS AND PATRICE ARE IN THE CAR TRAVELLING TO SCHOOL.

SIMON   It's going to be tricky to get girls to come to your dinner party I think.

WILL   What, because you all forgot and it's short notice?

SIMON   No, 'cos Louise Graham's quite popular. I think most people will be at hers.

WILL   Please say you'll at least try to bring girls. This birthday can't be as depressing as last year's.

NEIL   Why, because you got that briefcase?

WILL   No Neil, because my father left my mother.

SIMON   Maybe I'll see what Carli's up to?

JAY   Not being seen dead with you in a million years is what she's up to.

SIMON   Oh I'm sorry Russell Brand, who are you bringing again?

JAY   Don't worry about me, I'm up to my neck in sluts at the moment. Maybe I'll bring my new fuck buddy, that little blonde barmaid from the Fox and Hounds.

NEIL   You've pulled a barmaid? Nice.

WILL   Has she got any special dietary requirements? It's just I've never cooked for an imaginary woman before.

JAY   Well I know she's not allergic to nuts. My nuts.

SIMON   Brilliant.

JAY   Or my cock.

WILL   So she only eats small portions then?

JAY   Well I didn't hear your mum complaining . . . although her mouth was full at the time.

WILL   Yep, good one.

NEIL   Just drop us off here Si.

SIMON   Ah, don't you want a lift to school?

JAY   Yeah, but this is close enough. We don't want to be seen getting out of this shit heap.

NEIL   No offence mate.

JAY   See you later.

NEIL AND JAY GET OUT OF THE CAR. THERE'S A BEAT.

WILL   Actually I might get out too.

SIMON   Fine, see you at school.

PATRICE STAYS WHERE HE IS IN THE BACK OF THE CAR.

SIMON   Oh, do you want to get in the front Patrice?

PATRICE   *Non.*

SIMON   Great.

SIMON DRIVES OFF LOOKING LIKE A CABBIE.

———— SCENE 4 ————

INT. WILL'S KITCHEN

WILL V/O   *They say the quickest way to a man's heart is through his stomach. But I was hoping it would also be a good way into my female guest's knickers.*

WILL AND SIMON ARE SITTING AT THE COMPUTER, PATRICE IS STANDING LOOKING BORED BEHIND THEM. WILL IS GOOGLING RECIPES.

WILL   What about a chicken casserole?

SIMON   Why are you even asking? If it was up to me we'd all have Big Macs.

WILL   Did you not see *Super Size Me*?

SIMON   Yeah. It just made me really want a Big Mac.

THERE'S A PINGING NOISE ON THE COMPUTER.

WILL   Oh shit, Charlotte's online.

SIMON   Have you asked her along yet?

WILL   No. I don't know if I should, after everything.

SIMON   Oh go on, it'll be great. Message her now.

WILL   Really, do you think so?

SIMON   Yes, it'll be cool, just say hi.

WILL   All right. Done it. Oh wow, she's come straight back. She says 'Hi, whassup', smiley face. Urgh.

SIMON   Ask her out.

WILL   No, can't just jump in, not the way things have been with us. Have to charm her a bit first. I've written 'Just hanging out with Si and his French exchange'.

CHARLOTTE (MSN): oh, is he the handsome one?

WILL   She thinks you're handsome?

WILL (MSN): Simon?

CHARLOTTE (MSN): No silly, the French guy.

WILL   Oh no, she means Patrice, thank God.

WILL (MSN): Oh. Ha. I'm a div.

CHARLOTTE (MSN): :)

WILL   Hmm, another smiley face. Can't bring myself to send a smiley back. I suppose I could write 'lol' if I absolutely had to.

SIMON   Do that.

WILL (MSN): Laugh out loud.

CHARLOTTE (MSN): Smiley with tongue out.

SIMON   It's going well, mate, ask her out.

WILL   It is going well, isn't it?

SIMON   Definitely.

WILL   "It's my birthday, come for dinner"?

HE TYPES.

WILL (MSN): It's my birthday Saturday, come for dinner, 8ish?

THERE'S A PAUSE.

SIMON   That pause isn't good.

WILL   Calm down, it's only been a second.

SIMON   Although she was straight back every time before.

THEY STARE AT THE SCREEN AGAIN. BEAT. THEN MESSAGE APPEARS ON THE SCREEN: 'CHARLOTTE HAS LEFT THE CHAT'.

WILL   Holy shit, she's gone offline rather than have to actually answer whether or not she'll come to my birthday?

SIMON   Maybe the connection has dropped?

WILL   No, it was back and forth, back and forth, then a question about dinner, then she's gone. Oh brilliant, perfect, thanks a bunch.

SIMON   Look, she didn't say no, did she?

WILL   No. But she did hang up.

SIMON   So I'm sure she'll be there.

BEAT.

SIMON   Well not sure, but y'know.

WILL'S MUM (POLLY McKENZIE), COMES DOWN THE STAIRS AND SEES PATRICE.

POLLY McKENZIE   Oh hello Simon. Hello.

PATRICE   *Bonjour.*

POLLY McKENZIE   (BLUSHING SLIGHTLY) Oh, goodness, you're French.

SIMON   Um, this is Patrice, he's my sort of French exchange. Patrice, this is Will's mum.

PATRICE   Hello.

POLLY McKENZIE   OK, well, erm, I'm just off to play tennis. Don't know why I mentioned that. Bye then. *Au revoir*, Patrice.

PATRICE   *Au revoir.*

POLLY LEAVES.

PATRICE   Your muzzer is very sex.

WILL   Sorry?

PATRICE   She has the sex.

PATRICE LEAVES, HEADING FOR THE TOILET.

WILL   He's a strange one, isn't he?

SIMON   Yep, but he's just French, they're all weird aren't they?

WILL   Oh God, please don't be racist.

SIMON   That's not racist, I'm just saying that he barely says anything and when he does speak it's always about sex. Just like all French people.

———— SCENE 5 ————

INT. WILL'S KITCHEN

IT'S BREAKFAST TIME ON WILL'S BIRTHDAY. WILL'S MUM HAS PREPARED HIM A SPECIAL COOKED BREAKFAST. THERE IS A PRESENT AND A CARD LAID OUT ON THE BREAKFAST TABLE.

WILL COMES DOWN TO BREAKFAST IN A T-SHIRT AND BOXER SHORTS.

WILL V/O   *The next day was my birthday and Mum was serving me up her speciality, scrambled eggs and disappointment.*

POLLY McKENZIE   Happy birthday petal.

WILL   Thanks Mum.

POLLY McKENZIE   Here's your present. It's nothing big though, because I'm saving up for something special next year, when you can drive.

WILL   Next year? I can drive this year.

POLLY McKENZIE   I thought you had to be eighteen to drive?

WILL   No, it's seventeen.

POLLY McKENZIE   Oh right. Sorry. Your father used to deal with things like that.

WILL STARTS TO UNWRAP HIS PRESENT.

WILL   Oh thanks Mum. Calvin Klein.

WILL STARTS TO UNWRAP WHAT HE THINKS IS A T-SHIRT BUT QUICKLY REVEALS ITSELF TO BE A SINGLET.

WILL   It's . . . it's a tight vest top.

POLLY McKENZIE   Don't you like the colour?

WILL   Is this the only present you got me?

POLLY McKENZIE   What's wrong with it?

WILL   Well, when have you ever seen me wear something like that?

POLLY McKENZIE   You'll look cool. All the boy bands wear them.

WILL   I'm not in a boy band.

POLLY McKENZIE   Fine. Fine. I've got a receipt, you can exchange it. Sorry I've ruined your big day. I got it wrong about the driving and now I've got it wrong about this.

WILL   No, sorry Mum. Look I suppose it's not too bad.

POLLY McKENZIE   You don't want me to exchange it?

WILL   No, no, I'll wear it.

POLLY McKENZIE   Tonight?

WILL   Errrm, ooooh, not tonight.

POLLY McKENZIE   You hate it. Oh God, I'll change it.

WILL   No, fine. I'll definitely wear it tonight.

──────── SCENE 6 ────────

INT. SIMON'S KITCHEN

WE SEE SIMON TALKING TO HIS MUM (PAMELA COOPER) IN THE KITCHEN/DINER. SIMON IS CLEARLY PREENED READY FOR WILL'S DINNER PARTY.

PAMELA COOPER   Patrice spends an awfully long time in the shower, doesn't he?

SIMON   Oh yeah, about him. Since it's Will's birthday tonight, do you think you could look after Patrice?

PAMELA COOPER   No, you're meant to be learning from him Simon. Anyway, we're going out.

SIMON   Can't you take him with you?

SIMON'S DAD (ALAN COOPER) ENTERS.

PAMELA COOPER   It's a special night out for us. We don't really need a seventeen-year-old French boy tagging along.

ALAN COOPER   Things haven't got that bad in the bedroom yet.

SIMON   Jesus Christ.

PAMELA COOPER   Besides, he'll have much more fun with you and the boys.

SIMON   He doesn't. He just sits around rolling cigarettes and shrugging.

ALAN COOPER   Must be quite useful having a handsome Frenchman in tow when it comes to meeting the ladies.

SIMON   He's not handsome.

PAMELA COOPER   Patrice is handsome.

ALAN COOPER   Aye aye, I'd better watch it. Looks like your mother is lining up a toy boy.

SIMON   Oh God.

PAMELA COOPER   Chance would be a fine thing.

SIMON   Oh not you too.

ALAN COOPER   Just remember gorgeous, what I lack in energy I more than make up for in experience.

SIMON   Oh God, you two are disgusting.

ALAN COOPER   Oh come on Simon, you used to look at much worse on the internet.

SIMON STORMS OUT OF THE KITCHEN AS HIS DAD GRABS HIS MUM FROM BEHIND AND SORT OF SWAYS/LIFTS HER.

———— SCENE 7 ————

INT. JAY'S BEDROOM

WILL V/O   *Elsewhere on the internet the Dead Hand Gang was enrolling its latest recruit.*

WE SEE JAY ATTEMPTING THE 'SLEEPING BEAUTY' IN HIS BEDROOM. HE'S ON THE BED IN HIS PANTS AND SOCKS, WITH A LAPTOP SHOWING PORN ON IN FRONT OF HIM, AND HE'S SITTING ON HIS ARM. HE'S CHECKING THE TIME ON HIS WATCH, WHICH IS ON HIS OTHER ARM. HE LOOKS RIDICULOUS. THEN SUDDENLY HE HEARS THE DOOR HANDLE BEING TURNED.

MRS CARTWRIGHT   (OFF SCREEN) Jay, Neil's here for you.

JAY   What? He's early, don't come in, I'm getting changed.

JAY'S MUM WALKS STRAIGHT IN, FOLLOWED BY NEIL. JAY CAN'T REALLY MOVE
BECAUSE HE IS SITTING ON HIS ARM. THERE'S NO WAY THEY CANNOT SEE THE
HARDCORE PORNOGRAPHY ON HIS LAPTOP SCREEN. BEAT, AND JAY'S MUM
SURVEYS THE SCENE.

MRS CARTWRIGHT   Are you OK?

JAY IS DESPERATELY TRYING TO CLOSE THE LAPTOP DOWN BUT HIS ARM IS
TOTALLY LIMP AND DEAD.

JAY   It's just a film. A normal film. I'm getting changed. Get out.

HIS MUM LEAVES WITH HIM LIMPLY TAPPING THE KEYBOARD WITH HIS
VIRTUALLY PARALYSED HAND. NEIL IS STILL STANDING IN THE DOORWAY.

NEIL   What film's that then? . . . Oh, right.

——— SCENE 8 ———

INT. WILL'S DINING ROOM / EXT. FRONT DOOR

WILL V/O   *So whilst I was making my final preparations, including
putting on shit music girls would like, Patrice had been busy too . . .*

THE CURTAINS ARE SHUT AND WILL IS FUSSING OVER SOME CANDLES THAT ARE
PLACED IN THE MIDDLE OF THE TABLE.

WILL IS WEARING A SMART DINNER JACKET OVER A BLACK T-SHIRT, WHICH IS
ACTUALLY THE SLEEVELESS CALVIN KLEIN THAT HIS MUM GAVE HIM EARLIER.
SIMON IS JUST WATCHING IN SILENCE AS WILL FUSSES. PATRICE APPEARS FROM
THE DOWNSTAIRS BATHROOM.

PATRICE   I just had a really nice jerk thinking about your mother and
think some went on the floor . . .

WILL   Great, thanks Patrice.

PATRICE SMILES. BEAT. THE DOORBELL RINGS AND WILL AWKWARDLY WORKS HIS
WAY ROUND THE TABLE TO ANSWER IT.

SIMON   I'll get it. It could be Charlotte.

WILL   Well it's not going to be Charlotte.

SIMON   Cheer up, it might be. She's got the details, you said so your-self.

THEY GO TO THE FRONT DOOR AND OPEN IT. JAY AND NEIL ARE STANDING THERE.

JAY   All right, gays.

WILL V/O   . . . *oh happy birthday to me.*

——— SCENE 9 ———

INT. WILL'S DINING ROOM

WILL V/O   *It was eight thirty p.m. on my seventeenth birthday and my party was in full swing . . .*

IT'S A PRETTY STERILE AND BORING SCENE. THEY ALL HAVE A GLASS OF WINE, A BOTTLE IS ON THE TABLE. NO ONE IS REALLY SAYING ANYTHING.

WILL   Where's your plus one then Jay?

JAY   Not coming. She got a modelling job and had to fly to Paris.

SIMON   Barmaid by day, supermodel by night. Sounds likely.

JAY   And where's little miss stuck-up cock-tease?

SIMON   Do you mean Carli?

JAY   Yep.

SIMON   Oh yeah hmm, I don't think Carli will make it.

WILL   Why not? Is something up?

SIMON   No, nothing like that. I just sort of didn't invite her in the end.

JAY   Oh you really are a bollockless little twat, aren't you?

WILL   So there are going to be no women here then? None at all? I don't know why I bother.

JAY (SMIRKING AND LOOKING AT NEIL) Well I wouldn't say there will be 'no' women.

NEIL (ALSO SMIRKING) Yeah, not 'no' women.

WILL So there are some women coming then?

NEIL Maybe, maybe not.

WILL Look, it's very clear from your smirking faces and tone of voice that actually there are some women coming.

JAY We got you a special birthday treat.

WILL Did you?

NEIL A stripper.

WILL What?

SIMON Have you really booked a stripper?

JAY Yeah, she was only a hundred and fifty quid.

SIMON How did you manage to pay for that?

NEIL We haven't paid yet. We'll just have a whip-round when she gets here.

WILL A whip-round? Round who? The five of us? We haven't got thirty quid each.

JAY No, if we all put in a, um, wait, oh shit, yeah.

WILL Brilliant. So just to confirm, until an angry stripper turns up, we are without any female company? Oh thanks guys, this is a great birthday.

JAY God, if you're going to cry about it I'll go and get some local snatch in.

NEIL What about them birds we passed outside?

JAY Yeah, they were all right.

WILL Oh yes please, drag some random girls off the street for me.

SIMON Or we could go to Louise Graham's party?

JAY   Yeah, why aren't we there? It's got to be better than this shithole.

WILL   Thanks very much. More wine?

JAY   I bet it's crawling with clunge.

WILL   And I bet it's not.

JAY   Oh yeah, and you'd know.

WILL   Look I've put a lot of effort for this. I've made a really nice coq au vin.

JAY   A cock of what?

SIMON   You don't help yourself, do you?

WILL   Oh yes, I see, a 'coq au vin', very mature. It actually means chicken in wine, doesn't it, Patrice?

PATRICE   *Quoi?*

WILL   Well it does. And it doesn't mean cock in my arse, or a cock on my head, or I got a . . . er . . .

SIMON   You got some cock in the back of a van?

WILL   Or that I got a cock in the back of a van. Look, all I wanted was a civilised and sophisticated birthday. Just something a bit different from the usual parties, maybe even the sort of party girls are impressed by. OK, so there aren't any girls here, but why don't we at least attempt to have a sophisticated conversation. I know it's a tall order, and I'm not expecting sparkling, but let's give it a go AS IT IS MY FUCKING BIRTHDAY.

THIS EXPLOSION HAS ACTUALLY SHUT THEM UP. WILL DOES SEEM GENUINELY UPSET.

BEAT.

NEIL   How much Lego can you stuff up your bum?

WILL   Oh for Christ's sake.

NEIL   Not now, just when you was younger. How much did you get up there?

JAY   You are grim mate.

SIMON   Why were you sticking Lego up your bum?

NEIL   Not a lot, just like one of the rectangular ones and a long one. Couple of singles maybe.

WILL   Fine, fine. Let's go and see if we can get those girls from outside to come and join us then.

NEIL   (ENTHUSIASTICALLY) Yes.

PATRICE, NEIL AND JAY NEED NO SECOND ASKING. THEY ARE UP AND GET THEIR JACKETS.

SIMON   Are you sure, mate? I thought you wanted this to be special?

WILL   Why fight it? Charlotte's not coming, is she? And a skilful raconteur like Neil is wasted on just us.

JAY   Nice one. Now I can get myself a proper three courses – blowie, shag and anal.

WILL V/O   . . . *and so we headed into the night and found Jay's three courses sitting on a fence.*

──────── SCENE 10 ────────

EXT. ESTATE STREET

THE FIVE LADS ARE WANDERING THE STREETS. PATRICE IS SMOKING. THEY SPOT THREE GIRLS SITTING ON A WALL/BIT OF FENCE.

JAY   'Allo 'allo, here they are, the little lovelies.

NEIL   Nice.

SIMON   They look a bit rough.

WILL   Are they drinking in the street?

JAY   Dirty.

WILL   Not quite the sophisticates I had in mind, but at least they are female.

NEIL   You going over then, Jay?

JAY   Nah, Si should.

SIMON   What? Why me?

NEIL   Alphabetical.

JAY   You've got that bent look that girls go for.

SIMON   Fine, if you're going to be rude, you go then.

JAY   Ooh sorry for being 'rude'.

NEIL   Just go Si, it's freezing out here.

WILL   Si, come on. For me, yeah? For my birthday?

SIMON   God, all right then.

SIMON TAKES A DEEP BREATH AND THEN WALKS OVER TO THE GIRLS, WHO HAVE THEIR BACKS TO HIM. HE CALLS OUT.

SIMON   Hi there.

THE GIRLS TURN ROUND. THEY ARE MUCH YOUNGER THAN WE THOUGHT. ALSO THEY LOOK QUITE HARD. THE LEAD ONE (JULIE) HAS SHARP FEATURES AND A CROYDON FACE-LIFT.

JULIE   What did you fucking say?

SIMON   Erm, hello.

JULIE   And what?

SIMON   Um, I wanted to ask you to a party.

JULIE   I'm thirteen.

SIMON   Oh, right.

JULIE   And she's eleven, you nonce.

SIMON   Yep, well there's been a mistake, so . . .

JULIE   Like looking at little gels do ya?

ANOTHER, PARTICULARLY YOUNG-LOOKING, GIRL (MICHELLE) JOINS IN.

MICHELLE   Like getting them to go to parties where you can touch them do ya?

SIMON   No, God no. Look I'm going now.

SIMON STARTS A FAST WALK BACK TO THE OTHERS.

MICHELLE   Paedo.

JULIE   You fucking paedo.

MICHELLE   Yeah run, you paedo.

PATRICE STOPS A BIT, GRABS HIS CROTCH AND THRUSTS THE WHOLE AREA FORWARDS IN A MACHO GALLIC WAY, POINTEDLY AT THE GIRLS.

SIMON   Fucking hell, don't do that Patrice.

MICHELLE   Er, paedo.

JULIE   I'm going to get my fucking brother on you.

MICHELLE   That's it, run away, paedo boy.

JULIE   Keep going, paedo.

MICHELLE   Keep walking, you fucking paedo.

THE BOYS START WALKING AWAY.

———— SCENE 11 ————

EXT. ESTATE STREET BY WILL'S HOUSE

JAY   Nice work Si.

SIMON   Me? It was fucking Patrice who wound them up.

JAY   Yeah, but you're the one who tried to nonce them up.

SIMON   Right, not really in the mood for this Jay. Just warning you.

JAY   Ooh watch out, Uncle Simon might try and give me a special cuddle.

THEY ROUND THE CORNER AND SEE WILL'S HOUSE. AT THE DOOR IS A MIDDLE-AGED WOMAN WEARING A LONG COAT AND BOOTS AND UNDERWEAR AND

NOTHING ELSE. POLLY ANSWERS THE DOOR AND THEY SEEM TO BE HAVING A CONVERSATION.

WILL Oh fuck.

NEIL What's for pudding Will?

WILL A middle-aged woman demanding a hundred and fifty quid.

SIMON Oh shit. What are we going to do?

JAY I think we should just go to Lou—

WILL Yes, yes, fine, I give up. Let's go and try to get into Louise Graham's.

SIMON But what about your dinner party?

WILL Forget it. You can lead a horse to water but you can't stop it from sticking Lego up its bum.

WHILE WILL IS SPEAKING WE SEE PATRICE PISSING ON A DRIVEWAY.

SIMON Oh for Christ's sake Patrice, don't do that.

JAY God Si, he's a nightmare. We can't have him scaring all the muff away at the party, let's just ditch him.

SIMON I'm supposed to be looking after him. I can't leave him stranded in a strange country.

NEIL He comes from a strange country.

WILL Si, for once, Jay is right. Patrice is weird and boring. Do you really think girls are going to be impressed when we turn up with that?

SIMON Probably not.

JAY Come on, let's just leg it while he's got his back turned.

WILL It's now or never Si.

SIMON OK, fuck it. Come on then.

THEY TURN AND PEG IT UP THE STREET.

WILL V/O *So we ran away. Yep, ran away. Something I hadn't done since John Cook discovered wedgies in Year 8.*

———— SCENE 12 ————

EXT. ESTATE STREET

WE SEE A SHOT OF WILL, SIMON, NEIL AND JAY, JOGGING ROUND A CORNER. THEY LOOK LIKE THEY'VE JUST SLOWED DOWN TO JOGGING SPEED AFTER A SPRINT.

WILL   I've got a stitch.

JAY   All right, that should be enough.

SIMON TURNS ROUND.

SIMON   He's behind us.

WILL   No way.

THEY SEE PATRICE IN THE DISTANCE.

JAY   Run.

THEY ALL START TO RUN FAST, LOOKING BACK ALL THE WAY. PATRICE IS CLEARLY QUITE QUICK AND IS CATCHING UP.

SIMON   He's chasing us.

JAY   Fucking hell, he doesn't give up easily does he?

WILL   What does he think is happening?

AT THIS POINT PATRICE IS JUST BEHIND THEM.

NEIL   I think he's caught us up.

SIMON   Yeah, good spot Neil.

PATRICE HAS CAUGHT UP WITH THEM AND IS RUNNING ALONGSIDE THEM.

PATRICE   Simon, why we run?

SIMON   Erm, yeah, dunno.

PATRICE   You don't know?

SIMON   Yeah.

PATRICE   So we stop?

SIMON   Yeah, probably. Good idea.

THE FOUR BOYS AND PATRICE ALL STOP. THERE'S A BEAT AS THE BOYS STARE AT THEIR SHOES. IT'S A BIT EMBARRASSING.

NEIL   Shall we go to this party then?

WILL V/O   *So after trying and failing to outrun a boy in Cuban heels we headed for Louise Graham's party. Which we definitely wouldn't get into.*

——————— SCENE 13 ———————

EXT. LOUISE'S HOUSE

THE FIVE BOYS ARE NOW STANDING OUTSIDE LOUISE'S HOUSE. WE CAN SEE AND HEAR THAT A PARTY IS IN FULL SWING. THEY APPROACH THE DOOR. SIMON HAS FOUND HIMSELF AT THE FRONT.

SIMON   Who's gonna ask if we can come in? Will?

WILL   I don't even know her.

NEIL   I once stuck chewing gum in her hair when we were Year 8s.

WILL   Great. Anyone else fucked her off in her life?

JAY   Out the way you Kwik Shit Shitters, I'll sort this out.

JAY CONFIDENTLY STRIDES TO THE DOOR, THE OTHERS FOLLOW. HE THEN RINGS THE BELL AND JUST AS THE DOOR IS ABOUT TO BE ANSWERED HE SLIDES OUT FROM THE FRONT TO THE BACK AND PUSHES WILL FORWARDS – A CLASSIC CUNT'S TRICK. LOUISE ANSWERS THE DOOR.

LOUISE   Yeah?

WILL   Hello Louise. We've never been introduced. I'm Will.

LOUISE   You can't come in, there's too many here already.

WILL   Look, we'll be no trouble, I promise. I mean, look at us.

LOUISE DOES TAKE A LOOK AND SHE SUDDENLY NOTICES PATRICE HANGING AT THE BACK OF THE GANG.

LOUISE   One of you can come in.

WILL   One, five, there's hardly any difference, perhaps we could negotiate . . .

LOUISE   (POINTING AT PATRICE) Him. He can come in.

WILL   Oh, right, well the thing is Simon will have to come too then, because he's supposed to be looking after him.

PATRICE SHRUGS AND THEN SLIDES IN THE FRONT DOOR WITHOUT LOOKING BACK. LOUISE THEN SLAMS THE DOOR SHUT AS WILL IS STILL SPEAKING.

WILL   Great. So we can add Patrice to the growing list of people more popular than us.

JAY   (LOOKING THROUGH THE WINDOW) Fucking John's in there and he's with a girl.

NEIL   He's got his hand on her tit.

SIMON   This is too tragic.

NEIL   And Charlotte Big Jugs is in there.

WILL   Where?

HE LOOKS IN AND SEES CHARLOTTE WALKING THROUGH THE LOUNGE.

JAY   Right, looks like it's time for plan B.

WILL   Oh right, there's a plan B is there? It's just plan A was so brilliantly devised I wouldn't have thought we'd need a plan B. What is it? Climb over her fence?

——————— SCENE 14 ———————

EXT. LOUISE'S HOUSE, BACK GARDEN

WE CUT TO AN ALLEYWAY JUST BEHIND THE BACK GARDEN OF LOUISE'S HOUSE, WHERE WILL, SIMON, NEIL AND JAY ARE LOOKING UP AT AN 8-FOOT-HIGH FENCE.

WILL   It's a bit higher than I imagined.

JAY   Don't shit yourself, it's only a fence, it won't bite.

WILL   Yes Jay, except I'm not worried about it biting me, I'm worried about falling off and breaking my neck.

NEIL   Oh come on Will, it'll be a laugh, climbing and that.

WILL   Will it? There must be another way.

NEIL GIVES JAY A LEG UP TO LOOK OVER THE FENCE.

JAY   Oh it's full of clunge. Give us a push, Neil.

JAY JUMPS OVER. NEIL AND SIMON START TO CLIMB THE FENCE, HELPING EACH OTHER A BIT.

WILL   I'm just not made for climbing.

WILL   Maybe if one of these panels is loose.

WILL BENDS DOWN AND STARTS EXAMINING THE ROOTS OF THE HEDGE.

WILL   There's a gap here.

WILL STARTS TO WRIGGLE HIS BODY THROUGH THE GAP UNDER THE HEDGE. HE'S ABOUT SIXTY PER CENT INTO THE GARDEN WHEN THE OTHERS START TO LAND ON THE OTHER SIDE. WILL IS ALMOST THROUGH BEFORE HE STARTS TO GET A VERY STRONG WHIFF OF DOG SHIT. THAT'S BECAUSE HE'S CRAWLING THROUGH THE BEDDING WHERE LOUISE'S DOG DOES ITS BUSINESS.

SIMON   Come on, Will, hurry up.

WILL   Oh please no.

NEIL   Why's he always got to be different?

DUE TO THE NOISE AND THE RUSTLING, THE FEW PEOPLE THAT ARE IN THE GARDEN HAVE STOPPED TALKING AND ARE WATCHING THE NEW ARRIVALS CLAMBERING THROUGH THE HEDGE. WILL IS STILL ON HIS BELLY IN THE BEDDING.

JAY   Just fucking hurry up you twat, everyone's looking.

LOUISE HAS APPEARED THROUGH THE PATIO DOORS. SHE LOOKS ANNOYED.

LOUISE   What's going on?

WILL PULLS HIMSELF TO HIS FEET.

WILL   Oh, hi Louise. As I was saying earlier, it's quite important that we look after Patrice.

LOUISE   (LOOKING DISGUSTED AT HIS JACKET) Have you just crawled through my dog's shit?

WILL   Yes Louise, I have. But ask yourself why. The fact that you have excluded us from this party because of some vague rules about popularity is ridiculous. Although it may look like we've climbed over a fence and crawled through dog shit, in fact what we've done is challenged your social apartheid.

LOUISE   You weren't invited because I don't know you that well.

WILL   Yeah, that makes sense too I suppose.

LOUISE   God, if you're that desperate to come in then you can stay. And take that jacket off before you go inside.

LOUISE WALKS OFF.

JAY   Sweet, nice one.

SIMON   She's right about the jacket though, it stinks.

NEIL   Oh mate, that is rank. It's all up your sleeve, look.

WILL   Oh Christ.

WILL CAREFULLY TAKES OFF HIS DOG SHIT COVERED JACKET, REVEALING THE SINGLET UNDERNEATH.

JAY   What the fuck is that?

NEIL   Oh my God.

WILL   It was a present from my mum, all right?

SIMON   And you've worn it?

JAY   Has she been getting gift ideas from Neil's old man?

NEIL   Oi, my dad is not bent.

SIMON   Honestly, that is not a good look for you mate.

WILL   Well, we've just gatecrashed a party that John was invited to, so none of us are winning the cool prize at the moment.

JAY   Yeah, but you are losing by a mile.

WILL   Yes, but not for long. I'm going to find Charlotte and turn this birthday around.

NEIL   She'll be upstairs getting fucked most likely.

WILL   Neil, I've told you she's not like that.

BEAT.

WILL   I'll check upstairs first though.

WILL V/O   *The best thing about it being your birthday is that everyone has to do exactly what you want, and with this thought and a slightly dirtier one in mind, I went to find Charlotte.*

——————— SCENE 15 ———————

INT. LOUISE'S HOUSE

WILL IS LOOKING ROUND THE HOUSE, CLEARLY TRYING TO FIND CHARLOTTE. HE HEADS UP THE STAIRS, PAST THE VE KIDS SITTING ON THEM.

BOY A   Nice T-shirt.

GIRL A   Yeah, good look briefcase.

WILL   Thanks.

GIRL B   Someone's stolen your sleeves.

WILL   Yep, nice one.

BOY B   All right, where's the rest of Take That?

WILL   Retro, but a good one.

——————— SCENE 16 ———————

INT. LOUISE'S HOUSE, BY DOWNSTAIRS TOILET

THE PARTY IS BUSY, BUT NOT THAT GOOD – BUT NOT THAT SHIT – JUST A SLIGHTLY BUSIER THAN AVERAGE HOUSE PARTY. JAY AND SIMON ARE WAITING TO GO TO THE TOILET.

JAY   Come on, let me go first, you know I'm desperate.

SIMON   Unlikely.

JAY   Oh don't be a cock.

SIMON GOES TO PUSH JAY'S BLADDER SO THAT HE IS GOING TO PISS HIMSELF. IT'S A BIT OF A WRESTLE.

JAY   Oh no, don't. Seriously, come on, I'm bursting. Look, come on.

THE TOILET DOOR OPENS AND A PERSON COMES OUT. SIMON THEN GOES IN. AS HE SHUTS THE DOOR CARLI COMES OVER, LONG ENOUGH AFTERWARDS NOT TO HAVE SEEN HIM.

CARLI   Oh hi Jay, are you queuing?

JAY   Yeah, feel like I might piss my pants any minute.

CARLI   Oh.

JAY   Won't be too long, they've been in there a while.

CARLI   Oh, right. . . . So, I didn't know you lot were friends with Louise.

JAY   Oh we're not, we climbed over the fence.

CARLI   Right.

THE DOOR OPENS AND SIMON COMES OUT. JAY GOES PAST HIM QUICKLY.

SIMON   Carli, hi.

CARLI   Hi Simon, how are you?

SIMON   OK, yeah good, yeah, pretty awesome.

JAY   (BARELY INTO THE TOILET AS IF HE'S JUST BEEN HIT BY A WAVE OF STENCH. HOLDING NOSE THEATRICALLY ETC) Jesus Christ Simon, what the fuck have you done in there?

SIMON   What?

JAY   (AS IF WAVING SMOKE FROM IN FRONT OF HIM) Have you been eating cat food again? Oh God, you've left skids down the bowl too.

SIMON   Carli I didn't, I only went in for a piss.

JAY   Oh my God, I can taste it.

SIMON   Jay!

CARLI   I might go upstairs.

SIMON   (AS SHE'S LEAVING) No, don't, it was only a wee Carli. It was only a wee. I promise I didn't leave skids.

A FEW OTHER PEOPLE FROM THE PARTY ARE LOOKING AT HIM NOW. HE TURNS ANGRILY TO JAY.

SIMON   It doesn't smell at all, you fucker. It was a wee. Why did you do that?

JAY   Funny.

JAY SHUTS THE DOOR.

──────── SCENE 17 ────────

INT. LOUISE'S HOUSE, UPSTAIRS LANDING

WILL V/O   *OK, so things weren't going exactly to plan. If I could just find Charlotte, I was confident it could still be a birthday to remember.*

WILL HAS GONE UPSTAIRS. IT'S QUIET AND SEEMS EMPTY. THERE'S LAUGHTER FROM ONE THE ROOMS. WILL WALKS IN.

WILL   Charlotte?

HE TURNS ON THE LIGHT. IN THE BED WE SEE A DISHELLEVED-LOOKING CHARLOTTE. ON TOP OF HER IS A LAD WHO IS WRITHING AROUND. IT'S HARD TO MAKE OUT WHO IT IS AS WE CAN ONLY SEE HIS BACK AND SHOULDERS.

WILL   Oh hi Charlotte, there you are.

CHARLOTTE   Will. Um, can you go away?

THE PRESENCE OF WILL HASN'T REALLY DETERRED THE GUY WHO IS MAKING OUT WITH CHARLOTTE. HE STILL HAS HIS HEAD BURIED IN HER, NUZZLING HER NECK AND THE TOP OF HER CHEST. WILL WALKS OVER AND PUTS HIS HAND ON THE GUY'S BACK.

WILL   Time out, fella. You're not alone now.

WILL SEES THAT IT'S PATRICE.

WILL   Oh, Patrice, *salut*.

PATRICE   *Salut*.

WILL   Um, are you two . . . ?

CHARLOTTE   Seriously, Will, what are you doing?

WILL   I just thought we could hang out a bit maybe. Not right now, but maybe . . .

PATRICE ROLLS TO ONE SIDE OF CHARLOTTE WHILE REMAINING UNDER THE COVERS.

CHARLOTTE   Will, I don't know why you are doing this and what are you wearing?

WILL   I've got a bottle of champagne at home, and I remembered when we first met we had champagne, and as it's my birthday today I thought maybe we could . . .

CHARLOTTE GIGGLES A LITTLE, AND PATRICE IS SHIFTING HIS HANDS UNDER THE COVERS A BIT.

WILL   Is he touching you now?

CHARLOTTE   (STIFLING A GASP OF EXCITEMENT) Look, maybe we'll have a drink later.

WILL   Yeah later. Course.

CHARLOTTE   Oh Will, could you turn the light off?

PATRICE   No, leave on.

WILL   OK.

THE TWO OF THEM START KISSING AGAIN.

WILL V/O   *Great. And I'd rather hoped the singlet would be the worst birthday surprise.*

———— SCENE 18 ————

INT. LOUISE'S HOUSE, FRONT DOOR

WILL V/O   *Meanwhile, my mates were making the most of finally getting into a cool party. By standing in a corridor not talking to anyone.*

WILL COMES QUITE QUICKLY DOWN THE STAIRS. HE SEES NEIL, JAY AND SIMON TOGETHER.

SIMON   All right? Did you find Charlotte?

WILL   Um yeah, yeah I did.

SIMON   Where is she then?

WILL   She's upstairs being fucked by Patrice.

NEIL   Knew it.

JAY   Ooh, unlucky.

WILL   Can you make him stop please Simon? As a birthday present?

SIMON   Um, not really. Sorry, that's just too weird.

WILL   Yeah. Yeah, you're probably right. Shall we go then?

WILL WALKS TOWARDS THE DOOR, THE OTHERS SORT OF HALF FOLLOW HIM. AS HE GETS NEAR THE DOOR, MARK DONOVAN COMES IN. HE NARROWS HIS EYES AS HE SEES WILL, BUT WILL JUST KEEPS GOING.

WILL   Oh hi Mark, I'm just off, but if you were looking for Charlotte, I think she's upstairs.

MARK DONOVAN   Fuck off you prick.

WILL   Have a fun night.

THE THREE OTHERS PILE OUT AFTER WILL.

———— SCENE 19 ————

EXT. ESTATE STREET

WILL V/O   *So ironically it was Donovan who gave me the best gift this year. A savagely beaten French kid.*

THE FOUR BOYS ARE WALKING DOWN A STREET ON THE ESTATE.

SIMON   What if Donovan kills him?

WILL   Good.

SIMON   Mum'll go mental if Patrice is hurt, though.

JAY   What's she going to do, get you a shitter car?

SIMON   Fair point.

JAY   Look, fuck him, all right. You never see him again, so what?

SIMON   I think I'm meant to stay at his at half-term.

WILL   Do you want to go to France?

SIMON   Not really.

WILL   Well shut up then.

What about me? It's my birthday and I just saw Patrice trying to mount Charlotte, the fucking baguette-eating dickhead frog.

SIMON   That's a bit racist.

WILL   He's made me racist.

NEIL   Did you get to see her boobies?

WILL   No Neil. Funnily enough, through my tear-filled eyes I couldn't see any tits.

NEIL   Bad luck.

WILL   Oh God, what if my birthdays just get worse and worse from now on? What'll happen next year?

JAY   You get Aids?

WILL   I'd have to have sex for that to happen.

NEIL   Or fuck a monkey.

WILL   Technically that still counts as sex.

SIMON   Or drink from the same cup as Neil's dad.

NEIL   Oi, my dad does not have Aids.

JAY Your dad is so Aids he was the one who gave it to monkeys.

NEIL Take that back.

JAY That's what the monkeys said to him.

SIMON Oh come on mate, let's get back to yours. I'll let you beat me at Pro Evo if you like.

WILL You don't need to, I can beat you anyway.

SIMON Well we'll see, won't we?

WILL SMILES, THEN SUDDENLY FROM BEHIND THEM THERE'S A SHOUT:

JULIE That's them. Fucking paedos.

THE BOYS TURN AROUND AND SEE THE GIRLS FROM EARLIER, A PROPER HARD-LOOKING BLOKE WITH THEM. THE BLOKE STARTS RUNNING TOWARDS THEM.

NEIL Run.

WILL Again? Oh good.

THEY ALL RUN, THAT KIND OF BREATHLESS SPRINTING FOR YOUR LIFE.

JULIE Paedo!

SIMON Split up, he can't get us all.

JAY He's got a fucking cricket bat.

THEY DO SPLIT UP, BUT WILL AND SIMON ARE STILL RUNNING THE SAME WAY. NEIL FOLLOWS THEM.

SIMON Neil, go away.

WILL This, this is the tin hat. Worst birthday ever.

WILL V/O *So my birthday, or dog-shit, singlet, heartbreak day, as I've now come to think of it, was over. And it's fair to say, it hadn't been the best . . .*

. . . but I had learnt one important life lesson. If you go round to Neil's, don't play with his Lego.

Episode 4

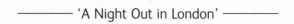

——————— 'A Night Out in London' ———————

I think one of the reasons that for a long time we only had five scripts was because we had put at least double the amount of words into this episode. We always write long, and then edit and cut down to the good bits, but this episode was ridiculous at more than twice the length it needed to be.

This was probably partly because we planned this as the opening episode and we were trying really hard to make it as funny as possible, and partly because growing up on the outskirts of London we both had had many nights out in town with friends, so there was an enormous pool of stories to work from.

The original draft was long, rambling and not especially good, to be honest. The finished episode still feels to me a little short of our best stuff, but it did contain an actual shot of a pair of shoes that are Damon's and he thinks are stylish ('flippas'), as well as the now familiar 'bus wankers' scenes. 'Bus wankers' came from a friend of Damon's who, some twenty years ago, standing at a bus stop near Gravesend, was greeted with 'Bus wankers' yelled out of the window of a moving Fiesta. It had always seemed almost perfect as an insult to us, because it was so pointless and yet cutting and totally unfair. For the record, I hadn't owned a car for ten years when we wrote this episode, and can still tell you the routes of at least twelve buses in London (the 8 being a favourite), so if anyone's a bus wanker, it's me.

——————— SCENE 1 ———————

INT. COMMON ROOM

WILL V/O   *In case you're interested, at my old school the day began with prayers followed by hymns and then an inspirational reading. Here it began with Jay showing me a pornographic video.*

SIMON, WILL, JAY AND NEIL ARE HUNCHED ROUND JAY'S NEW LAPTOP, WHICH HAS A WIRELESS INTERNET CONNECTOR ON THE SIDE. JAY IS PLAYING THEM THE '2 GIRLS, 1 CUP' VIDEO (LOOK IT UP ON THE INTERNET).

JAY   Right, watch this.

THE DISTINCTIVE MUSIC TRACK STARTS.

SIMON   This is tame, they're not even naked. Oh wait a minute, is she going to?

WILL   Oh my God. That can't be real. That's got to be chocolate.

NEIL   They should've got a bigger cup.

JAY   How tame is that then?

NEIL   Oh Christ, I'm gonna heave.

WILL   Jesus wept. Don't lick it.

NEIL   She's gonna vomit.

SIMON   I'm gonna vomit.

JAY   This is the best bit, look.

THERE IS A MOMENT WHERE IT LOOKS LIKE NEIL, WILL AND SIMON ARE GOING TO VOMIT.

SIMON/NEIL   Ooh!

WILL   Is it possible to 'unsee' things?

SIMON   (STILL IN A STATE OF SHOCK) I don't like girls any more.

WILL   So you get a new laptop and the first thing you did was find that?

JAY   No, it wasn't the first thing, this was the first thing.

JAY HITS THE KEYBOARD AND WE HEAR SOME HEAVY-DUTY MOANING, CLEARLY FROM A US PORN FILM. A GROUP OF GIRLS SITTING NEARBY LOOK OVER.

GIRL   You lot are such saddos.

WILL   (SLAMMING JAY'S LAPTOP SHUT) That's it, we can't carry on like this.

SIMON   Carry on like what?

WILL   We can't spend another term treading water, being the same old sad cases.

JAY   Well I'm not a sad case.

WILL   You just got called a sad case. Look, we've got to do something.

SIMON   What do you mean?

WILL   Carpe diem.

NEIL   Go fishing?

WILL   Seize the day. Do something unexpected. Reinvent ourselves, show the girls and everyone else who we really are.

SIMON   Reinvent ourselves as what?

WILL   I don't know. Literally anything. Something cool. We could . . . start going clubbing in London.

SIMON   My dad would never let me drive to London.

WILL   Thanks Si. That's the spirit.

NEIL   I could drive us. I got a car last weekend.

JAY   You got a car? You haven't even passed your test.

NEIL   Yeah I have.

WILL   And you never thought to mention it?

I love this shot as it's pretty much the whole team (minus parents). I'd guess that this is pre-series two, and of particular note for *Inbetweeners* fans are Miles, who plays "David" (far left on the bottom row) who has never had a line but been in almost every episode, which takes some stamina; Richard Hart (middle back, next to Donovan) who plays David Glover and can often be seen hanging round the pool table, and Isabella Laughland (back, other side of Donovan) who played Louise Graham and is a very fine actress who you might recognise from *Harry Potter* or *Black Mirror* by Charlie Brooker. Also of note is Kennedy's hand (the hand of real-life brilliant comedian Waen Shepherd) on Neil's shoulder.

The four of them outside the school in Ruislip where we filmed a lot of series one. I'd guess that Joe and James have just said / done something naughty by their smirks. Those two tend to drive the off camera jokes and are something of a weird Essex double act.

Above:

Simon Bird as Will. Actually a very handsome man and a very natty dresser. But not here.

Below:

Joe Thomas as Simon. His hair got spikier and madder as the show went on. Still no-one is claiming responsibility / credit for it.

Above Left:
Hotel rooms for the cast
can be expensive during
the shoot, and this is
one way the boys chip in
to save costs.

Above Right:
Blake Harrison as Neil
modelling the blue
jumper, and behind
him the actual working
lockers of the school
we shot in. Meaning
some poor kid's stuff is
getting rifled through
every time you see a
scene where they start
in a locker.

Left:
James Buckley as Jay
in the bowl-cut years,
meaning this was
probably taken around
series two.

Right:

Early Days. This is the very first week of filming ever, at Thorpe Park. An innocent time - none of us had any idea that the show would be watched by anyone at all - and the boys look suitably relaxed. Two interesting things about this photo. One, Simon is the only one to go for a lolly, despite loving ice cream so much he asks for it specifically from the catering truck. And two, I'll bet five hundred quid that Blake has something unnatural stuffed in those Speedos.

Above:

Emily Head is a dream to work with. Funny, nice, professional: much more so than any of the boys, and she's also a really good laugh to hang out with. We made Carli noticeably less nice than when she started, especially by the film, and Emily still somehow made her believable and sympathetic. Cheers Em.

Right:

Phil Gilbert, played by clinical giant Greg Davies, is named after a lovely producer in the Bwark office (Phil Gilbert, obviously) who's been around on the show since series one. Bless you Phil, may the Lord bless Phil.

Below:

Backstage at the fashion show. I remember this photo shoot as we didn't want to give too much away. Unlike Simon on the catwalk. I think it's fair to say that Carli has no future as a fashion designer with her weird double denim / S&M *Moulin Rouge* inspired collection.

Sarah-Jane and the amazing make up team make sure that everything is just right. Even the graffiti cocks. About three months after I took this I was in a cast myself, not falling off a garage like Neil, but getting so drunk in Malia when I was meant to be working that I fell off a dance floor during a dance-off with Damon.

Rehearsal. This is from the episode that Damon and I directed, and is the scene and the moment where Neil says thanks to Gilbert for the advice about getting a girl pregnant, an leaves. I think in the final cut w got Simon Bird to not smile and loo straight down the lens.

Simon and Tara - in The Venue in Blackhorse Lane, which you may recognise from an episode of *Peep Show*. Hannah Tointon is far more glamorous in real life than Tara, and I'm pretty sure she's never puked on th floor of a pub. 80% sure.

Above and Right:

Shoe shop / clothes shop in Waterside, which was actually the Pavilions shopping centre in Uxbridge. They stepped in at very short notice and let us film there after our preferred location dropped out at the last minute citing 'issues with the script'. (Not funny enough? Too many tall jokes? They never said.) When we shot there loads of people came to watch us, which is usually a disaster, but not a single one shouted to ruin a scene, or made noise, or did anything dickish. You were all amazing, thanks so so much, and for those two reasons I will always love Uxbridge.

Right:

This is Blake and James mocking a part of the script that called for them to spy on Will. You can see from their faces that they are taking the piss at the cartoonish nature of what they have been asked to do, the gits. But they were right, it did look stupid, and this kind of kids show acting is one of the many ways they let us to realise that we've written something shit.

In the woods - I think this was taken just after they have come back from chucking Joe in a muddy hole. Not for the show, for fun. We were out in these woods for the last bit of filming the last episode of the last series. And they are all still friends. If anything, they grew closer as the years went on, and the shoots became more and more fun. I miss them all.

TV Quick / TV Choice awards. Always a brilliant night, honestly those two mags know how to throw a party. It's full of proper TV stars, and because there are no TV cameras, everyone really goes for it and enjoys themselves, and it's even better when you win. A grinning Ben Palmer far left is dwarfed by Greg Davies, despite Ben being over six foot himself. Have we mentioned Greg's height enough yet?

NEIL   You never asked.

WILL   Of course, I forgot that's how it works. We have to ask you every single thing that might have happened in case it did.

JAY   That's brilliant Neil, now we won't have to drive around in Simon's little bitchmobile.

SIMON   Oh right. No more lifts for you then.

WILL   What about that then Si? If you don't have to drive, will you come?

SIMON   It's not the driving I'm worried about, it's more that we won't get in anywhere, won't get served and might get robbed, stabbed or killed.

JAY   Bullshit. All right, I go up to London all the time.

SIMON   When do you ever go up to London?

JAY   All the time. I went last weekend. Fucked some girl up there.

SIMON   Did you? Where was that then?

JAY   Was in the Tower of London.

WILL   The Tower of London? What did you do after you'd fucked her – cut her head off? Showed her the crown jewels.

JAY   She'd already seen the crown jewels, thanks. My bell-end.

WILL   Brilliant.

THEY ALL GET UP TO LEAVE FOR CLASS.

———— SCENE 2 ————

INT. SCHOOL CORRIDOR

WILL V/O   *Reinventing ourselves as clubbers was a brilliant idea of mine. Obviously we wouldn't actually get in anywhere, but Simon could at least give it a go.*

THE BOYS ARE ALL WALKING TOWARDS THE LUNCH HALL.

WILL   Go on Si, please come along.

SIMON   It'll be expensive, won't it? Don't some of those clubs charge thirty quid to get in?

JAY   I've already told you, I know the bloke who runs all the doors. He'll just slip us in.

SIMON   And when that turns out to be bullshit, what then?

FROM AROUND THE CORNER CARLI AND HER FRIEND (RACHEL) COME INTO VIEW. CARLI COMES OVER TO SPEAK TO SIMON.

CARLI   Hi Simon.

SIMON   Carli!

CARLI   How's your stomach?

SIMON   Oh, I . . . fine.

CARLI   (TO HER FRIEND) Simon had a really bad diarrhoea over the weekend. Really bad.

SIMON   Look, we're going up to London on Saturday, clubbing. Do you want to come?

CARLI   Sounds fun. We'd love to go. Which club are you going to?

SIMON   Um . . .

HE LOOKS DESPAIRINGLY ACROSS AT WILL, JAY AND NEIL.

NEIL   Spearmint Rhino

CARLI   Isn't that a strip club?

WILL   No, he's made a mistake. We're going to one of the big ones. One of the big cool ones right in the middle of London.

RACHEL   Oh right. Which one?

WILL   Um, the Land of . . .

SIMON   The Sound of . . .

CARLI   We usually go to the Astoria.

WILL   And that's exactly where we are going.

CARLI   Cool.

NEIL   And I'm driving if you want a lift?

CARLI   Nah, we're cool, we'll probably go up early, check out the shops. A lift back would be great though.

NEIL   No problemo.

SIMON WINCES JUST A TINY BIT AS NEIL SAYS THIS.

RACHEL   (POINTEDLY TO WILL) So do you go clubbing a lot then?

WILL   Me?

RACHEL   Yes, you.

WILL   Erm, yeah, yeah, course. Dancing on the podium probably or up by the speakers where it's, if anything, too loud.

RACHEL   Great. See you there.

CARLI   See ya.

SIMON   Great, see you later then.

THE GIRLS WALK AWAY.

JAY   (JUST AS THEY GET OUT OF EARSHOT) What did I tell you? London and muff go hand in hand.

SIMON   Fucking hell. I'm going on a date with Carli.

JAY   It's not really a date.

SIMON   I think it is.

NEIL   (TO WILL) I reckon you're in there too.

WILL   Me? Why do you think that?

NEIL   'Cos she touched her hair. In body-language speak that means she wants you.

JAY   Well in London on Saturday night there will be plenty of girls round me touching their hair.

WILL   Their pubic hair presumably?

JAY   No. Their, um, long . . . no, yeah, their pubic hair.

——— SCENE 3 ———

EXT. STREET BY NEIL'S HOUSE

WILL V/O   *Saturday rolled around and we were all incredibly excited about our night out in London. Rachel, an actual girl with a working face, had asked me if I was going, Simon got to continue his stalking of Carli, Neil just liked being out in the open like a Labrador, and Jay was up for some more make-believe sex in a tourist attraction. Maybe a hand job at Madame Tussaud's . . .*

MONTAGE OF THE BOYS GETTING READY.

WILL V/O. . . *of course I had no idea how we'd actually get into a club, but I wasn't taking any chances and wore my smartest shoes . . .*

. . . *something Simon didn't do . . .*

JAY, WILL AND SIMON ARE WALKING ALONG THE STREET TOWARDS NEIL'S HOUSE. THEY ARE WEARING THEIR BESTEST GOING-OUT CLOTHES. YOU CAN SMELL THE HAIR GEL COMING OFF SIMON. JAY AND WILL HAVE SHOES ON, SIMON IS WEARING HIS NEW NIKES. WILL'S SHOES LOOK FAR TOO BIG FOR HIM AND BEND UPWARDS AT THE END.

WILL   Why are you wearing trainers Si?

SIMON   Because they look good.

WILL   I specifically said no trainers. Not if we want to get into clubs.

SIMON   Everyone wears trainers.

WILL   Jay hasn't got trainers on. I haven't got trainers on.

JAY   You've got fucking flippers on. What size are they?

WILL   Size eight. My size.

SIMON   Oh yeah, Ronald McDonald called, he wants his shoes back.

WILL   There's nothing wrong with these. They're Italian.

JAY   (IN ITALIAN ACCENT) Ehhh, where-a are-a my flippas.

SIMON   At least you'll be all right if you fall in the Thames.

WILL   Yep, very funny. Would it have killed you to wear shoes just to be on the safe side?

SIMON   Whoa . . . check out Neil's car.

SITTING ON THE DRIVEWAY IS NEIL'S NEW CAR – A PIMPED-UP RED VAUXHALL NOVA WITH A SPOILER AND TINTED WINDOWS.

JAY   Yeah. Shit hot.

WILL   I'd say half right. It's shit.

WILL V/O   *. . . but a rubbish red Nova wasn't the main attraction at Neil's house.*

SIMON RINGS THE DOORBELL.

NEIL'S SISTER (KATIE) ANSWERS THE DOOR. SHE IS VERY ATTRACTIVE AND IS WEARING A DRESSING GOWN, WHICH DISPLAYS A BIT OF CLEAVAGE. SHE'S A COUPLE OF YEARS OLDER THAN THEM, BUT IT SEEMS LIKE DECADES.

SIMON/JAY   Hi Katie. / Hello.

KATIE   He's upstairs.

SIMON   So, how's things with you?

JAY   Yeah. Feel like I haven't seen you in ages.

THE BOYS ARE STRUGGLING TO KEEP THEIR FOCUS OFF HER BREASTS.

KATIE   (IGNORING THEM AND SHOUTING UPSTAIRS) Neil! Your friends want to know if you're coming out to play.

NEIL   Coming.

JAY   So Katie, d'you like clubbing?

KATIE   Can you stop staring at my tits please?

SHE GIVES THEM ONE LAST CONTEMPTUOUS LOOK BEFORE SHE TURNS AND GOES BACK INSIDE.

JAY   She must be on the blob.

NEIL BOUNDS DOWN THE STAIRS.

NEIL   All right. What do you think of the car then?

JAY   It's like a tractor beam for fanny. I love it.

NEIL   It's got a huge exhaust and a well-smart body kit. My sister's boyfriend is helping me do it up. He's a mechanic.

SIMON   Must be nice for your dad to have a man around the house Neil.

NEIL   What does that mean?

JAY   It means 'Does your dad suck him off?'

NEIL   No.

WILL   But your sister does.

NEIL   No. Well, I mean she might do.

SIMON   Oh she definitely does.

JAY   (POINTING OUT THE STICKER ON THE BACK OF THE CAR) Oh nice 'Porsche Engineering' sticker.

NEIL   I know. I put that on myself, it's gotta be worth at least a hand job.

SIMON   So how fast does it go then?

NEIL   Who knows? I haven't got it going yet.

SIMON   This'll be the first time you've driven it?

NEIL   No, it don't work. It hasn't got an engine. Dave's still trying to find me one.

WILL   But I thought you were driving us up to London?

NEIL   Yeah, so did I.

SIMON   So how did you plan to drive us up there without a car?

NEIL   I thought I was going to drive your car.

SIMON   But you're not insured to drive my car Neil.

NEIL   Yeah, I wondered about that.

WILL   Oh well, Simon you're going to have to drive us.

SIMON   No. I said no, and my dad will go mental if he finds out I've driven to London.

WILL   He won't find out.

JAY   And even if he does you'll have too many fingers up Carli to care.

WILL   Please Simon.

BEAT.

SIMON   Oh, Christ. Thanks a lot Neil.

NEIL   You need to be clearer about things I reckon.

SIMON   Oh OK, is this clear enough? You're a fucking idiot.

JAY   Calm down, I'll get some beers for the trip.

SIMON   I can't drink and drive.

JAY   Course you can, it's just a saying.

SHOT OF JAY TAKING LAGER FROM THE FRIDGE IN HIS DAD'S GARAGE

─────── SCENE 4 ───────

INT./EXT. SIMON'S CAR

WILL V/O   *So Jay liberated a few of his dad's lagers and we were off. The plan was simple. Get to London, get into a club, and pull Carli and Rachel and return to school on Monday morning to find our credibility at an all-time high. Yes, I said it was simple, not realistic. In the meantime we could enjoy the enlightening conversation . . .*

JAY   Here, who would you rather fuck? Will's mum or Neil's sister?

WILL   Oh good.

NEIL   Oi, leave it out.

BEAT.

NEIL   Will's mum.

WILL   Don't join in Neil.

JAY   Neil's sister would have the tighter snatch, I guess.

NEIL   Leave it out.

JAY   But Will's mum has huge tits.

NEIL   They are amazing.

WILL   Thanks Neil.

SIMON   Although Neil's sister looks like she'd be better at sucking dick.

WILL   Like father like daughter.

JAY   Oh yeah, I could see her going at it like a dog eating hot chips.

NEIL   Shut up Jay.

SIMON   I'd put my cock in them both.

WILL   That's a touching sentiment.

JAY   I'd be touching your mum's sentiment.

WILL   That doesn't mean anything.

JAY   It means I'd touch her bumhole. With my cock.

WILL   Nice one.

NEIL   I've thought about it. I'd definitely rather fuck Will's mum.

SIMON   Are you sure Neil? What about your sister's tight snatch?

NEIL   Nope, totally sure.

SIMON   Well that's good then.

JAY SEES SOMETHING UP AHEAD. IT'S A SHORT QUEUE OF PEOPLE WAITING AT THE BUS STOP.

JAY   Hang on. Slow down a bit Si.

SIMON BRINGS HIS SPEED DOWN TO AROUND 20MPH, JAY WINDS DOWN HIS WINDOW AND SHOUTS:

JAY   Bus wankers!

THE PEOPLE IN THE QUEUE LOOK A BIT MYSTIFIED. IT'S INCREDIBLY PUERILE.

THE BOYS LAUGH HYSTERICALLY.

SIMON   Where did that come from? Bus wankers.

JAY   I dunno, just felt right.

WILL   You could see their little faces drop as they thought, We must be the bus wankers.

NEIL   Pull over Si. I need a piss.

SIMON   Oh I can't pull over, there's a bus lane.

NEIL   Oh please. I'm desperate mate.

WILL   You'll just have to hold it Neil, we're late enough.

NEIL STARTS FIDDLING WITH HIS CROTCH.

WILL   What are you doing?

THERE'S A TINKLING NOISE.

SIMON   Are you pissing in my car?

NEIL   Nah.

SIMON   What's that noise then?

NEIL   I'm pissing in a can.

SIMON   What the fuck? You'll get piss on the floor.

NEIL   Don't worry, it won't overflow, I've got my chap's eye right in there so I can't miss. No problemo.

JAY   It stinks, Neil.

NEIL   Uh-oh. It don't want to stop.

SIMON   What do you mean, 'it'?

WILL   Just stop pissing yourself Neil.

NEIL   Quick, pass me another can.

WILL   That is not happening.

NEIL   Quick. It's filled up to the top, got to get it out.

THERE'S A QUICK MOVEMENT FROM NEIL AS HE WHIPS HIS PENIS OUT OF THE CAN.

NEIL   Ahhh-owwww, shit. My helmet. I've cut it on the can. Oh I think it's bleeding.

SIMON   Fuck bleeding. Is it still pissing?

NEIL   Ahhhh it stings.

WILL   Does anyone want to swap seats?

NEIL   I will.

WILL   Not you Neil.

SIMON   Get rid of it Neil!

WE SEE THE CAN BEING HOYED OUT OF THE CAR WINDOW.

JAY   Oh Neil.

WILL V/O   . . . *so, high on the smell of Neil's urine, we headed for the bright lights of London.*

————— SCENE 5 —————

INT. CAR / EXT. CENTRAL LONDON STREET

WILL V/O   *'Look out, ladies' phase one was complete . . .*

. . . we finally made it to London. And we even managed to see all the sights. Because Simon got us totally fucking lost.

THE BOYS ARE IN LONDON. THERE IS A SENSE THAT THEY ARE A BIT LOST.

WILL   It must be somewhere round here.

SIMON   I knew we'd get lost. Thanks a lot Neil.

NEIL   Is it my fault you're a shit driver?

SIMON   I don't want Carli to be pissed off if I'm late.

NEIL   You need to grow some balls I reckon.

JAY   Look, why don't we just pull over and ask someone where the club full of clunge is?

NEIL   I've got Google maps on my phone. Should be able to find it, no problemo.

SIMON   Neil, you have to stop—

JAY   (INTERRUPTING) Aye aye.

UP AHEAD HE HAS SEEN A BUS STOP WITH A QUEUE OF PEOPLE WAITING AT IT.

SIMON   No Jay, because—

NEIL   Go on.

JAY   (SHOUTING OUT OF THE WINDOW AGAIN) Bus wankers.

HE LEANS BACK INTO THE CAR LAUGHING THEN LOOKS AT SIMON, WHO ISN'T LAUGHING.

JAY   Why you slowing down?

UP AHEAD IS A SET OF TRAFFIC LIGHTS, AND THEY ARE RED. THEY'VE STOPPED ABOUT TEN YARDS FROM THE BUS STOP.

SIMON   I tried to say. Oh Christ Jay.

WILL   Oh shit.

TWO HARD-LOOKING BLOKES FROM THE BUS QUEUE ARE WALKING TOWARDS THE CAR.

JAY   Oh no, they're coming. Shit. Drive.

SIMON   Where? Where am I meant to drive to?

WILL   Anywhere.

JAY   Oh shit.

SIMON FLOORS IT AND TURNS THE WHEEL LEFT, TOWARDS THE PAVEMENT. HE SLOWLY MOUNTS THE PAVEMENT AND IS NOW TOTALLY STUCK.

WILL   Anywhere but the pavement.

THE TWO BLOKES NOW REACH THE CAR.

ONE OF THE BLOKES IS ON SIMON'S SIDE. AS SIMON IS APOLOGISING, THE
BLOKE REACHES IN WITH ONE HAND AND STARTS TO THROTTLE HIM.

SIMON   Listen mate. Sorry, I'm sorry, I'm really sorry. I'm really—

BLOKE   Who's a wanker?

SIMON   —sorry.

BLOKE   I'm a wanker, am I? Yeah?

SIMON   Sorry, I'm sorry.

WILL   He said sorry.

BLOKE   Yeah?

SIMON   Sorry, I'm really . . . I'm really sorry, please, sorry.

BLOKE   I'm a wanker, yeah?

WILL   He's really sorry.

SIMON   I'm sorry. Sorry.

SIMON IS STILL APOLOGISING AND FRANTICALLY WINDING UP THE WINDOW.
WHEN THE BLOKE'S HAND IS ALMOST TRAPPED, HE PULLS IT AWAY AND WALKS
OFF LAUGHING.

BLOKE   I'd rather be a bus wanker than drive that piece of yellow shit.

JAY   Oh fucking hell, you two shit yourselves.

WILL   What?

JAY   Oooh, I'm sorry, sorry, don't hurt me, sorry.

SIMON   You got me fucking throttled.

NEIL   Ooh, sorry. Ha.

SIMON   Oh fuck off.

JAY   Oooh, sorry I'm on the pavement.

NEIL   Sorry, sorry, sorry for my shit little car.

JAY   Oooooooooh, I'm just so sorry I'm alive and a bender.

SIMON   Just fuck off.

BEAT.

NEIL   Sorry Si.

JAY   Sorry I'm such a tit.

NEIL   Sorry I've done a poo in my pants.

JAY   Ooh, sorry my neck is stuck in your hand.

THEY LAUGH.

SCENE 6

EXT. SOHO STREET

WILL V/O   *Simon's a good friend. But it's fair to say he drives like a retard . . . but eventually, in Chinatown, just a few hundred yards from the club, we found the perfect parking space. Well, almost perfect . . .*

THEY ARE STANDING OUTSIDE THE CAR, LOOKING UP AT A SIGN ABOVE THE SPACE THEY HAVE PARKED IN. THE SIGN IS IN BOTH ENGLISH AND MANDARIN. IN ENGLISH IT SAYS 'NO PARKING. WE RESERVE THE RIGHT TO CLAMP. RELEASE FEE £200'. IT LOOKS LIKE THE SPACE IS IN FRONT OF SOME GARAGE DOORS.

SIMON   I don't think I can park here.

WILL   Simon, we've been driving round for an hour looking for a parking space. This one is perfect, let's just get going.

SIMON   But this says we'll get clamped.

JAY   Nah, it's a weekend. Different rules.

WILL   I'm sure he's right Si, and no one clamps any more.

NEIL   Please can we get going, I really need to check my knob. I think I've got a big problemo.

SIMON   Can you stop saying 'problemo'?

NEIL   What?

SIMON   It's not cool or funny, it's just embarrassing.

JAY   Don't worry Neil, he'll say sorry in a minute.

SIMON Maybe I should move it?

WILL Simon, listen to me. Carli has agreed to go clubbing with you, that is a big step forward, but in the hour it'll take us to find another parking space she could have gone off the idea.

NEIL Yeah, she could be wanking off the DJ by now.

WILL I doubt that's happening, but the point is valid. This is a great parking spot, let's get a move on.

JAY We are wasting valuable boning time.

SIMON Fine. Fine. Come on then.

JAY Don't bother locking it. If you're lucky someone might nick it.

SIMON Yeah, good one.

──────── SCENE 7 ────────

EXT. NIGHTCLUB

WILL V/O . . . *so despite the odd throttling and cut penis, we made it to the club safely. And the girls even seem pleased to see us.*

THERE'S QUITE A LONG QUEUE OUTSIDE THE CLUB. SIMON IS LEADING THE BOYS PAST THE QUEUE. CARLI, LOOKING PRETTY FANTASTIC, IS WITH A COUPLE OF FRIENDS NEAR THE FRONT.

SIMON SPOTS HER.

SIMON Carli.

CARLI Oh hi Simon, I wondered where you were.

SIMON Did you? You're actually here.

CARLI Yes.

SIMON You weren't lying about coming here then.

CARLI No. Why would I be lying?

SIMON Dunno. Don't know why I said that.

WILL Great, well we'll see you in there then?

WILL GOES TO WALK TO THE BACK OF THE QUEUE. JAY GRABS HIM.

JAY   Don't be a tit, just stand here.

HE AND THE OTHERS SORT OF TRY TO PUSH IN.

CARLI   Oh, are you joining us?

JAY   Yeah.

SIMON   Yeah, I think so.

THE PEOPLE DIRECTLY BEHIND THEM SHOUT.

CLUBBER ONE   You fucking pushing in?

CLUBBER TWO   Er, those arseholes pushed in.

WILL   (IGNORING THEM) So, great. You're near the front.

AN EMPTY COKE CAN HITS WILL ON THE BACK OF THE HEAD. HE TRIES HARD
NOT TO REACT.

RACHEL   Yeah, well we've been here long enough.

WILL   Suppose you have.

RACHEL   I just really want to get inside and dance now.

WILL   Yeah, me too. There's something very animalistic about our
need to dance, isn't there?

A SCREWED-UP BURGER WRAPPER HITS HIM ON THE NOSE.

RACHEL   I think those lads are throwing stuff at you.

WILL   Don't think so. They're probably frustrated because they want
to get inside too. They're saying, 'Let us in, we've got bloody great
dancing ants in our pants.'

RACHEL DOESN'T LAUGH AT THIS AND IS CLEARLY EMBARRASSED TO BE
STANDING BESIDE WILL. ANOTHER MISSILE HITS HIM IN THE BACK OF THE HEAD.

IRATE CLUBBER   Get to the back of the queue, you four-eyed prick.

RACHEL   Sorry, do you mind if I stand with my back to you? I don't
want them to think you're with me.

WILL   No, that's fine.

WILL V/O   *Rachel had the most beautiful back of a head I'd ever seen. Now all we had to do was get into the club . . .*

AT THE FRONT OF THE QUEUE THE BOUNCER WAVES CARLI AND HER FRIENDS THROUGH. SIMON IS THE FIRST TO FOLLOW, GRINNING. THE BOUNCER HOLDS UP AN ARM AND STOPS HIM.

BOUNCER   No trainers.

SIMON   What?

BOUNCER   No trainers.

SIMON   But they're . . . they're new.

BOUNCER   No trainers.

SIMON LOOKS DESPAIRINGLY AT CARLI.

SIMON   (TO CARLI) I'll see you in there in a minute.

HE LEAVES THE QUEUE AND THE THREE OTHERS FOLLOW HIM.

NEIL   Well that's us fucked then.

SIMON   Take it you don't know that bouncer then Jay?

JAY   What's this got to do with me? I'm not the one wearing trainers.

WILL   You fucking idiot. I am totally in there, like totally. Would it have killed you to wear shoes?

JAY   We could probably make another pair out of yours. And have enough leather left to cover a sofa.

SIMON   Doesn't matter anyway because I've sorted it. I'm going to borrow some shoes.

WILL   What?

WILL FOLLOWS SIMON'S GAZE OVER TO A TRAMP RIFLING THROUGH THE BINS.

TRAMP   (SHOUTING INCOHERENTLY) Hold it, sack!

WILL   Oh no.

Look, I'm going to level with you. I'm scared. London scares me. The bouncer scares me and that man really scares me. Let's just put this one down as another character-forming experience and go home.

SIMON   Oh come on Will. It's for Carli, she'll love it. It's romantic.

WILL   Yes. It's not quite *Romeo and Juliet* is it? These are old tramp's shoes we're talking about.

SIMON IS WALKING OVER, WILL IS FOLLOWING HIM.

SIMON   (TO THE TRAMP) S'cuse me mate.

SIMON   Mate, 'scuse me. Can I borrow your shoes?

TRAMP   Eh?

SIMON   I want to borrow your shoes. I'm trying to impress a girl.

TRAMP   Gi' us a blow job.

SIMON   What?

TRAMP   I'll give you a blow job.

SIMON   No, God no, no blow jobs, I just want your shoes.

TRAMP   All right. Twenty quid.

SIMON   Great.

TRAMP   And your shoes.

SIMON   Oh, of course.

THE TRAMP HOLDS OUT HIS HAND. SIMON GIVES HIM THE MONEY AND THEN TAKES OFF HIS SHOES. WILL WATCHES HORRIFIED AS THE TRAMP TAKES HIS SHOES OFF. SIMON HANDS THE TRAMP HIS TRAINERS AND PUTS ON THE TRAMP'S SHOES. THERE'S A DEFINITE SQUELCH.

WILL V/O   *. . . good old Simon. I could always rely on him to add a touch of class to proceedings. In many ways, though, it proved how much he valued Carli. Certainly more than he valued his dignity . . .*

SIMON   They're a bit wet.

TRAMP   Aye, that'll be my piss.

SIMON   OK. Thanks.

THE BOYS WALK BACK TO THE CLUB ENTRANCE.

THE BOUNCER LOOKS THEM UP AND DOWN AND GIVES THEM THE NOD TO GO IN.

WILL V/O   *. . . I'm not saying it was a dodgy club, but you have to question a door policy that says no to trainers but a big thumbs up to piss-soaked tramp shoes.*

———— SCENE 8 ————

INT. NIGHTCLUB

WILL V/O   *But we were in. We had got in, yes in the club, an actual club. Yes.*

THE FOUR BOYS PURPOSEFULLY STRIDE INTO THE NIGHTCLUB. THE PLACE IS HEAVING AND THERE ARE SOME SCANTILY CLAD FIT GIRLS.

JAY   I've died and gone to clunge heaven.

NEIL   Oh nice.

WILL   Well, this is what we wanted. This is it, the first day of the rest of our lives.

JAY   One small step for a man, one giant leap for your flippas.

WILL   You won't be laughing when we pull Carli and Rachel.

JAY   No I won't, cos it ain't gonna happen. Right, you can spend your evening talking to little girls, me and Neil are gonna find ourselves some proper women with experienced snatches.

WILL   Good luck with that. Just so you know, I think the Tower of London is closed now.

NEIL AND JAY SLIDE OFF ONE WAY WHILE SIMON AND WILL HEAD OFF TO FIND THE GIRLS.

——— SCENE 9 ———

INT. NIGHTCLUB, DANCEFLOOR

SIMON AND WILL SEE CARLI STANDING ON HER OWN AT THE UPPER BAR. RACHEL IS NOWHERE TO BE SEEN.

SIMON   Right, there she is. How do I look?

WILL   You look good.

SIMON   Obviously. Where's Rachel?

WILL   Don't worry, she's keen, I'm sure she'll find me. Away you go, mate.

SIMON   Wish me luck.

SIMON HEADS OFF TO TALK TO CARLI.

SIMON   Carli.

CARLI   Simon. You got in. I thought you were turned away.

SIMON   Well, Will was being a bit of a dick with the bouncers and there was a thing with my shoes . . .

AS HE TALKS, A HANDSOME AND, CRUCIALLY, OLDER-LOOKING GUY RETURNS TO CARLI, CARRYING A COUPLE OF DRINKS.

ADAM   They're out of ice already. Can you believe that?

CARLI   Oh Simon, this is Adam. He's a mate of Rachel's.

SIMON   Oh. All right?

ADAM   Yeah. You?

WHILE SIMON NODS, ADAM TAKES A SNIFF OF THE AIR.

CARLI   Simon's an old friend of the family.

SIMON   Not just that though.

ADAM   Can you smell piss?

SIMON   Um?

CARLI   Eurgh, yes. That's totally rank.

ADAM   Must be the toilets. We should move.

SIMON   Yeah, good idea.

———— SCENE 10 ————

INT. NIGHTCLUB, STAIRS

WILL V/O   *Meanwhile, Jay and Neil headed downstairs to discuss the nuances of sexual politics.*

NEIL AND JAY ARE STANDING AT THE FOOT OF THE STAIRS OGLING GIRLS THAT PASS INTO VIEW.

JAY   Oh, she'd definitely get it.

NEIL   Most definitely. What about her? I think she looked over.

JAY   Nice body, frightening face. You'd have to do her from behind.

NEIL   What about her?

JAY   Bit big, but then fat birds are more grateful.

THEY SEE ANOTHER SEXY GIRL.

NEIL   Check out the jubblies on that.

JAY   Oh, she'd get it. Until it fell off.

THEY WATCH HER SHIMMYING ON THE DANCE FLOOR.

NEIL   Oh please don't.

JAY   Please do.

NEIL   Oh no, she's giving me a boner and my cock's hurting worse than ever. I better go and check it out.

JAY   All right, but I might not be here when you get back. That one keeps giving me the 'I'm going to milk your balls dry' look.

CLEARLY 'THAT ONE' IS OBLIVIOUS TO JAY STARING AT HER. NEIL LEAVES TO FIND THE TOILETS.

JAY STANDS ALONE NODDING HIS HEAD TO THE MUSIC.

———— SCENE 11 ————

INT. NIGHTCLUB, MALE TOILETS

WILL V/O   *And in the toilets, Neil had a very big problemo. With his cock.*

NEIL IS AT THE URINAL INSPECTING HIS CUT COCK. A LOT. AND MAKING WINCING NOISES AS HE TURNS IT AROUND AGAIN AND AGAIN IN HIS HANDS. A MAN NEXT TO HIM HASTILY LEAVES.

ANOTHER MAN COMES IN. HE'S ABOUT TO USE THE URINAL. HE HEARS NEIL MAKING WINCING NOISES THAT COULD BE MISTAKEN FOR QUIET SOUNDS OF SEXUAL PLEASURE. HE CHANGES HIS MIND AND LEAVES.

———— SCENE 12 ————

INT. NIGHTCLUB, PRIVATE ROOM

WILL V/O   *I had my own difficulties in the cock department. Rachel was sitting next to one.*

WILL HAS TRACKED DOWN RACHEL, WHO IS CHATTING AND LAUGHING WITH ANOTHER GUY. WILL CUTS IN:

WILL   Rachel, there you are. Found you. Ready to put on your dancing shoes? I know I am.

RACHEL   That's good.

WILL   Hi, I'm Will.

DEAN   Dean.

WILL   So do you come here often Dean?

DEAN   I bet you say that to all the girls.

WILL LAUGHS THROUGH GRITTED TEETH.

WILL   He's got some chutzpah, I'll give him that. Anyway, nice to meet you, Dean, but we're off.

RACHEL   What? I'm good here, thanks.

WILL   Come on Rachel, it's getting a bit crowded round here, hey Dean?

DEAN   Sorry mate?

WILL   Look, come on mate, you've had a good run. Believe me, if I was in your shoes and I saw a gorgeous girl sitting on her own, I'd have made the move, but I'm here now, so . . .

DEAN   So what?

WILL   So do the honourable thing and step aside, because I was in with her first.

RACHEL   No you weren't.

DEAN   Is this guy for real? He talks like he's from a black and white film.

WILL   (TO RACHEL) Yes I was, I stood with you in the queue.

RACHEL   Behind me.

WILL   Well, more beside you. And you specifically asked me to come along tonight. I have got witnesses.

RACHEL   Will, I think you've got the wrong end of the stick.

WILL   Evidently. So is that it? So shall I just go away and leave you to it?

RACHEL   Yes. Go away.

WILL   Fine. Fine. That's the last you'll see of me. Thanks Dean, thanks a lot mate.

WILL STORMS OFF.

 SCENE 13

INT. NIGHTCLUB, MAIN BAR

WILL V/O   *I was starting to go off Rachel, she wasn't really my type. Elsewhere, my friends were faring no better.*

SIMON, CARLI AND ADAM HAVE MOVED TO A DIFFERENT AREA.

CARLI   I can still smell it.

ADAM   It's following us.

CARLI   Simon, I'm not being rude, but I think that smell might be you.

SIMON   Right. These shoes do kick up a bit.

CARLI SEES SIMON'S DISGUSTING SHOES.

CARLI   Jesus, what the fuck is on your feet?

SIMON   Oh, no, these aren't my shoes. I had to borrow them to get in.

CARLI   Who brings spare shoes to a nightclub?

SIMON   Oh no one. I swapped them with a bloke outside the club.

CARLI   What was he, a tramp?

SIMON   I think you're supposed to say homeless now.

CARLI   Sorry, you're wearing a tramp's shoes?

ADAM   Mate, that is weird.

SIMON   Yeah. Maybe.

——————— SCENE 14 ———————

INT. NIGHTCLUB, MALE TOILETS

WE FOLLOW JAY INTO THE TOILETS. NEIL IS STILL STANDING IN THE CORNER AT THE URINAL CHECKING OUT HIS COCK AND MOANING.

JAY   What's taking so fucking long?

NEIL   Oh mate, it's not good. Get us some bog roll, it's bleeding. Look.

NEIL TURNS TO JAY.

JAY   Oh Jesus, put it away.

NEIL   I can't. It stings when it rubs on my pants.

JAY   Well take your pants off then.

NEIL   Then it'll rub on my jeans.

JAY   Neil, no matter what your old man says, you can't walk round London with your knob hanging out.

AS THEY STAND THERE FACING EACH OTHER TWO BOUNCERS STORM INTO THE TOILETS. THEY MOVE IN, GRAB JAY AND NEIL AND MARCH THEM OUT.

NEIL   What? I didn't do nothing. I wasn't doing anything.

———— SCENE 15 ————

INT. NIGHTCLUB, MAIN BAR

WILL   So she didn't see the romantic intention behind the tramp shoes?

SIMON   Not immediately, but if that prick Adam hadn't been there it would've been different.

WILL   To be fair to him, the smell is appalling.

SIMON   You don't have to tell me, I'm breathing through my mouth. What happened with Rachel?

WILL   Oh, the usual. It was all going quite well, then she realised that I'm a massive dickhead and she pulled some other bloke.

SIMON   Right.

It's shit here, isn't it?

WILL   Yeah. Shall we go?

SIMON   Yeah.

THEY SEE JAY AND NEIL BEING DRAGGED OUTSIDE BY THE TWO BOUNCERS.

SIMON   Oh no.

NEIL   (SHOUTING) I wasn't wanking.

SIMON   Oh great.

NEIL   My cock's cut. MY COCK'S CUT.

WILL V/O   *So we were chucked out, out of the club. The actual club chucked us out. Exactly twenty-five minutes after it started, our life as cool London clubbers was over.*

──────── SCENE 16 ────────

EXT. NIGHTCLUB, ALLEY

SIMON   So what happened?

NEIL   I don't know. All I was doing was looking at the cut on my cock. Jay was helping me out.

WILL   Sorry, Jay was helping you out?

NEIL   He got me some tissues.

JAY   It's not how it sounds.

WILL   Because it sounds like you were watching Neil wank in the toilets.

NEIL   I wasn't wanking, I was just rolling it round in my hands.

WILL   All right, spare us the details.

SIMON   Oh fuck, what if Carli is getting off with that bloke?

AS THEY ARE WAITING, THE TRAMP FROM EARLIER HOVES INTO VIEW.

JAY   Don't cry Si, at least you can get your trainers back.

SIMON   What? Oh brilliant.

AS THE TRAMP GETS NEARER, SIMON CAN SEE HE'S STILL GOT THE TRAINERS ON BUT THEY ARE FUCKED, COVERED IN WHAT LOOKS SUSPICIOUSLY LIKE SHIT.

SIMON   How the hell have you done that?

TRAMP   What?

SIMON   You've only had them an hour.

NEIL   Maybe he's been out?

WILL   Technically he's always out.

SIMON   Right, that's it. Let's go. I've had enough. Standing sober in an alleyway stinking of piss and wearing tramp shoes wasn't what I had planned for this evening.

WILL   Out of interest, did you think it would go better or worse than this?

WILL V/O   *So the night was over and all we wanted to do now was get back in Simon's shit car and go home.*

──────── SCENE 17 ────────

EXT. SOHO STREET

THEY ROUND THE CORNER TO THE ALLEYWAY WHERE THEY LEFT THE CAR. SIMON CAN SEE VERY CLEARLY THAT IT'S BEEN CLAMPED.

SIMON   Oh fuck. Oh fuckety fuck. Fucko.

JAY   Ooh shit.

SIMON   Right, how much money have we got between us?

JAY   No, you chose to park there.

SIMON   Fucking hell Jay.

Will?

WILL   Sorry mate, I don't have any money left – getting in cleaned me out. I think you'll have to call your dad.

SIMON   It's one in the morning. He's going to go fucking mental.

And I told him I was staying at Neil's.

NEIL   Unlock it Si, I'm freezing.

WILL   He loves you. I'm sure he'd rather come and get you than see you suffer.

SIMON STARTS TO CALL HIS DAD.

SIMON   Dad, it's Simon. Simon. Don't panic, nothing's wrong. Just calm down. No I'm not dead. Well if I'm dead how can I be talking to you?

JUST THEN A HARD-LOOKING CHINESE BLOKE COMES OUT OF THE GARAGE.

CHINESE MAN   Oi. You owe me two hundred pound.

SIMON   I'll call you back.

WILL   Sir, as I am sure you are aware, private clamping is illegal. In addition to that it is a weekend—

CHINESE MAN   I couldn't get my fucking van out.

SIMON   Look, I've just called my dad and—

CHINESE MAN   I couldn't give a fuck. Two hundred pounds – now.

SIMON PANICS AND HE AND WILL GET INTO THE CAR AND LOCK THE DOORS. JAY AND NEIL ARE IN THE BACK.

SIMON   I don't have it.

WILL   We don't have it.

CHINESE MAN   I want two hundred pounds.

SIMON SITS IN THE FRONT AS THE BLOKE BEGINS TO ROCK THE CAR. JUST THEN CARLI AND RACHEL WALK PAST. THEY ARE WITH ADAM AND DEAN.

CHINESE MAN   Can't you fucking read? No fucking parking. I missed all my fucking deliveries.

SIMON LEANS OUT OF THE WINDOW TO SHOUT AT CARLI.

SIMON   Carli.

SHE DOESN'T HEAR HIM AT FIRST, FORCING HIM TO REALLY TURN THE VOLUME UP.

CHINESE MAN   I want my fucking money now.

SIMON   Carli. CARLI!

CHINESE MAN   I'll fucking kill you unless you give me that fucking money.

SIMON   Do you still want that lift?

CARLI   Erm, no, I'm fine, thanks.

SIMON TRIES A HALF SMILE AND A WAVE AS HE SITS IN HIS CAR, WHICH IS NOW BEING ROCKED BACKWARDS AND FORWARDS BY THE REALLY IRATE SHOUTING CHINESE GUY. CARLI WALKS AWAY.

SIMON   Great. See you Monday.

CHINESE MAN   Two hundred pounds. I'll fucking kill you unless you give me the fucking money.

WILL V/O   *So we had successfully reinvented ourselves, but not as the boys who go clubbing . . .*

. . . oh no. We were now the boys who freaked out girls . . .

SHOT OF KATIE LOOKING AT THE BOYS.

NEIL'S SISTER   Can you stop staring at my tits.

WILL V/O   *. . . apologised a lot . . .*

SHOT OF SIMON APOLOGISING WHILE THE BLOKE THROTTLES HIM.

SIMON   Sorry, I'm really sorry.

WILL V/O   *. . . wore tramp shoes and wanked in public toilets.*

SHOT OF SIMON WEARING THE TRAMP'S SHOES.

SHOT OF NEIL BEING DRAGGED OUTSIDE BY THE BOUNCERS.

BACK WITH THE FOUR BOYS INSIDE SIMON'S CAR, STILL BEING ROCKED BACKWARDS AND FORWARDS BY THE IRATE SHOUTING CHINESE GUY.

NEIL   I think I've got a big problemo.

SIMON   Please just shut up Neil.

NEIL   Alright.

JAY   Maybe you should try saying sorry over and over. Oh sorry for parking like a knob.

SIMON   Just fuck off!

Episode 5

Damon and I didn't participate in the Duke of Edinburgh's Awards Scheme when we were at school, but we knew a few friends who did. Investigating it for research for the show (including asking Facebook and Twitter 'friends' for help), it turns out it's actually both a hugely worthwhile and a massively time-consuming activity. Anyone who gets a gold DofE Award will have put in more hours than you can imagine, certainly more than I could ever countenance putting into one activity myself (unless that activity was ISS Pro Master League on the PS2, into which I put months of work).

Will, of course, doesn't put in the work. He's just thinking about a combination of, the variety he'll need on his CV to get into university, and his cock. Which, sadly, is a pretty fair reflection of my motivations at that age. That and football.

And talking of his cock, or my cock, or cocks in general, the pubic-wig story was a coming together of one of my anecdotes and one of Damon's. Damon and his mates once poured Immac down their friend's pants when he had passed out drunk. He woke up, showered, all his pubes fell out, and they forgot to tell him what they'd done until many years later. In the meantime, the victim had sleepless nights and visited various medical specialists, until finally they grew back. My anecdote was that I once glued a massive ball of false black hair to my groin because I was playing in a representative football match and I had no pubes at the time. I thought, incorrectly as it turned out, that a huge ball of wiry black theatrical hair would be a good match for my colouring and would make me less conspic-uous in the dressing room than being bald down below. As I say, I was incorrect.

——————— SCENE 1 ———————

INT. MR GILBERT'S OFFICE

WILL V/O   *I was no stranger to Mr Gilbert's office. I often popped by with a complaint or a suggestion on how I thought the school could be better run. But today was different . . . He'd actually invited me.*

WILL POPS HIS HEAD ROUND THE DOOR.

MR GILBERT   Sit down McKenzie.

WILL   Actually, I'm glad we've got this opportunity to chat as there's a couple of things I wanted to—

MR GILBERT   Shut up.

WILL   Sure.

MR GILBERT   The Headmaster in his infinite wisdom has decided it would be good for the Sixth Formers to participate in the Duke of Edinburgh Awards Scheme. So I'd like you to coordinate it.

WILL   Me? Really? The Duke of Edinburgh representative for the entire year?

MR GILBERT   Yes.

WILL   I'm honoured, sir, thanks very much. Why me?

MR GILBERT   You're a virgin, aren't you McKenzie?

WILL   Sorry?

MR GILBERT   A virgin. You haven't had full sexual intercourse.

WILL   Um, no I haven't.

MR GILBERT   Well there's your answer. Now get out.

WILL   Maybe we should arrange a weekly meeting just so you check on my progress?

MR GILBERT   You can if you like, but I won't be there.

WILL   Or, maybe, I could compose a regular memo with how it's all going?

MR GILBERT   OK, why don't you drop that in my pigeonhole?

WILL   Great, where's that sir?

MR GILBERT   Any bin. Any rubbish bin you see in, or indeed out of, the school. Just pop all your thoughts in a rubbish bin and they'll get to me. Goodbye McKenzie.

WILL LEAVES.

─────── SCENE 2 ───────

INT. SCHOOL COMMON ROOM

WILL V/O   *So, now I was Will McKenzie by royal appointment. But like all great leaders I'd need some idiots to use as cannon fodder . . .*

. . . now where would I find some idiots.

JAY, SIMON AND NEIL ARE LOOKING AND LAUGHING AT SOME PHOTOS ON THE INTERWEB. THE FIRST PHOTO IS OF A MAN WHO HAS A BEARD, A BRA AND 'I LOVE COCK' DRAWN ON HIS BODY IN BLACK MARKER. HE'S CLEARLY VERY DRUNK AND ASLEEP.

JAY   Here look at this one.

THE SECOND PHOTO IS OF A MAN WHO HAS A HUGE BALD PATCH DOWN THE MIDDLE OF HIS HAIR AND HAS A COCK DRAWN ON HIS NECK IN BLACK MARKER.

SIMON   Holy shit. This poor fucker's had all his hair removed with Immac.

NEIL   What's that?

JAY   It's what birds use to get a nice smooth fanny.

SIMON   I think my mum uses it for her legs.

JAY   She wants to try using it on her moustache . . . and the back of her hands.

SIMON   Brilliant.

WILL COMES OVER. HE'S CARRYING SOME DUKE OF EDINBURGH AWARD
PARAPHERNALIA.

WILL   Gilbert's just told me some great news.

JAY   The school's handing out free briefcases to speccy twats?

WILL   No.

NEIL   Your mum's giving out free blow jobs?

WILL   Nothing to do with my mum.

SIMON   You've been asked to appear on *Who's the Gayest?*

WILL   Don't think that's even a real show.

What's happened is, Gilbert has registered the school for the Duke of
Edinburgh Awards and I'm the coordinator.

SIMON   Oh sorry, I thought you said you had good news.

WILL   This is good news. Think how good a Duke of Edinburgh Award
will look on our UCAS form.

SIMON   Oh now it sounds awesome.

WILL   Simon, trust me, this will look great on your uni applications
because we get to help the community but also do some pretty incredible activities like white-water rafting, abseiling, even mountain climbing.

JAY   Sounds like a queer adventure holiday.

NEIL   Just who is this Duke of Edinburgh? Does he teach it?

JAY   Course he doesn't teach it you fucking idiot, the Duke of
Edinburgh is Prince Charles.

WILL   Um, no he isn't. It's his dad.

NEIL   King Philip?

WILL   No, that is the Duke of Edinburgh you're thinking of, but he's
not the king.

NEIL   He fucks the Queen though.

WILL   Ooh.

JAY   Probably up the arse.

WILL   Look, do you want to sign up or not?

JAY   You've got to be fucking joking. There's no way I am going to get bummed by some royal bloke on a mountain.

NEIL   Yeah, fuck it, I'm in.

JAY   What? Why you twat?

NEIL   I've never met the Queen.

WILL   Simon?

SIMON   I'll think about it.

WILL   Come on, you can't just have 'moping after Carli' on your UCAS form.

SIMON   I actually do loads of things in my spare time.

WILL   Masturbating doesn't count as a hobby Simon.

SIMON   Oh fuck it, go on then.

WILL   Brilliant, I'll go and register us now. See you Sunday.

SIMON   Sunday?

WILL   Yes, Sunday. My mum's BBQ? Do you remember anything I invite you to?

SIMON   Not really.

JAY   Don't worry, I'm coming. Wherever your mum's snatch is, I'll be there.

——— SCENE 3 ———

EXT. WILL'S GARDEN

WILL V/O   *So the good news . . . for fans of overcooked meat, tedious small talk and weird neighbours was that it was the day of my mum's BBQ and it was rocking . . .*

THE BARBECUE IS IN FULL SWING, AND A NUMBER OF ADULTS AND CHILDREN ARE PRESENT. NEIL, JAY AND SIMON ARE ALL WATCHING THE PROCEEDINGS FROM THE PLASTIC E-Z-UP.

NEIL   This is a shit party.

SIMON   It's a middle-aged woman's BBQ. What were you expecting, the playboy mansion?

JAY   Still shit.

WILL ENTERS.

WILL   Um, Si, I just saw your mum inside, she looked pretty upset.

SIMON   Oh no. Blubbing?

WILL   She was a bit, yeah.

SIMON   Oh bloody hell. She's been a total baby since Dad moved out.

WILL   Your dad's moved out?

SIMON   It's no biggie. They've not been getting on lately so he's moved out for a few weeks while they sort stuff out.

JAY   What, like her face? It'll take more than a few weeks to sort that mess out.

SIMON   Shut up you cock.

WILL   Do you maybe want to check if she's OK?

SIMON   Not really, I've had it all bloody week. It's so embarrassing. Do you want me to get rid of her?

WILL   Erm, no, it's fine. Alright then, I'd better go and mingle.

Don't break anything and don't steal anything.

JAY   Alright, alright, we'll just go inside and get a beer.

WILL   No. You are banned from going inside.

NEIL   Why?

WILL   Because you'll do something like steal my mum's knickers to sniff and then wank with.

JAY   With?

WILL   Yes, with. And then you'll take great pleasure in telling me how you wrapped my mother's knickers round your cock and use the friction generated whilst thinking about her tits to make you come.

SIMON'S MUM (PAMELA COOPER) APPEARS, SLIGHTLY RED-EYED, BEHIND WILL.

PAMELA COOPER   Hello Will.

WILL   Oh, hello Mrs Cooper.

PAMELA COOPER   Simon, do you mind if we go?

SIMON   Oh bloody hell, really? OK, fine.

AS HE LEAVES WITH HER, HE ROLLS HIS EYES AT THE OTHERS.

—————— SCENE 4 ——————

EXT. WILL'S GARDEN

WILL V/O   . . . *whilst Simon offered his mother a surly shoulder to cry on, I mingled with a fellow tank-top enthusiast . . .*

WILL IS CHATTING WITH AN ADULT FRIEND OF HIS MOTHER'S.

ROY   Shouldn't you be revising?

WILL   Ha, yes. One day off won't hurt.

ROY   It might do. My nephew went to Center Parcs six weeks before his entrance exam to Oxford. Didn't make the cut so he decided to take a year out. All his friends went to university and by the time they returned for Christmas he'd hanged himself.

WILL   Right, thanks Roy.

WILL TURNS ROUND AND ALMOST BUMPS INTO A GIRL (DAISY). SHE'S A LITTLE BIT OLDER THAN HIM, PRETTY IN A SORT OF BOOKISH WAY.

WILL   Oh, sorry.

DAISY   Hello Will. You probably don't remember me? I used to babysit for you.

WILL No, of course I do. You're Daisy, Maggie's daughter. Wow. Nice to see you again. You look really different.

DAISY You don't, I recognised your glasses straight away. And your funny walk? Do people still laugh at your funny walk?

WILL Did people laugh at my walk?

DAISY No. A bit.

WILL Great.

DAISY Sorry, it's not that funny. It's just different.

WILL To a normal one?

DAISY Yes. But who wants normal?

WILL Well me now.

DAISY Oh come on, there's a guy at uni with six toes, everyone loves him.

WILL Right, good to know. So what are you doing here?

DAISY Well I was invited.

WILL Yes. Of course.

DAISY And I'm working part-time at the old folk's home up the road, so I thought I'd pop by.

WILL Wow, what an incredibly selfless thing to do.

DAISY Not really. I'm hoping one of the rich ones might write me into their will.

WILL Sounds amazing. Amazing.

DAISY Well, we're always on the lookout for volunteers.

WILL Really? We're doing a volunteering scheme at school, maybe you could get us into the home?

DAISY It's volunteering at an old people's home, there's not a long waiting list.

WILL Yes. Sorry, course.

DAISY   So you're still at school?

WILL   Technically yes, but I'm very mature.

OVER HER SHOULDER WILL CAN SEE JAY AND NEIL GOING INSIDE THE HOUSE.

WILL   Oh God, look, sorry, I've just got to deal with something.

DAISY   Oh, what's happened?

WILL   Two of my friends have just gone into my house.

DAISY   Doesn't sound catastrophic.

WILL   You don't know them. Look, can you wait there?

DAISY   Um, I'm off soon, but do get in touch about the volunteering. Now let's do that funny walk again.

WILL   Really?

DAISY   For old times' sake.

WILL   OK. I don't really know how I do it.

HE LEAVES. (SIMON BIRD DOESN'T HAVE TO SPECIFICALLY ACT HERE, HE JUST WALKS AS HE DOES IN REAL LIFE.) SHE LAUGHS.

DAISY   There it is.

WILL V/O   . . . *Daisy was perfect for me. . . she was older and more sophisticated, and caring, and best of all owned her own nurse's uniform.*

─────── SCENE 5 ───────

INT. SCHOOL COMMON ROOM

JAY, SIMON AND NEIL ARE LOUNGING AROUND. WILL ENTERS.

WILL   I've got some great news. I've spent the morning setting up our first DofE assignment. It starts today after school.

SIMON   The what?

WILL   DofE. Stands for Duke of Edinburgh. It's what people on the course refer to it as.

NEIL   Do we need to pack? Is it mountain climbing?

WILL   No.

SIMON   Shit, I really hope it's white-water rafting.

WILL   Nope.

NEIL   Oh God this is killing me, what are we doing?

WILL   We're doing voluntary work at an old people's home.

NEIL   Up a mountain?

WILL   No, round the corner from school.

SIMON   Oh Will, for fuck's sake.

NEIL   But Prince Charles'll be there?

WILL   No.

SIMON   Will, do we have to do this?

WILL   Well there are several different modules you have to pass, and this is one of them, so yes.

JAY   Oh I am well glad I'm not doing it.

THE BELL GOES AND THEY GET UP AND START LEAVING.

WILL   I'm glad you're not doing it because you always fuck things up. And as this scheme is really important to me I didn't want you anywhere near it.

JAY   Yeah, it's important for you to spend time at an old people's home because you're a paedo.

WILL   Well, if I did fancy old people, which I don't, it would make me the opposite of a paedophile.

SIMON   He is right.

JAY   Well then he's an OAPaedo.

WILL   Brilliant.

JAY   You're desperate for a gum job.

WILL   Am I?

JAY   Ooh, 'Hello, I'm Will. Pop your teeth out Doris, and have a little nosh on this.'

WILL   Right. Any more?

JAY   Yeah give us a minute.

Something about you needing a queering aid?

─────── SCENE 6 ───────

INT. OLD PEOPLE'S HOME, MAIN ROOM

WILL V/O   *I decided not to mention that Daisy was the real reason we had to spend the next three weeks nursing the elderly. Instead, I focused on the positives.*

NEIL, WILL AND SIMON ARE WALKING IN FROM RECEPTION TOWARDS THE MAIN ROOM IN THE OLD PEOPLE'S HOME.

WILL   This will be great guys, think of the stories these people will have, how much we can learn from them.

NEIL   Is it going to be boring like reading?

THEY TURN A CORNER INTO THE MAIN ROOM WHERE A NUMBER OF ELDERLY PEOPLE ARE SITTING IN HIGH-BACKED CHAIRS.

SIMON   (THE SMELL HITTING HIM) Oooh, fuck.

NEIL   It don't smell great.

WILL   Guys. It is such a cliché that old people smell. I thought you were better than that.

NEIL   But it does smell in here.

WILL   In here, granted, it does smell. But the point is we are here to change things for these people, that's what the DofE awards are about.

SIMON   Oh great, let's skip the abseiling and just watch this lot sleep then.

WILL   Simon, I promise this will be worth it.

AN OLD LADY (PHYLLIS) TURNS AND REALISES THEY ARE THERE. SHE LOOKS AT WILL. SHE SEEMS VERY NICE BUT HAS A CURLY BLACK WIG ON, LIKE THOSE NICE BUT SLIGHTLY MAD OLD LADIES DO.

LADY   Hello.

WILL   Hello.

LADY   I think I've done a poo.

——————— SCENE 7 ———————

INT. OLD PEOPLE'S HOME, CORRIDOR

WILL   (OFF SCREEN) Oooh, that's not good. Wait there.

WILL COMES OUT OF THE TOILETS LOOKING WORRIED AND FLUSTERED. WITH RELIEF AND NO SMALL DEGREE OF DELIGHT, HE SEES DAISY, IN HER UNIFORM.

WILL   Oh, thank God. Daisy.

DAISY   Oh hello again.

WILL   Great to see you. Now I've got a bit of a problem.

DAISY   Is it the smell? You get used to the smell, don't worry.

WILL   No, it's that I've helped an old lady to the toilet, and now she's in the toilet and I didn't realise that the help would extend to helping her go and I don't think it's right for me to see her, you know . . .

DAISY   Fanny?

WILL   Erm, yes.

DAISY   You don't like fannies then?

WILL   No, love them, love the fannies, it's just an old lady's fanny. Not that she isn't a person, it's just her fanny. Is hers. And is private. Why am I talking to you about old ladies' fannies? Why am I talking about fannies at all? How has this happened?

DAISY LAUGHS.

DAISY   Is she in there?

WILL   Yeah.

DAISY   It's fine, you get used to the fannies. And the balls. They are lovely old boys here, but my goodness some of their balls.

WILL LOOKS SHOCKED.

DAISY   Wish me luck.

SHE POPS INTO THE TOILET.

 SCENE 8

INT. OLD PEOPLE'S HOME, MAIN ROOM

NEIL   So what do we do then?

SIMON   Just keep an eye on them, I guess.

NEIL   To make sure we don't lose any?

SIMON   I don't think they're planning an escape Neil.

NEIL   I had a tortoise once. It kept running away.

SIMON   What's that got to do with anything?

NEIL   That was old and wrinkly. Dead now of course.

 SCENE 9

INT. OLD PEOPLE'S HOME, CORRIDOR

WILL'S WAITING OUTSIDE THE TOILETS. PHYLLIS COMES OUT FOLLOWED BY DAISY. PHYLLIS HOBBLES OFF BACK TO THE LOUNGE.

DAISY   Off you go, Phyllis. Just give us a bit more warning next time.

WILL   Sorry, I was a bit useless there.

DAISY   It just takes a bit of practice. We'll soon turn you into the Florence Nightingale of wiping old arses.

WILL   (IN AWE OF DAISY) How do you do it?

DAISY   Front to back.

WILL   No, I mean dedicating your life to helping others.

DAISY   It's just a job, Will. And actually I'm not feeling particularly dedicated today.

WILL   Anything I can do to help?

DAISY   Not really. I can't get tomorrow off to go to my best friend's hen party.

WILL   Well, I'll be around tomorrow. And so will my friends, we could cover for you?

DAISY   That's sweet of you to offer, but I'd need cover for the overnight shift too.

WILL   I'll do that myself. I'll stay up all night if I have to.

DAISY   Seriously?

WILL   Absolutely. You shall go to the ball Cinderella.

DAISY   Ha, you're such a twat, but a very sweet one. Thanks, I owe you one.

SHE KISSES HIM ON THE CHEEK.

WILL   Then let me take you to dinner.

DAISY   Dinner?

WILL   Yes, dinner.

DAISY   Don't you think I might be a bit old for you?

WILL   I promise I am very mature for my age. Normally it's a curse, but right now it seems worthwhile.

DAISY   Alright, go on then. Friday?

WILL   Great.

DAISY   Cool, I'll see you then.

Thanks again, toy boy.

WILL V/O   *Yes, I'd done it. My ex-babysitter had agreed to go out with me, and all I had to do was ask her.*

——————— SCENE 10 ———————

INT. SCHOOL DINING HALL

WILL V/O   *Oh, and pretend that my mates were happy to spend their free time bathing geriatrics . . .*

JAY   So how was your evening with the zombies then?

SIMON   Creepy. Glad I'm not going back.

WILL   What?

SIMON   Oh yeah, sorry, I can't do it any more.

WILL   What do you mean? You've got to cover an extra shift tonight, they're short-staffed. You can't do this to me.

SIMON   I've gotta go and see dad tonight. Now he's moved out apparently I've got to spend time with him. It's such a wind-up.

WILL   Fuck, oh this is a fucking disaster. I promised Daisy the three of us would cover for her.

NEIL   Oh there's a bird involved. Now I get it.

WILL   Oh God, I can't let her down, she's agreed to go to dinner with me to say thanks for covering.

JAY   Ooh dinner?

SIMON   Maybe she won't mind.

JAY   Course she'll mind, she's only going out with him 'cos he's doing her a favour. It's tragic.

WILL   Oh God.

NEIL   Jay, why don't you cover?

JAY   Fuck off, I got better things to do.

WILL   What did you do last night then?

JAY   Went down the park.

WILL   The park? Did you play on the swings?

JAY   Say what you like, but at least I don't have to wipe old arse for the next three months just to get a duke of spastic award.

WILL   Oh come on Jay. Just think of it as doing me a huge favour.

JAY   Why would I want to do you a favour?

NEIL   For money?

JAY   Actually, I would do it for money. How much?

WILL   That was Neil's idea. I'm not going to pay you to do voluntary work.

JAY   Thirty quid and I'll do it.

NEIL   Forty.

WILL   *Neil!*

JAY   Listen, if you get this nurse bird to nosh you off then it's a bargain.

WILL   You really are a vile human being. Tenner?

JAY   Twenty.

WILL   Oh God, all right then, done.

JAY   Yep.

WILL V/O   *. . . sometimes you just have to dance with the devil. Or do voluntary work with a sex pest.*

——— SCENE 11 ———

EXT. CHEAP HOTEL

WILL V/O   *Without doubt the worst thing about your dad leaving home is having to eat at places like Little Chef and the Big Steakhouse while he tries to bond with you . . .*

WE ARE IN THE CAR PARK OF A CHEAP MOTORWAY SERVICE STATION HOTEL, VERY GROTTY AND BASIC. SIMON AND HIS BROTHER (ANDREW COOPER) ARE SAYING GOODNIGHT TO THEIR FATHER (ALAN COOPER).

ALAN COOPER   Look, er, I know this stuff with your mum is tough for you guys. You've probably got a lot of questions.

SIMON   Can I get a new car?

ANDREW COOPER   If he gets a new car, then I want a new computer.

SIMON   You had a new computer last year.

ANDREW COOPER   Yeah, well, you got a new car six months ago.

SIMON   Yeah, but it's shit.

ALAN COOPER   Boys, boys, I meant questions about your mum and me.

ANDREW COOPER   Not really. Can I go now?

ANDREW GETS INTO THE CAR.

ALAN COOPER   It's been really good to see you Simon, I'm just sorry to dump on you like this, but I've not really got anyone else to talk to.

SIMON   It's OK Dad, I understand.

ALAN COOPER   It's just things are complicated with your mum and me. And not just sexually.

SIMON   It's getting late now Dad.

ALAN COOPER   She used to have an incredible appetite for it, incredible.

SIMON   Please, I don't want to hear about you—

ALAN COOPER   I wish I could just switch off my urges, problem solved. I'm a very sexual person, always have been – is it the same for you?

SIMON   I'd better get going.

ALAN COOPER   Oh, yeah, OK.

SIMON   Dad, everything is going to be all right, isn't it?

ALAN COOPER   I hope so. Look, maybe at the weekend we can go and have a look around some car lots, see if we can't find an upgrade on the yellow peril?

SIMON   Ah thanks Dad, that would be brilliant.

ALAN COOPER   . . . oh Simon, one more thing. Can I borrow your laptop for a few days? The, er, movie channels in here are a little bit soft if you get what I mean.

———— SCENE 12 ————

INT. OLD PEOPLE'S HOME, MAIN ROOM

WILL V/O   . . . *so whilst Simon was struggling to keep his mixed grill down, in his place I had Jay helping me out at the home. Lucky me.*

JAY AND NEIL ARE IN THE MAIN SEATING AREA. JAY HAS SOME BANDAGES AND IS WINDING THEM ROUND HIS ARMS, OVER HIS CLOTHES, SO HE LOOKS A BIT LIKE A BADLY DRESSED MUMMY. AND HE IS DOING 'MUMMY' NOISES AS HE COMES OVER TO NEIL, WHO BASICALLY IGNORES HIM.

JAY   (MUMMY NOISE) Urrgghhhh.

NEIL   Careful Jay, you'll wake Brian.

JAY   Fucking hell, if you love Brian's old cock so much, why don't you marry him. This is boring. I'm going for a quick tug.

NEIL   What in here?

JAY   Nah. There must be a spare room around here somewhere.

NEIL   There's a bedroom just down the hall they cleared out this morning.

JAY   Perfect.

NEIL   But they cleared it out because someone died in it. What if it's haunted?

JAY   Well haunted or not, it'll be covered in ectoplasm when I'm finished.

NEIL 'Cos of the ghosts?

JAY No,'cos I'm going to spunk all over it.

JAY PICKS UP A COUPLE OF SLIGHTLY DOG-EARED MAGAZINES LIKE *NOW*.

JAY The problem pages in these (INDICATING THE MAGAZINES) are always wanking gold. See you later you mug.

——————— SCENE 13 ———————

INT. COMMON ROOM

WILL V/O *So my plan to impress Daisy was working perfectly, apart from Jay masturbating into a resident's sink, and me being so knack-ered from covering the overnight shift that I fell asleep at school. Never a good idea . . .*

WILL IS FAST FAST FAST ASLEEP ON A CHAIR. JAY AND NEIL COME IN.

JAY Here he is, 'sleeping ugly'.

NEIL LAUGHS AS THEY SIT DOWN NEXT TO WILL. JAY NUDGES WILL.

JAY Get any grey minge last night then, eh? I know that's why you were really there over-night, you've got a geriatric girlfriend, ain't ya? I bet you creep into her room, kiss her on the false teeth and then slide up into her powdery old fanny.

THERE IS NO REACTION WHATSOEVER FROM WILL. HE IS ABSOLUTELY OUT COLD.

NEIL He's asleep I reckon.

JAY Oh my God, I don't believe it, this is perfect.

JAY GOES INTO HIS BAG AND PULLS OUT SOME IMMAC.

NEIL What you got there?

JAY Hair-removal cream. Like in them photos. I nicked it out of Sadie Cunningham's bag during registration. Her bush'll go out of control, but this'll be well worth it.

NEIL Oh no way.

HOLDING THE IMMAC, JAY GENTLY PULLS WILL'S TROUSERS OPEN. WILL STIRS SLIGHTLY.

JAY   Give us a hand Neil.

Shouldn't need too much, he's probably only got about four pubes, and he pisses through one of them.

JAY PULLS WILL'S TROUSERS TOWARDS HIM AND POURS THE IMMAC INTO WILL'S PANTS. JAY AND NEIL LAUGH.

──────── SCENE 14 ────────

INT. WILL'S BEDROOM

WILL V/O   . . . *so unbeknownst to me, I'd been robbed of my pubic hairs. The date with Daisy was only a few hours away, and I had alopecia of the ball bag. Terrifyingly, Simon was my only hope . . .*

WILL AND SIMON ARE IN WILL'S BEDROOM. THEY'RE IN UNIFORM AS IF THEY HAVE JUST COME BACK FROM SCHOOL.

SIMON   This business with my dad is doing my head in.

WILL   I know it's upsetting mate, but it will get better.

SIMON   I bloody hope so. Christ he's boring. He keeps trying to talk to me 'man to man'. I can't bear it.

WILL   We still need some help at the old people's home, if you're interested?

SIMON   Anything so I don't have to hear about my parents' sex life.

WILL   Is that a yes?

SIMON   Yes, can I have my creepy, shitty, voluntary job back please?

WILL   Great. I get to sack Jay then, that'll be good.

Are you sure you're OK about your mum and dad Si?

SIMON   Yeah, yeah, they'll sort it out.

WILL   Well, I just want you to know that I'm here for you.

SIMON Thanks, mate.

WILL Just like I know that you're there for me if I need you.

SIMON Yeah, course.

WILL Good, because I need you to do something for me.

SIMON OK. What is it?

WILL Have a look at my cock.

SIMON Um . . .

WILL Not in a gay way, it's just something's gone wrong.

SIMON I think looking at your cock at all is a bit gay.

WILL Please, I'm serious. All my pubes have fallen out.

SIMON What?

WILL I was asleep at school. I must have had a wet dream because it was all sticky.

SIMON You spunked in the common room?

WILL Yes, but listen, I went home to clean up and all my pubes came off in the shower.

SIMON Sorry, you spunked your pants, in the common room, during the day, when there were people around?

WILL Yes.

SIMON And then your pubes fell out?

WILL Yes.

SIMON I think this is way out of my league.

WILL Just take a look at it. Normally it wouldn't matter, but I've got that date with Daisy in about two hours. What if she wants more than a snog?

SIMON Even a snog's unlikely, no offence, but go on.

WILL Well, if the miracle does happen and she touches, or worse, sees the bald old fella, what's she going to think?

SIMON   That you're a porn star?

WILL   Look at me. I don't think she'll think I'm a porn star Simon.

SIMON   Maybe you could draw some pubes on with a marker pen?

WILL   Oh OK, good idea. And after that maybe I'll draw a six-pack on my stomach? Or a longer cock.

SIMON   Or what about wearing a wig down there?

WILL   Oh, good idea, a cock wig. What sort of idea is that? Fucking wig.

SIMON   Look, if you don't want my help, I'll go.

WILL   I'm sorry if I seem a little stressed, it's just I've got no fucking pubes!

WILL   Sorry Simon, I do want your help. Please look at my cock.

SIMON GETS UP TO LEAVE. AS HE DOES SO, WILL TURNS TO OPEN HIS TROUSERS.

SIMON   No.

WILL V/O   . . . *Simon was useless, and all too soon it was time for my date. Despite my alarming lack of pubes I tried to put on a brave face.*

———— SCENE 15 ————

INT. OLD PEOPLE'S HOME, CORRIDOR

WILL IS IN THE HOME, A BIT DRESSED UP. DAISY COMES OVER. SHE IS WEARING A DRESS AND LOOKS NICE, BUT NOT TOO NICE.

DAISY   You look nice. I'm just going to wash my hands and then we'll go, shall we?

WILL   Yeah, great.

DAISY   Meet you outside.

WILL   Fantastic.

DAISY GOES INTO THE TOILET.

WILL LOOKS AROUND AND NOTICES A ROOM WITH AN OPEN DOOR. ON THE DRESSING TABLE HE CAN SEE A BLACK CURLY WIG ON A WIG STAND. HE HAS A QUICK DOUBLE CHECK TO MAKE SURE NO ONE IS AROUND BEFORE SLIPPING INTO THE ROOM AND SWIPING THE WIG, WHICH HE STUFFS AWKWARDLY DOWN HIS PANTS.

WILL V/O   *It may have been a rush of blood to my head, or maybe the slight chill around my balls, but suddenly Simon's cock-wig advice seemed like my best shot . . .*

DAISY COMES OUT OF THE TOILET.

DAISY   Are you ready?

WILL   Yep, sure am.

THEY WALK OFF OUT OF THE HOME. FROM THE BACK WE SEE WILL WALKING A BIT STRANGELY.

WILL V/O   *. . . it was itchy, but I kind of liked it.*

——————— SCENE 16 ———————

INT. SIMON'S HOUSE, FRONT ROOM

NEIL, SIMON AND JAY ARE PLAYING 'PRO EVO' ON THE PS3.

JAY   I cannot believe that plum Will is going to pay me for yesterday when all I did was watch TV and slope off for a crafty wank. I'm being paid to wank, it's my perfect job. Tomorrow I get paid twenty quid to do it all again.

SIMON   You go to an old people's home and wank off? Doesn't that seem weird to you?

JAY   Sometimes I even slip a finger up my arse while I'm doing it.

SIMON   Yeah, well, I'm going back tomorrow, so you'll need to find somewhere else to bash one out.

JAY   Oh no, I'll still be there. It's the easiest money I've ever earnt.

SIMON   Will's not going to pay you if he doesn't need you there.

JAY   Yes he will, he's got to give me notice. I'm a paid voluntary worker, I've got rights.

THERE'S A KNOCK AND SIMON'S DAD STICKS HIS HEAD ROUND THE DOOR. HE'S WEARING A SILK KIMONO, BUT NOTHING ELSE. SIMON IS SURPRISED TO SEE HIM THERE.

ALAN COOPER   Oh, hi Simon.

SIMON   Dad? What you doing here?

ALAN COOPER   Er, me and your mum are just talking things through.

SIMON   Oh great, that's great.

ALAN COOPER   Yeah, yeah. Listen, have you got any johnnies?

JAY AND NEIL SNIGGER WHILE SIMON LOOKS LIKE HE'S GOING TO VOMIT.

——————— SCENE 17 ———————

EXT. PIZZA EXPRESS

WILL V/O   *So whilst Simon's parents had noisy unprotected sex, my first ever dinner date was going rather well, especially considering I had a pensioner's wig in my pants . . .*

DAISY AND WILL COME OUT OF THE RESTAURANT. SHE'S LAUGHING.

DAISY   Did I just drink a whole bottle of Pinot Grigio?

WILL   I wasn't keeping score, but it looked very much like that.

DAISY   Oh God. I only really came to dinner to say thank you for doing my shift the other night.

WILL   My pleasure. It was easy. The home was as quiet as a place directly before the grave.

DAISY   You're funny.

WILL   I try. No I really do try.

DAISY   Oh God, come here.

SHE GRABS HIS FACE AND KISSES HIM.

WILL Wow. Nice.

DAISY What am I doing, you're so young?

WILL Um, yes, I am, but . . .

DAISY (INTERRUPTING) No, for god's sake don't talk. Just come back with me. Oh I can't believe I'm doing this, I'm going to blame the white wine.

THEY WALK OFF HAND IN HAND, WILL WITH A HUGE GRIN ON HIS FACE.

WILL V/O . . . *this was amazing.*

 SCENE 18

INT. DAISY'S FLAT

WILL V/O *And although in her role as a nurse I was sure Daisy had seen genitalia much more horrific than mine, what she probably hadn't seen was someone with a wig stuffed down there . . .*

. . . so after seventeen years of trying to get girls to touch my penis, I was now doing everything I could to prevent it . . .

DAISY AND WILL ARE ON THE BED SNOGGING. IT'S A PRETTY GROWN UP SNOG. DAISY'S HANDS HEAD DOWN TOWARDS WILL'S TROUSERS. HE MOVES THEM UP A BIT. THEY GO DOWN A BIT. WILL MOVES THEM UP AGAIN. THIS TIME SHE'S NOT TO BE RESISTED, SHE UNZIPS WILL'S TROUSERS, PULLS THEM DOWN A BIT AND THERE IS A MASSIVE BLACK WIG. THIS STOPS HER IN HER TRACKS A BIT, AND SHE PULLS IT OUT OF HIS PANTS AND HOLDS IT UP.

DAISY What the fuck is this?

WILL Daisy, I'm sorry, please let me explain.

DAISY Is it a wig?

WILL It's a long story but I've just not got any hair down there.

DAISY SITS UP FEELING A BIT SHOCKED.

DAISY No, no, of course you haven't. I forget how young you are. I shouldn't be doing this, you're a child.

WILL   No, no, no, it's not that, I have had hair . . .

DAISY   I'm sorry Will, please forgive me. I know you're not ready and you should be allowed to mature at your own pace.

WILL   Look forget about the hair. It still works. Just touch it, you might like it.

DAISY   I'm sorry.

SHE DOES A DOUBLE TAKE AT THE WIG.

DAISY   Is this Phyllis's wig?

WILL V/O   . . . *so my stupid hairless gonads had ruined it for me. And even worse, we still had two weeks' tedious voluntary work left.*

———— SCENE 19 ————

INT. OLD PEOPLE'S HOME, MAIN ROOM

JAY AND NEIL ARE IN THE MAIN ROOM.

JAY   Can't believe you're still here and not getting paid for it.

NEIL   I like the old people; they're just like people too.

JAY   You fancy them is what you mean.

NEIL   Nah, it's not that. It's just people like Brian, they've lived.

JAY   I think they're boring.

NEIL   Oh yeah, they're boring. But it's a different boring, know what I mean?

JAY   No.

Right, I think it's about that time, Neil.

NEIL   What again?

JAY   Look, when you've got as much spunk as I have you need to release the valve a couple of times a day. Plus I've got it down to about thirty seconds now.

NEIL   You want a copy of *Hello*?

JAY   Nah, I've done that cover to cover. Definitely need some new material. Even had a wank over Fern Britton the other day. If you see baldy bollocks, cover for us.

JAY HEADS OFF TO FIND AN UNUSED BEDROOM.

———— SCENE 20 ————

INT. OLD PEOPLE'S HOME, CORRIDOR

DAISY IS WALKING DOWN TOWARDS RECEPTION. WILL HAS CAUGHT UP WITH HER TO APOLOGISE AND MAYBE GIVE IT ONE LAST GO. THEY TALK AS THEY WALK.

WILL   Daisy, listen to me, I just wanted to try and clear the air about last night.

DAISY   Will, sorry, I'm just too embarrassed. And I've got to go and sort out a new resident.

WILL   But I wanted to explain. I don't know what happened, I used to have loads of hair down there.

DAISY   Will . . .

WILL   It went down the sides, all over my balls, and I've still got loads in my arse crack.

BEAT.

DAISY   Will, sometimes it's better just not to say anything.

———— SCENE 21 ————

INT. OLD PEOPLE'S HOME, BEDROOM

WILL V/O   *So while I was flogging a dead horse, Jay was thinking about flogging something else. And in his never-ending quest for fresh material, he plumbed new depths.*

JAY IS IN THE ROOM. THE CURTAINS ARE DRAWN BUT THERE'S ENOUGH LIGHT FOR HIM TO SEARCH THE DRESSER FOR MATERIAL FOR A WANK. HE FINDS A

PICTURE IN A FRAME OF A WOMAN FROM THE 1940S AT WHAT LOOKS LIKE THE LOCAL LIDO. SHE'S IN A BATHING SUIT. THAT'LL DO.

JAY GETS DOWN TO BUSINESS, HAVING A WANK STANDING UP BY THE DRESSER. HE IS JUST HITTING THE VINEGAR STROKES WHEN HE HEARS A VOICE FROM THE BED:

OLD LADY Hello? Who's that?

THE OLD LADY TURNS HER BEDSIDE LIGHT ON. JAY TURNS ROUND HORRIFIED. HE SEES AN OLD LADY SIT UP IN THE BED. HE CAN'T STOP HIMSELF THOUGH AND HE COMES INTO HIS HAND.

JAY Oh God. Oh I'm so sorry.

OLD LADY Don't worry love. I've seen it all before.

JAY IS MORTIFIED AND IS JUST DOING UP HIS FLIES ONE (LEFT)-HANDED (HAVING A PALMFUL OF SPUNK IN THE OTHER HAND).

JAY I thought it was empty.

THE DOOR OPENS AND DAISY ENTERS WITH A MIDDLE-AGED MAN, HAVING A CONVERSATION AS THEY ENTER.

DAISY Your mum's settling in OK, I think. Oh and this is Jay, he's helping out as part of the Duke of Edinburgh scheme.

MAN How nice. Thanks for looking after Mum.

HE REACHES OUT FOR JAY'S HAND TO SHAKE IT. THERE'S A BEAT WHERE THEY BOTH WORK OUT THAT SOMETHING ISN'T RIGHT WITH THIS HANDSHAKE.

OLD LADY He did that looking at me.

———— SCENE 22 ————

INT. CORRIDOR OUTSIDE MR GILBERT'S OFFICE

WILL, JAY, SIMON AND NEIL ARE SITTING ON CHAIRS OUTSIDE MR GILBERT'S OFFICE.

WILL Thanks a bunch Jay. Nice job.

JAY I didn't do nothing.

WILL   Really? Didn't sound like nothing.

JAY   It was a misunderstanding. God, I don't know why you're being so fucking menstrual about it.

WILL   Well, I'm a bit 'menstrual' about it because not only have you got me chucked off the Duke of Edinburgh course, but you've also blown it for me with a sexy older woman.

JAY   And that was my fault, was it?

WILL   Yes. It was.

JAY   How?

WILL   You wanked at an old lady.

JAY   Oh right, and you putting a wig down your pants had nothing to do with it.

SIMON   That was a terrible idea mate.

WILL   That was your idea.

NEIL   A wig – what were you thinking?

WILL   Maybe I was thinking Neil, what am I going to do, my pubes have fallen out because my friends thought it would be funny to pour hair remover over my balls.

JAY   And it was.

SIMON   On the bright side, at least Daisy touched your cock.

WILL   Ah, no she didn't. She couldn't get her hand through the lining.

JAY   Oi, don't forget you owe me forty quid for those two shifts.

WILL   I think you may be waiting a while for that payment.

JAY   We fucking shook on it.

WILL   Yes, well we know what happens when you shake on things.

THE DOOR OPENS AND MR GILBERT MENACINGLY BECKONS THEM IN.

WILL V/O   *They say every defeat is a victory if you learn from it. Well, not this one. It had simply been a credibility-crushing . . .*

SHOT OF MR GILBERT TALKING TO WILL.

MR GILBERT   You are a virgin, aren't you McKenzie?

WILL V/O   . . . *pube-losing* . . .

SHOT OF DAISY HOLDING THE WIG.

WILL V/O. . . *granny-wanking* . . .

SHOT OF JAY WANKING IN THE BEDROOM.

JAY   Oh God.

WILL V/O   . . . *royal disaster.*

WE ARE BACK WITH THE BOYS, WHO ARE WALKING INTO MR GILBERT'S OFFICE.

NEIL   Is Prince Charles cross with us sir?

Episode 6

——————— 'Exam Time' ———————

Episode Six came out of another thing that everyone goes through: exams. We also wanted to do something different with the Simon/Carli storyline, and Simon ruining his exams for a chance of kissing Carli seemed to make sense.

The end of term is intrinsically an end in itself and everyone understands that, so we didn't have to force a large part of the script. This is the end of the series, we get it, because it's the end of the year. I remember us writing this script relatively quickly and being happy with it and how the stories panned out. We then delivered the first draft to Caroline, who promptly informed us that the stories did indeed work nicely, but that it was possibly the least funny script she'd read from us. In fact, she compared it unfavourably to a popular teen soap opera. That is one of the many reasons Caroline is so brilliant. She pushes us to our limits all to make the script as good and as funny as it can be. We're writing comedy, not drama, and sometimes it's easy to be seduced by the pathos. But Caroline never lets us get away with that. It can often feel brutal, but we've known her for a long time and take the brutality in the spirit it's intended. So if you find this episode funny you have Caroline to thank, as I think we would have sat back at draft one and admired our story-telling.

In terms of where the stories came from, I remember someone at my school crying in an exam and I think we started there for Will. For Simon, getting together with Carli seemed like a nice end to his story, and Jay getting a girlfriend was something we'd always wanted to play with. Personally I think James Buckley gave us something above and beyond in this ep. We knew the line 'my cock was too big for her' as he starts crying was funny on the page, but he made it something else. At the first read-through he more or less got a standing ovation for it, and that's hard enough at the best of times, let alone when you've been shut in the same hot room for nearly three hours and the biscuits have run out.

Another thing I remember about writing this script is that I genuinely spent at least three hours sitting thinking of ways in which Jay's dad might think women were like fairground rides. As I stared at that one line, hundreds of tortured analogies followed ('they make you sick', 'they loop the loop', 'you have to keep your arms inside the vehicle') before, as a place marker as much as anything, I wrote 'fucking mental', because in its simplest form that was what his fundamental thought would be. Anyway, Damon laughed when he read it, so there was no need to change it, and that was that.

 OPENING MONTAGE

WILL V/O   *All in all it had been a strange few months for me and my friends. My plan to raise our social standing had been a qualified success; to be honest, if anything we had slipped down the social ladder. Although I did now know the worst way to impress a girl . . .*

SHOT OF WILL DOING YODA FROM *STAR WARS*.

WILL   Feisty one you are.

WILL V/O   *. . . or kill a fish.*

SHOT OF NEIL PUNCHING A FISH.

SCENE 1

INT. COMMON ROOM

WILL V/O   *But the end was in sight. The end of term, the end of year. And if I didn't pass my AS levels, the end of my life. But at least Simon wasn't feeling the pressure . . .*

SIMON HAS A SOCIOLOGY TEXT BOOK NEXT TO HIM, BUT HE'S ASLEEP. HE HAS A CAN OF PEPSI IN HIS HAND. CARLI APPROACHES HIM WITH HER FRIEND (RACHEL).

CARLI   Hi Simon.

SIMON WAKES WITH A BIT OF A START AND SPILLS THE DRINK ON HIMSELF.

SIMON   Oh shit.

CARLI   Revising hard.

SIMON   Oh yeah. (SPILLS DRINK) Shit.

CARLI   Are you OK?

SIMON   Sorry, bit wet. Mum'll get it out though, not to worry.

CARLI   Sorry to disturb you. I wanted to ask if you could do me a favour?

SIMON   Yes.

CARLI   You don't know what it is yet.

SIMON   Sorry, go on.

CARLI   Can I come over to yours and revise sociology with you?

SIMON   Yes. God yes, come over any time. Come over now.

CARLI   Well I can't come over now.

SIMON   No, no, course not.

CARLI   But this is really great of you Simon. It's so hard to revise at the moment because we've got the builders in.

SIMON   Oh right, is that, is that a euphemism?

CARLI   Sorry?

SIMON   You know, like, um, like having the painters in.

CARLI   Sorry, I don't really get it.

SIMON   Oh, don't worry, wasn't that funny.

RACHEL   What did you mean?

CARLI   Come on Simon, what does it mean?

SIMON   Oh, just 'having the painters in' means being on your period, right? So when you said you couldn't concentrate because you've got the builders in, I thought it might be a euphemism for you being on your period.

CARLI   Right. OK, I see.

SIMON   It wasn't that funny really.

CARLI   No, it's fine. I get it. See you tonight then?

SIMON   Cool. See you tonight.

CARLI AND RACHEL WALK AWAY.

RACHEL   You're actually going to that freak's house?

WILL V/O . . . so despite him behaving like a tool, Carli was actually going round to Simon's and even stranger things were happening at Jay's . . .

 SCENE 2

INT. JAY'S BEDROOM

JAY IS SITTING ON HIS BED SNOGGING A GIRL (CHLOE).

JAY TENTATIVELY PUTS HIS HAND TOWARDS THE GIRL'S BREAST. AS IT LANDS, SHE PULLS AWAY.

CHLOE No Jay. I'm not ready, sorry.

JAY No, I'm sorry. I don't want to rush things either.

CHLOE Really?

JAY Yeah, I'd hate for you to think I'm only after you for sex. But just so you know, if you do want to touch me downstairs, I'm totally fine with that.

CHLOE I'm OK for now. I'd better go, though, my mum's expecting me, and shouldn't you be revising?

JAY Yeah maybe I should. But when you are near me, I can't think about anything else.

CHLOE You're so sweet.

JAY Come on, I'll walk you home. Unless you want to . . . (HE SORT OF LOOKS AT HIS COCK)

CHLOE Um, no thanks.

JAY No, sure. Come on.

──────── SCENE 3 ────────

INT. WILL'S BEDROOM

WILL V/O　*Unlike the others, my revision strategy, went beyond trying to get into girls' knickers. I was studying hard. By hard I mean doing literally anything to avoid revising . . .*

WILL IS SAT AT HIS DESK, LAPTOP OPEN, BOOK OPEN, COLOUR-CODED SCHEDULE OPEN, JAR OF PRO-PLUS, HIGH-TAURINE DRINKS AT THE READY. HE IS NOT DOING ANY WORK AT ALL.

THE DOOR OPENS, AND WILL JUMPS BACK TO THE BOOKS AS IF HE'S BEEN STUDYING HARD.

WILL　I've said no Mum, I had a bath yesterday.

SIMON　Alright?

WILL　Oh, it's you.

SIMON　Yeah, what is all this shit?

WILL　It's not shit, the schedule alone took me two days to make.

SIMON　Well anyway, listen, you'll never guess—

WILL　Don't sit down.

SIMON　What?

WILL　Don't sit down.

SIMON　I've only come round 'cos I've got the most amazing news. Carli asked me, *she* asked *me*, if she can come round to my house to revise. Amazing, yeah?

BEAT.

WILL　(HANDING HIM THE SCHEDULE) Just have a look at this for me will you Simon?

SIMON　Sure. What is it?

WILL　It's my revision schedule.

SIMON　What am I looking for?

WILL   Does it say anywhere 'listen to Simon witter on about his futile crush on Carli D'Amato'?

SIMON   Don't be a dick, we're mates, and I wanted you to be the first—

WILL   Goodbye Simon.

SIMON   Come on, I just wanted to talk—

WILL   Goodbye.

SIMON   God, twat.

SIMON LEAVES, AND WILL GOES BACK TO HIS REVISION. THE DOOR THEN CREAKS OPEN AND WILL TURNS ROUND SHOUTING:

WILL   Look, Simon, I've told—

HE IS CUT SHORT BY SEEING NEIL STANDING THERE.

WILL   Neil?

NEIL   Alright?

WILL   Did you just see Simon?

NEIL   No, your mum let me in. She is looking hot, if I may say.

WILL   You may not.

NEIL   Right. Anyway, I need help revising.

WILL   What subjects do you do?

NEIL   What, now?

WILL   Yes, now.

NEIL   Tech and design and PE.

WILL   PE?

NEIL   Yep.

WILL   And that's an actual AS level at the school I now attend, is it?

Oh God, I don't know Neil, go for a run or something.

NEIL   Oh yeah, hadn't thought of that, nice one.

——————— SCENE 4 ———————

INT. SIMON'S BEDROOM

WILL V/O   . . . *Neil jogged home. And later that evening Simon had Carli where he had always wanted her. In his bedroom. Unfortunately she was fully clothed and discussing sociology.*

SIMON AND CARLI ARE SITTING ON THE BED FACING EACH OTHER, WITH OPEN BOOKS. THERE IS NOTHING SEXUAL ABOUT THE BODY LANGUAGE, MUCH AS SIMON WOULD LIKE THERE TO BE.

SIMON   And I suppose the big thing is that Parsons description of the family is one of a traditional nuclear family, so that means that what he says might not be relevant for everyone.

CARLI   Yeah. You could be stronger on that. Like, it clearly doesn't mean that all his work on the family is invalid, but it's a pretty important qualification.

SIMON   Right, course. Do you want to watch a DVD?

CARLI   Overall, was his theory evolutionary or revolutionary?

SIMON   Um, revolutionary?

CARLI   Evolutionary.

SIMON   Shit, I knew that.

THERE'S A KNOCK ON THE DOOR AND SIMON'S MUM (PAMELA COOPER) COMES IN WITH A TRAY OF BISCUITS AND TWO DRINKS.

PAMELA COOPER   Oh Simon, I've just brought you some biscuits.

AS THE DOOR STARTS TO OPEN, SIMON JUMPS UP TO STOP HIS MUM ENTERING.

SIMON   What do you think you are doing? You know you're not allowed in here.

PAMELA COOPER   All right, all right, I'm going, I'm going. Say hello to your mum for me Carli.

SIMON SHUTS THE DOOR ON HER FACE, THEN SITS BACK DOWN.

SIMON   Go away. God she's a nightmare.

CARLI   My mum's the same. It's like when I split up with Tom, she was like always hanging around when I was on the phone and stuff, trying to listen in.

SIMON   Right. Yeah, cool.

BEAT.

SIMON   Sorry, did you say that you've split up with Tom?

CARLI   I thought everyone knew?

SIMON   Oh yeah, course, they do.

He's a stupid lanky twat, isn't he?

CARLI   I don't really want to talk about it.

SIMON   No, of course. I might put some music on.

HE PUTS ON SOME VERY CLICHÉD SEXY MUSIC.

SIMON   Jay got me into this.

CARLI   Simon, do you mind if we do something different?

SIMON   Not at all, what were you thinking? Maybe we could watch that DVD . . .

CARLI   I'm really shitting myself about my last exam. I know you don't do geography, but would you mind helping me out with it a bit? I'm finding it really hard.

SIMON   Now? No, no problem at all. My pleasure.

CARLI   Thanks, so I thought we'd do longshore drift first.

SIMON   Just turn that off.

SIMON LEANS OVER TO SWITCH THE MUSIC OFF. CARLI HAS THE BOOKS OUT.

──────── SCENE 5 ────────

INT. COMMON ROOM

WILL V/O   *So while Simon was cramming for an exam he wasn't sitting, Neil had his own learning difficulties . . .*

WILL IS SITTING AT A DISTANCE, BUT STILL WITHIN EARSHOT OF SIMON AND NEIL. WILL HAS AN OPEN BOOK AND IS TRYING TO STUDY.

SIMON   How's your revision going?

NEIL   Terrible. I think I pulled a hamstring.

JAY WALKS IN.

JAY   Alright benders, you missed me then?

NEIL   Jay! Alright mate.

SIMON   Where have you been?

JAY   I been busy.

SIMON   Doing what?

JAY   I've met a girl.

SIMON   Oh yeah, what's this one, a Russian lap dancer?

JAY   No. Her name's Chloe and she goes to St Claire's. We met at the bus stop, and just got chatting and that.

NEIL   Did you fuck her behind the bus shelter then?

JAY   No Neil.

NEIL   Fingers.

JAY   No.

SIMON   Let's see a picture then.

NEIL   Yeah, of her strumming herself.

JAY   Neil, can you stop talking like that.

NEIL   Why?

JAY   Because I've never felt like this about a bird before. Chloe's special.

NEIL   What, more special than them twins that only wanted anal?

JAY   What, them? No, yeah, nah, this is different, that was . . . that was purely sexual. Chloe's a real lady.

SIMON If she's real you should have a photo.

JAY There you go.

HE SHOWS THEM A SHOT OF CHLOE ON HIS PHONE.

NEIL Hot stuff.

SIMON Oh, she seems nice mate.

JAY Yeah, yeah, she's good.

WILL (WHO HAS APPEARED OVER SIMON'S SHOULDER) You've nicked that photo off some random girl's Facebook site.

SIMON I thought you were revising?

WILL I'm trying to, but it's almost impossible with the amount of noise you idiots are making.

JAY Look, here we are together. I've got loads of 'em.

HE FLIPS UP A REALLY CUTE SELF-TAKEN SHOT AND SHOWS WILL. WILL LOOKS, THEN PASSES IT BACK.

WILL Hmm. Doesn't prove anything.

WILL WALKS OFF, BACK TO HIS BOOKS.

SIMON And do you love her then?

JAY Fuck off.

SIMON No denial. You fucking love her.

JAY (SMILING AND ALMOST BLUSHING) Shut up.

NEIL (STILL LOOKING AT PHOTO) Oh yeah, I thought I recognised her. She pulled David Glover, didn't she?

JAY Don't be a tit, Neil, course she hasn't.

NEIL I think she has.

JAY Look, one, she's not like that, and two, she doesn't know anyone from our school.

NEIL I'll ask. Oi David.

NEIL SHOUTS OVER AT A BLOKE (DAVID GLOVER) WHO IS PLAYING POOL.

DAVID GLOVER   What?

JAY   Neil, don't. Seriously, don't. Please don't.

NEIL   Oh, nothing.

DAVID GLOVER   Twat.

JAY   Honestly Neil, she don't know anyone from our school, ask her yourself. We're going to go down the Fox and Hounds after the last exam on Friday. Come along.

SIMON   And what, not get served?

JAY   Nah, Chloe reckons she gets served there all the time. Oh and, er, wear your wellies, Neil.

NEIL   Why's that?

JAY   'Cos you'll be knee-deep in grammar-school clunge.

──────── SCENE 6 ────────

INT. SCHOOL LIBRARY

WILL V/O   *. . . so somehow, Jay had an actual, non-fictional girlfriend, but I wouldn't let it distract me from my new revision strategy: staring at books and praying something went in . . .*

WILL IS SITTING SURROUNDED BY BOOKS, DRINKING ENERGY DRINKS. SIMON WALKS IN WITH SOME GEOGRAPHY BOOKS UNDER HIS ARM. HE SITS NEAR WILL.

SIMON   Hello.

WILL   Hello.

Sorry about the other night. It's just, politics is really important to me and it's my last exam. I didn't mean to be a dick.

SIMON   You were a dick.

WILL   Fine. Better get back to it.

SIMON   Sure.

WILL   Why are you revising geography? You don't do geography. They aren't letting you do an extra AS level, are they?

SIMON   Oh no, it's for Carli. She just needs a bit of extra help.

WILL   So when are you revising for your own exams? You know, the ones that are in the next couple of days.

SIMON   I'm not really. I can always resit.

WILL LOOKS AT SIMON AS IF HE'S GONE TOTALLY MENTAL.

SIMON   How's your revision going?

WILL   Yeah, not bad, pretty good. Got an excellent schedule sorted out, colour-coded, and balancing my time well, have some drinks to help, Pro Plus, that sort of thing.

SIMON   Right.

WILL   And nothing's fucking going in. Nothing. I mean look at this – I must have read about the 'Accountability of Legislatures to Citizens' fifty times and I still don't know what it means. I'm starting to doubt if 'Legislature' is even a word. It doesn't look like a word any more, none of them do. They just look like squiggles on a page.

WILL   (HOLDING UP A BOOK TO SIMON) I mean, is this a word?

SIMON   Yes. 'Council'.

WILL   Is it? It doesn't look right.

SIMON   I think you probably need a bit more sleep, mate.

WILL SWIGS SOME MORE ENERGY DRINK.

SIMON   And maybe lay off the power drinks a bit?

WILL   It's full of electrolytes, which if they exist are good for the brain.

SIMON   Think of your stomach, though. Even one of those drinks makes my shits come out too fast.

SIMON   I'm just saying. Like rusty water.

WILL V/O ... *it was a novel revision tip, I'll give him that, but when it came to advice, the real man to go to was Mr Cartwright.*

———— SCENE 7 ————

INT. JAY'S LIVING ROOM

JAY'S DAD (TERRY CARTWRIGHT) IS SITTING WITH A BEER.

JAY   All right Dad?

TERRY CARTWRIGHT   All right there.

JAY   Dad, can I ask your advice about something?

TERRY CARTWRIGHT   What is it, woman trouble?

JAY   Yeah, it is.

TERRY CARTWRIGHT   That little piece you were with the other day?

JAY   Chloe, yeah. See, there's this guy at school, right—

TERRY CARTWRIGHT   So she's dumped you for this bloke? That's a lucky escape, because I thought she was a fucking pig.

JAY   No, she's not dumped me Dad. I think I love her.

TERRY CARTWRIGHT   So you're back with the pig?

JAY   Dad, we didn't split up and please, don't call her a pig. It's just that I'm getting a bit jealous because I think she might have seen a few more people than I have.

TERRY CARTWRIGHT   I'd say that's a given, isn't it? If she's got off with more than one person she's beaten you hands down.

HE LAUGHS.

TERRY CARTWRIGHT   Look mate, women are like fairground rides – fucking mental. Your only hope is when she wants some, do the best you can with your tiny equipment. Oh, and check where she is the whole time, that's the only way you'll be totally sure she's not sucking off this other bloke.

JAY   Right. Thanks Dad.

TERRY CARTWRIGHT   Although let's face it she probably is. Fancy a beer?

──────── SCENE 8 ────────

INT. CHLOE'S BEDROOM

CHLOE IS SITTING AT A DESK. JAY IS SITTING BEHIND HER ON HER BED.

CHLOE   Thanks for coming round, it's a really nice surprise.

JAY   S'alright. Just wanted to be near you. Check how and where you are.

CHLOE   Oh, that's sweet. I'll just get this last bit done and then I'm all yours.

JAY   Cool.

Did you pull David Glover?

CHLOE   What?

JAY   David Glover, did you pull him?

CHLOE   I don't know who that is.

JAY   It's just Neil said.

CHLOE   Oh, your friend Neil?

JAY   Yeah, do you know him too?

CHLOE   No, it's just you mention him a lot.

JAY   Right, course. Anyway, do you want to come round mine tomorrow?

CHLOE   Oh I can't.

JAY   Where are you going?

CHLOE   Well, nowhere.

JAY   So you'll be at home then?

CHLOE   Yes. Shouldn't you be revising as well?

JAY   Nah, not allowed. Teachers say 'cos I got a photographic memory wouldn't be fair on the other kids.

CHLOE LOOKS PUZZLED.

 SCENE 9

INT. NEIL'S LIVING ROOM

WILL V/O   *If Jay's made-up memory story was a bad revision plan, then Neil's topped it, sitting on his arse playing computer games.*

NEIL IS SITTING IN HIS PE KIT IN HIS LIVING ROOM, PLAYING 'PRO EVO'. HIS DAD (KEVIN SUTHERLAND), POPS HIS HEAD IN. HE'S WEARING HIS BADMINTON KIT.

KEVIN SUTHERLAND   Oh Neil. I really think you should be revising.

NEIL   I am, this is football.

KEVIN SUTHERLAND   Well, what about your other subjects? What about tech and design?

NEIL   I put that shelf up, didn't I?

KEVIN SUTHERLAND   Was that for your exam?

NEIL   Yeah. Well it was 50 per cent of it.

SCENE 10

INT. SIMON'S BEDROOM

WILL V/O   *So whilst Neil wasn't revising for an exam he was taking, Simon was revising for an exam he wasn't . . .*

SIMON AND CARLI HAVE SOME GEOGRAPHY BOOKS OUT. SHE ANSWERS A QUESTION AND THEN HE SHUTS THE BOOK.

SIMON   Perfect answer. You're perfect. At this.

CARLI   God, I think I do know it. Amazing.

SIMON   You've done really, really well. Honestly.

CARLI   I couldn't have done it without you, thank you so much.

SHE LEANS OVER AND GIVES HIM A KISS ON THE CHEEK. SHE THEN PULLS BACK AND GIVES HIM A KISS ON THE MOUTH.

SIMON   Wow.

CARLI   It's late, I should go.

SHE GETS UP, TAKING HER STUFF.

SIMON   Oh, sure.

CARLI   God maybe I'll actually pass geography now. Thanks again. Bye.

SHE GIVES HIM ANOTHER KISS ON THE MOUTH AND LEAVES.

WILL V/O   . . . *so he had finally worn her down and Simon didn't know whether to come in his pants or text his friends. In the end he did both.*

————— SCENE 11 —————

INT. WILL'S KITCHEN

WILL V/O   *It was the day of my last exam and I'd just got in a good eight hours' revision. Unfortunately it was during the eight hours I should have been sleeping . . .*

WILL IS SITTING AT THE BREAKFAST TABLE WITH A SCHOOL BOOK. HE IS DRESSED IN HIS SCHOOL UNIFORM, WITH HIS BRIEFCASE, READY TO GO. THE CLOCK READS HALF PAST SIX. HIS MUM (POLLY McKENZIE) WALKS IN WEARING A NIGHTDRESS.

POLLY McKENZIE   What are you doing up so early? I thought the politics exam wasn't until this afternoon?

WILL   It is, but this way I can get a full morning of revision in. Better to be prepared. Also I've not really been to bed, so what's 'early'?

POLLY McKENZIE   I am worried about you petal. Have you had any breakfast?

WILL   No, I'm a bit, you know, my stomach.

POLLY McKENZIE   Oh yes, I do know. Would it have killed you to wipe down the back of the toilet bowl?

WILL V/O   . . . *so while the world was falling out of my arse, Simon was on top of it.*

———— SCENE 12 ————

EXT. SCHOOL PLAYGROUND

JAY, SIMON AND NEIL ARE WALKING IN.

SIMON   I can't believe she kissed me.

JAY   Calm down, it was only a kiss. Come back to me when you're wanking over her arse as she frigs herself off.

SIMON   It was two kisses actually, and she's already told me she's going to the Fox and Hounds tonight so I reckon there's more coming. How's Chloe?

JAY   Yeah, she's good. Not seen much of her 'cos she's revising, but I know where she's been, and I text her fifteen, sixteen times a day to keep in touch, y'know.

NEIL   Good idea.

JAY   And send her Facebook messages and that. Bebo, Myspace, just to let her know I'm thinking of her.

SIMON   Like a stalker.

JAY   Fuck off. How's Count Spacula been getting on?

SIMON   Going mental I think. We'll probably see him when we finish, his last exam is straight after ours.

Good luck with your PE.

JAY   Yeah, don't forget your kit.

NEIL   Oh fuck.

NEIL TURNS AND SPRINTS OFF HOME.

——————— SCENE 13 ———————

INT. EXAM HALL / EXT. PLAYGROUND

WILL V/O *The moment had arrived. The last exams. Simon and Jay both knew they had sacrificed their chances of good grades for a shot at love. A sweet if remarkably short-sighted decision . . .*

. . . while Neil had sacrificed his chances of keeping his balls in his boxer shorts . . .

SIMON IS SITTING DOWN IN THE EXAM ROOM AND BEING PRESENTED WITH THE SOCIOLOGY PAPER. HE LOOKS AWKWARDLY AT IT, THEN STARTS TO DRAW A HEART WITH 'CARLI' IN IT ON THE ANSWER SHEETS.

JAY GETS HIS PAPER AND LOOKS AT IT. HE GETS HIS PHONE OUT AND STARTS TO TEXT CHLOE. MR GILBERT IMMEDIATELY CONFISCATES IT. JAY LOOKS BEREFT. NEIL HAS FORGOTTEN HIS KIT. HE ENDS UP RUNNING ROUND THE TRACK IN HIS PANTS.

INT. CORRIDOR BY EXAM HALL

WILL V/O *. . . but then, for them, it was all over bar one last bollocking from Gilbert . . .*

SIMON AND JAY ARE WALKING OUT OF THE EXAM HALL. MR GILBERT COMES OVER AND HANDS JAY HIS PHONE BACK.

MR GILBERT I checked your texts, and despite almost making me vomit they obviously weren't about the exam. Count yourself lucky.

JAY I was texting a girl sir.

MR GILBERT Well good luck with that Cartwright, and all I can say is she can't be too keen because it didn't buzz once. Now piss off and let me get this final piece of hell over with.

MR GILBERT LEAVES.

SIMON AND JAY BUMP INTO WILL WALKING IN. HE LOOKS TRULY TERRIBLE.

JAY Fuck me, it's Shaun of the dead.

SIMON You look dreadful mate, really tired.

WILL   Why do you think I'm drinking these energy drinks? They perk me up.

HE DOES A MASSIVE FACIAL TWITCH.

JAY   Have you washed?

WILL   You can't revise in the shower Jay, the books get wet.

SIMON   Yeah, well do us a favour and have a shower before tonight, yeah? Seven at mine.

WILL   You betcha.

SIMON   Right, see you later then.

JAY   Yeah, good luck stinky.

WILL HEADS INTO THE EXAM ROOM.

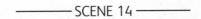

─────── SCENE 14 ───────

INT. EXAM HALL

WILL V/O   *. . . it was the most important exam of my life. And as I sat there, two thoughts occurred to me. The first was what's the point, seriously I mean what is the point, in being alive? And secondly, I really need a shit . . .*

THE EXAM HAS BEEN GOING FOR A WHILE. MR GILBERT IS WALKING UP AND DOWN THE AISLES. WILL LOOKS VERY UNCOMFORTABLE, AND IS TWITCHING A BIT NOW. HE LOOKS AROUND AND SHOOTS HIS HAND UP. MR GILBERT COMES OVER.

MR GILBERT   What is it now McKenzie?

WILL   Sir, I need to go to the toilet.

MR GILBERT   Again?

WILL   Yes.

MR GILBERT   Well you can't.

WILL   Sorry?

MR GILBERT   That will be the fourth time in a hour. You'll have to wait.

WILL   I'm pretty sure you can't do that sir.

MR GILBERT   If I have reason to believe you are cheating I can. And I do, so I have. Now get on with your paper.

HE WALKS OFF.

WILL   Oh God, no. Phil! (DESPARINGLY AFTER GILBERT)

MR GILBERT TURNS ROUND LOOKING LIKE THUNDER.

THERE'S A WET FARTING NOISE. EVERYONE ELSE AROUND HAS THEIR HEADS DOWN, BUT IT'S LOUD ENOUGH TO MAKE A FEW LOOK UP.

WILL   Phil!

WILL   Oh no, Phil.

MR GILBERT   Oh Jesus.

THE NOISES STOP.

WILL   I thought it was a fart, sir, I thought it was safe.

MR GILBERT SHAKES HIS HEAD AND LEADS WILL OUT OF THE HALL.

WILL V/O   . . . in a term of low points, this was it. Literally the bottom and yet as I waddled to the toilet, I felt strangely optimistic. Things couldn't get any worse. Painful as it may seem, in a way I was free to reinvent myself as whatever I wanted. Right after I changed my underpants.

 SCENE 15

INT. PUB

WILL V/O   And at least I still had my friends, who waited a whole ten minutes before going to the pub without me . . .

SIMON   What do you think's happened to Will? He's not normally late, he's normally irritatingly early. I hope he's all right.

JAY He's probably on the internet looking up the answers to the exam questions.

NEIL And then having a wank.

SIMON What?

NEIL Well, it's impossible, innit. I don't think I've ever been on the internet and not ended up having a wank.

SIMON Do you think Chloe and Carli will get on?

JAY Sure, it'll be like a cool double date. Ending with both of us getting some.

NEIL Maybe they'll lez off?

JAY Neil, I've told you, that's your last warning.

SIMON Do you honestly think you'll get served here?

JAY Yeah, course. I've got ID.

JAY WALKS TO THE BAR.

JAY G'day.

BARMAN What can I get you?

JAY Two jars of lager and a coke.

BARMAN Stella all right?

JAY (DROPPING THE ACCENT) Er, yeah. Cheers.

SIMON Fucking hell.

NEIL Nice.

SIMON The one time we get served and I'm driving. Bollocks.

JAY It'll be better to be sober when you see Carli. I mean Chloe prefers it. You know what I used to be like with the drink.

SIMON Erm, no?

THE DOOR TO THE PUB OPENS AND WILL WALKS IN. HE IS WEARING HIS BLAZER AND A PAIR OF TRACKSUIT BOTTOMS. IN HIS HAND HE IS CARRYING A CLEAR PLASTIC BAG WITH A PAIR OF PANTS AND TROUSERS IN IT.

WILL   Hello.

JAY   Fuck me, I thought you dressed like a twat normally, but even for you that's shit.

SIMON   Where have you been?

WILL   Just finished my exam.

SIMON   It started six hours ago.

WILL   I was a bit delayed.

SIMON   You look mental. Take your tie off at least. Why are you wearing tracksuit bottoms?

WILL   The tracksuit bottoms are from lost property, as are my new underpants, which I won't show you.

SIMON   And what's in that bag?

WILL   Well, in there are the trousers and pants I wore to school this morning.

NEIL   What's going on? Are you doing a fashion show or something?

WILL   It's a long story Neil, but the salient facts are these: recently I've had a bit of a nervy tummy, due to stress, I think.

SIMON   And all the energy drinks and Pro Plus.

WILL   Perhaps, and in the exam I took a risk and it backfired. I went to fart, and instead shit myself.

SIMON   You're joking.

WILL   No, I'm not.

JAY   In front of everyone?

WILL   Yep.

NEIL   Oh my God.

THEY ARE ALL LAUGHING IN DISBELIEF NOW.

WILL   Yes, and because of my high heart rate the school nurse spent three hours calming me down before I went back into the empty exam hall to finish. Hence I am late. Apologies.

NEIL   How do you think you did?

WILL   I think I might have failed Neil. I was a bit distracted.

SIMON   Why didn't you go home and change first? People are going to take the piss, mate.

WILL   Just to reiterate – I loudly shit myself in front of the school. There's no point in trying to hide it, life doesn't get much more embarrassing than that. This get-up is a mere fly in the ointment.

SIMON   Have you gone mad?

WILL   Possibly, hard to tell. Drinks anyone?

WILL TURNS TO THE BAR.

WILL V/O   . . . *now what could make this day worse? Oh yeah, not getting served.*

THE BARMAN APPROACHES WILL.

WILL   Good day. Could I have a pint of lager, please.

BARMAN   Stella?

WILL   Sorry, you may have misheard. I said I'd like a pint of lager.

BARMAN   Yes. Stella?

WILL   Yes. Right, well what if I want two pints?

BARMAN   Two pints.

There you go.

WILL   Well what about this?

WILL DOWNS THE FIRST PINT. THEN, AS NEIL, JAY AND SIMON WATCH, HE DOWNS THE NEXT PINT TOO.

NEIL   He's going to get drunk I reckon.

SIMON   Being dressed like that is weird enough, but that bag's got his shitty clothes in it. No one brings a bag of shit to a pub.

JAY   Your dad does.

SIMON   Does he?

JAY Yeah, your mum.

SIMON Brilliant.

BARMAN That'll be £6.20, please.

WILL Interesting. I'll have another pint then please.

CHLOE COMES OVER.

CHLOE Hi Jay.

JAY Chloe! Darling, this is Neil and Simon. This is Chloe.

CHLOE Nice to meet you.

SIMON Hi.

NEIL Alright?

JAY Do you want a drink babes?

CHLOE Um, actually Jay, could we go and have a quick chat outside?

JAY Yeah, course. I only want to be with you anyway, I see these twats all the time.

HE LAUGHS, AND SIMON AND NEIL LAUGH.

NEIL Yeah, go on, muff before mates.

JAY SMILES AND HEADS OFF WITH CHLOE.

SIMON Just the two of us then.

NEIL And Will.

THEY TURN ROUND AND SEE WILL DOWNING ANOTHER PINT.

SIMON Yeah. Not sure he'll be joining us.

NEIL We'll still have a laugh though. Me and you.

SIMON Yeah, course. Cheers mate.

NEIL Cheers.

——————— SCENE 16 ———————

EXT. PUB GARDEN

CHLOE AND JAY ARE ALONE OUTSIDE.

JAY Nice idea. This is much more private. I've been waiting to kiss you for ages. I've missed you so much.

HE TRIES TO KISS CHLOE AND SHE PUSHES HIM AWAY.

CHLOE No Jay, listen, we need to talk.

JAY Yeah, I know. Yeah, yeah. I love our talks, where you tell me about how you've, like, fallen out with one of your mates and then how you've made up later or something.

CHLOE No, I mean talk about us. It's not you, it's me, but I just don't feel this is right any more.

JAY What's not right? What, coming to the pub? We can leave if you like.

CHLOE No Jay, me and you. I just don't think that it's right that we see each other any more. I think you are a bit too sensitive for me.

JAY No I'm not. I'm really not, I promise you.

CHLOE You are for me, and you're a bit needy, and it's scared me because I'm not ready for that kind of thing. All the texting, all the calls, it's too intense, it's too much.

JAY Well I can change. I'll change. I won't call for ages, for weeks. Tell me what you want me to be and I'll be exactly that. Exactly that, just please don't split up with me.

CHLOE I'm sorry Jay, I've made up my mind. Hope we can be friends?

JAY (NUMB) Right. Yeah. Course.

CHLOE Cool. Well, have a nice evening. See you later.

SHE LEAVES AND JAY SITS DOWN SHELL-SHOCKED.

———— SCENE 17 ————

INT. PUB

WILL V/O *While Jay struggled to cope with his problems, I found an excellent way to deal with mine . . .*

WILL IS CLEARLY PISSED NOW.

WILL This is fantastic. No wonder so many people drink away their whole lives. Barkeep, another pint please.

BARMAN Sure.

WILL V/O *. . . so while I gave my liver a kicking, Simon and Neil were enjoying each other's company.*

NEIL Oh why don't we go—

JUST THEN CARLI COMES INTO THE PUB.

SIMON Hang on a second. Carli.

SIMON LEAVES NEIL STANDING ON HIS OWN AND GOES RUSHING OVER TO CARLI.

SIMON Carli.

HE GOES TO KISS HER ON THE LIPS BUT SHE TURNS AND HE GETS AN EAR AND SOME HAIR.

CARLI Hi Simon.

SIMON Hi. I've made you a CD.

HE HANDS HER A CD.

CARLI Oh right, thanks.

SIMON Oh it's nothing. Although the songs on there really do say a lot of the things I want to say, but sort of better.

CARLI Simon, listen, there's something I've got to tell you.

SIMON Oh God, I know. I feel it too. I've always felt it, for years, and now it's happened and here we are.

CARLI I'm back with Tom.

TOM WALKS IN BEHIND HER.

TOM   All right Simon? Get us a seat Carls. I'll get the drinks, yeah.

TOM HEADS TO THE BAR.

SIMON   Oh, you're back with Tom.

CARLI   Yes.

SIMON   Yeah. So that was what you wanted to say, not that you lo—

CARLI   I'm really sorry Simon. Do you want to join us for a drink?

SIMON   Um, nah, I'd better get back to Neil, I left him on his own.

CARLI   OK.

SIMON   Maybe I should take that CD back as well, thinking about it.

CARLI   Oh, can't I keep it?

SIMON   No, I've got to have it back.

CARLI   (LOOKING AT IT) Oh, that's a shame, it looks . . . Are these drawings of me?

SIMON   They're not all you.

CARLI   And is that you?

SIMON   (SNATCHING IT OFF HER) Erm, no. See ya.

─────── SCENE 18 ───────

EXT. PUB

WILL EXITS THE PUB, AND CHUCKS HIS TROUSERS INTO THE LARGE BIN NEARBY. HE HEARS A NOISE BEHIND HIM AND TURNS ROUND. IT'S JAY.

WILL   Goodbye cruel pants. Alright, you big poof? Where's your bit then? Thought you'd be out here up to your nuts in guts.

JAY   Nah. I had to er, I had to give her the boot.

WILL   Did you? I thought you were really into her?

WILL SITS DOWN NEXT TO JAY.

JAY   Nah, she was, like, frigid. And she wouldn't have this threesome even though I organised it with a top lezza model, and . . .

JAY'S VOICE CRACKS AND HE STARTS TO CRY.

JAY. . . my cock was too big for her.

JAY BREAKS DOWN & STARTS SOBBING PROPERLY NOW WITH HIS HEAD IN HIS ARMS. WILL TENDERLY PUTS AN ARM ROUND HIS SHOULDER.

WILL   It's all right mate, it'll be OK.

SIMON AND NEIL COME OUT OF THE PUB.

NEIL   Have you two been getting off with each other?

SIMON   What's wrong with Jay?

WILL   Oh, it's OK. He's split up with Chloe.

JAY   I dumped her. Make sure you tell people that.

WILL MOUTHS 'HE DIDN'T' AND DOES THE 'SPANISH ARCHER' (GIVING THE ELBOW) SIGN.

SIMON   Yeah, course mate.

NEIL   What, even if it isn't true?

SIMON   Neil! Come on, let's go. This place is cursed.

NEIL   Oh my God, it's haunted?

SIMON   No Neil.

NEIL   Well it might be. Like one of those ghost stories like *Harry Potter* or the Bible.

WILL   Maybe I could have one more pint? I did shit myself in front of the school today.

THEY ALL WALK TO THE PUB CAR PARK.

SIMON   Nope, we're off.

WILL   Aren't you going to wait for Carli?

NEIL   Nah. She dumped him.

SIMON   I wasn't dumped, it was more a mutual decision.

WILL   She mutually decided she fancied her boyfriend more?

SIMON   Yes. Come on Jay.

NEIL   Come on mate, it'll be all right, we'll get you some chips.

THEY GATHER ROUND SIMON'S YELLOW FIAT.

WILL   Think now's a good time to tell you I'll probably puke in your car.

SIMON   Great.

JAY   Ah don't worry, won't make this shit heap any worse. Shotgun?

SIMON   You've perked up.

JAY   Yeah, well, s'pose there's plenty more clunge in the sea.

NEIL   Yeah, that's it, and next term we'll be the top year which means pick of the birds.

SIMON   Oh yeah.

WILL   Oh God, next term. Do you think anyone's going to remember my little accident?

SIMON   Yes of course they will.

JAY   At least they won't call you briefcase mong any more.

WILL   Well that's good.

JAY   Now they'll call you shit-pants mong.

NEIL   Or Shitty Shitty Bang Bang.

WILL   Any more?

SIMON   Wayne Pooney. Take Shat.

NEIL   Doctor Poo.

JAY   The Lion, the Witch and the Specky Kid Who Shit Himself.

SIMON   We can keep this up all summer, you know.

WILL   Brilliant, looking forward to it.

THEY CLIMB INTO THE CAR.

SIMON   Brad Shit.

JAY   Bumdog Millionaire.

THEY DRIVE OFF.

WILL   All right. How about Vladimir Pootin!

NEIL   Who?

SERIES 3

Episode 1

——— 'Fashion Show' ———

Series Three presented many challenges, the main one being that three of the four main actors insisted on ageing (Joe Thomas stayed obligingly baby-faced), so we decided to cover the whole school year in one series. We also thought we'd maybe have a try at covering subjects we always shied away from – vandalism, pregnancy, actual relationships with girls – because we'd thought of them as the mainstays of teen dramas to the point of cliché.

But, as ever, we looked for stories or ideas that we thought people could identify with, and also things that we thought were funny. I remembered having a very similar reaction to Will when I found out there was a fashion show at my school, and my sense of it being simply about vanity and not about 'fashion' at all (no one was premiering their own lines of clothes, after all, just wearing stuff from TopMan) was heightened when I wasn't selected to model.

There was also a Post-it note left over from Series Two which said 'accidental ball out'. The idea was inspired by a story Bret McKenzie from *Flight of the Conchords* told us, about a time he and a friend played doubles tennis against two girls they fancied. His friend's shorts were too small for him, and early on one of his balls popped out. No one mentioned it, and he didn't notice until after the match. So when people ask us 'Where do you get your ideas from?' a truthful answer would be 'We steal them from funnier people.'

—————— OPENING MONTAGE ——————

WILL V/O   *My name is Will McKenzie, and my first year in state education has been an unqualified success. And by unqualified, I mean I failed all my exams . . .*

. . . that said, I have made three friends. Yep, three whole friends in one whole year. And they are the sort of friends everyone should have. Ones that are so tragic, they almost make someone like me look normal . . .

SHOT OF WILL DOING YODA FROM *STAR WARS*.

WILL   Feisty one you are.

————— SCENE 1 —————

EXT. ESTATE

WILL V/O   *But things are going to be different this year. For one, Jay can now drive, meaning we had a choice of which shit embarrassing car we got a lift to school in. Simon's was more yellow, but Jay's was more dangerous . . .*

WILL, SIMON AND NEIL ARE STANDING ON A ROADSIDE PAVEMENT, HANGING ABOUT. THEY ARE IN SCHOOL UNIFORMS.

JAY PULLS UP, ERRATICALLY DRIVING AT THE BOYS BEFORE STOPPING.

JAY   Morning benders. Jump in the mingemobile.

WILL   Strange thing to call your mum's car.

THE BOYS GET IN AND JAY DRIVES OFF.

———— SCENE 2 ————

INT./EXT. JAY'S MUM'S CAR

WILL V/O ... *Jay driving us to school really did make me feel like royalty. Unfortunately the royalty I felt like was Princess Diana ...*

JAY IS DRIVING, NEIL IS IN THE FRONT, WILL AND SIMON SIT IN THE BACK.

WILL Roundabout, Jay!

JAY DOESN'T SLOW DOWN AND CUTS UP ANOTHER CAR ALREADY ON THE ROUNDABOUT. THE DRIVER BEEPS HER HORN AND BRAKES HARD.

JAY Oi, give way to the fucking left! Stupid old bint.

JAY FLIPS THE BIRD AT THE WOMAN.

NEIL I think it's the right, mate.

JAY Is it? Oh yeah, that does sound familiar.

SIMON What's that in your ear?

JAY Oh, it's a piercing. Just a stud for now, but my dad's mining me a diamond to put in it.

NEIL Cool.

SIMON Hang on, have you had the left ear pierced?

JAY Yes.

SIMON Isn't that the one you get pierced to show you're gay?

JAY Fuck off.

NEIL Oh yeah, that is the gay one.

JAY Well there's a quick way to tell, which ear has your dad got pierced?

NEIL Neither, 'cos he's not bent.

SIMON Course not. Will which ear is gay?

WILL I'm the last person to ask.

NEIL I thought you knew everything?

WILL Well, I don't know any men who've had their ears pierced because I went to a private school.

SIMON Why have you had that done anyway?

JAY I like to keep my look fresh. Plus I'll probably need it for the fashion show tomorrow.

WILL Oh yes, the school charity fashion show. Where only people deemed good-looking enough by other good-looking people get to take part and raise money.

NEIL Well there's gonna be special guests.

WILL Special guests? Ooh, I wonder who that's going to be? Maybe Beyonce and Jay Z? The Obamas?

JAY Look, I don't give a shit what you think about it, because when I'm up there modelling I'll have my pick of the snatch. Everyone knows male models get all the pussy.

NEIL I didn't know they'd asked you to model Jay?

JAY They haven't yet. They haven't asked anyone.

SIMON I think they have.

JAY I'm telling you they haven't 'cos no one's asked me.

NEIL But it's tomorrow.

JAY Are you deaf? I've not been asked. I'd be first in line for any modelling work, look at me.

SIMON Well, I've been asked.

JAY Fuck off.

SIMON Carli's one of the organisers and she asked me to model.

JAY You? Who wants a model that looks like a spotty baby crossed with the Statue of Liberty.

NEIL Statue of Liberty?

JAY His hair.

NEIL Oh yeah.

WILL V/O . . . *it was hard to know where Jay got the idea that he should be a male model. It seemed it just stemmed from thinking that Simon was spectacularly ugly.*

 SCENE 3

INT. SCHOOL COMMON ROOM

JAY   Seriously, what clothes are going to look better on you than me? Apart from a paper bag for your fucking head.

SIMON   Brilliant. Shall we give it a rest now Jay?

MR GILBERT ENTERS.

MR GILBERT   Good morning. Shut up and let's get this over with.

MR GILBERT   Right, wait a minute. Cartwright, what is that?

HE'S POINTING TO JAY'S EAR.

JAY   It's a stud sir, and I don't mean the earring.

MR GILBERT   Take it out or I will rip it out.

JAY   But what about my human rights?

MR GILBERT   You have to be human for those to apply Cartwright. Out now.

JAY REMOVES THE EARRING. MR GILBERT TURNS TO THE REST OF THE COMMON ROOM.

MR GILBERT   Right, now, I'm sure most of you will remember Alistair Scott. Yes Sutherland?

NEIL   I don't.

MR GILBERT   You sat next to him in registration for four years.

NEIL   Oh Alistair.

MR GILBERT   Well, thankfully, after a tough year they found a donor and he's finally on the mend. In preparation for his return to school he's coming in at lunchtime to answer any questions you might have about his illness. Yes Sutherland?

NEIL   Can I catch it?

MR GILBERT   No, you cannot catch kidney failure. McKenzie, my office ten minutes.

MR GILBERT LEAVES.

SIMON   What's Gilbert want?

WILL   Probably wants me to act as a chaperone for that Alistair kid. Poor guy, imagine what he's been through.

JAY   He's a dick.

WILL   Jay!

JAY   What, he is a dick. I never liked him when he was well, I never liked him when he was ill, and I don't like him now he's getting better. Simples.

SIMON   Oh he was all right.

JAY   No he wasn't. He was a complete bell-end. He was worse than briefcase.

WILL   Thanks very much. Look, he's had a hugely traumatic time, maybe he's changed?

JAY   He's not going to have got more interesting in a hospital bed attached to a drip for a year, is he?

WILL   What a sympathetic view of a life-threatening illness.

JAY   And he used to stink. I'm not going.

NEIL   Oh come on Jay, there might be sausage rolls.

SIMON   Why would there be sausage rolls?

NEIL   We had sausages rolls when my nan died.

WILL   He's not dead Neil.

NEIL   Isn't he? They still might have sausage rolls though.

JAY   Fine, fuck it, I'll come, but I'm warning you he's a dick.

———— SCENE 4 ————

INT. MR GILBERT'S OFFICE

WILL V/O   *Well, if Jay thought Alistair was a dick, he was almost certainly a nice bloke, unlike Mr Gilbert.*

WILL   You wanted to see me sir?

MR GILBERT   Want is an overstatement. I'm putting you in charge of collecting the money for tomorrow's fashion show. Last time they had a collection for charity nearly half the money went missing, and then the organisers started turning up in new trainers.

WILL   Well sir, whilst I'm really pleased that you think I'm trustworthy enough to—

MR GILBERT   Oh it's not that. I just know that if anything did happen I could break you.

WILL   Right. Well the thing is I object to the fashion show on a moral level.

MR GILBERT   I'm sorry?

WILL   It's not about raising money, it's a popularity parade. It's just the self-elected attractive people using charity as an excuse to show off.

MR GILBERT   Well, this is a first. As it happens McKenzie, I agree with you.

WILL   You do?

MR GILBERT   Yes.

WILL   Great, so you understand why I'd rather not compromise my principles?

MR GILBERT   Yes I do, totally. Unfortunately for you it's not the First World War. You can't conscientiously object. So, you either collect the money or it's detention, starting now and continuing indefinitely.

WILL   But . . . you said you agreed with me?

MR GILBERT   Yes I know, it's a tricky one isn't it?

WILL   OK, fine, I'll do it. But I'm still exercising my right to protest.

MR GILBERT   Good. Just make sure it's not a dirty protest like the last one.

──────── SCENE 5 ────────

INT. SCHOOL HALL

WE ARE AT THE WELCOME LUNCH FOR ALISTAIR. HE IS IN A WHEELCHAIR AND A BIT THIN, BUT OTHER THAN THAT HE LOOKS FINE. CARLI IS TALKING TO HIM. ON A TRESTLE TABLE THERE'S A SPREAD OF FOOD. THE FOUR BOYS HAVE SEPARATED THEMSELVES FROM THE GROUP A BIT, AND ARE EATING SAUSAGE ROLLS.

WILL V/O   *Just as a stopped clock gives the correct time twice a day, once a term Neil gets something right . . .*

NEIL   Told ya there'd be sausage rolls.

JAY   Look at him, fucking milking it.

WILL   Jay, he's in a wheelchair.

NEIL   He was always a bit lazy though.

WILL   I don't think it's that Neil.

SIMON   Why is Carli finding him so funny? I mean what can he be saying that's so funny? He was never funny.

ALISTAIR   Um, excuse me, everyone, quiet, I want to talk.

(EVERYONE STOPS CHATTING)

I wanted to say super thanks to everyone who's given up their time to take part in the fashion show tomorrow to raise money for a new dialysis machine for St Margaret's. Especially all the sexy girls.

THERE'S ANOTHER SORT OF LAUGH, AND PEOPLE START CHATTING AGAIN.

SIMON   Did he just say 'super thanks'?

JAY   Nobody told me we was raising money for that twat. Might think twice about modelling tomorrow then.

WILL   You're not modelling anyway.

NEIL   Oh it's gonna be a gash-a-rama. I'm gonna try getting a job helping out backstage, so that way I get to see some close-up flange, but for charity.

CARLI COMES OVER TO THE BOYS.

CARLI   Hi Simon, you coming to the rehearsal after school?

SIMON   Yeah, course.

WILL   How much rehearsal does it take to walk up and down in a straight line wearing clothes?

CARLI   It's more for timings and stuff really.

NEIL   Do you need any helpers Carli?

CARLI   Oh brilliant, we do actually. Hardly anyone has volunteered and we really need people to help get the models dressed.

WILL   Christ, I knew they were stupid but can't they even dress themselves?

CARLI   It's for the quick changes actually. Whip one outfit off and another on. If you're sure you don't mind Neil?

NEIL   Are you joking?

CARLI   Great, thanks.

SHE LEAVES.

ALISTAIR ROLLS UP.

ALISTAIR   Hey guys, everybody cool?

WILL   Hi I'm Will by the way, I'm relatively new.

ALISTAIR   Are you the kid who shit himself in the exam?

WILL   Nice to meet you too. Now I was wondering if you and I could have a little chat about other ways to raise money, ways that could include everyone, the whole school, whatever they look like?

ALISTAIR   Yeah, could do, only you're not as pretty as Carli, so I think right now I'm going to chat to her, yeah? See ya . . .

ALISTAIR LEAVES.

JAY   Dick.

SIMON   You don't think him and Carli are . . . ?

NEIL   If they are, I bet he's 'wheely' good at it.

SIMON   Brilliant.

JAY   I'm going to have to go. I've got a missed call from Ralph Lauren.

JAY LEAVES.

SIMON   Didn't even ring, did it?

NEIL   Oh I'm well excited. Imagine the birds I'm going to get to see as a dresser.

WILL   It's not top international models Neil, it's just a load of the girls from school that you see every day.

NEIL   Yeah, but I think I'd fancy them a lot more if I saw them naked.

WILL V/O   . . . *I'll say this for Neil, at least his ambitions were simple: see tits and/or fanny.*

——————— SCENE 6 ———————

INT. SCHOOL HALLWAY

WILL V/O   . . . *Jay's were a lot more unrealistic.*

JAY STARTS STRUTTING OVER TO CARLI LIKE HE'S ON THE CATWALK, AND STOPS LIKE A MODEL AT THE END OF THE RUNWAY.

JAY   Erm Carli. Can I have a word?

CARLI   I'm a bit busy. What's up?

JAY   I was wondering if you needed any more models for tomorrow?

CARLI   No, we're fine.

JAY   Good, good. Don't know if you noticed but I've had my ear pierced.

CARLI   Oh, right.

JAY   So do you think you might be able to fit one more in now?

CARLI   Well no, because we've only got a certain amount of clothes.

JAY   Well, I could wear my own clothes.

CARLI   We're probably OK.

JAY   So I'm like a 'first reserve' then?

CARLI   Well, we haven't really got any reserves, so sort of no.

JAY   Cool. Cool, cool. Simples. How about a free ticket instead?

CARLI   Well it's for charity, so there aren't really any free tickets . . .

JAY   Yeah, nice one Carls. I'll catch you later, yeah.

———— SCENE 7 ————

INT. SIMON'S HOUSE, KITCHEN

WILL V/O   *So Jay had a size zero chance of becoming a model. But Simon was practising hard. Simon's my best friend. This bloke is my best friend . . .*

SIMON IS IN HIS KITCHEN PRACTISING HIS MODEL WALK. HE IS REALLY GETTING INTO IT. HE HEARS A GIGGLE AND TURNS ROUND TO SEE HIS MUM (PAMELA COOPER), DAD (ALAN COOPER) AND BROTHER (ANDREW COOPER) ALL WATCHING HIM.

SIMON   What the fuck do you think you're doing? You're spying on me? Spying, is that how you get your kicks?

ALAN COOPER   It's all right, it just looks like we've found the new David Beckham.

SIMON   Right, that's it. That is it. I am sick of you people. I'm leaving.

PAMELA COOPER   You're not going out now, you've got school tomorrow.

ALAN COOPER   Yeah, run away at the weekend when you've got your car back.

SIMON   Well I'm not spending another second in this house with you utter twats.

ALAN COOPER   Where you going, Paris or Milan?

SIMON   Fuck off!

SIMON'S FAMILY LAUGH AS HE STORMS INTO THE GARDEN AND STARTS TO CLIMB ON THE SHED ROOF.

ALAN COOPER   He's just like Naomi Campbell.

WILL V/O   . . . *so Simon was well on the way to becoming a super-model. He had the temperament, now all he needed was bulimia and a cocaine addiction.*

 SCENE 8

INT. OUTSIDE THE AUDITORIUM

WILL V/O   *The next night was the fashion show. And I realised in my role as doorman, I had the perfect opportunity to ruin everything for everyone . . .*

WILL IS SITTING AT THE CASH DESK AT THE ENTRANCE TO THE MAIN SCHOOL HALL. HE IS IN CONVERSATION WITH A MIDDLE-AGED WOMAN.

WILL   I'm not saying don't give to charity – do give to charity. I'm just saying you can give without supporting this egotistical vanity fest.

WOMAN   My daughter is one of the models.

WILL   Then you have failed her.

WOMAN   What?

WILL   God, five pounds please.

SHE WALKS IN. AS WILL SHAKES HIS HEAD AT HER, CARLI ARRIVES.

CARLI   Will I think it's so great you're helping out. I knew you'd come round.

WILL I haven't come round. I still feel exactly the same about this sham popularity parade.

CARLI You're being such an arse. What is wrong with you? Alistair nearly died. God.

AS CARLI STORMS OFF, UPSET, SIMON AND NEIL ENTER.

SIMON Carli? What did you say to her?

WILL Nothing. Maybe a small dose of the truth.

SIMON Will, seriously, you have to stop cock-blocking with all this principled shit.

WILL Simon, if Nelson Mandela hadn't stood up for his beliefs where would we be now?

NEIL We wouldn't have Nelson's column for a start.

WILL Yes, we would.

SIMON I'd better have a piss before this starts.

NEIL And a poo Si.

JAY ARRIVES. HE NOW HAS TWO BIG HOOP EARRINGS.

WILL What have you done?

JAY It's my new look.

SIMON What, the Pat Butcher look?

WILL I think it's more *Pirates of the Caribbean*.

JAY Exactly.

WILL If the pirates shopped at Matalan.

JAY Yeah, well, you won't be laughing when I'm getting all the pussy 'cos I'm up on the catwalk.

SIMON You're not going to be on the catwalk, you aren't modelling.

JAY I'm first reserve.

WILL What, in case one of the models fancy themselves so much they actually eat themselves.

NEIL   Ah, you would if you could though.

WILL   What?

NEIL   Suck yourself off.

WILL   That's not what I meant.

JAY   I bet you've tried it. We all have.

NEIL   I managed to lick the tip once, but it took a lot of stretching, twice a day for a couple of weeks.

WILL   Well, thanks for sharing Neil.

SIMON   Right, I've got to go, I'm desperate for a piss.

SIMON, NEIL AND JAY WALK INTO THE AUDITORIUM.

——— SCENE 9 ———

INT. BACKSTAGE, MALE CHANGING SPACE

WILL V/O   *Neil may have had dirty stretching powers, but what he really needed was X-ray vision . . .*

THERE'S A LARGE CURTAIN DIVIDING THE ROOM, AND THERE ARE ONLY BOYS ON THIS SIDE OF THE CURTAIN. NEIL AND SIMON ARRIVE.

NEIL   What the fuck is this?

SIMON   It's a curtain.

NEIL   Where's all the birds? I thought it would be wall to wall poon-tang in here.

SIMON   Presumably they're on the other side of the curtain.

NEIL   Well, why have they done that? We can't see them getting undressed now.

SIMON   For that exact reason Neil.

NEIL   Oh fucking bollocks, that is a spanner to my plan. There's got to be a hole.

SIMON   Come on, you're meant to be getting my clothes ready.

NEIL   Yeah, I think this is a little bit more important.

CARLI APPROACHES.

CARLI   Are you ready to go yet Simon?

SIMON   Yeah, nearly ready.

CARLI   Great, we're having an after-party in the common room later. Mark Donovan's got some booze, so you'll come to that, yeah?

SIMON   Yeah, obviously. Amazing.

SHE LOOKS DOWN AND SEES HE HAS QUITE A LARGE WET PATCH ON HIS BOXERS. HE LOOKS DOWN, SEES IT, COVERS IT UP, AND LOOKS BACK AT HER.

SIMON   I was washing my hands and it splashed back on to my lap.

CARLI   It's fine. Just make sure everything is spotless for the runway yeah?

SIMON   I'm really sorry.

CARLI   It's OK. I've got to run, there's still a million things to deal with. Neil, do you know which boys you're dressing?

NEIL   Boys? I thought I was dressing the girls?

CARLI   Ha, no, of course not. You and Mr Kennedy are dressing the boys. You were the only volunteers. See ya later.

NEIL   Oh no.

SIMON   Paedo Kennedy? I suppose at least if you run out of space you'll be able to hang the clothes off his erect cock.

——— SCENE 10 ———

INT. OUTSIDE THE AUDITORIUM

WILL V/O   . . . *so, no naked girls for Neil, just a sexual predator in a waistcoat. Meanwhile, I was having difficulty convincing proud parents to join my boycott . . .*

WILL IS STILL SITTING AT THE FRONT OF HOUSE, GRUMPILY COLLECTING THE MONEY.

WILL   Charity not vanity.

CHARLOTTE   Hello stranger.

WILL   Charlotte!

CHARLOTTE   Hi.

WILL   Charlotte! Here.

CHARLOTTE   Yes, good spot.

WILL   Yes, ha, no, I mean, what are you doing here?

CHARLOTTE   I had a reading week so I thought I'd come home. I didn't know this was your sort of thing – you know, fashion.

WILL   It's not. I think it's shit, and everyone taking part in it is a vain, talentless twat.

CHARLOTTE   I'm in it.

WILL   Apart from you. And maybe Si. Why did no one tell me you were in it?

CHARLOTTE   Well I didn't know if I could make it, so they put me down as like a special guest or something really embarrassing just 'cos I once did some catalogue modelling.

WILL   Underwear?

CHARLOTTE   No. You are going to come and watch me though, aren't you, even though I'm a talentless twat?

WILL   Oh yeah, no, no, I was only joking about that. I'm really behind this whole thing, taking the money, helping set it up.

JUST AS THEY ARE SPEAKING, ALISTAIR ROLLS UP.

ALISTAIR   Why are you trying to ruin this event McKenzie?

WILL   Good timing.

ALISTAIR   Do you think kidney patients like me should die, is that it?

WILL   Now come on mate, that's a bit extreme.

ALISTAIR   Is he trying to stop you coming in too?

CHARLOTTE   No, I'm one of the models.

ALISTAIR   Oh you must be Charlotte. Oh wowzeroony. Are you aware that this weasel is trying to stop people giving money to charity?

CHARLOTTE   Will?

WILL   No, no, that's not entirely correct. Look Alistair, why don't we go and have a chat about this somewhere different . . .

ALISTAIR   No, let's talk about it here.

WILL   Sorry, it wasn't a request. See you later Charlotte.

WILL ATTEMPTS TO ROLL ALISTAIR'S WHEELCHAIR AWAY FROM CHARLOTTE, INTO ANOTHER ROOM, BUT IS QUICKLY THWARTED AS ALISTAIR APPLIES THE BRAKE.

ALISTAIR   What are you doing? Are you trying to wheel me away? This thing's got brakes, you know. You can't just roll me off . . .

PANICKING NOW, WILL DECIDES TO DO THAT REALLY ANNOYING THING OF SORT OF MAKING NOISE LOUDLY OVER WHAT ALISTAIR'S SAYING TO DROWN HIM OUT.

ALISTAIR   You are trying to sabotage this event.

WILL   Baa baa baab—

ALISTAIR   I won't stand for it.

WILL   Baab up dup—

ALISTAIR   I won't have it.

WILL   Dup dup dup boop etc.

ALISTAIR   This is my special day and you're trying to ruin it.

CHARLOTTE   I'm going to go and get ready.

WILL V/O   . . . well, I think I got away with that. Brilliant.

——————— SCENE 11 ———————

INT. BACKSTAGE, MALE CHANGING SPACE

WILL V/O   *At the school fashion show, Simon's big moment had almost arrived. And Neil didn't give a shit . . .*

SIMON IS STRUGGLING WITH A SHIRT, TRYING TO GET CUFFLINKS IN. NEIL ISN'T HELPING AT ALL, HE'S JUST SURVEYING THE CURTAIN.

SIMON   Neil, can you give me a hand please?

NEIL   Oh mate this is torture. I've spent all week thinking about the snatches back there.

SIMON   I'm in a rush Neil.

NEIL   I reckon Sarah Bell's got lovely big nipples, and I bet Jo Larken shaves her pubes.

GIRL'S VOICE   (OFF SCREEN) We can hear you, you pervert.

NEIL   Who said that?

GIRL'S VOICE   (OFF SCREEN) It's only a curtain. We can hear everything you're saying.

SIMON   Shit, he's really sorry.

GIRL'S VOICE   (OFF SCREEN) I recognise one of the voices. It's Simon Cooper.

SIMON   Do something Neil.

NEIL   How big are Sarah Bell's nipples?

GIRL'S VOICE   (OFF SCREEN) Right, that's it, I'm getting a teacher.

SIMON   Shit, thanks Neil good job.

JAY ARRIVES.

JAY   All right Yves Saint le Ponce, what's going on here then?

SIMON   Neil's getting me in shit.

NEIL   They've put a curtain up so we can't see the clunge. It's totally sexist.

JAY   The crafty fuckers. They tried this when we did the school play, but we just cut a hole in the curtain and stuck our knobs through. It was well horny. We were getting noshed off between scenes.

GIRL'S VOICE   (OFF SCREEN) We can still hear you.

GIRL'S VOICE   (OFF SCREEN) And that never happened.

CARLI COMES ROUND FROM THE RUNWAY.

CARLI Simon, you're on hon.

CARLI SPOTS JAY.

CARLI It's models only back here.

JAY Yeah, but look. Two.

JAY PRESENTS HIS EARLOBES TO CARLI TO SHOW THAT HE HAS BOTH EARS PIERCED.

CARLI (STRESSED) The left one looks infected. Please hurry up Simon, you're on next.

CARLI RUSHES OFF.

SIMON Can someone just help me with my fucking cufflinks please?

JAY Alright precious, I'll help you, but if you haven't got them on in thirty seconds I'm going out in your place.

SIMON No you aren't.

SIMON MOVES OVER TO THE ENTRANCE TO THE CATWALK. JAY FOLLOWS HIM TO THE EDGE OF THE STAGE. MR KENNEDY ARRIVES AND APPROACHES NEIL, WHO HAS HIS BACK TO HIM.

MR KENNEDY The girls said there was some sort of problem back— Oh.

ON SEEING THAT IT'S NEIL, KENNEDY GOES TO HELP HIM UNDRESS, PULLING AT HIS TROUSERS.

MR KENNEDY Come on, we'd better get you out of these clothes.

NEIL But sir, I'm not modelling.

MR KENNEDY Oh. You should be.

WILL V/O . . . *so as Neil tried to swerve the advances of a man it seemed incredible the school continued to employ, the world's least stylish fashion show got under way.*

———— SCENE 12 ————

INT. AUDITORIUM

MR GILBERT ANNOUNCES THE FIRST 'COLLECTION':

MR GILBERT   'Our first collection's theme is glamorous nights and is put together' – incorrect tense – 'by Carli D'Amato. Modeling' – that should be two Ls – 'these gorgeous outfits are the equally gorgeous' – Christ, who wrote this? – 'Stephen DeBell, Richard Murray and Simon Cooper.'

SIMON AND TWO OTHER BOYS STRIDE DOWN THE CATWALK. WILL IS STANDING AT THE BACK WATCHING. ALISTAIR SPOTS HIM.

WILL V/O   *I'm not sure what the word for the opposite of cool is, but I think I know what it looks like. Sadly, I couldn't enjoy Simon's dreadful modelling for long. I had a two-wheeled nightmare on my case.*

WILL LEAVES. ALISTAIR FOLLOWS.

———— SCENE 13 ————

INT. OUTSIDE THE AUDITORIUM

WILL IS PACKING UP HIS MONEY TIN. ALISTAIR WHEELS UP TO HIM.

ALISTAIR   McKenzie, you try anything like that again and I will—

WILL   Alistair, I think we've got off on the wrong foot . . .

ALISTAIR   Is that meant to be a joke about the chair? I can walk you know, I just get tired easy.

WILL   No, no, no, it's not that, I think we just differ on ways to raise money. I happen to think that this is exclusive and about vanity.

ALISTAIR   And I happen to think you're a wanker.

WILL   That's not very mature is it?

ALISTAIR   Even in this chair I could kick your arse. Kick your arse right in.

ALISTAIR STARTS ROLLING HIS WHEELCHAIR INTO WILL'S LEGS AND SHOVING HIM. A COUPLE OF PEOPLE ARE LOOKING.

WILL   Look, let's not make a scene.

ALISTAIR   Come on then.

WILL   You're mental. He's mental.

ALISTAIR   Fuck you.

CHARLOTTE COMES RUSHING UP. ALISTAIR STOPS FIGHTING WILL.

CHARLOTTE   Will, you've got to help me.

ALISTAIR   Oh hi sexy.

CHARLOTTE   I was supposed to be modelling with Paul Keenan but he got so nervous he drank a bottle of vodka and passed out in the staff toilets. Please will you take his place?

WILL   Me? Um . . .

ALISTAIR   He won't do it, he thinks it's 'exclusive vanity'.

CHARLOTTE   Right.

WILL   No. He's talking shit, it's the painkillers. Of course I'll do it.

CHARLOTTE   Great.

ALISTAIR   What? You hypocrite.

WILL TAKES THE TABLECLOTH HE'S BEEN HOLDING AND STARTS TO WRAP IT AROUND AND OVER ALISTAIR.

WILL   Right you, time for a sleep.

ALISTAIR   Don't touch me.

WILL DRAGS CHARLOTTE AWAY AS ALISTAIR STRUGGLES BENEATH THE TABLE-CLOTH.

WILL   Come on.

CHARLOTTE   Is he OK?

WILL   Yeah, he's fine. He gets very grumpy when he's tired.

——— SCENE 14 ———

INT. BACKSTAGE, MALE CHANGING SPACE

SIMON COMES BOWLING BACK THROUGH THE CURTAIN, ELATED. JAY AND NEIL
ARE BACKSTAGE WAITING.

SIMON   Yes, this is going really well. Amazingly no cock-ups so far.

JAY   Ooh well done, you've mastered walking like a knob and looking
like a dick at the same time.

SIMON   This is actually enjoyable, in an 'I'm shitting myself' kind of
way.

NEIL   If you've shit yourself in them trousers I ain't touching them.

SIMON   Of course I didn't.

NEIL   You walked like you did.

WILL SUDDENLY ARRIVES WITH A LOAD OF CLOTHES IN HIS HANDS.

WILL   Neil, quick, I need help getting dressed.

NEIL   You are dressed.

WILL   No, dressed in something else. This. For the fashion show. I'm
modelling in the fashion show.

JAY   That's not happening, I'm first reserve.

JAY SNATCHES THE CLOTHES FROM WILL.

WILL   No, no way.

SIMON   What's up with you, I thought this was the worst sort of
vanity?

WILL   Yeah, well, I've changed my mind. Somebody pulled out, and
Charlotte's asked me to fill in so GIVE ME THE CLOTHES.

HE YANKS THEM BACK FROM JAY.

SIMON   Oh right, now it makes sense. One flash of Charlotte's tits
and your morals go out the window.

WILL   Yes, well we can discuss my morals later, after I get these fucking jeans on. God they're tight. I mean it can't be comfortable to walk around in jeans this tight every day, can it?

NEIL   Here. Let me help.

JAY   This is fucking bang out of order. I'm first reserve.

WILL   It was me Charlotte wanted, she chose me, that's the only reason I'm doing it.

JAY   Yeah, well, they'll be sorry. I'll show them.

WILL   Columbine massacre show them, or futile gesture show them?

JAY   Whatever's worse.

NEIL'S HELPING WILL GET DRESSED.

WILL   Um, Neil, you just brushed my penis there.

NEIL   Yeah.

WILL   That's the second time.

NEIL   Yeah I know.

WILL V/O   *Of course the only reason I was taking part in the fashion show was to get my penis brushed, but by Charlotte, not Neil.*

———— SCENE 15 ————

INT. CATWALK BACKSTAGE AREA

CHARLOTTE IS WAITING FOR WILL BY THE CURTAIN.

CHARLOTTE   Well done for getting ready so quickly.

Exciting, isn't it?

WILL   Yeah, yeah. Look, I just wanted to say I'm really pleased you picked me. It means a lot.

CHARLOTTE   I didn't have a choice really, did I?

WILL   Didn't you?

CHARLOTTE   No, we had to find someone to fit the clothes and I was like, who do I know that's really short? And then obviously I thought of you.

WILL   Oh. Is that really the reason?

CHARLOTTE   No, not really. They let me choose who I wanted, and I chose you.

WILL   Thanks Charlotte.

CHARLOTTE   Although it did have to be someone short.

WILL   Right.

MR GILBERT   (OFF SCREEN) And the next theme is – Seventies Disco.

WILL   Oh brilliant.

THE CURTAIN IS PULLED BACK. CHIC'S 'LE FREAK' PLAYS AND WE SEE CHARLOTTE (VERY COMFORTABLE) AND WILL (AWKWARD BEYOND BELIEF) 'BOOGIE' OUT DOWN THE CATWALK.

WILL V/O   *I'm a principled man and one of those principles turns out to be, I'll do literally anything a girl I fancy asks me to.*

 SCENE 16

INT. AUDITORIUM,

WILL V/O   *All right, I'm willing to admit I also got a bit carried away, but they do say a woman can tell a lot about what a man's like in bed from the way he dances. Which meant that if I did pull Charlotte, she'd be expecting surprise and enthusiasm along with finger work and an abrupt stop when I remembered where I was.*

CHARLOTTE AND WILL WALK OUT ONTO THE CATWALK. SHE'S LOVING IT, HE'S A LITTLE MORE NERVOUS. THEY GET TO THE FRONT OF THE CATWALK AND DANCE WITH EACH OTHER, DISCO STYLE. WILL LOOKS TERRIBLE DOING THIS, BUT HE SLOWLY STARTS TO GET INTO IT. HE STARTS TO LET LOOSE, BUT THEN CATCHES MR GILBERT'S EYE, WHICH SORT OF STOPS HIM IN HIS TRACKS.

INT. BACKSTAGE, MALE CHANGING AREA

WILL V/O   *Meanwhile, backstage, Neil was finally experiencing some job satisfaction.*

CARLI COMES RUSHING UP TO SIMON. SHE'S WEARING A SORT OF MOULIN ROUGE OUTFIT.

NEIL   Oh fucking hell. At last.

CARLI   Simon, there's been a slight change of plan. Chris Yates was meant to be wearing this for my sexy finale.

SHE HOLDS UP A TINY PAIR OF SPEEDOS, A TOP HAT AND A LEASH.

CARLI   But he's just taken his shirt off and his back is disgustingly hairy so I've sacked him.

SIMON   I thought this was for charity?

CARLI   You know when you get loads of hair caught round the plug-hole in the bath, and it gets all matted and wet?

SIMON   Yes.

CARLI   Well his back looked like that; it nearly made me vomit, so he's sacked. Anyway, it means that I need you to wear this instead for the sexy finale.

SIMON   Are they speedos? Um . . .

CARLI   Simon, you've been brilliant all night plus you've got a great body. Please, for me?

SIMON   Of course.

CARLI   Thanks. See you out there. You've got one minute.

CARLI RUSHES OFF.

JAY   This is so fucking unfair. So I'm not even second reserve now. Who's she going to ask next, John?

SIMON   Well, do you want to wear the speedos?

JAY   No. Oh what's the point.

JAY TAKES OUT HIS EARRINGS, SNAGGING THE LEFT ONE QUITE BADLY. IT BLEEDS.

JAY   Ahhh.

NEIL   Oh mate, your ear don't look great, it's covered in pus.

JAY   Oh fucking hell. I'd better get this looked at. Good luck, boner. Try not to get a stiffy in them speedos.

NEIL   He's right, you're in trouble Si. I nearly shot my bolt just looking at her, and all she was doing was standing here being moany.

SIMON   Neil did you hear what she said? She thinks I've got a great body. If I could just do this one thing for her and who knows what could happen?

NEIL   I know, you'll get a boner in front of the whole school. And in speedos there's no hiding it, trust me.

SIMON   Oh it's only a couple of minutes, I can do it. I can do this.

CARLI   (OFF SCREEN) Simon, are you ready yet?

SIMON   Will you give me a hand Neil?

NEIL LOOKS AT SIMON IN HIS PANTS, HOLDING THE TINY SPEEDOS.

NEIL   Nah, you're all right.

CARLI   (OFF SCREEN) Simon!

──────── SCENE 17 ────────

INT. CATWALK BACKSTAGE AREA

CHARLOTTE   That was so amazing, so brilliant. Oh my God, I couldn't have done it without you.

CHARLOTTE GIVES WILL A HUGE HUG AND A BIG KISS ON THE CHEEK.

CARLI COMES RUSHING UP TOWARDS THEM.

CARLI   How was it?

CHARLOTTE   He was brilliant.

CARLI   Was he?

CHARLOTTE   Yeah, he was all like 'yaaaaaaayy'.

CARLI   Yaaaayyyyy.

WILL   I wasn't entirely 'yaaayy'.

MR GILBERT   (OFF SCREEN)   'And now, ladies and gentlemen, it's time for the grand finale' – which I definitely didn't sign off on –

SIMON JOINS THEM. HE IS A PICTURE OF CONCENTRATION, TRYING DESPERATELY NOT TO LOOK AT CARLI.

CARLI   Come on Simon, we're on.

WILL   Are you all right?

MR GILBERT   (OFF SCREEN)   – 'a sexy' – that's inappropriate – '*Moulin Rouge*-inspired collection by Carli D'Amato.'

SIMON   Please don't distract me.

WILL   But, but . . .

WILL V/O   *Simon was concentrating so hard on not getting a boner that he was oblivious to what can only be described as quite a serious wardrobe malfunction.*

——————— SCENE 18 ———————

INT. AUDITORIUM

SIMON AND CARLI WALK OUT TO WOLF WHISTLES AND CHEERS.

SIMON CONFIDENTLY STRIDES DOWN THE CATWALK, DOING A FULL STRUT, BUT SOME PEOPLE ARE TURNING AWAY AND A FEW ARE LAUGHING. HE CAN'T SEE WHAT'S WRONG SO IS PUZZLED BUT NOT CONCERNED. CARLI IS IN FRONT OF HIM, HOLDING HIS LEAD, AND SO ALSO CAN'T SEE WHAT THE PROBLEM IS.

WE CAN: WE SEE ONE OF HIS BALLS HANGING OUT OF HIS SPEEDOS.

——— SCENE 19 ———

INT. CATWALK BACKSTAGE AREA

WILL AND CHARLOTTE ARE WHERE WE LEFT THEM, BY THE CURTAINS.

CHARLOTTE   I loved that. Seriously, thank you Will, I'm really grateful.

WILL   Oh, it was nothing, just what was left of my dignity.

CHARLOTTE   Oh come on, it wasn't that bad. And what other guy would have done that for me? I mean, uni's great, but there's no one there like you.

WILL   Shut up.

CHARLOTTE   No seriously, all I want is a boyfriend like you. I mean you're funny, sweet and you're kind to me. I think I'd be happy if I had someone in my life just like you.

BEAT.

WILL   Well, what about me?

CHARLOTTE   (LAUGHING, GENUINELY UNAWARE) No, no, not you. No, someone like you. You're so funny, not you obviously.

WILL LOOKS TOTALLY CRUSHED.

CHARLOTTE   Come on lovely, let's go for a drink?

SHE DRAGS WILL BY THE ARM.

WILL   Um, no, I'm OK, thanks. I'll just wait here I think.

CHARLOTTE   OK cool.

CHARLOTTE LEAVES. WILL SLUMPS DOWN, THERE'S A MOMENT AND THEN ALISTAIR ROLLS UP TO HIM.

ALISTAIR   Nice one, twatface, good dancing. All that whining and complaining for what? Nothing. You are what they call a sanctimonious prick.

WILL   Yes, well good to talk to you again Al, is that all?

ALISTAIR   No. I hope one day you get a serious illness too.

WILL   Oh fuck off Alistair, you dick.

ALISTAIR   You're a dick.

WILL   You're a dick.

——— SCENE 20 ———

INT. CATWALK BACKSTAGE AREA

SIMON FOLLOWS CARLI THROUGH THE CURTAIN BACKSTAGE.

SIMON   You were great.

CARLI   Yeah, bit of a weird reaction. It wasn't meant to be funny, it was meant to be glamorous.

THEY ARRIVE TO FIND ALISTAIR AND WILL INSULTING EACH OTHER:

ALISTAIR   You're a dick.

WILL   No, you're a dick.

SIMON   Guys, come on, calm down, don't spoil a good evening. We've put on a great show and raised a hell of a lot of money, haven't we Carls?

ALISTAIR LOOKS AT HIM DISDAINFULLY. AT ALISTAIR'S EYE LEVEL IS SIMON'S TESTICLE.

ALISTAIR   You know your testicle is sticking out?

SIMON   What?

CARLI   Is that why everyone was laughing? Has it been out the whole time? Oh my God, you've been walking behind me, mocking me. You've ruined my big night. I thought you liked me. You arsehole.

CARLI STORMS OFF. ALISTAIR LEAVES TO FOLLOW HER.

ALISTAIR   Hey Carls, it's all right, it's cool . . .

SIMON   Carli, listen, please . . .

WILL   Bit overdramatic. It was only a bollock.

SIMON   Fucking hell, I'm going to kill Neil.

WILL   Did you not feel a draught?

SIMON   Well it was tingling, but I thought it was nerves. Oh God, do you think people saw?

WILL   Yes. It was eye level for most of the audience.

SIMON   Oh God. Noooo. Noooo.

MR GILBERT ENTERS.

MR GILBERT   I suppose you thought that was funny, did you? Well your little joke has just got you into a lot of trouble.

SIMON   Please sir, honestly, it wasn't a joke.

MR GILBERT   No, there is nothing funny about testicles Cooper, as you'll discover tomorrow in my office.

SIMON   What?

WILL   Sorry, sir, that sounded a bit weird.

MR GILBERT   No it didn't. See me tomorrow.

———— SCENE 21 ————

INT. BACKSTAGE, MALE CHANGING AREA

WILL V/O   *It did sound weird, and talking of weird.*

NEIL IS TRYING TO CUT A PEEP HOLE IN THE CURTAIN WITH A PAIR OF SCISSORS AND MR KENNEDY CREEPS UP BEHIND HIM.

KENNEDY   Right then, let's get you out these clothes.

NEIL   Sir, I told you, I'm not modelling.

KENNEDY   Oh no, no, no, you are, I had a word with the man. The man said.

NEIL   And the show finished ten minutes ago.

KENNEDY   Ohhh.

NEIL   Have you been drinking, sir?

MR GILBERT SUDDENLY ARRIVES AND PUTS A HAND ON MR KENNEDY'S
SHOULDER.

MR GILBERT   Come on John, let's go and get you some fresh air.

GILBERT LEADS KENNEDY OFF.

MR GILBERT   I'm putting my fucking neck on the line for you John.

———— SCENE 22 ————

INT. SCHOOL CORRIDOR

WILL V/O   *So we headed home, Simon having learnt at least one
thing: never put on speedos in a rush.*

SIMON AND WILL WALK ROUND THE CORRIDOR.

WILL   I mean, why did you agree to wear it in the first place?

SIMON   Carli told me to.

WILL   Even with your whole sack covered, you'd look ridiculous.
Speedos, DMs, top hat and a leash – what maniac designed that? Who
thought: you know what's fashionable, dressing like an upper-class
mental patient.

NEIL ARRIVES.

NEIL   All right. Did you get that boner then Si?

SIMON   No.

NEIL   Oh well done.

SIMON   But my left bollock was sticking out the entire time.

NEIL   Fucking hell. Unlucky.

SIMON   I blame you.

JAY ARRIVES, WITH A HEAVILY BANDAGED EAR.

JAY   All right gays.

NEIL   How's your ear Jay?

JAY   Perfect, that's why I've got to wear this massive bandage.

NEIL   I suppose that's your modelling career fucked then.

WILL   He never had a modelling career.

JAY   Yeah, but I'm not bothered, 'cos I fucked the nurse who looked after me.

WILL   The St John's Ambulance lady?

JAY   Yes.

SIMON   Isn't she Warren Dunkley's nan?

JAY   Nah, there's another one who looked like Lucy Pinder.

WILL   Course there was.

NEIL   Are we going to this party then?

SIMON   I'm definitely not going.

WILL   Nor me. I think I'll burst into tears.

NEIL   Oh, what, 'cos you're so unpopular?

WILL   No Neil, because of Charlotte.

NEIL   Oh what happened with her then?

WILL   She basically told me I had no chance, at all, ever.

JAY   Yeah, well, I told you that.

WILL   Yes, but funnily enough it hurt more coming from her.

NEIL   You know I snogged her once.

WILL   No, I did not know that.

NEIL   I could have sworn I told you.

WILL   I think I would have remembered such crushing news.

NEIL   Well don't worry, it was after you.

SIMON   That makes it worse.

WILL   Yes, now it's like a betrayal too.

JAY Was it just a snog?

WILL Neil, please.

NEIL Yeah, course mate. Course. Just a snog.

WILL Well that's something.

BUT AS WILL WALKS AHEAD OF THEM, JAY LOOKS OVER TO NEIL, WHO BEHIND WILL'S BACK, SHAKES HIS HEAD AND THEN SNIFFS HIS FINGERS. JAY AND SIMON LAUGH.

WILL V/O *I'd learnt a few things that week myself. None good, all bad . . .*

SHOT OF JAY DRIVING.

WILL Roundabout, Jay!

WILL V/O *. . . Jay's driving is worse than his fashion sense . . .*

JAY Fucking left!

WILL V/O *. . . Neil is catnip for paedos, just because you've only got one kidney doesn't mean you're not a total dick and Simon has extremely hairy balls.*

SHOT OF MR KENNEDY AND NEIL.

SHOT OF ALISTAIR.

SHOT OF SIMON WEARING SPEEDOS.

Episode 2

We originally intended this to be the first episode of Series Three. We thought it might be a 'surprise' to the fans because it contains drugs and actual success with a girl, two things that had never appeared before in *The Inbetweeners*. In the end it was decided that a bollock popping out would probably be a funnier surprise, so 'Fashion Show' ended up as number one, and this ep went out second.

Casting Tara took a long time and we were extra-cautious because we wanted to get the first '*Inbetweener* girlfriend' right. We saw a large number of brilliant actresses, but no one who really seemed to embody what we were looking for. We saw Tara as having a kind of naivety and naughtiness wrapped up in the teenage bravado of someone going through a new rebellious phase now that she was in the Sixth Form. She had to be a fundamentally sweet girl, but also someone who had the strength to make a move for the older boy she'd always fancied from afar. On the last day of casting Hannah Tointon came in and was perfect.

In terms of the drugs, we felt it was realistic that at some point in their Sixth Form they would come into contact with soft drugs at least, and it would also make sense that Jay would think he was the man who knew all about them. In terms of Will's reaction to the drugs, this is another anecdote drawn directly from life. I had never taken any drugs at all before – or since – but in my first year at university I accidentally (long story, I thought it was a chocolate chip) ate some sort of cannabis. A short while later whilst at a student-hall bar, I was in a bubble, everything was flat and I was having random arm movements. A short while after that I was in an ambulance on the way to the Bristol Royal Infirmary. It was strange when after the show went out I saw comments saying 'That isn't what happens when you eat drugs,' because I can categorically say that's what happened to me.

——— SCENE 1 ———

INT. JAY'S CARAVAN

WILL V/O   *Jay was full of helpful tips and this morning's were about how to make the most of the space in your caravan . . .*

NEIL, SIMON AND WILL ARE SITTING AROUND THE TABLE. JAY IS STANDING AT THE END, VIGOROUSLY HUMPING AND SORT OF IMAGINARY FINGERING TO DEMONSTRATE HIS 'TECHNIQUE'.

JAY   So I had one bent over the table here, there was one up here I was fingering, I was just toe-fucking the one on the floor.

WILL   Whilst your parents were sleeping in bunk beds just over there.

NEIL   Quality. It's amazing just how good you are with birds Jay.

JAY   What can I say? It's a gift.

WILL   So when do we get to meet these three lucky ladies?

JAY   Well you can't, they've gone back to the Playboy Mansion.

WILL   Of course, because if you lived in the Playboy Mansion, you'd definitely holiday in Great Yarmouth.

JAY   Well they did. I told you you should have come on holiday with us, Si.

SIMON   I don't want made-up Playboy models. I just want a nice girl-friend, who'll maybe have sex with me.

NEIL   I read in my sister's *Grazia* that birds like it if you ask them questions. If you want to get a girlfriend you should probably try that.

SIMON   Really?

JAY   Yeah, that works. Course the only question I ask them is which hole do you want it in first.

SIMON   Great, thanks.

JAY'S DAD (TERRY CARTWRIGHT) ENTERS.

TERRY CARTWRIGHT   What are you lot up to? Is Jay showing you where he used to shag the cushions? He thinks me and his mum don't know about that.

JAY   Come on Dad . . .

TERRY CARTWRIGHT   We've had to replace the covers twice.

NEIL   Jay was just telling us about the birds he pulled in Norfolk.

TERRY CARTWRIGHT   Oh right, was he?

JAY   Yeah you remember, right Dad?

TERRY CARTWRIGHT   Well he's a total bullshitter then. 'Cause the only pussy he's ever touched was his mum's when he fell out of it. See ya later.

JAY   Ha, ha, he's such a wind-up merchant.

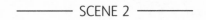

——————— SCENE 2 ———————

EXT. SCHOOL

WILL V/O   . . . *so with Mr Cartwright confirming that Jay hadn't hosted an orgy on the fold-out table, we began to question a few other things he'd said.*

THE FOUR BOYS ARE WALKING TO SCHOOL.

JAY   What else have I ever said that's bullshit?

SIMON   That your mate can squeeze himself into a microwave?

JAY   Yeah, a good-sized one.

WILL   That your dad fought Muhammad Ali as an amateur and beat him.

JAY   It was on a points decision.

WILL   And those are just from this morning. I could go on.

THEY WALK PAST MARK DONOVAN WITH TWO OF HIS MATES, WHO ARE SMOKING A LARGE SPLIFF. THE BOYS GO QUIET AND TRY NOT TO MAKE EYE CONTACT BUT IT IS VERY CLEAR WHAT DONOVAN IS DOING.

MARK DONOVAN Wankers.

ONCE THEY'VE PASSED DONOVAN, THE BOYS START SPEAKING AGAIN.

NEIL His fags smelt funny.

WILL Holy shit, was Donovan smoking drugs? In the open? And on a school day?

JAY STOPS AND TURNS.

JAY Don't shit yourself Talk to Frank. It was just a bit of puff. Everyone does a bit of puff.

WILL Oh right, do they? It's just I don't, you don't and nor does anyone we know.

JAY What are you talking about? I do it all the time.

SIMON Oh do you?

JAY Yeah, but obviously not with you saddos. I do it with my older mate.

SIMON Has this imaginary mate got a name then?

JAY Look, I go round his, we get nicely stoned listening to music, bit of reggae, or we go to gigs. Everyone does it at gigs, you just pass the puff round, share the love, the birds love it.

NEIL Is it true it makes your teeth feel funny?

JAY Yeah, but I'm hard core, so it doesn't really affect me.

WILL Well it is true that the effects are lessened if you only pretend to take it.

JAY Not that I have to prove anything to you mugs, but the other day we got his dog stoned and it got the munchies so it ran away for an hour. When it came back it had nicked a packet of Hobnobs from the all-night garage.

WILL What does that even mean?

JAY All you need to know is I can get as much gear as you like, whenever you like.

WILL I don't want any, ever.

NEIL   I suppose when you think about it everything is drugs innit?

WILL   No, not really.

NEIL   Yeah, you know like beer, disprin, coffee, trainers, chicken nuggets, cling film, elastoplast . . .

SIMON HAS BECOME DISTRACTED BECAUSE UP AHEAD HE'S SEEN CARLI GOING INTO SCHOOL.

SIMON   Right, I've got go.

HE RUNS AFTER HER.

NEIL   . . . plants, clothes, car tyres, calculators, wasps . . .

JAY   Yeah, that's right. And Simon's off to get his fix now.

NEIL   What, Si's doing drugs?

JAY   Yeah, he's addicted to crack Neil. Carli's crack.

NEIL   Oh yeah. Nice one.

——— SCENE 3 ———

INT. SCHOOL COMMON ROOM

WILL V/O   *I'm not an expert, but here's a tip: don't literally run after a girl you fancy, it makes you look needy and unless they're desperate or mental, it won't work.*

SIMON RUNS INTO THE COMMON ROOM, FOLLOWING CARLI. SHE WALKS OVER TO A REALLY GOOD-LOOKING BOY. NOW SIMON CAN'T GO OVER AND, TRANSFIXED, HE GOES TO SIT DOWN. HOWEVER, HE DOESN'T LOOK WHERE HE'S SITTING AND, WITHOUT REALISING IT, GOES TO SIT DOWN ON TOP OF A SEXY, COOL, INDIE-LOOKING GIRL (TARA) WHO HAS JUST SAT DOWN A SECOND BEFORE AND IS READING THE *NME*.

SIMON   Oh, sorry.

TARA   It's OK.

SIMON   No, God, I really didn't mean to sit on you.

TARA   No, 'cos that would be weird.

SIMON   Huh, yeah. Totally.

BEAT.

SIMON   Are you in the Lower Sixth?

TARA   Yeah. You've probably never noticed me before because I've just dyed my hair. And suddenly grown a pair of tits.

SIMON   Um, I'm Simon by the way.

TARA   I know. Tara.

SIMON   What are you reading?

TARA   The *NME*. I hate it, it's always wrong. It's basically shit. Still doesn't stop me from buying it every week.

SIMON   Right. Every week?

TARA   Yep.

SIMON   So you buy it every week?

TARA   Yeah.

SIMON   Not every week, though?

TARA   Yes, every week.

SIMON   So every week?

TARA   Are you broken? Have you got a head injury?

SIMON   So you're into music then?

TARA   Yeah, massively. I'd die without Spotify and I love going to gigs.

SIMON   Oh yeah, the same.

TARA   The same what?

SIMON   Same as what you said.

TARA   Right. So have you been down the Enterprise then?

SIMON   Um . . .

TARA   They have loads of brilliant up and coming bands.

SIMON   Um . . . can't quite, er, dunno . . .

TARA   It's cool if you haven't.

SIMON   No, don't think so.

TARA   Well you should. It's awesome. There's this band playing Friday, Failsafe, they're amazing. Me and a mate are going.

SIMON   Sounds cool, I love gigs. Went to a big gig last year, my mum took us to Take That at Wembley Arena.

TARA   Oh.

SIMON   It was good. Yeah. We were quite far back, sort of on the side, but, um, no, they were awesome, yeah. My mum went mental for it.

WILL, JAY AND NEIL WALK INTO THE COMMON ROOM. WILL SPOTS SIMON TALKING TO TARA, AND PUTS A HAND OUT TO STOP THE OTHERS. THEY WATCH, AMAZED.

TARA   Oh well to be honest I don't think you'd like Failsafe. It's a slightly different vibe to Take That.

SIMON   Oh no, I would, I love all vibes. Failsafe, Take That, reggae. I'd love to come and I'll even bring the puff if you like?

TARA   Drugs? I didn't think that was your scene.

SIMON   Didn't you? No, when I'm at gigs I always pass the puff round, share the love.

TARA   Really?

SIMON   Yeah. I'm pretty cool like that but I try to keep it on the down-low.

TARA   Wow, well you're doing a great job.

SIMON   Great, well I'll see you Friday then and I'll bring enough spliff puff for everyone.

TARA   Even enough for your mum?

SIMON   Ha, no, she won't be there, stupid bitch. But I'll be there, with the drugs.

——————— SCENE 4 ———————

INT. SCHOOL CORRIDOR

THE FOUR BOYS ARE STANDING IN THE CORRIDOR WHILE SIMON IS PUTTING SOME TEXT BOOKS INTO HIS LOCKER.

WILL   Why the fuck did you say you'd bring drugs? You don't do drugs.

SIMON   I know, but she's fit and I panicked.

WILL   So you're going to supply her, like some sort of pimp to a drug-addled prostitute. Is that what you've become?

SIMON   Calm down Will, it's just a bit of puff, everyone does it. Jay you can sort me out, right?

JAY   Slight problem on that front.

SIMON   What, in the past fifteen minutes.

JAY   Yeah, my mate's fucked off on a gap year to Afghanistan trying to get some pure shit from the source.

WILL   Of course he has.

SIMON   Thanks a fucking bunch Jay. Will's right, you are a total bullshitter.

JAY   Don't blame me. Drug dealers are unreliable.

NEIL   You could ask Donovan Jay.

WILL   Unless you're scared of him.

JAY   Yeah, no, of course not. I've had a toke with Mark untold times. I sort him out with rizlas and ting.

WILL   Oh, so you're a newsagent now as well as a liar?

JAY   Alright, I'll ask Donovan. Then tomorrow night when thanks to me we're watching Simon get balls deep in Tara, we'll see who the liar is.

WILL   Fine, we will.

SIMON   Probably be a bit weird if you two are there.

——— SCENE 5 ———

INT. SCHOOL COMMON ROOM

WILL V/O   *I don't know what Donovan was smoking. But it made him spread butter like a maniac.*

IT'S QUIET IN THE COMMON ROOM. DONOVAN IS MAKING SOME TOAST AS JAY AND NEIL COME IN. JAY HESITATES A BEAT.

NEIL   What if he throws the toaster at you?

JAY   Why would he do that? We're mates.

NEIL   Are you?

JAY   Sort of.

DONOVAN TURNS ROUND AND SEES THEM LOOKING AT HIM.

MARK DONOVAN   What the fuck are you two queers doing? Checking out my arse or something?

JAY   Right, come on, let's go.

NEIL   Nah, we just wanted a word.

MARK DONOVAN   Prick. There's a word.

JAY   Right. Sorry.

JAY TURNS TO LEAVE BUT NEIL STANDS HIS GROUND.

NEIL   We wanted to ask if you could sort us some puff?

MARK DONOVAN   Have you lost your retarded minds?

NEIL   It's just 'cos Jay's mate's in Afghanistan.

MARK DONOVAN   What?

JAY   Nah, look, we'll pay.

DONOVAN STARES AT THEM. THERE'S A MOMENT. THEN HE LOOKS ROUND AT THE EMPTY COMMON ROOM.

MARK DONOVAN   How much you got?

JAY   About twenty quid.

JAY GETS HIS MONEY OUT. HE HANDS IT OVER TO DONOVAN.

MARK DONOVAN   All right, I'll do you a special team twat deal.

NEIL AND JAY SMILE AT EACH OTHER. DONOVAN PICKS UP A BOX OF TEA BAGS ON THE SIDE. HE TEARS OPEN THE TEA BAGS AND POURS THE CONTENTS INTO A BIT OF CLINGFILM. HE CALMLY WRAPS UP THE 'PUFF' AND HANDS IT TO JAY.

MARK DONOVAN   There you go.

JAY   Nah, come on.

MARK DONOVAN   What?

JAY   Nah, seriously Mark, come on, that's . . .

MARK DONOVAN   Puff.

JAY   No, that's tea. Like normal tea, we just saw you empty the bags.

MARK DONOVAN   Are you calling me a liar? You disrespecting me like that?

JAY   No, it's just . . . you did it in front of us.

MARK DONOVAN   I'm going to give you a chance to apologise for that.

JAY   Right, yeah, no, sorry. But . . .

MARK DONOVAN   But what?

JAY   Nothing.

MARK DONOVAN   And?

JAY   Thank you for the puff.

MARK DONOVAN   Don't smoke it all at once.

JAY AND NEIL LEAVE.

———— SCENE 6 ————

INT. WILL'S HOUSE, KITCHEN

WILL V/O   *It was the night of Simon's date with Tara, and to mark the occasion he'd dressed like a dick.*

WILL Are you actually going to wear that?

SIMON Yes.

WILL Interesting.

SIMON Look, if I'm going to get a girlfriend I'm going to have to try a different plan than the one I had for Carli.

WILL Oh, was there a plan with Carli? I thought you just lurched from one disaster to another.

SIMON You want to know what I need to do with Tara, just pretend to be someone that I'm not. That I go to gigs, wear hats and most importantly, sort out D.R.U.G.S.

WILL Shhh, my mum's in.

SIMON So.

WILL She can spell!

WILL'S MUM (POLLY McKENZIE) COMES IN.

POLLY McKENZIE Ooh, you two look very smart, where are you off to?

WILL We're just going to pick up Neil, then we're going to a gig.

POLLY McKENZIE A gig, wow. I remember my first gig. INXS, Hammersmith Odeon, one of the band members went offstage then came back, on a skateboard. We all screamed. Looking back, I'm not sure why he did it.

WILL We're going to go now.

POLLY McKENZIE Well, have fun, and if anyone does offer you any D.R.U.G.S. be careful.

WILL What?

POLLY McKENZIE I overheard you. It's OK petal, I know boys will be boys, but I can trust you to do the responsible thing. I'm very lucky to have you because you're so boring.

WILL Boring?

POLLY McKENZIE Well not boring, just scared of things.

WILL   Scared?

POLLY McKENZIE   Sensible, that's the word I'm looking for. Sensible, you're very sensible, so I don't have to worry about you as much. Because you're so scared.

WILL   Thanks Mum.

THE BOYS LEAVE.

——————— SCENE 7 ———————

INT. NEIL'S HOUSE, LIVING ROOM

WILL V/O   *Instead of drugs Jay had bought PG Tips, which he spent the last hour failing to roll up into a joint . . .*

JAY IS TRYING TO ROLL UP THE FIRST OF THE TEA JOINTS. WILL LOOKS UNCOMFORTABLE AND EDGY.

WILL   I still can't believe you're going through with this Si.

SIMON   Oh come on Will, it's just a 'Leeetle spleeeeef'.

SIMON, NEIL AND JAY ALL LAUGH. WILL DOESN'T.

WILL   Is that meant to be funny is it? Is that drug humour?

JAY   Alright, Cliff Richard, if you don't like it then fuck off.

WILL   No, I'll stay. And laugh at you.

NEIL   Jay, I think smoking is well bad for your chest. Can't we just make tea with it instead?

JAY   No, you can't make tea with this type, remember Neil.

NEIL   Oh yeah. Why not?

JAY   Because it's stronger if you eat it. We could bake it into choco-late brownies.

NEIL   Cool. Delicious. Who knows the recipe?

WILL   Nigella Lawson?

SIMON   Look, we haven't got time to fucking bake cakes, my dad will be here to pick us up soon. I just want to try it before I meet Tara.

NEIL   Well, I can cook toast. And eggs. What about putting it in egg on toast? Would that work Jay?

JAY   Um, yeah, might do.

WILL   Drugs on eggs on toast? Are you not worried it might lead to harder stuff? Like beans on toast, maybe a sausage.

NEIL   Or I can make jelly?

SIMON   Right, fuck it. I'm brewing some hash tea.

——————— SCENE 8 ———————

EXT. NEIL'S HOUSE

WILL V/O   . . . *the one thing Jay didn't want Simon to do with the tea was make tea, because he'd find out it was tea.*

THE FOUR BOYS COME OUT OF THE FRONT DOOR AND WALK TOWARDS SIMON'S DAD (ALAN COOPER)'S CAR. SIMON STORMS AHEAD.

JAY   I told you Si, there were supply issues.

WILL   The main issue being Donovan supplied you with tea.

SIMON REACHES THE CAR FIRST AND CLIMBS IN, SLAMMING THE DOOR BEHIND HIM.

ALAN COOPER   Oi.

WILL V/O   *And so refreshed but in no way high, Simon headed for his date with Tara.*

——————— SCENE 9 ———————

INT. SIMON'S DAD'S CAR

THE FOUR OF THEM ARE SITTING IN SILENCE AS SIMON'S DAD DRIVES THEM. SIMON HAS A PORK-PIE HAT ON.

ALAN COOPER   You lot seem very quiet tonight.

SIMON   Yeah, well it's better than hearing non-stop bullshit.

ALAN COOPER   Language. What's that on your head Simon?

SIMON   Um, I don't know Dad. Oh yeah, it's a hat. Obviously. God.

ALAN COOPER   Looks bloody stupid.

WILL   We tried to tell him.

ALAN COOPER   You look like a butcher.

SIMON   Pete Doherty wears them actually.

ALAN COOPER   Pete Doherty's butcher wears them.

SIMON   Oh, I forgot you were a comedian as well as a cab driver.

ALAN COOPER   Oi, I'm doing you a favour.

Why are you wearing it anyway? You've never worn anything like that before.

NEIL   He's meeting a bird.

SIMON   Neil.

ALAN COOPER   Knew it. You've got that look in your eye.

SIMON   What?

ALAN COOPER   It's a sort of animal look. I've seen it when you watch TV sometimes, *X Factor* and that.

JAY   When he sees Louis Walsh?

SIMON   Funny.

ALAN COOPER   No, thankfully, Cheryl Cole. If his mum's in the room he has to pop a pillow over his lap.

THE BOYS LAUGH.

———— SCENE 10 ————

INT. GIG VENUE

WILL V/O   *It wasn't exactly Take That at Wembley Arena, but the end prize had everything you could want from a local music venue. Bar staff who didn't ask for ID, a worrying lack of fire exits and a horrific smell from the toilets.*

THE VENUE IS BUSY WITH PEOPLE SORT OF MILLING ABOUT. THE BAND IS NOT ON STAGE YET. THE FOUR BOYS GO TO THE BAR. SIMON HAS HALF AN EYE ON THE BARMAN, TRYING TO GET SERVED, BUT IS ALSO LOOKING AROUND.

SIMON   Can you see Tara anywhere?

JAY   Just follow the puddles, she's that fucking wet for you.

SIMON   Can you hear something Will? I can smell bullshit, but I can't hear anything.

JAY   Oh, stop being a baby.

WILL   Simon, it's probably for the best that you don't have any drugs. I'm sure Tara will understand.

SIMON   Have you got a girlfriend?

WILL   No. You know that.

SIMON   Then you'll excuse me if I don't give a shit what you think.

NEIL   You can share mine if you like Si, I've got some tabs.

WILL   What? Like LSD?

NEIL   Nah, I've nicked some of my dad's sleeping pills. Apparently if you mix them with Ribena and red wine and cough mixture, it gives you a well good buzz.

WILL   Is the buzz crippling stomach acid?

JAY   Oh yeah, no, it's good that. Mix in some Lucozade, as well – it gives it more of a crunchy buzz.

SIMON   Thanks Neil, but I think Tara is expecting me to have some puff, so I'm fucked because someone is a total bullshitter.

JAY Fucking hell, if you're going to be so menstrual about it I'll go and score some shit here.

SIMON Oh yes, off you go to 'score' Scarface.

JAY I will. You coming Neil?

NEIL Yeah, all right. Get us a Ribena and wine Si? Half and half, yeah? It's got to be quite pacific.

WILL *SPECIFIC.*

 SCENE 11

INT. VENUE

JAY AND NEIL ARE LOOKING AROUND.

JAY Fucking Simon, I have to do everything for him. He'll probably want me to bone that girl for him too.

NEIL Show her how it's done properly.

JAY Exactly.

NEIL When you do it, do you more bump or grind?

JAY What?

NEIL Like, I was thinking about it and whether it's better to like bump or grind? 'Cos you can only do one or the other if you think about it.

JAY Not me mate, no I do both. And I slap. They all love a slap.

NEIL You're not bullshitting me are you?

JAY Oh, what? Neil, come on mate.

NEIL Sorry, it's just you keep saying you can get loads of drugs but so far the only drugs you've got is tea. Just makes me think . . .

JAY Neil, don't alright. Just don't OK. I've not scored any gear because where am I meant to get it from? My mate's in Afghanistan I can't help that. And there's no one dealing.

NEIL What about him?

JAY FOLLOWS NEIL'S GAZE AND THEY CAN SEE A GUY (STEPHEN) IN THE CORNER OF THE BAR. HE IS LOOKING AROUND AS HE EXCHANGES MONEY WITH ANOTHER PERSON WHO WALKS AWAY QUICKLY.

JAY   Shit, right, yeah.

NEIL   You going over then?

JAY   Yes, but you'd better come too. As muscle.

NEIL   Right, cool.

JAY   Look hard, this might get tasty.

JAY AND NEIL WALK OVER TO THE DEALER WITH THEIR SHOULDERS HUNCHED, TRYING TO LOOK ENORMOUS. JAY IS SWAGGERING A BIT AND NEIL IS PRETENDING TO CHEW GUM.

JAY   Oh, can I have some gum?

NEIL   I ain't got any, I'm pretending.

THEY REACH THE DEALER.

JAY   Alright mate.

STEPHEN   Alright?

NEIL   My mate wanted to say something to you.

STEPHEN   Yeah?

JAY   Sort me out then geezer.

STEPHEN   What?

JAY   Please sort me out geezer. I've got twenty quid.

STEPHEN   So what do you want from me?

JAY   You know, gear. Sweet Mary Jane, ganja man?

STEPHEN   Ah so you want to buy drugs and you came to me why?

NEIL   Well, 'cos we saw—

STEPHEN   'Cos I'm black. You saw a black guy at a gig and thought he must be a dealer?

JAY   No we didn't . . .

STEPHEN   You fucking white boys are all the same. Scratch beneath the surface just a little bit and you're racist. Yeah that's right I've said it, racist.

NEIL   But have you got any drugs?

STEPHEN   Yes I have but that's not the point. The point is that you assumed I had some just 'cause I was black.

JAY   Could we buy some please?

STEPHEN   Why should I deal to you? Why should I deal to two little suburban racists who see me as some kind of stereotype? I'm at university.

NEIL   But you are a drug dealer as well, yeah?

STEPHEN   Yes, I do deal, but you keep missing the point.

JAY   Look, here's thirty quid, can we just have some puff?

STEPHEN   Yes you can, but only because I'm a dealer, not because I'm black. Now fuck off.

NEIL AND JAY START TO LEAVE. JAY THEN STOPS AND DOUBLES BACK.

JAY   Can you roll it up for us please?

WILL V/O   *If ever there was an advertisement for drugs not being cool, Jay was it.*

——— SCENE 12 ———

INT. GIG VENUE

WILL V/O   *My first ever gig was in full swing. Whilst Simon searched for his date, I was enjoying it in a way . . .*

WILL   Do you like the taste of beer? I don't know if I do actually.

JUST THEN SIMON'S HAT IS PULLED SHARPLY OFF THE BACK OF HIS HEAD. IT'S TARA.

TARA   What the fuck's this?

SIMON   What? Oh hi.

TARA   Didn't realise Pete Doherty was coming along.

SIMON   Is he?

TARA   No, I mean you, you twat.

SIMON   Oh right, because of the hat?

WILL   No, because you fucked Kate Moss. Obviously it's the hat. Hi, I'm Will.

TARA   Are you the guy who shit himself in the exam?

WILL   Yep. Now Tara, don't you think it's just cool here? Great vibe, no need to drink too much or take anything to make it better. Couldn't get better, could it?

NEIL BOUNDS OVER.

NEIL   Jay's sorted it.

SIMON   No way.

NEIL   Yep, no bullshit, he's totally done it. The man even rolled one up for us.

TARA   Oh cool.

SIMON   Yeah, course.

NEIL   He's waiting outside.

WILL   I don't want to be a killjoy, but I just think you should remember that what you are about to do is illegal.

TARA   So's doing bombs in the swimming pool, but I do that. Because it's fun, yeah? Come on Simon.

SIMON AND TARA WALK AHEAD, EXCITEDLY.

WILL   Technically that's not illegal.

——— SCENE 13 ———

EXT. GIG VENUE, BY THE BINS

WILL V/O . . . *I didn't know which was worse, that my friend was about to do drugs, just to impress a girl, or the smug look on Jay's face.*

JAY Here we go boys and girls.

TARA Cool.

NEIL Nice.

SIMON So you've actually got it then?

JAY Listen, when I say I'm gonna deliver, I fucking deliver.

WILL Like a postman with tourette's.

JAY Right, who's first then?

TARA I've never done it before.

SIMON Haven't you?

TARA No, go on Simon, show me how.

SIMON Maybe Jay should go first because he sorted it. Only fair.

JAY Nah, I'm cool taking a breather. I've smoked one the size of a parsnip whilst I waited for you latecomers.

SIMON Or maybe ladies first? So that is you.

TARA No, I'm nervous. Go on.

SIMON OK. Alright, I suppose.

WILL V/O *I couldn't really blame Simon. If I thought a fit girl like Tara might get off with me, I'd probably mainline heroin into my eyeball . . .*

SIMON TAKES A DRAG BUT EXHALES IT ALMOST IMMEDIATELY AND THEN SWIFTLY HOLDS OUT THE SPLIFF TO TARA.

SIMON Great, that was really great. Here you go.

TARA   What? You didn't even inhale. You've got to take it right in like a cigarette.

SIMON   Oh, right, OK. Sometimes I do it this way, gets your, um, cheeks nicely stoned, but no, I'll have a go your way.

SIMON TAKES A HUGE MOUTHFUL, HOLDS IT IN HIS CHEEKS AND THEN GULPS IT DOWN. HE COUGHS A LOT.

SIMON   That definitely went in that time. Right in the lungs. Tara?

TARA TAKES THE SPLIFF AND SMOKES IT. SHE'S MUCH MORE CONFIDENT THAN SIMON WAS.

TARA   Cool.

WILL   How are your cheeks feeling now? Have they got the munchies?

JAY STICKS HIS HAND OUT, EXPECTING TARA TO PASS OVER THE SPLIFF, BUT SHE TAKES ANOTHER ENORMOUS TOKE ON IT.

JAY   Can I have a go, please?

TARA   Oh, right, sorry.

JAY   This is cool, just us here, smoking a foul doobie.

WILL   Oh yes, hanging out by some bins, near a skip in the cold, doing drugs, oh it's very cool. Very cool indeed.

JAY   Yep, that is good weed. Neil?

NEIL   Nah, I'm all right, I've got my sleeping tabs.

SIMON   What about the Ribena and wine?

NEIL   I had that earlier. It all gets mixed up in my tummy anyway, so it should be all right.

JAY   What about you, 'Just Say No'? Or are you still too scared?

WILL   Oh yes I'm scared. Scared that you three won't think I'm cool enough to hang out with any more. Oh no.

THERE IS AN ANNOUNCEMENT FROM INSIDE, A BIT MUFFLED.

TARA   Oh, Failsafe. Shit, we can't miss them.

SIMON   No way, José. Come on then guys.

THE OTHER THREE LOOK AT SIMON, AS HE LETS TARA DRAG HIM INSIDE.

JAY   Na, you're all right José.

——— SCENE 14 ———

INT. GIG VENUE, BACK OF HALL

WILL V/O   *I was questioning my beliefs. If winners don't do drugs, how come Simon was off with lovely Tara, whilst I was stuck with two morons, half a lager and a bottle of cough syrup.*

JAY STANDS WITH WILL AND NEIL. IT'S NOT AS NOISY OR AS CRAZY AS AT THE FRONT.

JAY   Ah, I'm definitely feeling something now, this is great. I might try and get a shipment in for Glastonbury.

WILL   Yes, I mean it's the next logical step from buying a small amount for you and a friend, dealing to seventy thousand people in a field.

JAY   Alright, alright. Keep it down. You never know who's listening.

WILL   Who?

JAY   Old Bill, undercover Bacon. These places are usually crawling with filth, I've got to keep on my guard.

NEIL   I think I'm coming up. How many singers are onstage? It looks like five.

JAY   Ask Professor Downer, he'll know.

WILL   Just because you've had a puff on your first joint doesn't make you Kurt Cobain.

JAY   Look, if you want to be a mummy's boy, that's fine. But stop trying to bring us down man.

WILL   Am I a mummy's boy because I refuse to bow to peer pressure, or am I in fact the opposite?

NEIL   You're a mummy's boy.

JAY   Go on petal, have a puff, show us you're not scared.

WILL   Well I would, but I don't smoke because of – what's that thing that you get when you smoke?

NEIL   Sex?

WILL   No, cancer Neil.

JAY   Fine, eat it then.

WILL   I could do, but as I keep explaining, I have no interest in getting, as you say, high.

NEIL   I feel brilliant.

WILL   Well from the outside you're basically the same but a bit more boring.

JAY   It's alright Neil, he's scared.

NEIL   Course, scared.

WILL   Give it here then.

JAY HANDS WILL THE BROWN LUMP. HE PUTS IT IN HIS MOUTH, CHEWS A BIT, TAKES A SWIG OF HIS DRINK AND SWALLOWS IT.

WILL   Right, happy now? So you can shut up about how you like to chase the bloody dragon. I've had some, I feel fine, let's move on.

JAY   Fucking hell, not all of it. You've eaten all of it.

WILL   Yes, so in my life I've done even more drugs than you and I still think it's pathetic.

JAY   I told you to keep it on the down-low. He looks federal.

JAY POINTS OUT A RANDOM IN THE HALL.

———— SCENE 15 ————

INT. GIG VENUE, MOSH PIT

WILL V/O *So while I tried to work out what 'federal' meant, Simon was experiencing moshing for the first time. Which is a bit like being beaten up to music.*

TARA This is so fucking cool.

SIMON Yeah. Fucking cool.

IT'S NOISY AND FAST, BUT THE PEOPLE DON'T SEEM TO MIND BECAUSE REALLY IT'S ABOUT BOUNCING AROUND AND GOING MENTAL. SIMON GETS SHOVED INTO TARA.

SIMON Easy mate.

HE GETS SHOVED FROM ANOTHER DIRECTION. THEN ANOTHER. THEN ANOTHER.

SIMON Ow, God, bit aggressive, but cool.

TARA Simon, you've got to mosh or they'll crush you.

TARA STARTS POGOING UP AND DOWN. SHE GIVES SIMON A SHOVE TO TRY AND GEE HIM UP.

SIMON Oh right, that's what we do, is it?

TARA LAUGHS AS SIMON JOINS IN. SIMON GIVES HER A BIG SHOVE IN THE BACK AND, COMPLETELY CAUGHT OFF BALANCE, SHE FLIES FORWARDS AND DROPS TO THE GROUND.

SIMON Are you alright Tara?

TARA Owww. MY NOSE. Aghhhh.

———— SCENE 16 ————

INT. GIG VENUE, BACK OF HALL

WILL V/O *Back at my Mensa meeting, things were starting to happen . . .*

NEIL Tuesday then, yeah?

WILL   Are you all right Neil? You're dribbling.

NEIL IS INDEED DRIBBLING.

NEIL   Yeah thanks. You can have it back Tuesday.

NEIL STUMBLES OVER TO THE MIDDLE OF THE HALL AND STARTS TO DO HIS
ROBOT DANCE, BUT A LITTLE MORE SLOWLY THAN NORMAL.

──────── SCENE 17 ────────

INT. VENUE, SIDE OF HALL

WILL V/O   *when it came to killing off brain cells, Neil had very little
room for manoeuvre. Meanwhile, Tara being a combination of stoned
and concussed was working in Simon's favour.*

SIMON AND TARA ARE SITTING ON A SOFA, AWAY FROM THE MOSH PIT NOW.

SIMON   Is your nose OK?

TARA   My nose is OK, but I still feel a bit queasy.

SIMON   If I see the guy that did it, I'll, grrr, y'know.

TARA   You'll what?

SIMON   Dunno.

TARA   Did you say 'grrr'?

SIMON   I think I did.

I'll 'grrrr'.

TARA   Like a tiger.

SIMON   I'm Tony the tiger. Grrrr.

SIMON MAKES SILLY CLAW MOVEMENTS.

TARA   More.

SIMON   Grrroowwwwwwwllllllll.

THEY ARE BOTH GIGGLING AND GETTING ON WELL, OBVIOUSLY A BIT STONED.

———— SCENE 18 ————

INT. GIG VENUE, BACK OF HALL

WILL V/O   *I'm sure pretending to be a big cat or a slow-moving robot wasn't the standard reaction to doing drugs, but I would have taken either of those over what was going on in my head.*

WILL IS STANDING WITH NEIL AND JAY AND STARTING TO LOOK EDGY.

WILL   I don't want to sound mental, but I'm starting to feel a bit like I'm in a bubble. Is this what being high is? Do you feel like you're in a thick bubble?

JAY   Nah, it's cool. I feel pretty nice. Up but down, but chilled, but like ready to do it.

WILL   Oh God, this isn't good, I feel unusual.

Why did you let me eat it? Why? My arms feel odd.

JAY   Oh just shut up, enjoy it.

WILL   Jay, I think I'm going wrong. Time is going by really, really, really, really slowly. You need to call an ambulance right now, because I can't use the phone. My arms don't work and my hands are sausages.

JAY   (LAUGHING) Fuck off.

WILL   Jay, I'm serious. You feel miles away. I think I might be dying. What if I'm a dead person? Please call an ambulance.

JAY   I can't call an ambulance because they'll bring the fucking police, I'll get done for dealing, and with looks like this, if I go to prison my anal virginity won't last a day.

WILL   But my hands?

JAY   I'm not calling an ambulance. So stop being a baby and just ride it out.

WILL   Oh God.

WILL SPOTS NEIL DANCING VERY SLOWLY NOW AND RUNS OVER TO HIM. WILL'S ARMS RANDOMLY JERK UPWARDS.

WILL　Neil, Neil, you've got to help me, everything's going flat and I think I might be dead.

NEIL　Eh?

WILL　Help me. I'm getting random arm movements.

NEIL　Sleepy time. Sleepy time.

NEIL STUMBLES TO THE SIDE OF THE HALL AND SLUMPS DOWN ASLEEP ON THE FLOOR. WILL IS MASSIVELY SPOOKED BY THE SIGHT OF NEIL, AND HIS RANDOM ARM MOVEMENTS ARE BECOMING MORE FREQUENT. HE LOOKS AROUND, BUT THERE'S NO ONE THAT CAN HELP HIM.

WILL V/O　*So I couldn't rely on Neil, but I knew one thing for sure. I had to stop my fucking arms.*

──────── SCENE 19 ────────

INT. GIG VENUE, SIDE OF HALL

SIMON AND TARA ARE STILL SITTING DOWN, GIGGLING. SIMON IS STILL DOING HIS TIGER IMPRESSION.

SIMON　Grrrrrrr.

TARA　Can I say something?

SIMON　I don't know, can you? You just did, so probably, yes.

TARA　OK, clever clogs, can I do something?

SIMON　Depends what it is.

TARA LOOKS A LITTLE WOOZY, LIKE SHE MIGHT FAINT.

SIMON　Tara. What did you want to do?

TARA　Oh this.

TARA LEANS TO KISS SIMON. HE CLOSES HIS EYES AND AS THEY GET CLOSER SHE SUDDENLY PULLS AWAY AND PUKES OVER HIS FEET.

TARA LOOKS UP AT SIMON AND WIPES A BIT OF SICK AWAY FROM HER MOUTH WITH THE BACK OF HER HAND. SHE GRINS A STONED GRIN AT SIMON, THEN SHE SNOGS HIM.

TARA I feel sick.

SIMON PICKS BITS FROM HIS MOUTH.

TARA It's got to be the joint. I shouldn't have done it.

SIMON Right. Um, maybe stick your fingers down your throat, get it all up, then we can go again?

TARA Yeah. I think I can make it to the toilet. Don't move.

AS SHE LEAVES, WILL COMES OVER, RANDOM ARM MOVEMENTS AND ALL.

WILL Listen Simon, this is very important information. Call an ambulance and tell them I'm in a bubble and everything is very flat.

SIMON I'm a bit busy here Will, can you look after yourself?

WILL I can't stop my arms. Look how random my arms are. Help me.

SIMON Look, I'm in here Will, so can you please fuck off.

TARA BOUNDS BACK OVER.

TARA Didn't make it.

SHE LEAPS ON SIMON'S LAP AND IMMEDIATELY STARTS SNOGGING HIM AGAIN. WILL LOOKS DESPERATE.

WILL V/O *I needed help. Jay was useless, Neil was getting an early night and Simon was too busy licking vomit off Tara's tonsils . . . I really needed help. How could I get help?*

——————— SCENE 20 ———————

INT. GIG VENUE, STAGE

WILL VERY STIFFLY CLIMBS ONTO THE STAGE AND SPEAKS INTO THE MICROPHONE. HE'S NOT HOLDING THE MIC THOUGH, DUE TO HIS NOW MORE REGULAR RANDOM ARM MOVEMENTS.

WILL Hello, hello everyone. Can somebody call me an ambulance, because I'm in trouble. Time is moving really, really slowly and everything is flat. I need you to call an ambulance or failing that my mummy. I really want my mummy because, and I'm not being dramatic, but I think I might be dead. Is that clear? Mummy or ambulance.

AS WILL IS NEARING THE END OF HIS PLEA, TWO BOUNCERS ARE CLOSING IN ON HIM, ONE FROM EACH SIDE OF THE STAGE, NOT IN A PARTICULARLY THREATENING WAY BUT THEY ARE DEFINITELY GOING FOR HIM.

WILL V/O   *I don't remember the details of that night especially well, but I do know that despite their love of violence the bouncers were surprisingly kind to me. Which could only mean I looked proper mental.*

——————— SCENE 21 ———————

EXT. MUSIC VENUE

THERE'S A SMALL CROWD OF INTERESTED SMOKERS, ALONG WITH SIMON AND TARA WATCHING WITH THEIR ARMS ROUND EACH OTHER AS WILL IS WHEELED IN TO THE BACK OF AN AMBULANCE. HE'S NOT ON A STRETCHER, BUT IN A SORT OF WHEELCHAIR WITH A BRIGHT RED BLANKET OVER HIS KNEES.

PARAMEDIC   Are you sure it was just cannabis you took?

WILL   I ate it, I'm really sorry. Is my mummy coming? Can you make my arms stop?

PARAMEDIC   We'll do our best.

THE PARAMEDICS ARE SHUTTING THE DOORS AS A TWITCHY AND NERVOUS-LOOKING JAY COMES OUT AND WALKS OVER TO SIMON AND TARA.

JAY   Whagwan?

SIMON   Someone called an ambulance and they're taking him away.

JAY   Oh fucking Jesus, oh no. It wasn't me that sold it right? Not me? Oh shit the blue lights.

SIMON   It's an ambulance.

JAY   That's what they want you to believe. Shit.

JAY RUNS OFF, THROWING STUFF (TISSUES ETC) OUT OF HIS POCKETS AS HE DOES SO.

WILL V/O   *It had been a week of firsts . . .*

. . . *our first gig, our first drugs. The first time we had to admit Jay delivered on one of his bullshit claims, Simon's first actual girlfriend, and the first time I spent two days in bed, silently crying and trying to make the walls stop moving.*

Episode 3

──────── 'Will's Dilemma' ────────

This episode was thematically entitled 'maintaining a girlfriend', something that I think is hard enough at the best of times (eh, fellas?), but is certainly difficult if you are the kind of blindly unthinking and selfish teenager that Simon Cooper is, or I was. Until I was about thirty-four.

Again, anecdotes played a large part in the writing of this episode (I fainted when I was on a double date in a cinema), including the opening. The motorcycle bullshit then crash was based on something that happened to Damon once, actually not that far from where we shot the scene in Dartford. I could write the story out verbatim, but it's pretty much exactly what's in the script. A friend bought a bike and then wasn't allowed to ride it home as he didn't have a licence. Damon claimed he had a licence and was an experienced motorcyclist, before getting on the bike in front of the owner and promptly crashing it straight into a wall. In the script we wrote 'Jay crashes into a wall' but luckily for us, and unluckily for him, the stuntman put himself through the door on take one, we all pissed ourselves, and take one was used.

Something we really wanted to get into this episode was the shopping-centre stuff, and especially the amazement you have when you live in suburbia and you see one of your teachers outside of school. It's a cross between seeing a celebrity and a monster (in Greg Davies' case, a literal giant) and your reactions can vary accordingly. Jay and Neil merely shouted his name, then ran off, and that seemed appropriate.

It's called 'Will's Dilemma' and I like to think for the character of Will it represented a genuine dilemma. He's desperate for some sort of sexual contact, partly to prove his normality, but if that contact comes from someone he considers 'abnormal', where does that leave him? Sure, he didn't have to call her 'the Empire State Building', but y'know, the rest was a dilemma.

———— SCENE 1 ————

EXT. MOTORCYCLE DEALERSHIP, GILLINGHAM

WILL V/O   *Neil was about to turn eighteen and to celebrate this landmark his mum was buying him an early grave.*

THE FOUR BOYS STAND OUTSIDE A MOTORCYCLE DEALERSHIP BESIDE A ROW OF BIKES. NEIL HAS HIS WRIST IN A PLASTER CAST. HE'S PROUDLY POINTING OUT ONE OF THE BIKES.

NEIL   What do you think?

JAY   Best. Present. Ever. Mate you're gonna hoover up the snatch on that.

NEIL   I know. Can't wait to get this cast off and go for a burn.

WILL   Does your mum usually buy you gifts this extravagant?

NEIL   Not really, but it is for my eighteenth.

JAY   And she did run off.

SIMON   Why are you getting a bike when you've already got a car?

NEIL   Motorbikes are cooler.

WILL   Until you hit a bus and kill yourself.

JAY   Don't listen to Captain Sensible, this is the ultimate clunge magnet. It's well known that if you can get a bird on the back of one of these they just cream their knickers 'cos of the vibrations.

WILL   Is it?

JAY   Yeah, that's why there are no female superbike champions. They all get too horny and have to stop and fud themselves off all the time.

WILL   Neil, how on earth is Jay allowed to ride your bike back without a licence or insurance?

JAY   Don't shit your pants health and safety. Neil can't do it 'cos of his arm, and the dealer's happy for me to take it 'cos I used to be a stunt rider.

WILL   It rhymes with stunt.

SIMON   Well we know that's bollocks.

JAY   Is it? 'Cos I can show you the DVD of me leaping over five lorries on *Blue Peter* if you like.

WILL   Wow, did you make it into the *Guinness Book of Fictional Records*?

JAY   Fuck off.

SIMON   I don't think Tara would be happy if I got one of these. She thinks they're death traps.

JAY   Beepedy beep beep . . . beepedy beep beep . . . time for another Tara update.

SIMON   What's that supposed to mean?

JAY   Nothing. Just because no one cares what Tara says or does, don't let that stop you from mentioning her every forty seconds.

SIMON   Don't be a dick. I don't mention her that much.

NEIL   You do mate.

SIMON   Oh pardon me for having a girlfriend.

JAY   Beepedy beep.

THE GUY WHO RUNS THE SHOP COMES OUTSIDE.

GUY   Who's taking it back then?

JAY   I am.

GUY   And you said you're used to motorbikes?

JAY   Course. My dad used to drink with Lance Armstrong.

GUY   What? The cyclist?

JAY   Um, yeah.

GUY   Right, well hop on, I'll just show you the basics in case it's different from what you've ridden before.

JAY GETS ON THE BIKE.

JAY   Can do.

GUY   These are the gears, these are the brakes.

JAY   And they're for stopping, right?

GUY   Yeah, I presume you want to stop.

JAY   Maybe.

GUY   Do you need me to show you that again?

JAY   Nah, it's alright. You never forget. It's like riding a bike innit.

JAY FLIPS DOWN THE HOOD ON HIS CRASH-HELMET, TWISTS THE THROTTLE AND JERKILY PULLS OFF, OUT OF CONTROL, TOWARDS THE WALL/SHOP FRONT. HE TRIES TO CHANGE COURSE, PANICS, AND ENDS UP HITTING THE WALL AND CRASHING THROUGH THE SHOP DOOR.

WILL   I think he's used to left-hand drive.

——— SCENE 2 ———

<u>INT. SIMON'S CAR</u>

WILL V/O   *If Jay's bike-riding skills weren't quite as good as he'd claimed, his ability to brazen it out was unparalleled.*

THE FOUR BOYS ARE DRIVING BACK FROM GILLINGHAM, STILL LAUGHING AT JAY.

JAY   I should fucking sue him, those tyres had no grip.

WILL   They don't tend to grip so well when they're up in the air.

NEIL   Oh my God, that was amazing, you looked such a knob.

WILL   What about your bike Neil?

NEIL   I know, the way he said he could ride it and then fell off and put his head straight through that door, it's got to be the funniest thing I've ever seen.

WILL   No, I meant what are you going to do about your bike? It's not only still in Gillingham, it's now fucked.

NEIL   Oh no.

WILL   So that's your mum's gift destroyed; what's your dad getting you?

NEIL   I'm getting this party on Friday, aren't I?

WILL   You mean you're having a party.

NEIL   No, I'm getting a party for my eighteenth. The party, that's my present.

JAY   Ha, you've got to be fucking joking. That's it?

NEIL   Why's that funny?

JAY   Look, I'm just saying, and no offence mate, but a party round your house is the pikiest eighteenth present I've ever heard of.

NEIL   Leave it out, he's not got much money at the moment.

JAY   Spent it all on butt plugs has he?

NEIL   No.

SIMON   Because he already owns every single one. In the world.

NEIL   Yeah, brilliant. Well done.

WILL   Who's coming then Neil?

NEIL   Mostly family, but I am allowed to invite ten friends.

SIMON   Ten, that's generous, considering you haven't got ten friends.

NEIL   Fuck off.

SIMON   All right, who are you going to ask then?

NEIL   Well I . . . Oh shit. How am I going to get ten people along?

JAY   Tell them your sister's going to be naked and your dad's promised not to bum them?

NEIL   Behave.

SIMON   I could ask Tara, see what she's up to?

JAY   Beepedy beep beep . . .

NEIL   Yeah nice one. She got any fit mates?

SIMON   S'pect so. I'm going to meet one of them after school tomorrow.

WILL   I thought we were going to Waterside tomorrow, to the cinema?

SIMON   Yeah, we are. But Tara and Kerry are coming too.

JAY   Oh I'm well up for that.

NEIL   Yeah I need to go Waterside anyway, I'm nearly out of pants.

SIMON   Um, you two aren't invited. It's like a double date.

WILL   Wow. What? I didn't agree to this.

SIMON   Oh come on. Apparently Kerry has been having a bit of a tough time recently, and Tara—

NEIL   Beepedy beep beep.

SIMON   —thinks you two would get along well, so I said you'd be cool.

WILL   Well, yes, but a date's quite a big thing? I mean do you know what she looks like?

SIMON   I've not seen her, but Tara says she's amazing and gorgeous.

JAY   I bet she's a right dog.

SIMON   Just 'cos you're not invited?

JAY   No, it's just that girls always think their mates are really fit, and then when you meet them they look like a pork scratching.

SIMON   To be fair, Tara's pretty spot on about most things.

NEIL   Beepedy beep beep . . .

SIMON   This conversation is specifically about Tara.

JAY   Look, at best I reckon this Kerry will be a mid-level munter.

SIMON   I'm sure she's not, honestly Tara says she's fit. Plus, and I probably shouldn't tell you this, but apparently Kerry has given her last three boyfriends blow jobs.

WILL   Seriously?

SIMON   Yep.

WILL   Well why didn't you say. What time are we meeting then?

——— SCENE 3 ———

INT. WATERSIDE SHOPPING CENTRE

WILL V/O   *Because I didn't own a tracksuit, I'd never seen the appeal of hanging out in a shopping centre. But whilst Simon and Tara explored the deepest recesses of each other's mouths, I was on a date with a girl who gave out blow jobs, so things were looking up. And by things, I mean me.*

SIMON AND TARA, WILL AND KERRY ARE ON THEIR DOUBLE DATE.

TARA AND SIMON ARE COMING UP THE ESCALATOR, SNOGGING. NEXT UP COMES WILL, LOOKING THOROUGHLY FED UP. BEHIND HIM IS KERRY, WHO IS NOT UNATTRACTIVE; WHAT SHE IS, THOUGH, IS TALL, MUCH TALLER THAN WILL.

TARA   This is fun. A fun double date.

WILL   Hah, we're just shopping.

TARA   Yeah, but after that we're going to watch the new *Saw* film. That's like a date.

WILL   Oh yeah, I might not make that actually.

TARA   You're not scared, are you?

WILL   No, I'm just not very good with blood.

SIMON   It's not real Will.

WILL   Yes Simon, thank you, I am aware of how cinema works. Any blood makes me feel queasy.

KERRY I'm the same, I don't like blood. Once I saw some and I didn't like it.

WILL Right.

TARA You two are so alike.

WILL Are we? Most people don't like blood.

TARA Yeah, you are. Anyway, I saw the best outfit for Simey in here. We won't be long. Why don't you two hang out?

TARA DRAGS SIMON INTO THE SHOP, LEAVING WILL AND KERRY ON THEIR OWN.

WILL Wait, I'll come with you and . . . right.

KERRY I like your glasses.

WILL Thanks.

KERRY Do you need them to see better?

WILL Yep.

——— SCENE 4 ———

INT. WATERSIDE SHOPPING CENTRE, CLOTHES SHOP

WILL V/O *So as I herded Kerry off, Simon was discovering that he wasn't just Tara's boyfriend, he was also her project.*

TARA AND SIMON ARE WANDERING AMONG THE RAILS, TARA BEAMING AND EXCITED AND SIMON LOOKING A BIT BORED.

SIMON Are we going to be looking round much longer? It's just my feet are really hurting.

TARA Oh my God, there it is.

A RAISED MANNEQUIN IN THE MIDDLE OF THE SHOP FLOOR IS WEARING THE OUTFIT SHE IS REFERRING TO. IT'S NOT VERY SIMON AND INCLUDES A CARDIGAN, A BOW-TIE AND FAKE GLASSES.

TARA You would look so cute in that.

SIMON   Yeah, um, the shirt is sort of nice.

TARA   Not just the shirt, the whole thing.

SIMON   Really? Do you think?

A MALE SHOP ASSISTANT COMES OVER.

SHOP ASSISTANT   Were you looking at this? I think it's great.

TARA   It's so great, isn't it? I was saying he'd look really good in it.

SHOP ASSISTANT   He would, he'd look really good in it.

SIMON   Not the cardigan though.

SHOP ASSISTANT   Especially the cardigan. And the bow tie.

TARA   The bow tie is amazing.

SHOP ASSISTANT   He should try it on.

SIMON   How are you suddenly so involved?

TARA   Yes, please just try it on, we don't have to buy it.

SIMON   But I'm going to look exactly like the dummy.

TARA   Please? For me?

SIMON   Do you not think it'll look weird?

TARA   Pleeeaaassse.

SIMON   God, alright, for you but not for him.

SHOP ASSISTANT   She's precious, isn't she?

TARA DRAGS SIMON TO THE DRESSING ROOM.

───── SCENE 5 ─────

INT. WATERSIDE SHOPPING CENTRE, CLOTHES SHOP

WILL V/O   *It was a mark of how desperate Simon was to lose his virginity that he was willing to let Tara dress him up like an eccentric posh child . . .*

SIMON COMES OUT OF THE DRESSING ROOM LOOKING VERY UNCOMFORTABLE, WEARING THE EXACT OUTFIT THAT IS ON THE MANNEQUIN, BAR THE GLASSES. THE SHOP ASSISTANT AND TARA ARE STANDING WAITING FOR HIM.

TARA   Oh my God.

SIMON   It's shit, isn't it?

TARA   You look adorable.

SHOP ASSISTANT   He looks fantastic, my creation has come to life. I have to tell everyone.

THE SHOP ASSISTANT GETS ON HIS INTERCOM:

SHOP ASSISTANT   All staff to dressing, all staff to dressing.

SIMON   No mate, come on.

TARA   You look amazing, I really fancy you in that.

SIMON   Do you?

TARA   Yeah. Put the glasses on.

SIMON DOES THIS SLOWLY AND THIS ELICITS ANOTHER SQUEAL OF DELIGHT FROM TARA.

SIMON   I'm going to take it off now.

SHOP ASSISTANT   Not yet. You're like my wet dream, I need to get a photo.

THE SHOP ASSISTANT GETS HIS PHONE OUT. SIMON LOOKS VERY UNHAPPY.

TARA   Oh come on Simon, smile.

TARA   Hands off everyone, he's mine.

WILL COMES OVER AND STARTS TO TALK TO SIMON BEFORE STOPPING DEAD.

WILL   Simon, can I have a word about Kerry, now—

BEAT.

WILL   Who has done this to you?

SHOP ASSISTANT   Out the picture you, geek chic was last year.

WILL V/O *. . . in a way it was a compliment, I'd never been called chic before.*

SCENE 6

INT. WATERSIDE SHOPPING CENTRE

WILL AND SIMON SIT ON A BENCH WHILE THE GIRLS SHOP.

SIMON   What is it with fucking girls? They think shop assistants are their friends. They're not, you've just met them and they are trying to sell you stuff.

WILL   Look, I think before this goes any further you need to tell Tara that Kerry isn't my type.

SIMON   What does that mean? You've only kissed three girls. Your type is 'anyone who will let you'.

WILL   Alright, fine, look, I don't want to seem really shallow but she's a bit big.

SIMON   Is she?

WILL   Oh, did it escape your notice that she's a giant?

SIMON   So she's tall. Come on, you're always saying how desperate you are, do you honestly think you'll get better?

WILL   Yes, I'd have thought so.

SIMON   Really?

WILL   May I remind you of Charlotte Hinchcliffe? She went out with me and she was not only fit and popular but also normal-sized.

SIMON   OK, so Kerry might not be the fittest girl ever, but she'll almost certainly give you a blow job if you stick with it.

WILL   Oh God, I know. My head is telling me to do one thing and my cock another. It's a genuine dilemma. I mean, is using her for sex totally unethical?

SIMON   She's offering to put your penis in her mouth, not pay you to ask questions in Parliament. You'd like a blow job wouldn't you?

WILL   Yes obviously. Oh God, this is a fucking nightmare. And having Neil and Jay follow us around isn't helping.

SIMON   What?

WILL   Are you going to come out then? We can see you, you're not even hiding.

NEIL AND JAY COME OUT FROM THEIR OBVIOUS HIDING PLACE, CHILDISHLY LAUGHING.

JAY   Your new girlfriend's big, isn't she?

WILL   She's not my girlfriend.

JAY   No, she's fucking Canary Wharf.

NEIL   You can bring your girlfriend to my birthday if you like Will.

WILL   Is that a joke?

NEIL   Nah, it'll help push the numbers up.

SIMON   It'll help push the height up.

WILL   Thanks Simon.

NEIL   So has she given you a blowie yet?

WILL   Here in Waterside? Oh yeah Neil, I've had two – one on the escalator and one in Nando's.

NEIL   Really?

WILL   No Neil, not really.

JAY   Are you going to go for it then? I mean she's a freak, but there's nothing like a blow job.

WILL   And you'd know because you've had so many blow jobs?

JAY   Yeah.

NEIL   When was your first then Jay?

JAY   Long time back, many suck jobs ago now. Years.

SIMON   Years ago? Bollocks.

JAY   I got one off the cleaner when I was twelve.

WILL Who was your cleaner, Gary Glitter?

NEIL Was it good?

JAY It was brilliant mate, I pissed right in her mouth.

SIMON What? Why would you do that?

WILL Is that even possible?

JAY Yes, that's how you finish blow jobs. And she said I was the best she'd ever had.

SIMON Through mouthfuls of piss.

WILL Before she had to get on with the hoovering.

TARA AND KERRY COME BACK.

TARA Oh, hi guys.

NEIL Alright?

TARA Come on Simon, we'd better get going, we don't want to miss the film.

JAY We're off too actually.

TARA Oh no.

JAY Yeah, off to get a Zinger Tower meal.

JAY AND NEIL LEAVE. SIMON STANDS UP AND TARA TAKES HIS HAND. KERRY TRIES TO TAKE WILL'S HAND BUT HE AVOIDS IT CAREFULLY.

WILL V/O *It was clear that tonight wasn't about me at all, and if he thought it would make Tara happy Simon would have set me up on a blind date with a plastic bag full of his own shit.*

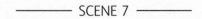

SCENE 7

INT. WATERSIDE SHOPPING CENTRE, HMV

JAY AND NEIL ARE WANDERING AROUND THE SHOP.

NEIL I don't think she's that bad, just a bit big.

NEIL PICKS UP A COMPUTER GAME.

NEIL Oh that one's meant to be awesome.

JAY Completed it.

NEIL It only came out last week.

JAY Completed it.

NEIL What about this?

JAY Championship Manager? Completed it mate.

NEIL You can't complete it.

JAY Yeah I know, but I got so good at it the FA offered me a role in the England set-up?

NEIL Did they?

JAY I took Woking from the conference to the champions League in six seasons, stuff like that doesn't go unnoticed Neil.

NEIL HAS FOUND A CARD STAND IN THE MIDDLE OF THE AISLE. IT'S ONE OF THOSE STANDS SELLING TACKY CALENDARS AND CAR STICKERS.

NEIL Oi Jay, look at this.

'Nice people swallow'. It means spunk.

JAY Yeah.

NEIL Or what about this: 'honk if you want a blow job'.

JAY We should stick it on Kerry, she loves giving blow jobs.

NEIL We'd have to get a bigger one.

JAY Yeah, good one. I know where this should go.

——————— SCENE 8 ———————

INT. WATERSIDE SHOPPING CENTRE

WILL V/O   *After becoming possibly the first people ever to actually laugh at a bumper sticker, Jay and Neil's day got even better when they saw something rare and exotic in the shopping centre.*

NEIL AND JAY ARE WALKING THROUGH THE SHOPPING CENTRE, WHEN NEIL STOPS DEAD. HE'S SEEN MR GILBERT IN A GIFT SHOP, LOOKING AT CUDDLY TOYS. IT'S CLEARLY AN UNGUARDED MOMENT.

NEIL   Oi Jay, look.

JAY   Fucking hell, what's he doing here?

NEIL   Dunno. Shopping?

JAY   (SHOUTING EVENTUALLY, BUT FIRST ONE A BIT SOFT) Gilbert. GILBERT!

MR GILBERT TURNS HIS HEAD BUT NEIL AND JAY ARE LEGGING IT AWAY, PISSING THEMSELVES LAUGHING.

——————— SCENE 9 ———————

INT. WATERSIDE CINEMA

WILL V/O   *A few years ago I'd seen King Kong at the cinema, now I was on a date with her . . .*

WILL   This is very violent.

SIMON   Yeah.

WILL   Do you feel all right? With the blood?

SIMON   Yes. Shush.

KERRY   Are you OK?

WILL   Fine thanks, yeah, bit hot.

KERRY   Remember, it's not real.

KERRY LEANS ROUND AND PUTS HER ARM AROUND HIM, THE SORT OF WAY A BLOKE WOULD WITH A GIRL.

WILL V/O . . . *Kerry's attempt to comfort me with her massive hand did the opposite. There was no way out, the horror, the hand, the horror, the hand, it was all too much. I told Simon I didn't like blood . . .*

WILL STARTS TO LOOK REALLY ILL AND THEN HE STARTS TO GET UP.

WILL Sorry, I think I need some air.

HE STARTS TO CLAMBER OVER KERRY, WHO IS NEXT TO THE AISLE, BUT HE SORT OF STUMBLES AND FALLS.

WILL I feel really faint.

HE DOES FAINT INTO THE AISLE. THERE'S LAUGHTER FROM THE BACK OF THE CINEMA AND POPCORN IS CHUCKED BY LAUGHING, SLIGHTLY YOUNGER, TEENAGERS. KERRY IS IMMEDIATELY OUT OF HER SEAT TO HELP HIM.

KERRY Fuck off, he's scared of blood.

WILL Oh dear.

──────── SCENE 10 ────────

INT. CAR / EXT. TARA'S HOUSE

SIMON IS DROPPING TARA OFF, AND THEY ARE PULLED UP IN HER DRIVE.

WILL V/O *I'll say this for Kerry – she made a great human popcorn shield. Meanwhile, by the time we'd driven Tara home, Simon was getting withdrawal symptoms because he'd gone more than five minutes without sticking his tongue down her throat.*

THEY GET OUT OF THE CAR.

TARA I think that went really well. I could tell Kerry likes him. She's amazing isn't she, so beautiful.

SIMON Yeah, sort of. She's quite tall.

TARA What do you mean?

SIMON LOOKS UP AND SEES THAT TARA'S MUM AND DAD HAVE COME OUT.

TARA Oh no, what are they doing?

SIMON   They know about me right?

TARA   Totally. Hence the welcome party.

Simon, this is my mum and dad, who happen to be stepping outside the front door for no reason just as we arrive.

TARA'S MUM   Hello Simon. I'm Tara's mum, she's told me all about you.

SIMON   Hello.

TARA'S DAD   Whereas because I'm Tara's father she's told me virtually nothing about you.

SIMON   She doesn't really know that much about me. Not that there's anything bad to know.

TARA'S DAD   This is your car, is it? At least you're not driving my daughter round in some souped-up death trap.

SIMON   No, it's just a stopgap really, until I get enough money to buy something less crap.

TARA'S DAD WINCES A LITTLE AT THE WORD 'CRAP'.

TARA   Mum and Dad don't like swearing Simon.

SIMON   Oh sorry. What did I say? Crap? Is crap a swear word? Crap?

TARA'S DAD   Let's just err on the side of caution with that one, shall we.

SIMON   Yeah, sorry.

BEAT

TARA'S DAD   It's OK. BEAT Someone's got a funny bumper sticker. What's this one say? 'Honk if you want a . . .' Oh.

SIMON   What?

SIMON MOVES AROUND TO SEE THE STICKER.

SIMON   That's not mine.

TARA'S DAD   Well it's on your car.

TARA   Dad, can you just go inside please? Mum tell him.

TARA'S DAD   It's all right Simon, I can see it's meant to be a joke.

SIMON   I literally have no idea how that got there.

TARA'S DAD   Just not very funny though is it. I mean why would you want to drive around with that on the back of your car? It just makes you look dirty.

SIMON   I'm not. It's not like I'm obsessed by blow jobs or cocks.

THERE'S A BEAT AS EVERYONE TAKES THIS IN.

SIMON   Honestly, I'm not.

TARA'S DAD   Say goodnight to Simon Tara.

TARA AND HER FAMILY GO INSIDE AS SIMON FRANTICALLY TRIES TO PULL THE STICKER OFF.

──────── SCENE 11 ────────

EXT. WILL'S HOUSE

WILL V/O   . . . *so whilst Simon struggled to get rid of something impossibly clingy, so did I.*

WILL AND KERRY ARE WALKING TO WILL'S FRONT DOOR.

KERRY   I don't think they should have thrown stuff. What kind of a person throws stuff at another person when they are not feeling well?

WILL   Anyway, thanks Kerry, but I think I'm meant to walk *you* home.

KERRY   I want to make sure that you get home safely.

WILL   Yes, well here I am, so thank you.

KERRY   You can kiss me goodnight if you want to.

WILL   Oh, OK, right.

WILL TENTATIVELY GOES TO KISS HER. KERRY PULLS HIM CLOSER, VIRTUALLY LIFTING HIM UP ONTO TIPTOE.

WILL   Right, well, I'd better go. Goodnight then. Get home safely.

KERRY GOES TO KISS WILL AGAIN, BUT HE'S BACKING BEHIND THE DOOR.

WILL   Nope, that's enough for tonight.

KERRY   Kiss me one more time.

WILL   No. Night, Kerry.

HE MORE OR LESS SHUTS THE DOOR IN HER FACE.

——— SCENE 12 ———

INT. SCHOOL COMMON ROOM

WILL V/O   *OK, I ran away, but she's still going on my kiss list. Number four – big Kerry. Considering it had the combined brain power of Jay and Neil behind it, the blow-job sticker joke worked amazingly well.*

SIMON   It's impossible to get off. Tara's dad was really angry.

JAY   Beepedy beep beep . . .

SIMON   I'll have to get the car resprayed I reckon.

NEIL   Try to pick a less shit colour.

SIMON   Brilliant. How's your girlfriend Will?

WILL   If you mean Kerry, she's not my girlfriend.

NEIL   How come she's changed her Facebook status to 'in a relationship' then?

WILL   Has she? How did you find her on Facebook?

NEIL   It's easy when you know where to look.

JAY   Which is in a group for lanky munters.

SIMON   Mate, I reckon it's all good. Tara—

JAY   Beepedy beep beep.

SIMON   . . . told me something very interesting about Kerry.

NEIL   She bangs her head wherever she goes?

SIMON No. She told me you kissed her last night.

JAY Did you use a fucking stepladder?

WILL No.

SIMON Why did you do it? I thought you weren't interested.

WILL I don't know, I can't decide, and at that moment it was easier to kiss her than not to kiss her.

NEIL Were you scared?

WILL A bit.

SIMON It sounds to me like you're closing in on that BJ, maybe it'll even happen at Neil's party.

WILL No I think it's all wrong. I'm going to de-invite her from the party.

NEIL Oh no way, she's got to come, I need to get the numbers up. With you three and Tara I'm stuck on five.

WILL Four.

NEIL But if Kerry comes as well, that'll make six.

WILL Five. Taking her to the party is a bit like admitting we're going out when all I really want from her is a blow job. It would be morally wrong.

SIMON Look, why don't you just get the blow job and then see how you feel?

NEIL I've got an idea. Why not get the blowie, ask for a fuck and if she says no then dump her.

WILL Brilliant. Well I'd just like to thank everyone for their fucking useless advice. Thank you.

JAY I don't know what your problem is. I've never been out with a girl I liked anyway.

WILL Oh apart from the last one, who made you cry.

JAY LOOKS CHASTENED.

SIMON   Will!

NEIL   Oh that is bang out of order.

WILL   What? After everything he's said?

SIMON   Yeah, but some things just aren't okay. You alright Jay?

JAY   Yeah, I'm fine.

SIMON   Apologise.

WILL   For that?

SIMON   Yes, for that.

WILL   I have literally no idea what the rules are then.

JUST THEN MR GILBERT WALKS PAST THEM, LOOKING AT A FOLDER.

NEIL   Oi Jay.

NEIL   (ALMOST UNDER HIS BREATH AS GILBERT PASSES) Waterside.

JAY   Waterside.

MR GILBERT HAS STOPPED DEAD. HE SPINS ON HIS HEEL.

MR GILBERT   What did you say?

NEIL   Nothing.

MR GILBERT   Right, a week's after-school detention.

For both of you.

NEIL   Oh what?

MR GILBERT   Two weeks.

JAY   Come on, sir . . .

MR GILBERT   Three weeks.

JAY   But sir . . .

MR GILBERT   Four weeks detention.

JAY GAWPS LIKE A GOLDFISH AT MR GILBERT.

MR GILBERT   Starting tonight. I'll see you later.

MR GILBERT WALKS OFF.

JAY   Oh fucking hell.

NEIL   Now I'm going to be late to my party.

WILL   Right, OK, I've made up my mind. You're right. Maybe a blow job is worth it. I think I'm going to play the long game with Kerry.

JAY   Just make sure you don't play the tall game.

SIMON   She'd win every time.

NEIL   Because she's tall.

WILL   Yes, I get it.

——— SCENE 13 ———

INT. NEIL'S HOUSE, LIVING ROOM

WILL AND SIMON ARE STANDING IN NEIL'S LIVING ROOM, DRINKING A SMALL BOTTLE OF LAGER EACH. TARA AND KERRY ARE WITH THEM. NEIL'S SISTER (KATIE) STANDS AT ONE END OF THE ROOM, CLEARLY NOT READY FOR THE PARTY, IRONING A PAIR OF TROUSERS ON AN IRONING BOARD.

WILL V/O   *That evening as we stared at Neil's impossibly attractive sister, two thoughts crossed my mind. Surely she must be adopted and could this party get any worse? Turns out it could . . .*

THE DOOR TO THE LOUNGE OPENS AND NEIL'S DAD (KEVIN SUTHERLAND) ENTERS WEARING A SHIRT BUT NO TROUSERS.

KEVIN SUTHERLAND   Oh I say. What must you all think of me, racing around the house in my briefs like we're in some sort of Roman orgy.

HE PULLS HIS TROUSERS ON.

KEVIN SUTHERLAND   Neil will be back in a minute, he's just finishing up at chess club.

HE LEAVES JUST AS TARA AND KERRY COME OVER. SIMON IS IN THE WATERSIDE ENSEMBLE.

KATIE SUTHERLAND   You know it's not fancy dress, Simon?

SIMON   I'm not in fancy dress.

TARA   It's a new look for Simon. I chose it.

KATIE SUTHERLAND   You should get your girlfriend to dress you too Will. You look like shit.

KATIE LEAVES WITH HER IRONING.

KERRY   She's really rude to you. Did you two have a thing?

SIMON   With Katie? He wishes.

KERRY   I don't understand.

TARA   Come on Kezza, let's go and get our men some more drinks.

KERRY   Lager for William?

THE GIRLS GO TO THE KITCHEN.

WILL   Maybe the cheap French beer will numb the shame of being seen in public with her.

SIMON   Oh come on, it's fine, she's nice.

WILL   Is the definition of 'nice' someone who is a bit boring and embarrassing and much taller than you?

JAY AND NEIL ENTER THE ROOM.

JAY   Aye aye Si, you never told me you'd joined JLS?

SIMON   Brilliant.

JAY   And you've come as a nerd.

WILL   Yes, very droll.

NEIL   Is the Bigfoot here? You know, your girlfriend.

WILL   Oh God, I can't go through with it. I don't fancy Kerry and I can't keep stringing her along, it's not right, is it? Or is it?

NEIL TAKES HIS JACKET OFF TO REVEAL HIS PLASTER CAST HAS BEEN DRAWN ON. IT IS LITERALLY COVERED IN COCKS.

SIMON   That's nice.

NEIL   Fucking Donovan did it, he pinned me down in detention.

NEIL'S DAD IS PASSING.

KEVIN SUTHERLAND   Oh Neil, what is that monstrosity?

NEIL   It was an accident, you remember, I fell off the garage.

KEVIN SUTHERLAND   Not the cast, what's on it? Cover it up. Your granny's going to be here in a minute. Oh Neil.

HE LEAVES, DISAPPOINTED.

JAY   I thought he would have liked it.

NEIL   Why?

JAY   It's covered in cocks.

NEIL   Oh behave.

SIMON   How was detention?

NEIL   It was all right, apart from that. I even managed to give out a couple more invites.

JAY   Did you?

THE DOORBELL GOES.

NEIL   Yeah, whilst you were getting changed. I told them to be here early, so that should be them now.

JAY   Please be fit. Please be fit.

NEIL OPENS THE DOOR WITH THE OTHERS EXPECTANTLY BEHIND HIM. IT'S JOHN AND DAVID.

JOHN   Hello.

JAY   Brilliant, it's a bring-a-freak party.

NEIL   Say what you like, but with these two, us four and your girl-friends that's got me up to the magic ten.

WILL   Eight.

NEIL Oh shit.

JOHN Neil, is it OK if I brush my teeth?

NEIL No it is not.

——————— SCENE 14 ———————

INT. NEIL'S HOUSE, KITCHEN

WILL V/O ... *well, John and David made it official. Neil's was the worst eighteenth birthday party ever. Unless you were Simon.*

SIMON AND TARA ARE IN THE KITCHEN SNOGGING. NEIL COMES IN JUST AS SOME OF THE ADULTS WALK AWAY DUE TO THE KISSING.

NEIL Oh get a room.

SIMON Sorry mate. Actually, can we use your room?

NEIL Depends. What for?

SIMON What do you think?

NEIL You've lost me.

SIMON I want to spend some time alone, and not in your kitchen, with Tara.

NEIL Oh right, time together, yeah. What for?

SIMON You know.

NEIL Oh yeah, right. That. Go on then.

SIMON Cheers mate.

AS SIMON AND TARA HEAD OUT OF THE KITCHEN, AND HIS GRAN COMES IN, NEIL SHOUTS AFTER THEM DOWN THE HALLWAY:

NEIL Try not to spunk on the sheets. (THEN TO HIS GRAN) Do you want some more crisps Gran?

NEIL'S GRAN LOOKS PRETTY HORRIFIED.

———— SCENE 15 ————

INT. NEIL'S HOUSE, LIVING ROOM

WILL V/O   *And I was left with Kerry, who might give me a blow job, but might also swallow the rest of me.*

KERRY FINDS WILL SITTING ON THE SOFA.

KERRY   Oh there you are.

KERRY KISSES WILL'S CHEEK AND THEN SITS DOWN ON HIS LAP.

WILL SLIDES HER OFF.

WILL   Woooah.

KERRY   Oh sorry, am I a lump?

WILL   No, it's not that.

KERRY   Why don't you come and sit on my lap instead?

WILL   There's plenty of room to both sit down.

KERRY   OK Mr Grump Grumps.

WILL   Kerry we need to talk.

KERRY   We are talking.

WILL   No, not here. In private.

KERRY   Oh good, more kissing. You're a really good kisser. Am I a bad kisser? I bet I'm a rubbish kisser, aren't I? Do you think—

WILL LOOKS UP TO SEE JAY AND NEIL OVER KERRY'S SHOULDERS. JAY IS KNEELING NEXT TO A STANDING NEIL, DOING A CRUDE IMPRESSION OF WILL AND KERRY, AND THEY ARE PRETENDING TO KISS.

WILL   OK Kerry, I'm really sorry to do this.

KERRY   What?

WILL   We're not going out.

KERRY   Yes we are.

WILL   No we aren't. I don't want to be your boyfriend and if anyone asks I never was. Alright?

KERRY   Oh.

WILL   That didn't come out perfectly but you know what I mean.

KERRY   I'll give you a blow job.

WILL   I'm sure you will, but I just can't accept.

KERRY   Is it because I'm a bit taller than you?

WILL   No.

KERRY STARTS BAWLING, LOUDLY. EVERYONE IN THE ROOM TURNS AROUND.

WILL   Calm down, you can't be that upset. We were never going out. We only met the other day.

ALL EYES ARE ON AN AWKWARD-LOOKING WILL.

WILL   She's just had some bad news.

—————— SCENE 16 ——————

INT. NEIL'S BEDROOM

SIMON IS KISSING TARA'S NECK, AND IS CLEARLY QUITE INTO IT BUT SHE DOESN'T SEEM THAT BOTHERED.

TARA   I really hope Will and Kerry are getting on OK.

SIMON   Mm.

TARA   She's such a sweetheart, and she's had such a rough time. I'd love it if she met someone really nice. What do you think?

SIMON   Yeah, definitely.

TARA   Does Will really like her?

SIMON   Whatever you want.

TARA   I said, does Will really like her?

SIMON   Can we not talk about Will right now? It's putting me off.

WE PULL WIDE TO REVEAL THAT TARA HAS BEEN GIVING SIMON A HAND-JOB THE WHOLE TIME THEY HAVE BEEN TALKING. THEN THEY HEAR A NOISE, A BIT LIKE VERY LOUD EMOTIONAL WEEPING, FROM DOWNSTAIRS. SHE STOPS.

TARA   Oh God, that sounded like Kerry. I'd better go and check she's OK.

SIMON   I'm sure she's fine.

TARA   Simon, you know what she's been through.

TARA GETS UP AND LEAVES.

SIMON   Oh for fuck's sake. Well don't fucking bother starting me off if you aren't going to finish it.

TARA POPS HER HEAD BACK AROUND THE DOOR.

TARA   Sorry, did you say something?

SIMON   No.

———— SCENE 17 ————

INT. NEIL'S HOUSE, LIVING ROOM

KERRY IS SITTING ON THE SOFA, SOBBING HYSTERICALLY. SHE IS BEING COMFORTED BY NEIL'S GRAN AND BY A NEIGHBOUR (MAGGIE).

KERRY   Hhhhheee dumped meeeee.

MAGGIE   Oh dear.

KERRY   He led me on.

WILL   That's not strictly true, is it Kerry?

KERRY   He, he tried to have sex with me and then dumps me.

WILL   Is that correct Kerry?

NEIL'S GRAN   You should be ashamed of yourself.

WILL   For what? I've actually been really nice.

NEIL'S GRAN   You took advantage of her.

WILL   No I didn't.

NEIL'S GRAN   I think that's pretty low.

WILL   Do you really?

TARA COMES DOWN.

TARA   What have you done? Are you OK Kezza?

KERRY   He dumped me.

WILL   No I couldn't have, because we were never going out.

KERRY   He used me and then he dumped me. Because I'm so big.

TARA   Will, I don't know how you can do this, especially after what Kerry's been through.

WILL   It hasn't been an easy ride for me either. Trying to stay out of her clutches.

TARA   Her dad died last month.

THIS ELICITS GASPS OF DISAPPROVAL FROM THE ADULTS.

BEAT.

WILL   Well that's awful, obviously, but not . . .

TARA   What?

WILL   Well it's not . . . not relevant, is it?

NEIL'S GRAN   You disgust me.

TARA   Will, I think you should leave.

WILL   But I've done nothing wrong. The dad timing is unfortunate, but it's not my fault. If you're interested in the truth, Kerry hands out blow jobs like they're going out of fashion, and by all accounts I'm one of the only people to have turned her down.

KERRY   I HATE YOU.

KEVIN SUTHERLAND   Will, I want you to leave.

WILL What, for turning down oral sex from the Empire State Building? For trying to let her down gently rather than placing my glans into her stupid boring mouth?

KEVIN SUTHERLAND Will, I want you to leave my house and never come back.

WILL Yeah, yeah, yeah.

WILL LEAVES.

──────── SCENE 18 ────────

INT. NEIL'S HOUSE, HALL

WILL IS LEAVING AS SIMON COMES DOWN THE STAIRS DOING UP HIS TROUSERS.

SIMON What's going on?

WILL I've been told to leave for dumping a girl I wasn't going out with.

SIMON Oh fuck.

WILL And by the way, did you not think it important to mention at any time that Kerry's dad had died?

SIMON Oh shit, yeah, I forgot.

WILL Didn't forget about the blow jobs though, did you? Oh no, you were all about the blow jobs, couldn't stop going on about the blow jobs, but the dead dad, that just slipped your mind? Well thanks very much Simon. See you at school mate.

WILL V/O *To be fair to Simon, I'd have probably forgotten my own mother's name if Tara had been wanking me off.*

──────── SCENE 19 ────────

INT. SCHOOL COMMON ROOM

WILL Life is so unfair.

SIMON   Yes, and?

WILL   Neil's dad phoned my mum and I've been grounded for three weeks. I did nothing wrong.

SIMON   Not nothing.

WILL   Yes, nothing. If anything I did the right thing by not letting her give me a blow job.

SIMON   You didn't handle it brilliantly though, did you?

WILL   Oh OK, so right and wrong don't matter, it's all about presentation is it?

JAY   It's like me with Gilbert, I did nothing and I get a month's detentions.

WILL   You did say 'Waterside'.

JAY   Yes, nothing. It's not offensive, it's not a swear word.

SIMON   Yeah, but . . .

JAY   Yeah but what? What? Do I have to draw you a fucking picture? I said 'Waterside' and got a month's detention. How is that fair?

WILL   Anyway, sorry for ruining your birthday Neil.

NEIL   Nah, not at all, it was awesome.

WILL   Was it?

NEIL   Yeah after you left and my dad went to bed, Kerry gave me a blowie upstairs.

WILL   What?

SIMON   Did she? Because Tara said—

JAY   Beepedy beep.

SIMON   Fuck off . . . Tara said she was still really upset the next day.

NEIL   Oh yeah, that was the only downside, she was still crying a little bit on the first one.

WILL   Oh God.

WILL V/O   *It may not have been extravagant, but Neil will always remember his eighteenth . . . mainly because Jay drove his mum's gift into a wall . . . Simon ejaculated on his duvet . . . and I ruined the evening by comparing the grieving girl I was supposedly seeing to an immense, cock-sucking American landmark.*

Episode 4

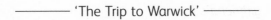

——————— 'The Trip to Warwick' ———————

'The Trip to Warwick' is another one of my favourite episodes. I like the way that we took them all away, we had four stories for them, and they all came together in a disaster at the end. I'd also say it's one of the rudest episodes we've ever written, but clearly by this point we'd offended anyone we were going to offend as the show didn't get any complaints. Funnily enough the show has never attracted many complaints, something that delights me as we never meant to offend and also it means that people really 'get' it, so thanks for that. Only punching the fish ever caused any real fuss.

So this episode is rude thematically, but I like it because it's one of the ones where it feels like we got a lot of the one-liners really right. I remember Blake Harrison (lanky gormless Neil in the show, and in real life) texting me when they first got the scripts for the new series with the words 'i'm going to fuck your fucking fanny off you twat?' and nothing else. It's texts like this that give you the sense that lines might work. We also enjoyed Jay's one-liners in this ep, including 'shit down my arm' and 'If she fucks like she complains you're in for a treat.' But my favourite is when Neil worries that university might be boring, 'just like a load of Wills hanging around'. Despite what we say in the intro about not remembering who wrote what, I am very confident that is a Damon line.

——— SCENE 1 ———

INT. SIMON'S BEDROOM

WILL V/O   *I'd not seen a lot of Simon in the past few weeks because he had a new hobby: spending as much time as was humanly possible munching his girlfriend's face off.*

SIMON AND TARA ARE SNOGGING ON HIS BED WHEN THE BEDROOM DOOR SWINGS OPEN AND SIMON'S MUM AND DAD (PAMELA AND ALAN COOPER) COME IN.

ALAN COOPER   Aye aye, what's going on in here?

SIMON   What the bloody fuck do you think you're doing?

PAMELA COOPER   Language.

ALAN COOPER   Coming to check up on you.

SIMON   Check up on me? What are you, like the thought Nazis police?

PAMELA COOPER   Hello Tara.

TARA   Hello Mrs Cooper.

SIMON   Jesus Christ, we're just studying.

ALAN COOPER   Yeah, but you don't do biology.

SIMON   Is that meant to be funny?

PAMELA COOPER   We'd like you to stick to what we agreed. We don't mind you having girls up here, but you've got to leave the door open.

ALAN COOPER   Yeah, so we don't miss any of the good stuff.

SIMON   Oh Jesus.

ALAN COOPER   Only kidding Tara. But seriously, you do have to keep the door open.

SIMON   Yes, fine.

PAMELA COOPER   We'll leave you then.

ALAN COOPER   Yep, leave you 'to it'.

SIMON   Oh go away you sad man.

MR AND MRS COOPER LEAVE. SIMON AGGRESSIVELY LUNGES FOR TARA AGAIN.

TARA   Simon. What if they come back?

SIMON   They won't.

HE LUNGES AGAIN.

TARA   Simon, shush, they'll hear.

SIMON   Oh God, I'm just so horny.

TARA   I know you are. Look, it feels like we've been going out for ages now, so I was thinking that maybe we should, you know, have sex.

BEAT.

SIMON   I'm sorry?

TARA   I'm ready. I mean we love each other, right?

SIMON   Yeeeeeaaaaahhhhhh.

TARA   So I was trying to work out where. Where we'd be alone, away from our parents and everyone.

SIMON   Down the bottom of the garden.

TARA   What?

SIMON   There are some bushes at the bottom of my garden, we could do it there. I'm pretty sure you can't be seen from the house.

TARA   Simon, I'm not having sex in your garden.

SIMON   What about in my car?

TARA   No.

SIMON   I know it's not perfect but I think we both need to compromise, yeah? Yeah?

TARA   Look, my sister is at Warwick Uni. It's not too far and she's always saying I should go and visit. I've told her I'm coming up with you for the weekend.

SIMON   Right, great. Why?

TARA   So we can have lovely sex together.

SIMON   This weekend?

TARA   Yep.

SIMON   Lovely. That will be lovely. The sex.

TARA   You do want to make love to me, don't you?

SIMON   Yes.

TARA   Well tell me then.

Talk to me to get me in the mood. I like imagining things.

SIMON   Um . . . Is this like dirty talk?

TARA   Yes, Simon, just try it. It's naughty.

SIMON   OK. Um, well, I'd like to kiss your boobs.

TARA   (GIGGLING) Oooh, good, see? I like that.

SIMON   Good, OK. Well, God, my penis is really hard for you.

TARA   Oooh, and what are you going to do to me?

SIMON   Um, I'm going to fuck your fucking fanny off you twat.

AS HE SHOUTS THIS, HIS BROTHER (ANDREW COOPER) WALKS PAST THE OPEN DOOR.

TARA   Um, OK.

ANDREW COOPER   Oh God.

SIMON   Fuck ooofff.

HE SLAMS THE DOOR. THERE'S A VOICE FROM DOWNSTAIRS.

ALAN COOPER   (OFF SCREEN) Open that door.

———— SCENE 2 ————

INT. SCHOOL COMMON ROOM

WILL V/O *Simon had hit the jackpot. A girl who still wanted to have sex with him, even after getting to know him, which meant I got to spend some quality time with Jay and Neil. Low-quality time . . .*

NEIL IS SITTING DOWN, PLAYING ON HIS NINTENDO DS LITE. WILL IS READING *A PORTRAIT OF THE ARTIST AS A YOUNG MAN*, A LITTLE BIT APART, WHEN JAY ENTERS.

JAY Oi Neil, d'you hear about Chris Wharton from the paper shop?

NEIL No, what?

JAY He was mucking about up the rec and got his head wedged in the bottle bank. Got stuck there all night. By the time someone found him in the morning he'd been arse-raped eighteen times.

NEIL Oh mate, that's grim.

WILL I have a few questions.

JAY Like what?

WILL Well, one – why was he sticking his head in the bottle bank?

JAY Looking for bottles you mug.

WILL OK. Number two – what you're saying is that the first eighteen people to have discovered him in this state just happened to be opportunistic homosexual rapists?

JAY Looks like it. Here, where was your dad last night Neil?

NEIL Badminton, why?

JAY Course he was.

WILL And finally why, after what was at best a humiliating evening, would he as the victim tell anyone, let alone you, about it?

JAY I used to sit next to him in woodwork.

WILL Of course, well thanks for clearing that up. Much as I'm enjoying our morning chats, I can't help wishing Simon was around more.

NEIL Who?

WILL Simon.

JAY You can forget about him mate, he's probably off with his 'girlfriend'.

NEIL Yeah, as per usual, 'girlfriend'.

JAY Yeah, he's all like 'Oh everyone look at me, I've got a girlfriend, and I love going round her house and listening to her shit music and laughing at her shit jokes, and pretending that she's fit when she's not even that fit.'

SIMON WALKS IN.

SIMON Who's not that fit?

JAY Your mum.

SIMON Nice.

NEIL She isn't though.

SIMON You can say what you like, because guess who's getting laid this weekend?

NEIL Dunno. Is it someone famous?

SIMON It's me Neil.

NEIL Well don't say before I've guessed.

WILL Not really? Really? Shit, that's amazing. With Tara?

SIMON We're going to her sister's house in Warwick, it's going to be brilliant.

WILL This is a big deal. A very big deal.

SIMON I know.

JAY You got your plan of action all sorted then? You know, for the shagging.

SIMON   The what? No. The what?

NEIL   Ooh, shit.

JAY   Ooh, fucking hell, good luck then.

SIMON   I don't need a plan.

NEIL   Uh-oh.

JAY   Oh mate, you are in serious trouble. Course you need a plan. Bloke I knew didn't have a plan on his first time, went in too quick, broke his knob in half.

WILL   Bollocks, you don't need a plan. I didn't have a plan with Charlotte.

JAY   Oh right and how did that go?

WILL   I pogoed on her stomach for five seconds, she asked me to leave and I'm still a virgin, but that's not the point.

SIMON   No offence, but I really don't want any sexual advice from you.

WILL   I have taken some offence.

SIMON   It'll be fine, I'll be OK. I just need to get some condoms, that's all.

JAY   Oh for fuck's sake, don't wear a johnny, it's a guaranteed hard-on killer. That's why they call it safe sex, 'cos you can't get it up.

WILL   Well, that isn't the reason.

JAY   Look, if you have to bag it up then at least get her to put it on for you, that way you might get a few more seconds of wood.

SIMON   Really? Does that work?

NEIL   Get her to pop it on with her mouth.

JAY   Mouth's a good idea. Or arsehole.

WILL   What?

JAY   Sometimes I like to get them to put it on with their bum. Back into it.

SIMON   I don't know if I can ask her that. It's her first time too.

JAY   Yeah, it's probably a bit specialist, but you're going to have to do something to make sure you stay hard.

SIMON   Oh God, this is a nightmare. Should I write this down?

JAY   These are the basics mate. If you want, me and Neil can come along and talk you through it beforehand? Make sure you don't embarrass yourself.

SIMON   Really?

NEIL   What about her minge Jay? You never even mentioned that.

JAY   We've not even started on the minge. Now the minge has two main parts, the flaps and the clitty.

NEIL   What about the hole?

JAY   Alright, three. But really it's mainly all about the clitty.

SIMON   Oh God.

 SCENE 3

EXT. SCHOOL

WILL V/O   *Jay's encyclopaedic sex tips continued all day. From analingus to a zookeeper he once fucked. And as we walked home, he had even more good news for Simon.*

JAY   Right, I've made a few calls, moved some stuff around, and good news, me and Neil can come with you to help out.

SIMON   That's gonna look weird, isn't it?

JAY   It'll look weirder when you try and fuck her in the ear because you don't know what you're doing.

SIMON   And what am I going to say to Tara when she asks why you're there?

JAY   Oh I dunno, tell her we're your mates and have known you longer than her and to shut her fucking whining.

NEIL And you could mention I've got a lot of fingering experience.

SIMON Fine, God, alright.

JAY Nice one. And then while you're finally putting your knob to good use, Neil and me will be tapping up the campus clunge.

NEIL Won't university be a bit boring though, just like a load of Wills hanging around?

WILL GIVES NEIL A LOOK OF 'I AM HERE, YOU KNOW'.

JAY No, everyone knows it's where posh birds go to set their gash free.

NEIL Nice.

JAY Oh and Si, as we're doing you a favour, I'm not paying petrol money.

SIMON Fine whatever. I'll pick you up at one.

JAY AND NEIL LEAVE.

WILL Cool, see you tomorrow then.

SIMON Well you're definitely not going.

WILL But Warwick is one of my choices, so . . .

SIMON So what? Go to the open day, don't come with me when I'm trying to get laid.

WILL Alright, look the truth is I don't want to be left out. I get lonely.

SIMON Oh for fuck's sake, all right, I'll see you tomorrow then.

 SCENE 4

INT. SIMON'S CAR

WILL V/O *So Simon whisked Tara away for their romantic weekend, and it's fair to say, it wasn't exactly as she'd imagined it . . .*

THE CINQUECENTO IS FLYING UP THE M40. SIMON DRIVES, TARA IS IN THE BACK, SQUEEZED BETWEEN WILL AND JAY.

JAY I bet you've never had a boyfriend with a car this embarrassing eh Tara?

TARA Actually I like Simon's car. It's so tragic at least I know he's not out picking up girls in it.

JAY Oh Christ, she's done you.

SIMON I've picked up girls before in this.

JAY No you haven't.

SIMON Yes I have.

TARA And did you make these girls sit in the back too because your mate called shotgun?

NEIL It's the rules.

SIMON It is the rules Tara.

TARA Well can you slow down a bit at least Simon?

SIMON OK Tars. Sorry.

JAY We're only doing fucking sixty-five.

TARA I get carsick. Especially in the back.

SIMON There's no rush, let's enjoy the drive.

WILL Yes, this really is one of the more beautiful stretches of anonymous British motorway.

SIMON It's not Tara's fault she gets carsick.

TARA I can speak for myself Simon.

JAY Ooooooooh.

SIMON Jay, shut up.

TARA Ow, something hard's digging into my leg.

JAY Don't look at me. Although it could reach from here.

NEIL LAUGHS. TARA IS STRUGGLING UNCOMFORTABLY.

TARA Shit, what is this?

SHE PULLS OUT AN ENORMOUS FOUR LITRE BOTTLE OF ORANGEADE.

NEIL   Oh that's mine.

WILL   Why are you taking a four litre bottle of orangeade to Warwick?

NEIL   Polite, being a good guest, bring a bottle and that.

SIMON   Bring a bottle means alcohol Neil.

NEIL   Nah, everyone likes orangeade. You can make cocktails like vodka and orangeade or whisky and orangeade or wine and orangeade.

WILL   Those aren't cocktails, that's just the names of some drinks with orangeade added to the end.

NEIL   Yeah, well at least I'm being polite.

TARA   Well thank you Neil, I'm sure my sister will appreciate it.

NEIL   I know what she wouldn't appreciate.

NEIL GIGGLES. TARA LOOKS CONFUSED.

JAY   Oh no, Neil, you haven't?

TARA   What?

WILL   Unbelievable.

TARA   Urghhh, my God that stinks.

SIMON   Neil, have you farted again?

NEIL   Not sure. Could be a fart, could be worse.

SIMON   For fuck's sake, open your window.

WILL   You should go and see a bowel specialist.

JAY   Or he could ask his dad. He likes inspecting men's anuses.

TARA   I feel really ill, Simon can you pull over?

NEIL   Calm down, it was only a sausage and egg McMuffin.

TARA   Ew.

THERE'S ANOTHER POP FROM NEIL.

NEIL   Oop, that's the hash brown.

WILL   Jesus Christ.

TARA   Someone please open a window?

──────── SCENE 5 ────────

EXT. SOPHIE'S HOUSE

WILL V/O   . . . *fortunately, Neil's McFarts calmed down just outside Warwick. Which is more than can be said for Tara.*

THE GANG ARE WALKING TOWARDS THE FRONT DOOR. TARA AND SIMON WALK A LITTLE BIT IN FRONT OF THE OTHERS.

TARA   Either they're getting the train back or I am.

SIMON   Look, it'll be fine, let's just remember why we're here, yeah?

TARA'S SISTER SOPHIE HAS COME OUT TO MEET THEM.

SOPHIE   I didn't know there'd be so many of you.

TARA   They've just come to hang out OK?

NEIL   Apart from him, he's lonely.

WILL   No, ahem, you see some of us are going to university next year and so I thought I'd come along, check the place out, maybe even make a few friends in case the worst comes to the worst and I end up at Warwick.

SOPHIE   Meaning?

WILL   Well, just that it's not my first choice.

SIMON   It's your last choice, isn't it?

WILL   But it is a choice, I think that's the key point here.

NEIL   I've bought some orangeade for the party.

SOPHIE   There isn't a party.

JAY   We could make it a party?

SOPHIE   No, you couldn't. It's bad enough that Joe's idiotic friends descend on our front room practically every night.

TARA   Oh no, is he still a nightmare?

SOPHIE   God, he's a total tool, all he does is drink. I don't know why we agreed to share with him.

WILL   Interesting, a bit of a social hub is he? The big man on the campus, the go-to guy?

BEAT AS SOPHIE STARES AT WILL BEFORE IGNORING HIM.

SOPHIE   Right well, Christian's away so I suppose those three can sleep in his room. I'll share with Heike, though she's got flu so that'll probably mean me catching it. Tara you and him can have my room.

TARA   Aw thanks sis.

SOPHIE   I'm not mad keen on you having sex at all, but at least this way I'll know you're doing it somewhere comfortable.

SIMON   Oh absolutely. Only in her vagina.

SOPHIE   I meant in my bed.

SIMON   Um, so did I?

JAY   Why'd you say 'vagina' then?

SIMON   Hmm.

SOPHIE   Come on Tara, I'll show you where the condoms and spare sheets are.

SIMON   Nice to meet you Sophie.

SOPHIE AND TARA WALK OFF.

NEIL   Who's Heike?

SIMON   Flatmate. Fit apparently. Dutch.

NEIL   I've never met a Dutch.

JAY   Always the filthiest.

WILL   Right, and you know that, do you?

JAY   Yes, I fucked a Dutch girl.

SIMON   Bollocks. You've never been to Holland.

JAY   Yeah I have, West Ham under-thirteens football tour.

WILL   Oh right, and what did she do to you when you were twelve that was so filthy? Give you a blow job in a windmill? Wank you off with clogs?

JAY   No, it was properly filthy, I shouldn't tell.

SIMON   Try us.

JAY   All right. When I fingered her she shit down my arm.

LONG BEAT, AS THEY TAKE THIS IN.

WILL   Shall we go and have a look at where we're sleeping then?

SIMON   Yeah.

WILL V/O   *And to think, I used to associate Holland with tulips.*

———— SCENE 6 ————

INT. SOPHIE'S HOUSE, LIVING ROOM

WILL V/O   *We'd only travelled as far as Warwick University, but Sophie's flatmate Joe and his friends seem to speak a different language . . .*

SOPHIE OPENS THE DOOR TO TWO BLOKES (DANIEL AND LEWIS) WITH ARMFULS OF BEERS. JOE COMES TO THE DOOR. WILL IS LURKING ON THE STAIRS.

JOE   Ah, good evening Commander, Bombardier.

DANIEL AND LEWIS (TOGETHER)   Good evening Admiral.

DANIEL   Alright Soph, where's this little sister of yours then?

SOPHIE   She's upstairs, with her boyfriend.

DANIEL   Ooh, boyfriend, denied.

LEWIS   Denied!

JOE   Denied. Come in gentlemen, and we'll commence.

SOPHIE   Don't break anything.

LEWIS　All right speccy?

WILL V/O　. . . *ah. An insulting nickname. I think it meant they liked me.*

SCENE 7

INT. SOPHIE'S HOUSE, BEDROOM

WILL V/O　*Meanwhile, it was a good job Jay and Neil had their sleeves rolled down, because there was a Dutch girl on the loose.*

NEIL AND JAY ARE IN THE BEDROOM. THE DOOR OPENS AND HEIKE WALKS IN, WEARING PYJAMAS, LOOKING LIKE A PRETTY GIRL WITH NO MAKE-UP ON WHO HAS A COLD.

HEIKE　Oh, hello.

NEIL　Well hello there.

HEIKE　You are Sophie's sister's friends?

JAY　Er, yeah.

HEIKE　OK, very welcome. I have a fucking cold, so I am looking for the bloody tissues.

SHE SNEEZES.

JAY　Bless you.

HEIKE　Thanks you. Ah, there are the bloody things. See you guys, have a super-fun night.

NEIL　Oh we will have a 'super-fun night'. Most definitely.

HEIKE　Great.

NEIL　Yep.

BEAT.

HEIKE　Bye to you.

SHE LEAVES.

NEIL　Fucking hell, she's fit.

JAY Yeah. She looks like she loves cock.

NEIL Do you have to do it different with a Dutch bird?

JAY There are three things you need to know about European birds Neil: they're filthy, they're hairy and they don't mind if you wipe it on the curtains.

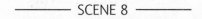

——— SCENE 8 ———

INT. SOPHIE'S HOUSE, LIVING ROOM

WILL V/O *I'd always imagined my evenings at uni would consist of study, heated intellectual debate and avoiding elderly homosexual lecturers. The reality of Warwick was a little different . . .*

WILL WATCHES JOE AND HIS MATES PLAYING DRINKING GAMES.

JOE Next game is fuzzy duck. Duckmaster General to my left, fuzzy duck.

LEWIS Fuzzy duck.

DANIEL Does he?

LEWIS Fuzzy duck?

JOE/DANIEL Wrong! Drink.

THEY ALL ROAR WITH LAUGHTER AS LEWIS HAS TO DRINK. WILL, SLIGHTLY SCARED, WALKS FORWARD.

WILL Hey fellas, you don't mind if I join you do you?

DANIEL Ooh, question!

LEWIS Two fingers.

WILL What? What does two fingers mean? Two fingers of what, this?

DANIEL Aaargh, pointing. A fine Admiral?

JOE The fine is ooooohhh.

JOE STARTS WOBBLING HIS FINGERS IN FRONT OF HIMSELF.

WILL Are you OK?

JOE   OOOOooooooh – down it.

WILL   All right, but after that can we talk normally for a bit? About Warwick . . .

JOE/DANIEL/LEWIS   Questions! Down it, down it.

WILL   Fine. I was going to drink it anyway for fuck's sake.

HE DOWNS HIS CAN INCREDIBLY SLOWLY.

JOE/DANIEL/LEWIS   Get it down, you Zulu warrior, get it down you Zulu chief.

WILL   What? Zulu? Why Zulu?

NEIL AND JAY WALK INTO THE ROOM.

JAY   All right, what's going on?

LEWIS   Question! Down it!

JAY IS HANDED A BEER.

WILL   I honestly have no idea.

NEIL   Can I play?

JOE/DANIEL/LEWIS   QUESTION!!!

HE HANDS NEIL A CAN. THE BOYS DOWN THEIR BEERS.

WILL V/O   . . . it seemed like a vaguely moronic drinking game. So as these guys were students, I assumed it was irony.

 SCENE 9

INT. SOPHIE'S HOUSE, KITCHEN

WILL V/O   In the kitchen, nothing ironic was happening . . .

SIMON AND TARA ARE KISSING. HE'S A BIT CARRIED AWAY AND STARTS REALLY DRY HUMPING HER HARD AGAINST THE WORK SURFACE. SOPHIE WALKS IN AND SIMON LEAPS AWAY FROM TARA.

SOPHIE   Not in the kitchen please, I eat in here.

SIMON   Hi, Sophie, hi.

SOPHIE   Tara, did you find those towels to put down?

TARA   Yep.

SOPHIE   And the flannel?

TARA   Yeah.

SOPHIE   Remember, it's when you're ready, not when he's ready OK? It doesn't have to be tonight, and it certainly doesn't have to be in the kitchen.

SIMON   Um, so what is it you're studying Sophie?

SOPHIE   Look, you probably won't enjoy it, but just make sure you don't regret it, OK?

SIMON   English, was it?

TARA   Jesus, give it a rest, please.

SOPHIE   Look, I'm only saying these things because I love you, yeah?

TARA   Yeah I know, but Simon loves me too.

SOPHIE   Does he?

SIMON   I should go and check on the others.

SOPHIE   No, don't worry, I'm going.

SIMON   Bye Sophie, great to chat.

TARA   I think she really likes you.

SIMON   She seems like she hates me.

TARA   No, she's probably just jealous.

SIMON   Really?

TARA   Yeah, 'cos I've got you. Let's not wait any longer, let's go to bed.

SIMON   Great. I just need to run that by Jay and Neil quickly first.

TARA   What are you going to ask them for advice?

SIMON   Oh shit, did Jay tell you?

TARA   I was joking.

SIMON   Um, me too. I do need to talk to them about dinner though. Jay can get really grumpy if he doesn't eat.

TARA   I don't give a fuck.

SIMON   Look, why don't you go upstairs and get yourself ready, and I'll just tell them there's some stuff in the fridge, yeah?

WILL, NEIL AND JAY WALK INTO THE KITCHEN. NEIL AND JAY ARE LAUGHING.

NEIL   Those guys are mental.

WILL   They're mentally ill. Do they even speak English?

JAY   You're just fucked off because we fit in with uni blokes 'cos we're a laugh and you don't 'cos you're a twat.

NEIL   I love it. I think I'll go to uni now.

WILL   I wouldn't bank on it Neil.

SIMON   Good times. Anyway Jay, I just wanted to talk to you quickly about 'dinner'.

JAY   What the fish supper you're having?

TARA   (SLIGHTLY PISSED OFF) Simon, are you coming?

SIMON   Um, yeah, one minute, I just need to sort this out.

TARA   God, fine.

SHE LEAVES.

JAY   If she fucks like she complains you are in for a treat.

WILL   Oh my God, is this it then Si? Are you going to do it right now?

SIMON   Listen, I need your advice. You know you said I'd have a problem getting it up. I've got the exact opposite problem, it won't go down. If she touches it I'm sure it'll go off, straight away. What am I gonna do?

WILL   Just be yourself, be honest with her.

JAY   Worst. Advice. Ever.

SIMON   Jay help me.

JAY   Look, it's simples. Go and have a quick tactical wank now, then when she puts some clunge round it you'll be able to go for hours.

SIMON   Right, good idea.

WILL   Is it?

JAY   Yes. Now get up there, knock one out, start on her and don't embarrass yourself.

NEIL   Yeah, try and forget about how this is the biggest moment of your life.

SIMON   Thanks.

SIMON LOOKS AT THEM AND HEADS UPSTAIRS.

———— SCENE 10 ————

INT. SOPHIE'S HOUSE, BATHROOM/LANDING

WILL V/O   . . . so Simon chose Jay's advice over mine and as a result was masturbating into a sink, whilst inhaling his girlfriend's sister's knickers.

SIMON'S IN THE BATHROOM DOING JUST THAT. THERE'S A KNOCK AT THE DOOR.

TARA   Simey, come on. Come to bed.

SIMON   Coming, um, I'm just . . . doing a . . . a poo.

HE WINCES.

TARA   OK. Wash your hands then.

SIMON   Yep.

———— SCENE 11 ————

INT. SOPHIE'S HOUSE, LIVING ROOM

WILL V/O   *Downstairs, after only a couple of hours in their company, I was already hoping the Commander, the Bombardier and the Admiral would get sent to Afghanistan.*

NEIL AND JAY REALLY DO LOOK DRUNK NOW. WILL IS WATCHING, UNIMPRESSED.

JOE   Oi Neil, dare you to down this?

HE HOLDS UP THE HALF-FULL ORANGEADE BOTTLE, WHICH IS NOW FILLED WITH A MIXTURE OF ORANGEADE, BEER AND FAG BUTTS.

NEIL   Oh what no way.

DANIEL   Go on.

NEIL   Oh all right then.

WILL   You don't have to bow to peer pressure Neil.

LEWIS   Your mate is fucking boring, isn't he?

JAY   Yep.

WILL   No Neil don't, it's disgusting. Look, it's got fag butts in it.

NEIL DOWNS THE DISGUSTING MIX, WILL LOOKS HORRIFIED AND ALL THE OTHERS CHEER.

WILL   Yes, cheer that. Because that was so impressive. What would you like for an encore, Jay to punch himself in the face?

DANIEL   Go on Jay.

JAY PUNCHES HIMSELF IN THE FACE.

JOE   You're boring mate.

WILL   No, no I'm not.

NEIL   You are a bit boring.

WILL   What because I don't do dares? It takes no time or effort or skill to down half a bottle of orangeade.

JOE   Takes balls though.

LEWIS   Yep.

WILL   Well I've got balls. More than you.

NEIL   More than two?

LEWIS   Go on then, do a dare.

JAY   He won't, he's boring.

WILL   So what, if I eat . . .

WILL LOOKS AROUND FOR SOMETHING AND SEES THE BONSAI TREE ON THE COFFEE TABLE.

WILL   . . . this bonsai tree, I automatically become fun and interesting, do I?

JOE   Yes.

WILL   Fine, well I'll eat it then and we'll see.

DANIEL   Go on then.

WILL   I will.

WILL LOOKS AT THE BONSAI. THEN HE LOOKS AT THE UNI LADS' DISDAINFUL FACES. HE BRACES HIMSELF THEN STUFFS THE WHOLE TOP OF THE BONSAI, LEAVES FIRST, INTO HIS MOUTH AND BITES DOWN.

——————— SCENE 12 ———————

INT. SOPHIE'S HOUSE, BEDROOM

WILL V/O   *Unfortunately, it turns out 'bonsai' doesn't mean 'delicious little tree' in Japanese. Upstairs, Simon was struggling to get some wood of his own . . .*

SIMON AND TARA ARE IN BED TOGETHER, SNOGGING UNDER THE DUVET.

SIMON   It is cold isn't it? Like really cold.

TARA   Well cuddle up tighter then.

THEY SNOG.

SIMON   Does your sister ever turn the heating on in here?

TARA   Your sex talk is getting worse Simon.

SIMON   Right. Is there a draught as well?

THEY SIT UP.

TARA   Look, she's a student, it's expensive, OK? Do you want to go and talk to her about gas prices?

SIMON   No.

TARA   Good.

THEY SNOG. SIMON TAKES OFF HIS T-SHIRT, SHE LEAVES HERS ON.

SIMON   Um, are you going to take your top off?

TARA   I'm cold too you know.

SIMON   Of course, sure we established.

TARA GETS A CONDOM FROM THE PILE ON THE SIDE THAT HER SISTER LEFT HER.

TARA   Get the condom on.

SIMON   Yeah, I meant to say about that, can you put it on me? It's sexier.

TARA   OK, if you want.

TARA UNWRAPS THE CONDOM AND IS ABOUT TO PUT IT ON SIMON'S COCK WHEN SHE HESITATES.

TARA   Are you ready? It doesn't look ready.

SIMON   No, it's fine. I just think it would help my, y'know, readiness a bit if you put it on with your mouth.

TARA   With my mouth?

SIMON   Or bum?

WILL V/O   . . . 'Or bum.' Those two little words every girl dreams of hearing on her first time.

——— SCENE 13 ———

INT. SOPHIE'S HOUSE, LIVING ROOM

WILL V/O   *Downstairs, I was halfway through dinner.*

THE LADS ALL LAUGH AS WILL CHEWS THE BONSAI, HIS EYES WATERING. THEN SOPHIE ENTERS AND THE LAUGHTER STOPS.

SOPHIE   Guys, I'm going to bed now, so please try and keep it down, yeah?

BEAT WHERE SOPHIE CLOCKS WHAT WILL IS DOING.

SOPHIE   What are you doing?

JAY   Question! Two fingers.

WILL   I'm sorry, but I was trying to satirise their bravado. If you think about it, it worked.

SOPHIE   You ate a bonsai tree.

WILL   Yes, but . . .

SOPHIE   I think you should go to bed, and you lot should leave.

JOE   Yeah, yeah, fine, we're going to the Union anyway. Nice one specs, thanks for ruining the evening. And Jay, remember what we told you about Heike.

JAY GIVES A THUMBS UP AS THE THREE LADS LEAVE. WILL MAKES A MOVE TO GO UP THE STAIRS TO BED BUT SOPHIE STOPS HIM.

SOPHIE   Where are you going?

WILL   Bed.

SOPHIE   Not without them you're not. Oh and if you fancy a midnight snack, there's a spider plant in the bathroom.

SHE LEAVES.

JAY AND NEIL ARE HAMMERED.

NEIL   This has been the best night of my life.

——— SCENE 14 ———

INT. SOPHIE'S HOUSE, BEDROOM

WILL V/O   *So while Neil got emotional about drinking orangeade and fag butts, Tara was also doing her best to get something disgusting in her mouth. Simon's flaccid penis.*

SIMON TAKES ANOTHER CONDOM AND PUTS IT IN TARA'S MOUTH. SHE LOOKS RIDICULOUS.

TARA   I can't put it on at all when it's like that. Is it nerves?

SIMON   Look, just stop talking about it, um, it's not helping, just get it on.

HE TAKES HER BY THE BACK OF HER HEAD AND SLIGHTLY TOO FIRMLY PUSHES HER TOWARDS HIS LAP. TARA POPS HER HEAD UP AS SIMON SLIGHTLY FIGHTS HER.

TARA   It's not working, it's too soft.

SIMON   One more time please.

TARA   God, OK, just don't push my head down so hard, yeah?

SIMON   Sorry.

SHE HEADS DOWN AGAIN, BUT STARTS TO CHOKE. SHE POPS BACK UP, CLEARLY CHOKING ON THE CONDOM, AND SIMON HAS TO SLAP HER ON THE BACK, HARD.

SIMON   You OK?

SHE SHAKES HER HEAD A BIT, SPLUTTERING, AND SPITS OUT THE CONDOM.

TARA   It's just not doing anything.

SIMON   Oh God, why won't it start. I think if I could see your boobs it would help.

─────── SCENE 15 ───────

INT. SOPHIE'S HOUSE, BEDROOM

WILL V/O   *Unlike Simon, I could see nipples. Unfortunately they were hairy and attached to a dickhead who would not shut up.*

JAY, NEIL AND WILL ARE ALL LYING DOWN. NEIL IS IN THE BED, SNORING, WILL IS NEXT TO HIM, AND JAY IS LYING ON THE FLOOR.

JAY   I know Heike wants a fuck. The way she looked at me after she sneezed.

WILL   Shh, sleepy times now.

JAY   I've got young meat, that's what she likes. The boys said!

WILL   Shhhhh.

JAY   The Commander says she loves a fuck.

WILL   Fine, great. Well, why don't you just go and ask her? Get out of the bedroom, let me sleep, and ask her for the fuck she so famously wants.

JAY   Alright, I will.

JAY GETS UP.

WILL   No Jay, come on, I wasn't serious.

JAY   I'm going to get my Dutch fuck.

WILL   Fine, fine, off you go. I'm sick of babysitting you twats anyway.

JAY LEAVES AND WILL ROLLS OVER AND IS FACE TO FACE WITH NEIL, ALMOST KISSING. HE TURNS BACK AND CLOSES HIS EYES.

WILL OPENS HIS EYES WILDLY AND QUICKLY.

WILL   Oh God.

HE JUMPS OUT OF THE BED LIKE HE'S BEEN ELECTROCUTED, AND QUICKLY TURNS ON THE LAMP ON THE BEDSIDE TABLE. WE SEE HIS FRONT IS A BIT WET.

WILL   Oh no Neil! Neil, wake the fuck up, you've pissed the bed.

NEIL WAKES UP WITH A START AND ROLLS OVER, SPRAYING AN ARC OF PISS EVERYWHERE.

NEIL   Oh no.

WILL   Stop it, stop pissing.

NEIL   I've got a problem with that.

WILL   Go to the loo then. Oh God, Sophie's going to go mental. Why's it so green?

NEIL   My head hurts.

WILL   Yes, I'll suspend my sympathy as I'm covered in your piss.

NEIL   It's good for you.

WILL   Oh right, I'll piss on you then, shall I? Get the fuck to the toilet.

NEIL STARTS TO GO OUT OF THE ROOM, WITH WILL FOLLOWING.

WILL   It smells like pissy sugar puffs.

——— SCENE 16 ———

INT. SOPHIE'S HOUSE, LANDING

NEIL IS WALKING TO THE TOILET, A WET WILL IS FOLLOWING HIM. THERE ARE A NUMBER OF DOORS.

NEIL   Oh I'm a mess, where's the bathroom?

WILL   More worryingly where's Jay?

THEN THERE'S A SCREAM FROM BEHIND A DOOR.

WILL   Oh there he is.

——————— SCENE 17 ———————

INT. SOPHIE'S HOUSE, HEIKE'S BEDROOM

JAY IS STANDING IN HIS PANTS, SWAYING DRUNK. SOPHIE AND HEIKE ARE SITTING UP.

JAY Come on, Heike, just give me a little fuck, I know you want to.

SOPHIE Get out. You've got ten seconds to get out of the house.

JAY Don't worry, I've got enough young meat for you both.

SOPHIE IS ON HER FEET.

SOPHIE Get fucking out.

——————— SCENE 18 ———————

INT. SOPHIE'S HOUSE, BEDROOM

WILL V/O *So while Jay had to get out, Simon couldn't get in.*

SIMON IS ON TOP OF TARA, GRUNTING A BIT.

TARA Simon, Simon, nothing's happening.

SIMON I know! Do you think I don't fucking know that? I know that better than anyone; I know it's floppy.

TARA Sorry, I was just saying—

SIMON Well don't just say, OK? I know better than anyone that my penis isn't fucking working.

TARA It's OK.

SIMON (LOOKING DOWN AT HIS COCK, SHOUTING) It's not fucking okay. It's not okay. Why won't you start? Every time I don't want one it's there, and yet the one time I actually need it, nothing.

TARA OK, you're scaring me now.

SIMON Just work you stupid fucking thing. Get big. Get big.

TARA Simon.

SIMON   Why aren't you doing it? Do it. Get big. Oh please just work you ugly cunt.

HE STARTS GOING MENTAL AND PUNCHING HIS COCK, REALLY SLAPPING IT AND PUNCHING IT HARD.

TARA   Simon stop it.

——————— SCENE 19 ———————

INT. SOPHIE'S HOUSE, LANDING

SOPHIE IS SHOVING JAY OUT OF THE ROOM, STRAIGHT INTO A PISS-COVERED WILL. NEIL IS SWAYING AND HIS BOXERS ARE WET.

SOPHIE   Oh my God, have you pissed in my house?

WILL   Look, none of this is ideal, I'm aware of that.

SOPHIE   You are disgusting, disgusting. Oh my God, the smell, the mess.

TARA COMES OUT OF THE BEDROOM AND RUNS INTO SOPHIE'S ARMS.

TARA   Sophie, Sophie. He's gone weird like you said he would.

SIMON COMES OUT OF THE BEDROOM, BOLLOCK NAKED.

SIMON   Tara, Tara, look, I've almost got it.

SIMON STANDS, SEMI-ON, IN FRONT OF THE ASSEMBLED CROWD.

SIMON   Oh, hi everyone.

SOPHIE   If you don't get out of my house right now I'm going to call the police. GET OUT!

SOPHIE STARTS TO DIAL ON HER MOBILE.

WILL   All right, it's not perfect, sure, but let's be reasonable, none of us have any clothes on.

SOPHIE CONSIDERS THIS FOR A MOMENT.

JAY   Are we having this threeway or what?

WILL   OK, OK. We're going.

THE FOUR OF THEM SCURRY DOWN THE STAIRS.

———— SCENE 20 ————

INT. SIMON'S CAR

WILL V/O   *No we weren't going to have a threeway, we were going to spend the night in Simon's car naked and then when we'd sobered up drive home at stupid o'clock the next morning.*

THEY ARE DRIVING BACK. JAY IS IN THE FRONT, RETCHING INTO A SMALL PLASTIC BAG.

NEIL   Didn't Tara want a lift back Si?

SIMON   I think she's OK Neil. Oh, I forgot to thank you all for the advice, by the way, it went perfectly. I'm so glad you lot came along.

NEIL   What exactly did you do to her then Si?

SIMON   Nothing, I think that was the problem.

SIMON'S PHONE BEEPS.

SIMON   Get that Will?

WILL READS THE TEXT.

WILL   It's Tara.

JAY   Beedpedy beep beep.

SIMON   Oh cool.

WILL   She says never contact her again.

SIMON   Cool.

WILL V/O   *I'd been inspired by my trip to Warwick.*

WILL V/O   *Inspired to get the best grades I possibly could so I didn't end up at uni with Jay and Neil. One good thing came out of the weekend. Tara dumping Simon meant I got my friend back . . .*

SHOT OF SIMON TALKING DIRTY TO TARA.

SIMON   . . . fuck your fucking fanny off you twat.

SHOT OF SIMON IN BED WITH TARA, PUNCHING HIS COCK.

WILL V/O   . . . *my silver-tongued slightly weird and still a virgin friend.*

Episode 5

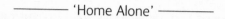

──────── 'Home Alone' ────────

I will always think of this as Damon's episode, partly because it was based on a short-lived burst of daffodil vandalism he and his friends perpetrated on his estate in the 1980s, and partly 'cos he's in it. There he is delivering beer to 'Polly Milf-kenzie', and doing a very fine job at it too. I've auditioned for parts in the show, the main one being the Scottish tramp in Series Two (for which I was considered a shoo-in), but have never been cast.

We tried to write about the boredom of being a teenager in suburbia and the effect that sometimes has on you, and also the unthinking nature of teenagers at times. None of Damon's friends were evil when they lopped the heads off the locals' daffodils with a nine iron (actually, I think they used a kind of long piece of wire); they were just incredibly thoughtless and bored. The same as the guys in the show, who never really think of how their actions might affect those around them, but it was key to us that they came across as unthinking rather than mean, and that was the line we tried to walk with the script. I hope you think we managed it. I realise, unlike the British Comedy Awards, we've not really thanked Simon Bird enough and this episode is just another example of how we take his brilliance for granted. Without knowing how incredibly consistently funny he is it would be impossible to ever begin an episode where the central premise is 'his character is at home'.

This episode also contains our second death in the show, this time of a squirrel. Again, Damon was the source of this story and I won't go into too many details, but it involved a bird, a car, boredom, some ovine piss-taking, and remorse that has yet to leave him.

SCENE 1

INT. JAY'S HOUSE, LIVING ROOM

WILL V/O   *Weekends in suburbia are a great time to wash the car, mow the lawn or insult your children . . .*

JAY'S FAMILY ARE GOING OUT. HE WATCHES THEM GO, THE DOG, BENJI, AT HIS FEET.

TERRY CARTWRIGHT   Right, we'll only be a couple of hours. Try not to break anything.

JAY   Don't you want to take Benji?

TERRY CARTWRIGHT   We're going to weed Grandad's grave you moron, why would we want to take that shitting machine with us?

JAY   He likes the fresh air.

TERRY CARTWRIGHT   Yeah well so do my bollocks, doesn't mean I take them out in graveyards. Dickhead.

SCENE 2

INT. JAY'S BEDROOM

WILL V/O   *. . . so with his parents gone, Jay did what pretty much every male human does when they think they might get five minutes alone in the house.*

JAY IS KNEELING ON HIS BED LOOKING AT PORN ON HIS LAPTOP, HE'S GOT A BIG ROLL OF TOILET PAPER AND SOME HAND CREAM. HE STARTS TO GET READY TO MASTURBATE AND THEN ALMOST THROUGH A SIXTH SENSE LOOKS OVER HIS SHOULDER.

WILL V/O   *Unfortunately for him, he wasn't alone. He had company.*

BENJI IS STARING STRAIGHT AT HIM, UNBLINKING, FROM THE FLOOR. JAY TRIES TO IGNORE HIM AND STARTS AGAIN, BUT HE CAN'T CONCENTRATE AND LOOKS BACK AT BENJI. HE GIVES UP.

JAY   Fucking hell Benji.

WIILL V/O   *Jay was into some pretty weird stuff, but even he drew the line at letting the family pet stare at his penis.*

—————— SCENE 3 ——————

INT. WILL'S HOUSE, LIVING ROOM

THE BOYS ARE ALL SITTING DOWN EXCEPT WILL, WHO IS ON HIS FEET, PLAYING TENNIS ON THE WII, GETTING REALLY INTO IT, WHILE HIS OPPONENT SIMON IS ON THE SOFA, CASUALLY FLICKING THE CONTROLLER.

SIMON   Why don't you just shut him out the room?

JAY   I've tried that, he goes mental, scratches at the door and howls. It's even more distracting.

SIMON   Or you could take him to a dog-training class?

WILL   I think traditionally they teach more sit, stay, beg. Not stop watching me wank, you're putting me off.

JAY   Why didn't you buy a PS3? Everyone knows that Wiis are for children and girls.

NEIL   And gays.

WILL'S MUM (POLLY McKENZIE) POPS HER HEAD ROUND THE DOOR.

POLLY McKENZIE   Will, I'm just heading out— oh sorry, didn't realise you had friends round. Hello boys.

SIMON   Hi Mrs McKenzie.

JAY   Hello.

NEIL   Alright?

POLLY McKENZIE   I see you are enjoying Will's new double u eye eye.

WILL   It's called a Wii.

POLLY McKENZIE   It's pretty neat isn't it? It's the only computer game I've ever been able to play.

NEIL   Would you like a game now Mrs McKenzie?

POLLY McKENZIE   Oh no, I'm not very good. Even Will can beat me.

SIMON   You must be terrible.

JAY   I'll give you some tips. With this one the trick is to bounce around a lot.

POLLY McKENZIE   Is it?

NEIL   Oh yeah, you really have to bounce. Up and down.

POLLY McKENZIE   Oh OK, maybe I'll give it a quick game.

WILL   No, you definitely won't. Did you want something?

POLLY McKENZIE   Oh, not really. I'm just going away for the weekend and I wondered if there was anything special you wanted from Waitrose?

WILL   You're going away? Where?

POLLY McKENZIE   To a friend's house in the Cotswolds.

WILL   You don't have any friends in the Cotswolds.

POLLY McKENZIE   Yes I do.

WILL   Who?

POLLY McKENZIE   Fergus.

WILL   Sorry, who?

POLLY McKENZIE   Fergus. We were friends at college and have just recently caught up again on Facebooks.

WILL   You're going away with a Facebook stalker? Do you not watch the news? Where's he taking you, a ditch off the A40?

POLLY McKENZIE   I know you're upset, but try not to overreact. Maybe we should talk about this later.

WILL   No, let's talk about it now in front of everyone. I've got nothing to hide, have you?

POLLY McKENZIE   Will, try and stay calm or you'll have an asthma attack just like you did that time when we lost Teddy.

WILL OK, fine, we'll talk about it later.

THE OTHERS ALL LAUGH AT HIM.

WILL V/O *For the record, it was an allergy, it wasn't Teddy's fault, but luckily the others didn't take the piss for too long because they were obsessed with the really big news of the day.*

—————— SCENE 4 ——————

EXT. ESTATE

SIMON, NEIL AND JAY ARE WALKING BACK FROM WILL'S HOUSE.

NEIL With Will's mum on Facebook that's tonight's wank lined up.

SIMON I doubt she's put anything too outrageous up there.

NEIL As long as it has the eyes, the eyes is all I really need.

JAY Why is she going away to get wrinkly old cock when she could stay at home and have my massive young pole? It's a mystery to me.

SIMON That is perhaps the greatest mystery of all time.

JAY Oi Neil.

JAY POINTS TO SOME FLOWERS AND KICKS THEM.

SIMON IS STARTING TO GET AGITATED BY THE FLOWER DECAPITATION.

SIMON Why do that?

JAY It's just funny.

NEIL And cool.

SIMON But that's someone's garden, it's vandalism.

NEIL Nah, vandalism is like smashing in people's windows or something. This is just a laugh. Give it a go Si.

SIMON Don't think so.

JAY What, in case you go to prison for killing flowers?

NEIL Don't worry Si, it don't hurt them, they ain't got feelings. Look

NEIL KICKS SOME FLOWERS TOO.

SIMON   I'll pass. Good luck with the landscape gardening. I'll see you later.

JAY   Where you going?

SIMON   Golf. Got the father-son tournament at the weekend.

JAY   Golf? Golf is for fat wankers in their forties. Do you know what it stands for?

SIMON   What?

JAY   Gay Outdoor Lifestyle with Fellas.

NEIL   Ha, brilliant.

SIMON   Well, it's not as entertaining as playing with flowers but I sort of don't care what you say because it turns out I'm quite good at it, we might actually win.

JAY   Ooh win, see ya later then.

JAY HAS STOPPED IN HIS TRACKS AT THE SIGHT OF A NEWLY PLANTED FLOWER BED ON THE ROUNDABOUT, WHICH READS 'WELCOME TO OUR VILLAGE'.

JAY   Oh mate, that is too perfect.

NEIL   Nice.

SIMON   Oh what, come on.

JAY   Listen Tiger Wuss, you should probably get off, you won't like this. Some flowers are about to get fucked up.

——————— SCENE 5 ———————

INT. SCHOOL COMMON ROOM

WILL V/O   *So while the other three were enjoying themselves, I was having a terrible week. Finding out your mum's on Facebook is bad enough, but finding out she's using it to look for cock is beyond the pale.*

WILL Am I overreacting? I've never been introduced to even the notion of a boyfriend; I think I'm entitled to be reasonably defensive about him. Neil your parents have been divorced longer than mine. What was it like when your mum had her first boyfriend?

NEIL It wasn't too bad. He was a bit like my dad. I suppose she's got a type.

JAY Gays.

NEIL Fuck off.

WILL It's still difficult though isn't it?

NEIL Yeah, no, I understand. Do you think this is the first knob she's had since your dad?

WILL Wooh, maybe we'll leave the heart to heart for now then Neil.

NEIL But we've established that this Fergus bloke is boning her?

WILL They're just going to Bath, for the weekend, sightseeing.

SIMON The major sight being her tits, in his mouth.

WILL I think it's the Roman baths actually.

JAY So when shall we come round for the party?

WILL Um, never?

NEIL Oh come on, if your mum's away you've got to have a party.

WILL No. I'm not going to be one of those idiots who advertise a small gathering on Facebook but then four thousand people turn up, the roof gets stolen and the next morning they are on the news saying 'things just got out of hand'.

SIMON Plus your mum would probably find out now she's on Facebook.

NEIL Yeah, tell her she hasn't replied to my friend request yet.

WILL Please stop looking at my mum on the internet Neil.

NEIL Did a lot worse than look at her last night.

WILL And that's an OK thing to say is it?

JAY   All right, let's keep this party simples. Just us, a crate of vodka and a jacuzzi full of clunge.

WILL   No parties and no imaginary orgies, that's the last thing I need. It's bad enough that my mum is practically internet dating.

MR GILBERT IS APPROACHING THE BOYS AND HIS EARS PRICK UP WHEN HE HEARS WILL DISCUSSING HIS MUM.

MR GILBERT   McKenzie. Did you just say your mother is internet dating?

WILL   Um, sort of.

MR GILBERT   Ah interesting, I'm single at the moment, and she's very much my type.

WILL   OK.

MR GILBERT   Maybe you could set me up with her, and then who knows, if things go well you could end up calling me daddy.

WILL   Was this what you wanted to see me about sir?

MR GILBERT   No. My office, now.

WILL V/O   *Right, now even Head of Sixth Form was doing jokes about my mum – at least I hoped he was joking.*

───────── SCENE 6 ─────────

INT. MR GILBERT'S OFFICE

WILL ENTERS.

MR GILBERT   As I'm sure you are aware there has been a spate of vandalism recently, culminating in someone adapting the flower display on the main road to read (LOOKS DOWN TO READ) 'we come tit village'.

WILL SNIGGERS SLIGHTLY.

MR GILBERT   Oh, you think it's funny do you McKenzie?

WILL   Well a bit. It doesn't even make sense. 'We come tit village'. What kind of morons would do that?

MR GILBERT   I think you know exactly who did it.

WILL   What? I don't know sir, honestly I don't.

MR GILBERT   Oh come on McKenzie, you're the sort of busybody who knows everything that goes on. You can't resist getting that beak of yours into other people's business.

WILL   Beak?

MR GILBERT   Yeah, your beaky nose. And if you don't tell me who did it, in my role as your UCAS referee I will fuck your application up.

WILL   I honestly don't know who did it. I don't. I would've grassed. You know I would've grassed. Straight away.

MR GILBERT   Yes, that is true. Well you've got until Monday morning to find out. Or it's goodbye first rate education, hello the University of Lincoln.

——————— SCENE 7 ———————

EXT. NEWSAGENT'S

WILL V/O   *This was serious. I'd been to Lincoln and it's a shithole. But luckily I was about to take part in the shortest investigation ever.*

THE FOUR BOYS ARE OUTSIDE A SHOP.

SIMON   What did Gilbert want then?

WILL   He thinks I know who vandalised the roundabout.

NEIL   Maybe you do.

WILL   Oh God, it was you two wasn't it?

JAY   I can't remember. Was it us Neil?

NEIL   I can't remember Jay.

JAY   Yeah, it was us.

WILL   Fucking brilliant. Well done you morons.

NEIL   Thanks.

SIMON   You gonna grass them up then?

WILL   Yes, of course.

SIMON   Will.

WILL   Fine, no then.

JAY AND NEIL LAUGH.

WILL   Yes hilarious, you vandalise something, I end up with the University of Lincoln.

JAY   I'll tell you what will be hilarious.

WILL   And what's that?

JAY   When Gilbert fucks your mum. He will crush her.

NEIL   Nah, her lovely big tits will cushion him I reckon.

JAY   If he's on top.

SIMON   But what about from behind Neil? Well can you imagine the size of his bollocks. It'll be like two massive wrecking balls smashing against her arse.

WILL   Lovely image.

JAY   She's going to be a mess when he's finished with her.

SIMON   Maybe he'll go twos up with that Fergus bloke?

WILL   What an enjoyable conversation this is about my actual mother.

NEIL   Oh yeah, I bet she's getting a load right now.

WILL   Well she isn't, because she doesn't leave till tomorrow. Simon, do you want to stay over?

JAY   Oh what? You said no one was allowed round.

WILL   It's for security reasons.

JAY   You mean you're too scared to sleep in the house on your own.

WILL   (LAUGHING IT OFF) No.

SIMON   I can't, sorry. Got the golf tournament at eight on Sunday so I promised my dad I wouldn't stay out late on Saturday.

JAY   Tell you what briefcase, I need a night away from the dog, so if you're gonna be scared I'll stay round. And I won't even charge. I just need some baby lotion and access to your mum's knicker drawer.

WILL   Well it's a lovely offer, but I think I'll pass. Neil are you around?

NEIL   As long as I can bring my PS3 so we don't have to play those shit Wii games.

WILL   Yeah, anything you like.

JAY   How comes he can fucking stay and I can't?

WILL   Well mainly because he's not planning to ejaculate over my mother's underwear.

NEIL   I ain't promising nothing.

——— SCENE 8 ———

EXT. WILL'S HOUSE

WILL V/O   *The next day my mum was all set to go. Now I'm not one for making rash judgements, but to me, Fergus looked like a massive ginger bell-end with a stupid car and I hated him.*

THERE IS A BMW ON THE DRIVE WITH A HANDSOME MAN (FERGUS) SITTING IN IT. WILL'S MUM KISSES HIM GOODBYE. NEIL IS STANDING JUST BEHIND WILL, PS3 UNDER HIS ARM.

POLLY McKENZIE   The fridge is full, but if you need anything else the Ocado account number is by the computer.

WILL   You are only going to be away for one night aren't you?

POLLY McKENZIE   Probably. I've left the heating on constant in case you get cold, and don't forget Mrs Springett has got a key, so she'll be popping in to check you're OK.

WILL   Well I'll look forward to an unscheduled appearance from her then.

POLLY McKENZIE   Oh and Neil, Will's a little bit stressed at the moment – me not being around might bring on one of his migraines. If that does happen there are special suppositories in the bathroom cabinet.

WILL   Mum.

POLLY McKENZIE   It's the only thing that works as he's usually a bit sick, can't keep painkillers down. You just need to pop two in.

NEIL   In where?

POLLY McKENZIE   Well, they are suppositories, so in his bottom.

WILL   Mum.

NEIL   For a joke?

POLLY McKENZIE   No, to stop his headache. Bye petal.

SHE KISSES WILL AND GETS IN THE CAR.

NEIL   Well, that is not happening. Seriously, I don't care if you're dying, I'm going nowhere near your arsehole.

WILL   No, sure, fair enough.

AS POLLY AND FERGUS DRIVE AWAY, WILL WATCHES THEM LEAVE.

WILL   OK, so they've gone then. That has actually happened. Fine, come on Neil, let's just run through a few house rules, nothing too crazy, just—

NEIL   Shotgun your mum's bed.

WILL   Right.

 SCENE 9

EXT. PARK

JAY IS WALKING IN THE PARK WITH HIS DOG, BENJI. JAY LOOKS THOROUGHLY PISSED OFF AND CHUCKS THE BALL FOR BENJI, WITH ONE OF THOSE PLASTIC BALL-THROWING THINGS, AND BENJI BRINGS IT STRAIGHT BACK. JAY THEN

LOOKS AS IF HE HAS AN IDEA. HE THROWS THE BALL AS FAR AS HE CAN AND THEN LEGS IT IN THE OPPOSITE DIRECTION.

WILL V/O   *As Neil made himself very much at home, Jay had come up with a plan to put some distance between his sexual organs and the dog. He'd temporarily lose Benji, run home and do what he had to do, do what he had to do again, and once more if it wasn't too painful, then head out with some photocopied lost-dog signs and a £20 reward. Unfortunately, Benji, a dog, was too smart for him.*

CUT TO JAY WALKING OUT OF THE PARK, SMILING. HE'S LOOKING OVER HIS SHOULDER A BIT. AS HE LEAVES THE PARK HE DISCOVERS BENJI, SITTING AT THE PARK GATES WITH THE BALL IN HIS MOUTH.

JAY   Oh fucking hell Benji.

——— SCENE 10 ———

INT. WILL'S HOUSE, KITCHEN

WILL V/O   *Back at mine, I was fighting a losing battle to house train my new pet . . .*

NEIL HAS A SLICE OF TOAST ON THE GO. HE IS ROOTING THROUGH THE FRIDGE AND PICKS UP A JAR AND EXAMINES IT.

WILL   Do you eat this much toast at home?

NEIL   Will, what's this 'pesto'? Is it for humans?

WILL   No, it's for extraterrestrials, that's why we keep it in the fridge. Of course it's for fucking humans.

NEIL   Can you have it on toast?

WILL   Please use a plate.

SUDDENLY JAY APPEARS IN THE KITCHEN DOORWAY.

JAY   Alright gays.

WILL   How did you get in?

JAY   Front door was open.

WILL   Neil, did you leave the front door open?

NEIL   Might have done.

JAY   Do us some toast Neil.

AS JAY WALKS INTO THE KITCHEN HE TURNS ON THE PORTABLE TV AND THEN TAKES A SEAT AT THE KITCHEN TABLE, NOT EVEN BOTHERING TO WATCH WHAT'S ON THE SCREEN. HE GRABS THE OPEN LAPTOP AND STARTS SURFING THE NET.

WILL   Sorry is there a sign outside, by the permanently open front door, saying 'this way to the toast bar'? Look you're not even watching the TV.

JAY   All right, calm down Home Alone. It's just force of habit.

WILL   Why are you even here?

JAY   I need to get away from my place because the dog is driving me fucking mad.

WILL   Because it stares at you while you masturbate.

JAY   Exactly.

NEIL   How long have you had him now?

JAY   About eight years.

NEIL   And has he always done it?

JAY   No, course he hasn't. I wasn't wanking a lot when I was ten, was I?

NEIL   I thought you got laid when you was nine? With the fit babysitter.

JAY   Yes, I did Neil. And that is why I wasn't wanking so much.

WILL   Something must have started him off.

JAY   Well I think he might have chewed on a tissue under my bed and now he's got a taste for it.

WILL   Jesus, that's some acquired taste, dry Kleenex and your ejaculate.

NEIL   Here y'are Jay.

NEIL THROWS JAY'S TOAST OVER TO HIM. IT LANDS FACE DOWN ON THE
KITCHEN TABLE. JAY PICKS IT UP AND EATS IT WITHOUT WIPING THE TABLE TOP.

JAY   Cheers.

WILL DIVES IN WITH A PIECE OF KITCHEN ROLL AND WIPES THE TABLE.

WILL   Can you try and be a bit tidier please?

JAY   I tell you what won't be tidy. Your mum's tits. I bet Fergus is
covering them in spooge right now.

WILL   Can we not talk about this?

JAY   Chuck us a drink Neil.

WILL   Erm, no one is chucking anything. If you want a drink then
pour yourself a glass. The glasses are up there.

JAY   God, it's like staying at The Ritz.

WILL   Famous of course for it's no chucking drinks or toast policy.

JAY   There's no fucking glasses.

WILL   Try the dishwasher.

JAY GOES TO THE DISHWASHER, PULLS OUT THE TRAY A BIT TOO FAR, AND A
GLASS FALLS OVER AND SMASHES.

WILL   Oh for God's sake. Right, we're going out.

NEIL   Out where?

WILL   I don't care. Outside. Out of here.

JAY   Fucking hell, I'll buy you a new glass if you're going to get so
menstrual about it.

WILL   It's not about the glass. You're like a plague of toast-eating
locusts.

JAY   Right, fine, we'll go out. Neil, I think it's time we took Will on a
pussy patrol.

———— SCENE 11 ————

EXT./INT. JAY'S CAR

WILL V/O   . . . *so I was taken along on the pussy patrol, and it was pretty much everything I dreamed it would be.*

WE SEE A WIDE SHOT OF THE BOYS IN JAY'S MUM'S MICRA. JAY IS DRIVING, NEIL IS IN THE FRONT SEAT, WILL IN THE BACK.

WILL   This is the pussy patrol, is it? Driving your mum's car very slowly round the estate?

NEIL   Sometimes we go down the shops.

WILL   Have you even got your licence?

JAY   Provisional.

WILL   So all the time you've been driving it's been illegal. Great.

NEIL   It's fine. If we get stopped we just say I'm giving him a lesson.

WILL   But you aren't allowed to give lessons till you've been driving for three years.

JAY   You just say disabled, then it's allowed.

WILL   Who's disabled? You or him?

NEIL   One of us. You say it's a mental disablement.

JAY   Yeah, I do a really good voice.

WILL   Oh, well I look forward to that then.

THERE IS A SQUIRREL ON THE ROAD, NEAR THE KERB, EATING SOMETHING.

NEIL   Watch that squirrel Jay.

JAY   He'll shit himself and jump out the way, they always do.

AS THEY DRIVE FORWARD, THE SQUIRREL DOESN'T MOVE. JAY REVS THE ENGINE A BIT, BUT THE SQUIRREL STILL DOESN'T MOVE AND JAY IS FORCED TO SWERVE. WILL AND NEIL LAUGH, AND JAY LOOKS A BIT FLUSTERED.

WILL   Hilarious, you just lost a game of chicken with a rodent.

NEIL   He's still there. He's mugging you off mate.

JAY Yeah, well we'll see who's the chicken.

JAY REVERSES BACK BUT THE SQUIRREL JUMPS OUT OF THE WAY. THEN, WHEN THEY LOOK OUT THE FRONT, IT'S BACK ON THE ROAD AGAIN.

NEIL Oh my God, he's jumped out the way. He's made you look a right mug.

JAY Oh fuck this.

JAY HAMMERS THE CAR FORWARD AND AGAIN THE SQUIRREL LOOKS UP BUT DOESN'T MOVE. THIS TIME JAY DOESN'T SWERVE. THERE'S A BUMP.

WILL Oh God.

JAY Ha.

JAY STOPS THE CAR AND THEY GET OUT. THERE'S A DEAD SQUIRREL ON THE ROAD.

NEIL Oh no, why did you do that?

JAY Not so clever now is he? Now who's the fucking mug?

WILL I don't think it was trying to make you look a mug, Jay.

JAY Fucking little pisstaker.

NEIL I'll get a spade, we'll bury him.

JAY Nah, fuck him.

BEAT.

JAY LOOKS DOWN AT THE ANIMAL FOR A SECOND.

JAY His eyes look sad.

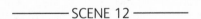

——————— SCENE 12 ———————

INT. WILL'S HOUSE, KITCHEN

WILL V/O *Great. So, so far in Jay and Neil's war against Mother Nature the death toll stood at fifty-two flowers and one piss-taking squirrel. Eventually, and with the blood of a defenceless animal on our hands and on Jay's wheel arches, we headed back to mine.*

WILL ARRIVES HOME TO FIND SIMON IN HIS KITCHEN.

SIMON   Alright. Where have you been?

WILL   Jesus Christ Simon, you scared the shit out of me. How did you get in here?

SIMON   Back door was open.

WILL   Neil!

NEIL   Oh yeah, sorry.

JAY   Mate, what the fuck are you wearing?

SIMON   It's a polo shirt and chinos.

NEIL   You look like my cousin when he went for a job interview.

SIMON   Oh, is he a golf pro?

NEIL   Nah, he's got Down's syndrome.

SIMON   This is just what everyone wears for golf. Can I make some toast Will?

NEIL   Oh pop one in for us, Si. I'm just going to shit out a poo.

WILL   Use the downstairs toilet. And open a window.

THE DOORBELL RINGS.

WILL   Who's that?

SCENE 13

INT./EXT. WILL'S HOUSE, FRONT DOOR

WILL OPENS THE DOOR TO AN OCADO DELIVERY MAN CARRYING A CASE OF 24 LAGERS.

DELIVERY MAN   Hello. This is for Polly Milf-kenzie.

WILL V/O   *If this was my dickish friends' way of taking my mind off what Fergus was doing to my mum, it wasn't working.*

———— SCENE 14 ————

INT. WILL'S HOUSE, KITCHEN

WILL ENTERS, CARRYING THE BEERS.

WILL   Who ordered these?

JAY   I know, I'm a genius. Your mum left her card details on a Post-it on the laptop.

WILL   That's for emergencies only.

JAY   It was an emergency, your house is fucking boring. Now we can get totally wankered.

WILL   No, I'm getting it refunded. I don't want to get wankered, I want everything to be the same as it was before she went away.

WILL WALKS OVER TO THE LAPTOP. JAY SITS BACK FROM IT A BIT, SNIGGERING, AS IS SIMON.

WILL   What?

JAY   Nothing. We haven't done anything, have we Si?

SIMON   Nope. We haven't been anywhere near your Facebook page.

WILL   Oh for fuck's sake, what have you done?

Oh, you've changed my profile pic to a fat naked man and you've changed my status to 'Will is fingering his cat'. Presumably you've changed the password too?

JAY   Yep. Do you like the picture? The knob's a bit big, but other than that it's definitely you.

WILL   Seriously, you've got to tell me the password. What if my mum sees this?

SIMON   She won't. I don't think Fergus can get Facebook on the end of his cock.

WILL   If you don't tell me the password I'm contacting the site administrator and reporting you.

JAY   Oooh, look out Si, he's going to get the Facebook police on to us.

SIMON   Oh no, I don't want to get told off by the nerds who run Facebook.

WILL   Please, I'm begging you.

JAY   OK. You can have the password if I can stay over.

WILL   I thought it was boring here?

JAY   Well it is, but you don't have a dog and I have certain needs to fulfil.

WILL   Oh Christ.

Alright, you can fucking stay. Now what's the password?

SIMON   I heart . . .

WILL   I heart . . .

SIMON   . . . my mum's vagina.

WILL   Brilliant.

WILL   And that's not even it. Jay?

JAY   Briefcase wanker.

WILL   Pricks.

WILL FRANTICALLY SETS ABOUT REMOVING THE OFFENSIVE ITEMS FROM THE PAGE. JAY OPENS A LAGER FROM THE CASE.

WILL   So, no longer fingering a cat, but now I can't return the lager. Thanks Jay.

JAY   You're welcome. Si?

SIMON   I can't really, I've got the tournament tomorrow.

JAY   Just one?

SIMON   Oh fuck it, I can probably have one can't I?

NEIL ENTERS THE ROOM.

NEIL   Toilet's blocked.

WILL   What do you mean 'toilet's blocked'?

NEIL It's blocked.

WILL So what you actually mean is, you've blocked the toilet.

NEIL Maybe, I dunno. I'm not a plumber.

SIMON I think I can smell it from here.

NEIL Yeah. It was a bad one to be honest. Like all the leftovers from Christmas dinner all in one go.

WILL Oh God.

NEIL So, as you'd expect, not a clean break. And you're out of toilet roll, so I had to use a wet towel.

WILL Jesus Christ. Well I'm sorry, but from now on, all toilets are now out of bounds to guests.

JAY Oh what.

SIMON Hang on, what if I need to go?

NEIL You could use your garden?

SIMON I'm not a dog Neil.

WILL OK, I'd assumed it was a given, but I'll make it clear now just in case, no one is to shit in my back garden.

WILL LEAVES.

JAY That's it.

SIMON What?

JAY I'll tell Dad that Benji did a shit in the house.

NEIL Did he?

JAY No, but if I say he did we'll have to keep him outside. And then I can wank freely without him judging me.

NEIL Your dad?

JAY The dog.

——————— SCENE 15 ———————

INT. WILL'S HOUSE, KITCHEN

WILL V/O   *I don't know what they have for Christmas dinner round Neil's house, but it smelt like turkey stuffed with rotten eggs and Pedigree Chum.*

THE ROOM IS EMPTY AS WILL RETURNS.

WILL   Well, he's right, it's definitely blocked.

THERE IS NOISE FROM OUTSIDE. WILL WALKS OUT TO FIND THE OTHERS.

——————— SCENE 16 ———————

EXT. WILL'S HOUSE, BACK GARDEN

SIMON, JAY AND NEIL ARE ON THE PATIO AT THE BACK OF WILL'S HOUSE. THERE ARE SOME PLANT POTS WITH DAFFODILS IN THEM NEARBY, AND NEIL HAS A GOLF CLUB. WILL APPEARS.

WILL   What's going on?

NEIL   Watch this.

NEIL TAKES A SWING AND SMASHES THE HEAD OFF ONE OF THE DAFFODILS, SENDING IT FLYING INTO THE GARDEN. JAY, NEIL AND SIMON LAUGH.

WILL   What the fuck are you doing?

JAY   This golf bat is perfect, it's exactly what we've been looking for.

NEIL SWINGS AND SENDS ANOTHER ONE FLYING.

WILL   Sorry, was that not clear? Stop fucking vandalising my garden.

SIMON   Oh come on Will, I thought that at first, but have a go, it's fun.

WILL   Not for me it's not.

JAY   They're only daffodils. Little fucking show-offs, ooh look at me, I'm out first, I'm all yellow.

WILL   Have you gone mental?

SIMON   Just have a go, it's fun. They go miles.

WILL   No. What are you going to do next, tag up my bedroom, piss through my letter box?

NEIL   Can we?

WILL   No. Right, come on, we're going out again. Come on.

─────── SCENE 17 ───────

EXT. ESTATE

WILL V/O   *Babysitting these three was exhausting, so I did what all good babysitters do. Hit the drink and let them get on with it.*

THE BOYS ARE WALKING DOWN THE ROAD WITH ONE OF SIMON'S GOLF CLUBS AND CANS OF LAGER IN HAND.

SIMON   Oh Christ, I've got to sober up. What am I going to tell my dad?

JAY   To leave your mum. She's a dog.

SIMON   Fuck off.

THEY COME ACROSS A HOST OF DAFFODILS IN SOMEONE'S FRONT GARDEN. THEY STOP.

JAY   Oh yes, nice.

NEIL   I thought we did all these the other night?

JAY   Yeah, they grow back every day, don't they.

WILL   Or the bloke has replanted them at some effort and cost.

NEIL   Nah, they're in pretty much the same place, so they must have grown back.

WILL   Someone has replanted them Neil.

NEIL   I doubt it.

JAY   They're *flowers*. They grow. That's what they do. That's why nobody minds us smashing them up.

SIMON You know a lot about gardening.

JAY Yeah, well my dad used to shag Delia Smith didn't he? Plus this is public ground anyway, so we can do what we like.

WILL No it isn't, this is someone's front garden.

JAY Where's the fence then?

NEIL TAKES A HUGE SWING AND SENDS ONE FLYING.

SIMON Nice.

WILL This isn't right, you shouldn't be doing this.

JAY Oh shut up for once.

NEIL No one cares Will, everyone does it.

WILL By the way, they definitely don't.

JAY In your whole life, have you ever just done something just because it's a fucking laugh?

JAY HAS A SWING AND CHOPS A FLOWER HEAD CLEAN OFF.

WILL Look at you, hanging round the estate drinking and smashing up people's gardens. You're just a teenage pregnancy away from an ASBO.

JAY Oh sorry, neighbourhood watch.

SIMON TAKES A SWING AT THE FLOWERS.

SIMON Oh come on Will, it is a laugh.

WILL But what would my mum say if she found out I was involved?

JAY I know what she's saying at the moment.

WILL Do you?

JAY Yep. 'Oh Fergus, oh Fergus, fuck me harder, in the mouth, now quickly get it in my arse Fergus.'

WILL Fine, give it here then.

WILL HANDS HIS CAN TO NEIL AND GRABS THE GOLF CLUB. HE SMACKS A DAFFODIL A REALLY LONG WAY.

NEIL Oi Jay, Nick Faldo.

SIMON See!

WILL To be fair, that was brilliant.

NEIL My go.

WILL No, one more.

WILL SMASHES ANOTHER ONE, THEN THEY ALL LOOK UP AS THEY HEAR A NOISY BANGING FROM ONE OF THE BEDROOM WINDOWS IN THE HOUSE. THERE IS A RED-FACED NEIGHBOUR BANGING ON THE WINDOW, AND SHOUTING.

NEIGHBOUR Oi.

NEIL Oh fuck.

NEIGHBOUR Stay there or I'm calling the police.

SIMON Run.

JAY Fuck off you fat old shit.

WILL Well that's not helping.

 SCENE 18

INT. WILL'S HOUSE, KITCHEN

WILL V/O *So I'd become what I hated. But thanks to the beauty of alcohol, I couldn't care less.*

THE BOYS ARE SITTING IN THE KITCHEN, DRINKING BEERS.

NEIL IS INSPECTING SIMON'S GOLF CLUBS.

NEIL 'Ere what do you reckon this one would do to a daffodil then Si?

SIMON I reckon it would smash the fuck out of it Neil.

NEIL Nice. I might have to borrow it and head over to that bloke's place when the flowers have grown back.

WILL Oh come on Neil, give the fat old shit one day off.

SIMON Yeah, or he'll call the police.

WILL That was amazing, wasn't it? I mean, did he think that for one second that would scare me. Fucking daff-loving idiot.

JAY FINDS A WOODEN ROLLING PIN IN ONE OF THE KITCHEN DRAWERS.

JAY Yes, found it, Will's mum's vibrator.

WILL That's a rolling pin.

JAY (SNIFFING IT) Oh it's still got the smell.

WILL It's a rolling pin.

JAY Right. I've got some unfinished business to attend to. Business pulling my cock with no dogs around.

WILL Not in my mum's bed.

JAY No, of course not.

SIMON That's something.

JAY No, Neil's going to be wanking in there.

NEIL Yeah found these in the wash basket. (HOLDING UP SOME PINK PANTIES) Oh yes they've still got that lovely arsey smell.

JAY AND NEIL HEAD UP THE STAIRS.

SIMON Game of Pro Evo – three shots for the loser?

WILL What about your golf?

SIMON Oh I'm a natural, everyone says it. A couple more drinks won't make any difference.

WILL Ah, the drink-drivers' charter, cheers.

THEY MOVE TO THE LIVING ROOM.

———— SCENE 19 ————

INT. WILL'S HOUSE, LIVING ROOM

WILL V/O   *The next morning, we were woken by a terrible banging. Either Jay was having the most aggressive wank ever, or something even more worrying was happening.*

WILL AND SIMON ARE SLOWLY COMING TO, BOTH VERY HUNGOVER AND GROGGY. THE DOORBELL IS RINGING REPEATEDLY AND THERE IS A BANGING AT THE DOOR.

SIMON   Uuurrghhh.

WILL   What? What's that?

SIMON   Oh fucking hell, my head is killing me. What's that noise?

WILL   I think it's someone at the front door.

SIMON   It's a bit early, isn't it?

WILL   It's not that early.

SIMON   What? Oh shit, oh fuck, it's past nine o clock. I should've been at golf an hour ago.

WILL   I wouldn't leave just yet.

SIMON   What do you mean? I'm already late.

WILL   Well, shall we find out who is trying to smash the door down before you head outside?

WILL PEERS OUT OF THE WINDOW AND SEES THE NEIGHBOUR FROM LAST NIGHT AT THE DOOR.

WILL   Oh fuck.

SIMON   Who is it?

WILL   It's the bloke whose garden we destroyed.

SIMON   What, the fat old shit?

WILL   Yes, except he's not fat, he looks fucking hard.

SIMON   I've got to get to golf, I've got seven missed calls, my dad is going to go mental.

JUST THEN THE GUY STOPS BANGING ON THE FRONT DOOR AND MOVES TO THE FRONT WINDOW.

WILL   Fuck, hide.

WILL AND SIMON DROP BELOW THE LEVEL OF THE WINDOWSILL, AS THE GUY LOOKS IN.

SIMON   Has he gone?

WILL LOOKS UP CAUTIOUSLY. HE SEES THE NEIGHBOUR WALKING TOWARDS THE GARDEN GATE.

WILL   Oh shit, he's going to try the back door.

SIMON   So?

WILL   What if Neil's left it open again?

SIMON   Oh shit.

WILL AND SIMON HURRIEDLY CRAWL ROUND AND OUT OF THE ROOM ON THEIR HANDS AND KNEES.

—————— SCENE 20 ——————

INT. WILL'S HOUSE, KITCHEN

SIMON AND WILL CRAWL FRANTICALLY INTO THE KITCHEN, ONLY TO FIND NEIL STANDING UP MAKING TOAST AND TEA.

NEIL   Morning.

WILL   Neil, back door.

NEIL   I locked it.

THE NEIGHBOUR LOOKS IN THROUGH THE KITCHEN WINDOW.

WILL   Neil, get down.

NEIL   What?

NEIGHBOUR   OI!

NEIL STARES AT THE NEIGHBOUR THEN DROPS BELOW THE LEVEL OF THE WINDOW.

WILL   Yep, that should have fooled him.

NEIL   He looks well angry.

SIMON   Shit, another missed call from my dad. What are we going to do?

NEIGHBOUR   I know you're in there.

NEIL   Let's go back to the living room.

WILL   How is that going to help?

NEIL   I just farted in here.

CRAWLING BACK TO THE LIVING ROOM.

WILL   Oh God Neil, I'm in its wake. It's like you're carrying it in your pants.

———— SCENE 21 ————

INT. WILL'S HOUSE, STAIRS

AS THE THREE OF THEM CRAWL PAST THE BOTTOM OF THE STAIRS, JAY COMES TO THE TOP, OBVIOUSLY JUST OUT OF BED.

JAY   What the fuck's all the noise?

NEIL   We're under attack from the daffodil bloke.

JAY   What?

WILL   He's basically correct. We're being threatened.

NEIGHBOUR   (OFF SCREEN) Come out here young man!

JAY   Does he know I'm here?

WILL   I don't see how he could.

JAY   Good, I'm going back to bed then.

JAY WALKS OFF. JUST THEN WE HEAR A KEY IN THE LOCK AND SEE THE DOOR START TO OPEN. SOMEONE IS CALLING FROM THE OTHER SIDE OF THE DOOR:

MRS SPRINGETT   (OPENING DOOR) Oh Will, just popping in to check that everything is OK, are you—

WILL SPRINGS TO HIS FEET, KICKS THE DOOR SHUT IN HER FACE AND PUTS THE CHAIN ON. MRS SPRINGETT SCREAMS AND FALLS BACKWARDS.

WILL   (ON HIS HANDS AND KNEES AGAIN) Fucking Mrs Springett.

——————— SCENE 22 ———————

INT. WILL'S HOUSE, LIVING ROOM

THE NEIGHBOUR IS NOW BACK AT THE FRONT OF THE HOUSE, BANGING ON THE WINDOW. WILL, SIMON AND NEIL ARE SITTING DOWN BELOW THE WINDOWSILL.

NEIGHBOUR   I know you're in there. I saw your mate. Come out and do some vandalism now then.

WILL   See, I told you it was vandalism.

SIMON   Oh my God, my dad is going to kill me.

WILL   I think this guy might kill you first.

NEIGHBOUR   I know your mum. I know your mum.

SIMON   Oh shit, he knows your mum.

NEIL   Everyone knows your mum.

WILL   Not now Neil.

NEIGHBOUR   I know you're there, I can see your feet.

WILL SEES THAT NEIL'S LEGS ARE OUTSTRETCHED.

WILL   Neil.

NEIL   I was getting cramp.

SIMON   Will, please try to talk to him. See if he'll just let me out.

WILL   Are you insane? Listen to him.

SIMON   Please mate? For my dad? This golf thing is massive for him.

NEIL   Go on Will, what's the worst he can do?

WILL   Hit me really hard.

SIMON   He won't do that. He won't. Please mate.

NEIGHBOUR   (OFF SCREEN) There's an old lady with a broken nose out here.

WILL   Oh God, fine.

WITH A LARGE BREATH, WILL STANDS UP AND FACES THE NEIGHBOUR THROUGH THE WINDOW.

WILL   Now sir . . .

NEIGHBOUR   Come out here you coward.

WILL   I think we should all take a breath, try and calm down.

NEIGHBOUR   You're telling me to calm down? Calm down? I'll smash the shit out your garden, see how you like it.

WILL   OK, I've got a really bad hangover, so if you aren't willing to have a sensible conversation about it, I'm just going to shut the curtains.

NEIGHBOUR   Are you taking the moral fucking high ground? Is that what you're doing?

WILL   OK, as I say, I'm going to close these now.

WILL HAS HIS HANDS ON THE CURTAINS, ONE EITHER SIDE OF HIM.

NEIGHBOUR   You think that's going to stop me?

WILL   OK, so I . . . I'm closing them now . . .

NEIGHBOUR   You think I give a fuck?

WILL   About to close . . .

NEIGHBOUR   You're a bunch of fucking vandals.

WILL   Closing, closing.

NEIGHBOUR   And I'd call the police but I want to deal with you myself.

HE SLOWLY CLOSES THE CURTAINS IN THE FACE OF THE STILL-RANTING NEIGHBOUR, WHO IS NOW EVEN ANGRIER IF ANYTHING.

WILL   And they're closed.

NEIL   He's gone. Nice one.

SIMON   That's your solution?

WILL   Do you have a better one?

SIMON   Oh God. Oh God, my dad is never, ever going to forgive me.

NEIL   Anyone want any toast?

WILL   Um, yeah, alright.

JAY ENTERS IN TEARS.

NEIL   You alright mate? What's up?

JAY   Just got a text from my dad. He's had Benji put down. Said once they start shitting indoors it's basically the end anyway. Kindest thing to do. What have I done? I'll never wank again.

NEIL GOES TO HIM AND PATS HIM ON THE SHOULDER.

NEIL   Come on, mate, you will.

JAY IS SILENTLY CRYING AND THEY HEAR A CAR PULL UP OUTSIDE.

SIMON   That'll probably be the police.

WILL RUSHES TO THE CURTAINS AND LOOKS OUT.

WILL   Oh shit.

SIMON   Is it them?

WILL   It's worse than that. It's my mum.

WE SEE WILL'S MUM OUTSIDE TALKING TO THE ANIMATED AND ANGRY NEIGHBOUR AND A DISTRAUGHT MRS SPRINGETT, WHO IS HOLDING HER BLEEDING NOSE.

WILL V/O   *It had been an interesting few days. I'd squashed my first squirrel, found out that I had a beak, and seen evidence that Jay and Neil were surprisingly creative.*

SHOT OF VANDALISED VILLAGE FLOWERS: 'WE CUM TIT VILLAGE'.

WILL V/O   *The only good news was that having spent the weekend being fucked by a ginger stranger, my mum was dumped immediately because, and I quote, he couldn't be dealing with a problem child.*

Episode 6

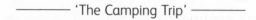

──────── 'The Camping Trip' ────────

We were pretty clear when we were writing it that this would be the last ever episode. We'd written a draft of the film at this point, but we didn't know if that would go ahead, so this could be the last time we could be certain that people would see Jay, Neil, Simon and Will interact.

And really that was what we wanted the episode to be about the most, just the four of them interacting with each other, and that probably meant taking them away somewhere. And something that most teenagers seem to try out at some point (certainly both Damon and I did) is a camping trip.

We also didn't want to end on a huge, neat moment. It felt to us that at that age things rarely come to an end neatly – friendships just kind of drift off rather than you having cataclysmic separations – and we wanted this ep to reflect that, even if it meant (and it did) some people finding it a little unsatisfying.

Incredibly, this ep marks the first time any of them have actually had sex. It felt like a momentous moment both in their lives and in the series, but we thought that rather than build it up too much or show it happening (both things we'd kind of done before with Will and Charlotte and Simon and Tara anyway), it would be funnier for Neil just to baldly announce that it had happened. And say that his legs ached.

I think this episode has some nice set pieces in it, from Simon and Carli's brother to Gilbert with Will and Neil, culminating with the car rolling in the lake, but really it's about them chatting – whether it's in the common room, round the fire, in the tent before they puke on each other, or as they wander off into the darkness. The series was always meant to be about language and friendship, and this episode is all about both those things.

SCENE 1

INT. SIMON'S HOUSE, KITCHEN

WILL V/O   *For a man with an internet history as exotic as Simon's, emergency meetings were never good news.*

THE COOPER FAMILY (PAMELA, ALAN AND ANDREW COOPER) ARE GATHERED IN THE KITCHEN. SIMON COMES IN AND SITS DOWN.

PAMELA COOPER   We've been waiting for you Simon.

SIMON   Sorry, I was busy. I have a life too you know. And what's so important we have to have a meeting like, like businessmen or something?

ALAN COOPER   Well, I don't really know where to start. My company are making a lot of people redundant. I've managed to keep my job but it means moving to Swansea.

SIMON   Where's that? Is it far?

PAMELA COOPER   It's in Wales. You must have heard of Swansea Simon.

SIMON   I haven't and I'm not moving to fucking Wales.

ALAN COOPER   Eh, mind your language.

PAMELA COOPER   Simon, I know it's a lot to take in, but please try and stay calm.

ALAN COOPER   It's been an incredibly tough decision for us to make. I mean, I would have been out of a job.

SIMON   Oh it's all about you, isn't it? What about me? What about my friends, my other relationships?

ANDREW COOPER   Your what?

SIMON   And my exams? I mean one minute you're all like 'revise revise revise' the next you're moving me to Swansea.

PAMELA COOPER   We've spoken to the examination board and you'll be able to sit the same exams in Swansea, you'll just do them at a local college.

SIMON   I'm not going. How's that suit your fucking plans? I'll get a flat with Jay, I'm eighteen, you can't stop me. Me and Jay'll get a flat and Andrew can come and live with us.

ANDREW COOPER   No thanks.

ALAN COOPER   Boys, I promise I'll make this work for us all. I love you both so much.

SIMON   Oh that's all right then. Well done.

SIMON GETS UP FROM THE BREAKFAST BAR AND STORMS OUT, STOPPING TO DELIVER HIS FINAL, LOUD, VERDICT:

SIMON   Brilliant, you've effectively ended my life. In fact why not go the whole hog and shoot me. Or better still have me taken to the vet's and secretly put down. Just like you did with Patch.

HE STORMS OUT.

——— SCENE 2 ———

INT. SCHOOL COMMON ROOM

WILL V/O   *But after he'd slept on it, Simon was even more unreasonable.*

THE BOYS ARE ALL SITTING AROUND CHATTING.

SIMON   He's a total selfish wanker. I don't understand why he doesn't just get another job. It's not even like he's well paid. He's in his fucking forties, his life is practically over.

NEIL   What is Swansea? Is it an animal?

SIMON   It's a place.

NEIL   It don't sound near.

SIMON   It's in Wales.

JAY   Oh mate, they say it's well grim up North.

WILL   Yes, they do, but Wales isn't up North Jay.

JAY   Wherever it is, Michael fucking Palin, it's not round here is it?

WILL   No, but on the plus side I've heard Swansea is quite nice.

SIMON   Really, who from?

WILL   A friend of my gran's.

SIMON   Is that supposed to make me feel better?

WILL   It's all I've got I'm afraid.

SIMON   That's pretty much it for me and Carli then.

JAY   Oh I dunno, maybe you could still 'not-have-a-relationship' long distance.

SIMON   Yep, good one.

NEIL   So can we have a crack at her then?

SIMON   No.

JAY   Oh go on, don't be a dick. I'd love a go on that.

NEIL   Think about that lovely snatch.

SIMON   Fuck off Neil, just fuck off. I'm having a nightmare here.

NEIL   All right, calm down, you're not the only one with problems.

SIMON   Really, what problems do you have Neil?

JAY   Bent old man . . . Wants to fuck own sister . . . Mum did a legger.

NEIL   Nah, none of them. I think I'm going to be a dad.

JAY   Neil, you have to fuck a girl for that to happen.

NEIL   I know. I did it with this bird from Asda and now she's pregnant.

BEAT.

WILL   Congratulations.

SIMON   Are you serious?

JAY   No. Fucking. Way.

SIMON   So you're not a virgin any more?

NEIL   Don't think so.

JAY   Nice one, mate. I knew you'd lose your V-plates before these sad pricks. Welcome to the shaggers club.

SIMON   Where only 50 per cent of the members have had sex.

WILL   Let's back up thirty seconds shall we. This is very serious. I have a couple of questions Neil.

NEIL   Yes.

WILL   Well, what did it feel like?

NEIL   It was alright.

WILL   'Alright'? Anything else? No one's expecting D. H. Lawrence Neil, but did you think anything other than 'this is alright'?

NEIL   My legs ached.

WILL   I give up.

SIMON   This is a big deal. How did it happen?

NEIL   We was both on the cheese counter and she was being well saucy and that. Then we went back to hers in our lunch break and did it. Now she's pregnant.

WILL   How romantic. Are you sure she's pregnant Neil?

NEIL   She texted me. Look "Did the test. It's positive. Thought you should know". Two dots and a diagonal line.

WILL   Worried smiley, dear God.

SIMON   Why didn't you use protection?

NEIL   Well, she told me she couldn't have any more kids.

JAY   Any more?!

WILL   Jesus Christ. How old is she Neil?

NEIL   Well I don't know, pretty old.

WILL Have you told anyone else about this?

NEIL Nah. I mean I can't really talk to my dad, can I.

JAY What, 'cos he's never seen a woman's fanny?

NEIL Shut up. He's seen my mum's.

JAY Well that don't count, everyone's seen your mum's.

NEIL Fuck off.

JAY Until she ran off.

WILL I think you need to talk to Gilbert about this. For all his flaws he's not a bad bloke and his role as Head of Sixth is pastoral as well as tutorial.

NEIL He's what?

WILL It's his job.

———— SCENE 3 ————

INT. MR GILBERT'S OFFICE

MR GILBERT IS SITTING BEHIND HIS DESK. NEIL AND WILL SIT OPPOSITE. MR GILBERT'S FACE IS THE PICTURE OF CONCENTRATION.

NEIL . . . then I pushed it in a bit, then out, then in a bit, then my legs ached, then out again, then in, then it went off. Now she's pregnant.

MR GILBERT OK, I think I get the picture Sutherland.

NEIL Cool.

MR GILBERT Look, isn't this exactly the kind of thing that Twitter or Myspace were invented for?

WILL No sir.

NEIL I was thinking about writing to the *Daily Star*'s problem page, you know the one with the photos, but it takes a week to find out the advice.

MR GILBERT   OK. And this 'encounter', did it take place on the school premises or with a fellow pupil?

NEIL   Nah.

MR GILBERT   Good. Well, what I think you should do is turn around, get out of my office and we'll pretend this conversation never happened.

NEIL   Alright, cheers for that.

NEIL GETS UP AND LEAVES.

WILL   But sir, what about your duty of care?

MR GILBERT   Listen McKenzie, that Sutherland has managed to pass on his genes may be a looming disaster for mankind but it is not my mess to clean up.

WILL   But what about the oath?

MR GILBERT   Sorry to disappoint McKenzie, but teachers don't start each day swearing allegiance to the education fairies under a photo of the Queen. It's not so much of a calling these days, more a graveyard for the unlucky and the unambitious. Between you and me, the only reason anyone teaches these days is because they've taken a more relaxed view on police checks in recent years. Goodbye McKenzie.

WILL V/O   *They say the art of teaching is aid and discovery, and Mr Gilbert helped me discover that he was a wanker.*

 SCENE 4

INT. SCHOOL CANTEEN

SIMON IS GETTING HIS LUNCH. HE HANDS OVER A TEN-POUND NOTE TO THE DINNER LADY. SHE STARTS FIDDLING AROUND BEHIND THE TILL. CARLI COMES OVER. SHE'S WITH HER FRIEND (RACHEL), WHO IS CLEARLY AGITATED ABOUT BEING LATE FOR SOMETHING.

CARLI'S FRIEND   . . . OK, two minutes.

CARLI   Simon, God, my mum just told me about you moving away.

SIMON   Oh right, yeah. It's basically the end of my life.

CARLI   It's so weird, I can't imagine us being that far apart.

SIMON   Hmm.

CARLI'S FRIEND   We're going to miss the bus.

CARLI   Anyway, I've got to go. See you soon.

SIMON   No. I'll come with you, I'm just waiting for my change. It's eight pounds. (TO THE DINNER LADY) Where's my change?

DINNER LADY   Manners.

CARLI   I'll see you. I suppose I just always thought we might, y'know, we might . . .

CARLI'S FRIEND   We have to go.

CARLI   I've got to go, I'm sorry. I'll see you Simon.

RACHEL DRAGS CARLI OFF. SIMON IS STUCK THERE.

SIMON   (CALLING AFTER CARLI) What? We might what? Say it. Come on . . .

SOME OTHER PUPILS HAVE CLOCKED HIM AND ARE LAUGHING AT HIM. HE'S NOW SHOUTING HOPELESSLY AFTER CARLI AS SHE DISAPPEARS ROUND A CORNER.

SIMON   Make love, was it make love? Carli, make love?

CARLI HAS GONE.

SIMON   (SCREAMING AT THE DINNER LADY) Where's my fucking change?

THE DINNER LADY HANDS SIMON HIS CHANGE.

SIMON   Thank you.

———— SCENE 5 ————

INT. SCHOOL DINNER HALL

WILL V/O   *So it had finally happened. Carli had made Simon's brain explode.*

NEIL, JAY AND WILL ARE ALL SITTING EATING IN THE DINNER HALL. SIMON COMES OVER.

SIMON   That stupid ugly bitch has ruined it for me with Carli.

JAY   What, has she been controlling your personality for the last eighteen years?

SIMON   Brilliant, yeah, good one.

WILL   Anyway Simon, I've been thinking, we should do something for you before you leave.

NEIL   What, like give him a makeover, sort his hair out an' that.

WILL   Could do. I was thinking more along the lines of a camping trip to the countryside. Pubs, long walks, no parents, no girls, just the four of us, the lads, a tent and a load of beers.

JAY   Sounds like a bent version of *Brokeback Mountain*.

WILL   Which would be a heterosexual version.

NEIL   Is this like a poshos' tradition? Did your mates do the same thing for you when you left Hogwarts?

WILL   Um, no they didn't.

NEIL   Oh right. Well, I'm up for it, do me a lot of good to get away for a bit, out in the country, get my head straight.

JAY   Bring your old man along; see if you can get him straight an' all.

NEIL   Fuck off.

SIMON   Dunno Will. Don't think I'd be much company.

JAY   Oh come on Si, it'd be a laugh. Although the last time I went to the country, I had a bit of bother.

SIMON   What from locals?

JAY   Nah, a cow. It charged me so I had to knock it out. One punch.

NEIL   Nice.

JAY   I had to leg it though because its mates saw what was going on and, no word of a lie, they stood up on their hind legs and started firing milk at me from their tits.

WILL   Udders.

JAY   Well yeah, there were loads of them.

WILL   Right. What do you reckon Si, fancy a weekend punching cattle?

SIMON   No, no. I've got two weeks left here and I'd rather spend them trying to finally get together with Carli than hanging round with you lot talking shit about cows and fucking camping.

BEAT

WILL   I'll put you down as a maybe then.

──────── SCENE 6 ────────

INT. WILL'S BEDROOM / EXT. ESTATE

WILL V/O   *That night at 2 a.m., I was lucky enough to be woken by a call from a steaming-drunk Simon . . .*

SIMON IS STANDING IN THE STREET OUTSIDE CARLI'S HOUSE WITH A BOTTLE OF WHISKY. WE INTERCUT TO WILL ON THE PHONE.

SIMON   Will, it's me, Simon.

WILL   Yes, I know.

SIMON   Man, you were right, I've got to make Carli believe in me, make the sort of gesture she'll never forget.

WILL   That doesn't sound like me. Are you drunk?

SIMON   I'm going in. This might be my last chance to see her, to kiss her, to maybe make love to her.

WILL   Right, fine, I'm coming to get you as long as you promise never to say 'make love' again.

———— SCENE 7 ————

EXT. CARLI D'AMATO'S HOUSE

WILL V/O   . . . *so, like a superhero, I went off to Simon's rescue, a superhero in slippers and a dressing gown.*

WILL COMES RUNNING ROUND THE CLOSE TO SEE SIMON CLIMBING INTO CARLI'S HOUSE THROUGH AN OPEN FIRST-FLOOR WINDOW.

WILL   Simon. Simon. Please. Oh Christ.

———— SCENE 8 ————

INT. CARLI'S HOUSE, BEDROOM

SIMON STANDS AT THE END OF THE BED AND WHISPERS:

SIMON   Carli, it's me Simon.

THERE IS NO MOVEMENT FROM THE BED. SIMON SITS ON THE END OF THE BED AND GENTLY STROKES THE COVERS ABOVE WHERE IT LOOKS LIKE THERE ARE SOME LEGS. THE SLUMBERING BODY STARTS TO TURN AND WAKE.

SIMON   What was it you wanted to say? Was it about making love?

AS HE'S STROKING, HE LOOKS MORE CLOSELY AT THE DUVET COVER AND REALISES THAT IT HAS FOOTBALLS ON IT. AS HIS EYES BECOME MORE USED TO THE DARK, IT'S CLEAR THIS IS A CHILD'S BEDROOM. SIMON STARTS TO BACK OFF AS CARLI'S BROTHER (CHRIS) WAKES UP.

CHRIS D'AMATO   Daddy?

SIMON   No, shh, sleep.

CHRIS D'AMATO   What's happening? Who's that?

SIMON   Shh. Please, please just shush your little fucking mouth.

CHRIS D'AMATO   You're not my daddy.

CHRIS STARTS TO SCREAM. SIMON RUNS TO THE WINDOW AND SCRAMBLES OUT.

SIMON   Oh fuck.

CHRIS D'AMATO   Mummy, Daddy . . .

——————— SCENE 9 ———————

EXT. CARLI'S HOUSE

WILL V/O   *Simon's intention was pure* Romeo and Juliet*; unfortunately the execution was pure* Crimewatch.

WILL SEES SIMON CLIMBING OUT OF THE WINDOW AND OFF THE ROOF, BEFORE SPRINTING OFF DOWN THE ESTATE. A LIGHT FLICKS ON IN CHRIS'S ROOM, AND WILL PANICS AND ALSO SPRINTS OFF.

——————— SCENE 10 ———————

INT. SIMON'S HOUSE, BATHROOM

SIMON IS THROWING UP.

ALAN COOPER   (OFF SCREEN, ON THE PHONE) Yeah, cheers Steve. No, there's no need to press charges. Don't worry. Sorry again.

ALAN COOPER WALKS IN.

SIMON   You're not going to shout at me, are you Dad? My head really hurts.

ALAN COOPER   Nah, I'm not going to shout. I think we need to have a talk, though. I know that the move is stressful for you and you might feel a little crazy.

SIMON   Um, yeah.

ALAN COOPER   But you can't go touching up children. Not now, not ever, not kiddies Si.

SIMON   Oh God no, no. No it wasn't that at all. I got the wrong bedroom. I wanted to touch Carli.

ALAN COOPER   Really?

SIMON   Yes, yes.

ALAN COOPER   Oh thank Christ. Thank God. I've been googling chemical castration all morning. Well, I think you need to forget about her for a while. You go near that house and her dad's going to fuck you up, his words not mine.

SIMON   Oh God.

ALAN COOPER   Maybe go to your nan's for the weekend?

SIMON   Will wanted to go camping.

ALAN COOPER   Camping? Yeah, that sounds good. Healthy, outdoors, no children around.

SIMON   Dad, I've loved her for ages, I don't know what to do.

ALAN COOPER   I totally understand mate. There was a girl I was crazy about once.

SIMON   Really?

ALAN COOPER   Yeah. She was gorgeous, funny, my best friend in many ways. But nothing ever happened, as much as I wanted it to.

SIMON   Because you never told her?

ALAN COOPER   No, she was frigid. Her knickers were about as wet as August in the Sahara.

SIMON   Oh.

ALAN COOPER   Then your mother came along, and she was a real tomcat, let me tell you.

SIMON STARTS RETCHING AGAIN.

ALAN COOPER   Didn't take long for me to forget about the Ice Queen with your mum around, if you get me.

HE BANGS SIMON ON THE BACK.

ALAN COOPER   Get it all up mate.

——————— SCENE 11 ———————

INT. SIMON'S CAR

WILL V/O   *Simon's choices were simple: stay at home and lose more of his stomach lining hearing about his mum's high sex drive, or take us camping.*

THE BOYS ARE ALL IN THE CAR. WILL IS IN THE BACK WITH CAMPING PARAPHERNALIA PILED HIGH ON HIS LAP. JAY, SITTING NEXT TO HIM, IS ANNOYED AND KEEPS SHOVING THE STUFF BACK TO WILL'S SIDE.

WILL   As we're getting near I thought we should run through the itinerary for the weekend.

NEIL   What's an itinerary?

SIMON   It's Will's way of taking the fun out of everything.

WILL   No, it's just a schedule of what we'll get up to and when we'll be doing it.

JAY   Right, item one, can you get your shit off my side of the car?

WILL   It's not just shit, it's essentials. I've brought it for everyone to make the trip more enjoyable.

JAY   Oh right, yeah, Monopoly. That's going to make it a proper lads weekend. All we need is beer and johnnies, and I've got plenty of both.

SIMON   Why have you brought a load of johnnies?

JAY   In case I get lucky.

WILL   We're camping by a river near a wood. What are you hoping to pull, a fish or an owl?

JAY   Listen, all these country birds love a bit of big-city cock.

WILL   You're not from the big city.

JAY   Anywhere with a train station and a Morrisons counts as a city to them.

SIMON   Neil, look at the map, please? Where is it?

NEIL LOOKS AT GOOGLE MAPS ON HIS PHONE.

NEIL   Oh, it's around here somewhere. Like the next left or something.

SIMON   And that's what Google Maps says, is it? The next left or something?

NEIL   Sorry mate, my head's a mess. What if I have to go to the birth? Can you imagine how grim that'll be, watching that baby getting squeezed out her arse?

WILL   Right, I've got some news Neil.

NEIL   Oh here it is. Turn in here Si.

SIMON   Jesus Christ, it stinks. Is it near a pig farm, Neil?

NEIL   Nah, sorry, that was me. It just slipped out.

SIMON/WILL/JAY   Oh Jesus, Neil . . . You are rank mate . . . It's making my ears hurt . . . You need to get that checked out . . . My nose is bleeding . . . I can see that, it's like a brown mist . . .

——— SCENE 12 ———

EXT. CAMPING AREA BY LAKE

WILL V/O   *Despite Neil's anxious bowels burning our eyes and choking our lungs, we made it. I'd researched this place online and it certainly delivered. Secluded, remote, beautiful . . .*

THE CAR STOPS AND THEY GET OUT.

NEIL   So where do we shit?

WILL   What?

NEIL   When we need to shit, where do we shit?

JAY   Hang on, he's right. Where are we going to shit?

WILL   Well, usually you'd place the trench at least twenty yards from the site, down stream of course . . .

SIMON   What trench?

WILL   The toilet trench.

NEIL   Where you put the toilets?

WILL   No, where you do a toilet.

SIMON   I'm not shitting in a trench.

JAY   You've gone mental. I'm not going anywhere near a hole filled with your shit.

WILL   No, we each get our own trench.

SIMON   Oh that's all right then.

NEIL   We're camping surrounded by shit?

JAY   No. No one is shitting in a trench.

NEIL   We'll have to drive to a pub or something and shit there.

SIMON   Good idea.

JAY   Agreed.

NEIL   That's decided then. Write that down Will, item two.

WILL   Hmm, could do. Or you could remember to shit in the pub when we're there? Right, let's get this tent up.

NEIL   I need to go now though.

WILL   What? Just hold it in.

NEIL   I can't, I get all emotional.

WILL   We've only just got here Neil. Camp first, poo second.

NEIL   I don't think I can. I'm honestly getting teary. It's like it's trying to push its way back into my stomach.

SIMON   Ah, I sort of need one too. What about the service station we passed?

NEIL   Oh God, the snake's out the cave.

WILL   Fine, everyone back in the car.

THEY ALL GET BACK INTO THE CAR.

WILL V/O   . . . *so our camping trip was delayed while Neil left what he described as King Kong's finger in the Welcome Break toilets.*

——— SCENE 13 ———

EXT. CAMPING AREA BY LAKE

WILL V/O   *Neil genuinely felt better after unloading a massive poo, and now the car was unloaded, so was I . . .*

ALL THE CAMPING PARAPHERNALIA IS UNLOADED IN A PILE. WILL TAKES CONTROL.

WILL   Right, first we need to clear the ground, make sure our site is safe and then put up our tent.

JAY   Fuck that, let's just crack open the beers and build a fucking massive fire.

WILL   You can't just build a fire, it takes preparation. I mean have we even asked the land-owner's permission?

SIMON   Will, I didn't come here for a refresher course in the Countryside Code, I just want to get pissed and have a laugh. I won't be able to do any of this in Wales.

NEIL   What 'cos there are no fields?

SIMON   No, 'cos I won't have any mates.

JAY   You won't need mates, Welsh birds are total filth.

NEIL   Are they?

JAY   Yeah, pretty much all British porn stars are Welsh. Most of them don't get paid, they just do it for cock.

SIMON   Oh OK, made-up sluts, now I'm glad I'm going to Swansea. Fucking hell, Swansea.

WILL   Fine Simon, look if you really want I'll build you a fire now.

You lot put the tent up, I'll go and find some suitable wood and kindling.

JAY   Alright Arkela.

WILL   But remember, fire is an element, it must be respected.

———— SCENE 14 ————

EXT. CAMPING AREA BY LAKE

WILL V/O . . . *camping is all about self-reliance and teamwork. And I knew I could rely on myself to create the perfect camp and my team to fuck it up.*

WE SEE WILL, WITH ARMFULS OF LOGS, COMING OUT OF THE WOODS. HE LOOKS OVER AND SEES JAY HOLDING A PETROL CAN AND A MATCH ABOVE A TWO-FOOT-HIGH, METRE-WIDE BONFIRE. JAY CHUCKS THE MATCH ON AND WILL WATCHES IN HORROR AS A HUGE FLAME ERUPTS. HE RUNS OVER.

WILL What the fuck have you done?

NEIL Alright Will, fancy a sausage?

JAY Calm down. I just got it going and I didn't even need a gays badge.

NEIL Nah, just some petrol.

WILL You've put petrol on it?

Wait a minute – is that my fold-out table in the fire, and my picnic basket?

NEIL I thought you said look for stuff to burn.

WILL Wood, burn fucking wood, not my stuff. Oh fucking hell. Why have you done that?

JAY Look someone had to take charge of this weekend or it was going to be all Monopoly and shitting in trenches.

SIMON Look, come on, sit down, have a beer, have a sausage. Just chill.

WILL I'll chill when you stop burning my fucking possessions.

JAY Oh, I thought they were for 'everyone'.

WILL Yes, for everyone to use, not to burn.

NEIL CHUCKS A CHAIR IN THE FIRE.

WILL What are you doing?

NEIL Fire's going down.

WILL   Stop burning my things.

NEIL   Oh alright, I forgot, Jeez.

WILL SITS DOWN AND SULKS.

WILL V/O   *We were barely an hour from home but somehow that meant that burning my possessions was not only OK but hilarious . . .*

WILL IS STILL SULKING. THE OTHERS ARE LAUGHING.

SIMON   Oh come on, we're sorry, it was just a joke. We'll do whatever you want to cheer you up. Anything you like.

BEAT.

WILL   Game of Monopoly?

THE OTHERS ROLLS THEIR EYES.

NEIL   Oh fuck off.

SIMON   Apart from that.

JAY   Look, if you want to play a game, I've got a proper game, not a shit one. Thinking about it, you lot are probably too pussy to play.

NEIL   It's not that game that you used to play with your weird neighbour in his shed is it?

JAY   Well that never happened.

NEIL   Yeah you told me about it years ago. Just after he moved away.

JAY   No I never. Shut up you knob. Right to start with we all have to swap phones.

THEY ALL SWAP PHONES. JAY HAS SIMON'S PHONE, WILL HAS JAY'S PHONE, NEIL HAS WILL'S PHONE AND SIMON HAS NEIL'S PHONE.

NEIL   Now what?

JAY   Now you text someone in their phone book. So right, you've got Will's phone right, so when you text someone, they'll think it's from him.

NEIL   So does that mean I've got to write it all posh and like 'ooh hurdy wurdy durdy'?

JAY   Nah. The only rule is you can write whatever you like and no one can stop you.

WILL   I just want to say for the record there's no way anything good can come out of this.

JAY   Ready, go.

THEY ALL TEXT FURIOUSLY.

WILL   I've only got five numbers in my phone, and three of them are you lot, so do your worst.

NEIL   Well as long as one of the others is your mum, you're still in trouble.

WILL   Neil, come on, that's too much.

SIMON   I think that is literally the point of the game.

WILL   Oh fuck.

JAY   Right gays, finished, that's it. Send 'em.

THE FOUR PRESS 'SEND' SIMULTANEOUSLY, SORT OF LAUGHING/SHAKING THEIR HEADS AT THEIR STUPIDITY.

JAY   Right, so I wrote, from Simon's phone to Carli: 'Carli, I love you from the bottom of my cock.

SIMON GROANS

JAY   'The thought of leaving you is making me cry.'

SIMON   Better.

JAY   'And I'm using those tears as lube to wank with.'

SIMON   Right.

WILL   Don't worry Si, I texted Jay's dad and wrote: 'Dad, I'm just thinking about you.'

JAY   Well that's all right.

WILL   'I'm in the bath and I'm hard.'

JAY   Oh fucking hell.

SIMON   Neil?

NEIL   Fairly standard to Will's mum: 'Mum, it's been seventeen years but I'd love another go on your big old tits.'

WILL   Oh no.

NEIL   'Then I'd like to smash in your back doors, brackets 'anus'.'

WILL   So it'll come up that I've sent her a text, she'll think, Oh good, he's just letting me know he's got there safely, then she'll read that?

NEIL   Yep.

WILL   Right then Si, what did you send to, I presume, Neil's dad?

SIMON   You presume wrong. I've gone for a slightly different flavour. I've written to the soon-to-be mother of his child.

NEIL   Oh what?

SIMON   At least that's who I guess 'saucy Asda Karen' is?

NEIL   It is.

SIMON   Good, 'cos I've written: 'Karen – I love you and love that you are to be the mother of my child. Marry me?'

NEIL   Oh fucking hell.

JAY   Brilliant.

WILL   That is good.

NEIL   I only met her a month ago. She smells of cheese most of the time.

JAY   What, 'cause of all the knob she's had?

NEIL   God, I thought coming out here would take my mind off it all. The countryside's really boring innit? It's just a load of fields and rivers and that. They don't do nothing, they just sit there, it's not like the London Dungeon where people jump out at you.

JAY   He's right, it's boring, shall we go back?

SIMON   No come on, we could go for a swim, skinny-dipping?

BEAT.

SIMON   Yeah, you're right, probably be a bit gay.

NEIL   Yeah.

WILL   But there's always Monopoly.

JAY   Fucking hell, fine, as long as I can be the dog.

SIMON   Why?

JAY   Reminds me of Benji.

——————— SCENE 15 ———————

EXT. CAMPING AREA BY LAKE

WILL V/O   *. . . this was great. Camping, playing board games round the fire as the sun went down. It was like I was back in Cub Scouts, but without the unpleasantness.*

THEY ARE ALL STILL PLAYING MONOPOLY, BUT THE FIRE HAS PRACTICALLY GONE OUT AND THEY ARE STRUGGLING TO SEE. JAY SEEMS REALLY INTO IT THOUGH.

JAY   Ha. Park Lane, with a hotel, that's £1500 you owe me top hat.

WILL   Can I pay you after I pass 'Go'? I'm nearly there.

JAY   Nope.

WILL   Well, will you take one of my properties then? Oh this is impossible, I can barely see.

SIMON   I've not been able to see anything for fucking hours. Let's just stop.

WILL   OK, we'll call it a draw.

JAY   Fuck off, just 'cos I'm winning and all you've got is stations.

NEIL   I'm happy to call it a draw.

JAY   Course you are, 'cause you were out about four hours ago anyway, you fucking idiot.

NEIL   You lot think I'm dumb but I've got street smarts.

SIMON   You got a woman from Asda pregnant in your lunch hour.

JAY   I'll build another fire.

WILL   It's too dark to collect wood, and you've burnt everything I own.

JAY   Well fine, get Si's car and shine the lights over here.

SIMON   Here you are then.

SIMON CHUCKS JAY THE KEYS AND JAY RUNS OVER TO THE CAR.

WILL V/O   *This was embarrassing, I hadn't lost a game of Monopoly since I was seven, yet I was about to be beaten by Jay, a man who took pride in the fact he couldn't count to a hundred.*

WILL   He really wants to win doesn't he? I never knew he was so competitive.

NEIL   I can't get enough of these sausages. I love them raw in the middle.

JAY DRIVES BACK TO THE SLIGHT SLOPE WITH THE LIGHTS FACING DOWN TOWARDS THEM, THEN JUMPS OUT, SLAMMING THE DOOR BEHIND HIM.

JAY   Right, sorted. Now you owe me fifteen hundred quid.

WE SEE SIMON'S CAR START TO ROLL DOWN THE SLOPE TOWARDS THEM.

SIMON   Jay, my fucking car. Handbrake?

JAY   Oh shit.

SIMON   Stop it! Jay, help!

SIMON, NEIL AND WILL GET IN FRONT OF THE CAR AND STOP IT.

JAY   Alright, alright.

SIMON TRIES THE DOOR.

SIMON   It's locked. Jay throw me the keys.

WILL, NEIL AND JAY ARE HOLDING THE CAR, AND SIMON IS CHECKING THE DOORS.

JAY   I gave them to you.

SIMON   No you didn't.

JAY Yeah I did.

SIMON No you fucking didn't.

JAY Oh brilliant, well someone's gone and lost the fucking keys then.

WILL Yes you, you've lost them.

SIMON You must have locked them in the car. Oh God, oh God.

WILL We'll have to smash a window.

SIMON Fucking hell Jay, you're paying for that.

JAY It's not my fault.

SIMON It's entirely your fault.

JAY I always lock my car like that. Yours must be different.

NEIL It's shitter for one.

SIMON Thanks Neil.

JAY If my old man was here he would be able to get in it in two seconds flat. He used to jack Ferraris for the mafia.

SIMON How is that total bullshit helpful?

WILL OK you two, hold it. We'll go and find something to smash the window with.

JAY Oi, why do me and Neil have to hold the fucking car?

WILL Obviously because you two are the strongest.

SIMON AND WILL RUN OFF TO FIND ROCKS. NEIL AND JAY ARE LEFT STRAINING AGAINST THE CAR TO PREVENT IT FROM ROLLING INTO THE LAKE.

JAY It's true, we are.

ON WILL AND SIMON.

SIMON Fucking hell, why are there no rocks? It's the countryside. Why are there not any fucking rocks? What are we going to smash the window with?

WILL Jay's face?

BACK TO NEIL AND JAY STILL HOLDING THE CAR BACK. IT LOOKS LIKE IRRITATING, RATHER THAN BACK-BREAKING, WORK.

NEIL   My arms hurt.

JAY   I don't know why they're bothering to get that rock. The way I look at it it's inevitable that the car's going to go into the lake.

NEIL   I suppose it's nature, you can't fight nature.

JAY   Exactly. It's going in anyway, my arms hurt, we might as well just let it go.

NEIL   D'you think Simon'll be annoyed?

JAY   How can he be, it's logical. We can't stop it.

NEIL   We are stopping it a bit now.

JAY   It's inevitable Neil, trust me. We'll let go after three, alright?

NEIL   Gotcha.

JAY   One, two . . .

JAY JUMPS ASIDE ON 'TWO'AND THEN NEIL SCRAMBLES QUICKLY TO THE OTHER SIDE OF THE CAR. IT STARTS TO ROLL, QUITE QUICKLY, TOWARDS THE LAKE. SIMON SPOTS THIS AND COMES RUNNING DOWN WITH WILL.

SIMON   Noooooooooooo! Oh God, oh God, oh God, oh God!

BUT IT'S TOO LATE: THE CAR HAS GONE AND THEY ALL WATCH AS IT SPLASHES INTO THE LAKE AND SITS THERE, THE BONNET SUBMERGED IN WATER. THERE'S A BEAT AND THEN NEIL CHUCKS A BRICK THROUGH THE BACK WINDOW.

SIMON   Why did you do that?

NEIL   You said smash a window.

SIMON   Nooooo! No, no, no!

SIMON RUNS INTO THE WATER AND TRIES TO DRAG THE CAR OUT. HE'S STRAINING AND SWEARING AND JUST ABOUT LOSING IT. WILL, NEIL AND JAY ARE STANDING ON THE SIDE WATCHING HIM GET MORE AND MORE SOAKED.

SIMON   You arseholes. You total pair of fucking wankers.

NEIL   It's all right Si, we'll just wait for the morning and rescue it when the tide is out.

SIMON   It's a fucking lake Neil, the tide isn't going out. I've wasted my life hanging around with you fucking morons. I can't wait to move to Swansea. I fucking hate you, fuck off. Fuck off.

SIMON SPLASHES THE WATER, HAVING A HUGE TANTRUM.

WILL   Come Si, come out the water and dry off, I'm sure we'll think of something.

SIMON   You never think of anything, you've just got an accent that makes us all think you're clever, but you're not. You're as much of a fucking idiot as these two.

WILL   Bit harsh.

SIMON   You wankers, you total total wankers. All of you. Oh God. Oh God. Oh God. Oh God.

SIMON SPLASHES THE WATER GETTING EVEN MORE ANNOYED WHILST THE OTHERS STAND ON THE BANK LOOKING BACK AT HIM. SIMON STOPS. THERE'S A BEAT.

NEIL   Do you want a lager Si?

SIMON   Yes.

NEIL GOES TO HELP HIM AND SIMON SLOWLY TRUDGES OUT OF THE WATER. JAY PUTS HIS HAND IN HIS POCKET AS HE AND WILL ARE WALKING UP THE BANK BEHIND SIMON AND NEIL.

JAY   Oh shit. I did have the keys.

WILL   Probably wouldn't mention it.

——————— SCENE 16 ———————

EXT. CAMPING AREA BY LAKE

WILL V/O   *So Simon's shitty yellow Fiat was gone for ever. But on the bright side, at least Jay didn't beat me at Monopoly . . .*

JAY, SIMON, NEIL AND WILL ARE SITTING ROUND WILL'S BURNING RUCKSACK.

WILL   Which do you think burns better Si, my rucksack or my sleeping bag?

SIMON   Nice try, but this is now officially the worst weekend ever. Let's just go home.

NEIL   How?

JAY   Call your dad Si. If you think about it, it's sort of his fault we're here.

SIMON   Can't face it. He's going to go ballistic about the car. What about your old man Jay?

JAY   Nah, he's out – a private poker tournament with Danny Dyer and the Krays.

WILL   Aren't the Krays dead?

JAY   No, that's just a cover story 'cause they done a bunk from prison. They're holed up in one of me dad's warehouses.

SIMON   Course.

WE HEAR A MOBILE PHONE TONE. WILL REACHES INTO HIS POCKET AND PULLS OUT A PHONE. IT'S JAY'S.

WILL   Ooh, looks like your dad has taken a break from the made-up poker tournament Jay. Just texted you back.

JAY   Oh shit, what does he say?

WILL   'You're sick son, your mum was right about sending you to that shrink.'

JAY   What's he on about the fucking wanker. Talking bollocks as usual.

THERE'S AN AWKWARD MOMENT, WHICH IS PUNCTURED BY ANOTHER PHONE BEEP. SIMON PULLS NEIL'S PHONE OUT OF HIS POCKET.

SIMON   Got a text too Neil, it's from your bird. Maybe you should read it.

SIMON HANDS THE PHONE TO NEIL. NEIL READS IT AND HIS FACE LIGHTS UP.

NEIL   Oh thank you God, thank you.

SIMON   She said yes to the marriage proposal then?

NEIL Much better. It says: 'You dopey prick, not pregnant tested positive for—' what's that say Will?

WILL Chlamydia.

NEIL Yes, get in!

THERE'S A SLIGHT BEAT.

NEIL What's chlamydia?

WILL Well, how shall I put this Neil? You no longer have a child on the way but you do have an STD.

NEIL Ha, I got an STD. Yes an STD, woow!

SIMON Go on then, check mine.

JAY PULLS OUT SIMON'S PHONE.

JAY Oh it's from Carli, let's have a little look then.

SIMON No!

SIMON SNATCHES THE PHONE FROM JAY AND LOOKS AT IT. HE SMILES.

WILL Well?

SIMON Brilliant. Should we go to bed then?

WILL What did it say?

WILL V/O . . . *Simon was never this cagey. When it came to Carli he normally wore his heart on his sleeve and his boner in his pants. Maybe he had other things on his mind.*

 SCENE 17 ————

INT. TENT

NEIL, JAY AND SIMON ARE LYING DOWN, STARING AT A LAMP HANGING FROM THE 'CEILING' OF THE TENT.

SIMON So we had a light all along then?

JAY Oh shit yeah, I forgot about that one.

SIMON　So my car went in the lake for no reason.

NEIL　I'm upset too Si, I got my first hand job in that car. Who's gonna want to give me a hand job when I'm a dad.

JAY　Your dad?

SIMON　You're not going to be a dad, remember Neil.

NEIL　Oh yeah.

JAY　He'll probably still give you one anyway. Look, even if we did get it out mate, I doubt it would work anyway. I think the engine's flooded.

SIMON　Is that supposed to be funny Jay?

NEIL　You'll get it on the insurance I reckon.

SIMON　Yeah, I've got a third-party, fire and your mates rolling it into a lake so it should be fine.

WILL COMES IN.

SIMON　How was the trench?

WILL　I had to wipe my arse with leaves.

SIMON　Jesus.

WILL　And I think there were some ants in there so I now literally have ants in my pants. And soil, and some earwigs.

THE OTHERS LAUGH. WILL TAKES HIS GLASSES OFF, GETS INTO HIS SLEEPING BAG AND LIES DOWN NEXT TO NEIL. IT'S A TIGHT SQUEEZE, BUT THEY ARE ALL IN THERE.

NEIL　Hey, do you remember the first time we slept in a tent in my back garden?

SIMON　Yeah, we had to come in the house at about midnight because Jay got scared.

JAY　Yeah, I was scared that Neil's dad would come out and bum us.

WILL　And on that familiar note, it's goodnight. Sorry about your car Si.

SIMON　Doesn't matter, it was a shit car anyway. Thanks for the send-off. I suppose when I'm away from you lot— Jesus, that stinks Neil. Is that a fart?

NEIL No, a burp. It ain't great though, I think it's them sausages.

SIMON Whatever, goodnight.

JAY Well I'll get the fucking light then, shall I? Goodnight gaylords.

JAY LEANS UP AND SWITCHES THE LIGHT OFF.

NEIL Si, I was wondering, when you're gone . . .

SIMON Yeah.

NEIL What do you want us to do with Will? Like look after him and stuff.

WILL I'm not a stray cat Neil.

JAY But you do shit in a hole in the ground?

WILL Brilliant.

NEIL I just worry about you that's all.

WILL I think I'll be fine. Goodnight.

WILL Thanks though Neil.

SUDDENLY, FROM NOWHERE, NEIL PROJECTILE VOMITS OVER WILL, WHO IS LYING NEXT TO HIM.

WILL Oh fucking hell, it's in my hair.

NEIL I think it's the sausages.

JAY SITS UP AND SWITCHES THE LIGHT ON, THEN HE MOVES TO THE FRONT OF THE TENT.

JAY Oh God, I've got to get out.

SIMON Oh God, the smell's so bad, I think I'm going to puke.

WILL Don't puke in here.

SIMON PUKES IN THE TENT TOO.

WILL Oh you have.

NEIL I don't feel well.

SIMON PUKES AGAIN, SO DOES NEIL.

SIMON   Oh the smell . . .

WILL   Jay, get the fucking tent open. Jay.

JAY IS STRUGGLING WITH THE ZIP.

JAY   I can't find the zip.

JAY PUKES ALL OVER THE TENT FLAP.

WILL   Great.

—————— SCENE 18 ——————

EXT. CAMPING AREA BY LAKE

IT'S DARK AND THE BOYS ARE BEGINNING THE LONG WALK HOME.

WILL   Oh, my mum's texted me back.

JAY   She up for some back-door action then?

WILL   No, it said, 'I love you too.' It's a template.

JAY   Well, if she is up for it Neil should get to bum her 'cause it was his text that got her frothy.

WILL   True. Obviously she's not up for it.

SIMON   How do you know?

NEIL   Did it say that pacifically?

WILL   Specifically.

JAY   Are you saying she only likes it in her axe wound?

WILL   Seriously, we've got a long walk ahead of us, I'm covered in puke, can we just drop the mum stuff?

JAY   I'd like to drop your mum's stuff . . .

WILL   Oh. We can't.

THE BOYS LAUGH.